Gender and American Law

The Impact of the Law on the Lives of Women

Series Editor

Karen J. Maschke

GARLAND PUBLISHING, INC.
New York & London
1997

Contents of the Series

The Employment Context

Edited with introductions by
Karen J. Maschke

GARLAND PUBLISHING, INC.
New York & London
1997

Library of Congress Cataloging-in-Publication Data

The employment context / edited with introductions by Karen J.
   Maschke.
      p. cm. — (Gender and American law ; 3)
      Includes bibliographical references.
      ISBN 0-8153-2517-7 (alk. paper)
      1. Sex discrimination in employment—Law and legislation—United
States. 2. Women—Employment—Law and legislation—United States.
I. Maschke, Karen J. II. Series.
KF3467.A75E48 1997
344.7301'4133—dc21   96-39889
                                  CIP

Printed on acid-free, 250-year-life paper
Manufactured in the United States of America

Contents

Series Introduction

From colonial times to the present, the law has been used to both expand and contract the rights of women. Over the last two decades, a body of literature has emerged that examines the ways in which the law has had an impact on the lives of women in the United States. The topics covered in this series include the historical development of women's legal rights, matters surrounding reproduction, sexuality and the family, equal employment opportunity, educational equity, violence against women, pornography, sex work, hate speech, and developments in feminist legal thought. The articles represent multidisciplinary approaches in examining women's experiences with the law and provide theoretical insights about the nature of gender equality.

A unifying theme in these articles is that women have been constructed historically as "different," and that this characterization "has had implications in regard to the way in which women are understood as objects and subjects of law" (Fineman 1992, p. 1). Biological differences between women and men and assumptions about the different "nature" of women and men have provided the basis for legal restrictions on women's ownership of property, guardianship of their children, ability to control their reproduction, and access to the workplace and educational institutions.

Even though women have more legal rights now than at any other time in history, many of the articles show that the law can both eradicate and reinforce women's subordination. Nineteenth-century child custody law is a telling example. While "judges granted women new legal power in family affairs," they also placed "severe limits on married women's overall legal rights" (Grossberg 1983, p. 235). On the one hand, by claiming the authority to determine which parent should be granted custody, judges dismantled the practice of fathers possessing unquestioned domain over matters of child custody and guardianship. Yet judges also "ensured that women's domestic powers did not translate into extensive external political and economic authority" (Grossberg 1983, p. 237).

The limitations of legal reform are also revealed by contemporary attempts to achieve gender equality. For example, in the 1970s many local governments adopted comparable worth wage policies. Such policies were "designed to correct historically discriminatory wages of female- and minority-dominated jobs" (Evans and Nelson 1989, p. 172). However, when some local communities were forced to raise women's wages to correct discriminatory practices, they eliminated or modified various jobs and social programs. Many of these programs, such as after school latchkey programs, were developed in response to the needs of two-paycheck and female-headed families. "In other words," note Evans and Nelson, "local governments are reacting to comparable worth with threats to renege on the emerging social commitment to policies addressing what have been traditionally defined as *women's* problems" (Evans and Nelson 1989, p. 183).

Other articles provide additional evidence of how legal reforms may actually disadvantage women in ways that are unanticipated. Furthermore, they reveal the problems in employing the model of equality as a basis for achieving gender justice. The emerging "difference theories" in feminist legal thought focus on the ways in which women and men live "gendered lives," and the ways in which legal and social institutions are shaped and operate according to gendered constructs (Fineman 1992).

The articles in this series also show how the law affects women in different ways. Women of color, poor women, and single mothers may experience the power of the law in ways that are different from the experiences of white, middle-class women. Poverty reform discourses are laden with images of single mothers as "bad" and often lump these women together "with drug addicts, criminals, and other socially-defined 'degenerates' in the newly-coined category of 'underclass'" (Fineman 1992, p. 283). Consequently, current welfare policies are not designed so much to help single mothers as they are to punish them for their bad behavior.

Several authors show how in the legal matters concerning male violence against women, "the experiences of women of color are frequently the product of intersecting patterns of racism and sexism" (Crenshaw 1991, p. 1243). These authors contend that theories of gender oppression must acknowledge the intersection of race and sex, the ways in which women have contributed to the social construction of race, and the oppression of black women. They also point out that the analyses of the law's role in women's oppression must take account of the intersectional identities of women and of how the law responds to, reinforces, and stigmatizes those identities.

The articles in this series bring together an outstanding selection from a growing body of work that examines how the law treats women and gender difference. They represent some of the most intriguing theoretical writing on the subject and reflect the strong multidisciplinary character of contemporary research on women and the legal order.

Notes

Cited works are contained in volumes five, three, seven, and two, respectively.

Crenshaw, Kimberle. 1991. Mapping the Margins: Intersectionality, Identity Politics, and Violence Against Women of Color. *Stanford Law Review* 43:1241–99.

Evans, Sara M. and Barbara J. Nelson. 1989. Comparable Worth: The Paradox of Technocratic Reform. *Feminist Studies* 15:171–90.

Fineman, Martha. 1992. Feminist Theory in Law: The Difference it Makes. *Columbia Journal of Gender and Law* 2:1–23.

Grossberg, Michael. 1983. Who Gets the Child? Custody, Guardianship, and the Rise of a Judicial Patriarchy in Nineteenth-Century America. *Feminist Studies* 9:235–60.

Volume Introduction

Women have greater employment opportunities today than at any other time in history. Yet they continue to face barriers that prevent them from attaining full equality with men in the workplace. Women earn less than men and are segregated in traditional female jobs such as nursing, teaching, and social work. When they enter professional occupations such as business and law, a glass ceiling operates to keep them from reaching the upper levels of the profession (McGlen and O'Connor 1995). These barriers are especially problematic for nonwhite women, who continue to suffer from racial discrimination.

Historically, women have been segregated in traditional female jobs and prohibited by law from working in some occupations or under certain conditions of employment. During the late 19th and early 20th centuries, states enacted "protective" labor laws that regulated women's hours of employment and that barred women from some jobs. Proponents of these laws claimed the laws were designed to "protect" women from harsh and dangerous conditions in the workplace. Yet many unions supported protective legislation for women because they wanted to "protect" their male constituents from female competition. While some of these laws did protect women from adverse conditions in the industrial workplace, they also perpetuated the view that women needed protection because of their physical characteristics and capacities.

Protective labor laws also reinforced the ideology of "separate spheres" for men and women. Justice Joseph Bradley's concurring opinion in the case of *Bradwell* v. *Illinois* (1873) is an example of separate spheres ideology. In *Bradwell* the U.S. Supreme Court upheld an Illinois court ruling that permitted the state to refuse to license women as lawyers. Justice Bradley contended that the state could take such action because

> [T]he civil law as well as nature itself, has always recognized a wide difference in the respective spheres and destinies of man and woman. Man, is, or should be, woman's protector and defender. The natural and proper timidity and delicacy which belongs to the female sex evidently unfits it for many of the occupations of civil life . . . The constitution of the family organization, which is founded in the divine ordinance, as well as in the nature of things, indicates the domestic sphere as that which properly belongs to the domain and functions of womanhood (*Bradwell* v. *Illinois* 81 U.S. 130 (1973) at p. 141).

It was not until Congress passed the Civil Rights Act of 1964 that a legal remedy was available to women to challenge discriminatory employment policies like the one faced by Myra Bradwell. Although the Civil Rights Act was designed to address the problem of racial discrimination, sex discrimination was included as an illegal form of discrimination under Title VII. This section of the Civil Rights Act prohibits private employers from discriminating against workers on the basis of race, color, religion, sex, and national origin. Congress amended Title VII in 1972 to protect public employees from discriminatory treatment in the public sector.

In the 1970s the courts began to rule that state protective laws for women violated Title VII. Women also brought lawsuits under Title VII challenging employment practices that discriminated against them because they were pregnant, that paid them lower wages than men, and that constituted sexual harassment. Courts initially were reluctant to apply Title VII to such forms of discrimination; over time, however, they ruled that the sex discrimination clause of Title VII prohibited employers from discriminating against women on the basis of pregnancy and from paying them lower wages than men who performed comparable work. Courts also have ruled that sexual harassment is a form of sex discrimination (MacKinnon 1987).

However, because gender is "rooted in and at the workplace," (Baron 1989, p. 179) women continue to experience subtle and not-so-subtle forms of discrimination that limit their ability to achieve full equality with working men. Phyllis Coontz reminds us that "gender conveys what it means to be female and male. In a workplace that is stratified and segregated by sex, the meaning conveyed is that women are not as valuable as men" (Coontz 1995, p. 3). Nowhere is this more apparent than in the labor market's wage structure. For example, in 1990 "women who were employed full-time year-round made just 70% of what men earned," and "the more female-dominated the occupation, the lower their relative earnings" (Coontz 1995, p. 3). That women continue to earn less than men raises questions about the limitations of legal reforms that were designed to advance equality in the workplace. Comparable worth was promoted as such a reform policy.

Comparable worth emerged in the 1970s as a "wage policy designed to correct historically discriminatory wages of female- and minority-dominated jobs." Its focus is on equal pay for "job classifications that are valued equally in terms of skill, effort, responsibility, and working conditions" (Evans and Nelson 1989, p. 172). Most comparable worth policies have been implemented by state and local governments through the use of job classification strategies. In Minnesota, women and minorities who occupied the lowest end of the pay scale received pay increases resulting from the implementation of comparable worth (Evans and Nelson 1989).

Studies of comparable worth policies show that while these policies may succeed in equitably distributing wages, they do not challenge the distribution of workers among jobs. Consequently, women continue to be "concentrated in the lowest paid jobs with fewest opportunities for advancement" (Evans and Nelson 1989, p. 171). This is especially problematic for black women, who traditionally have been segregated in service jobs such as "cashiers, maids, messengers, and child care workers." Because they are caught "in the interstices between sex and race," black women are particularly vulnerable to discriminatory treatment in the workplace. Thus, legal theories aimed at wage discrimination alone will not alleviate some of the inequitable conditions black women experience in the employment setting (Scales-Trent 1984, p. 53).

Sexual harassment is a problem to which black women are uniquely vulnerable (Ellis 1981), partly because they have been construed since the slave era as women who exemplify "promiscuity and sexual abandon"(Ellis 1981, p. 39), but also because they consistently remain at the bottom of the economic ladder. Although sexual harassment has always occurred in the workplace, the legal claim of sexual harassment was not recognized by the courts until the mid-1970s. Sexual harassment is a violation of the sex discrimination clause of Title VII and is defined as "unwelcome sexual advances, requests for sexual favors, and other verbal or physical conduct that enters into employment decisions and/or conduct that reasonably interferes with an individual's work performance or creates an intimidating, hostile, or offensive working environment" (Rubin 1995, p. 1)

Incidents of sexual harassment not only reveal the highly sexualized nature of the workplace, but also the ways in which the expectations and boundaries of masculinity and femininity are intertwined. While femininity is traditionally defined around the idea of passivity, "[M]asculinity is traditionally defined around the idea of power" (Karst 1991, p. 501). The idea of power extends to the sexual conquest and control of women, whether in the home or in the workplace. Yet masculinity also is at the center of the workplace, for gender is a fundamental "understructure" of the workplace (Acker 1992). Nowhere is this more evident than in traditional male occupations such as the U.S. military, where the "pursuit of manhood" is linked to sexuality and masculine power (Karst 1991). Consequently, it should come as no surprise that sexual harassment is a serious problem for women in the military (Murray 1994).

Gender is also an understructure of the legal profession, where sexist attitudes prevail. Women lawyers report that they see and experience gender bias, while men lawyers report that such bias does not exist. What Phyllis Coontz discovered was that gender bias occurs in the legal profession in ordinary ways and has become an accepted part of the professional legal culture (Coontz 1995). That such bias continues to persist in the workplace indicates that Title VII and other equal employment policies are insufficient for achieving equality in the workplace. What is needed, says Coontz,

> are strategies aimed at reconceptualizing gender and women's place in the workplace. Such strategies should target the sources of gender bias: socialization and educational practices that channel females and males into traditional gender roles; assumptions about family responsibilities that are gender-based; and cultural images that portray women and men in stereotypical ways (Coontz 1995, p. 19).

Until the sources of gender bias are eliminated, women will never be fully accepted and treated as equal members of the workplace.

Notes

* Articles marked with an asterisk (*) are included in this volume.

Acker, Joan. 1992. From Sex Roles to Gendered Institutions. *Contemporary Sociology* 2:565–69.

Baron, Ava. 1989. Questions of Gender: Deskilling and Demasculinization in the U.S. Printing Industry, 1830–1915. *Gender and History* 1:178–99.

Bradwell v. *Illinois*, 81 U.S. 130 (1973).

*Coontz, Phyllis D. 1995. Gender Bias in the Legal Profession: Women 'See' It, Men Don't. *Women and Politics* 15:1–22.

*Ellis, Judy Trent. 1981. Sexual Harassment and Race: A Legal Analysis of Discrimination. *Journal of Legislation* 8:30–45.

*Evans, Sara M., and Barbara J. Nelson. 1989. Comparable Worth: The Paradox of Technocratic Reform. *Feminist Studies* 15:171–90.

Karst, Kenneth. 1991. The Pursuit of Manhood and the Desegregation of the Armed Forces. *UCLA Law Review* 38:499–581.

*MacKinnon, Catherine A. 1987. Sexual Harassment: Its First Decade in Court. In *Feminism Unmodified*. Cambridge, Mass.: Harvard University Press.

McGlen, Nancy E., and Karen O'Connor. 1995. *Women, Politics, and American Society*, Englewood Cliffs, N.J.: Prentice Hall.

*Murray, Yxta Maya. 1994. Sexual Harassment in the Military. *Southern California Review of Law and Women's Studies* 3:279–302.

Rubin, Paula N. 1995. Civil Rights and Criminal Justice: Primer on Sexual Harassment. National Institution of Justice, Research in Action. Washington, D.C.

*Scales-Trent, Judy. 1984. Comparable Worth: Is This a Theory for Black Workers? *Women's Rights Law Reporter* 8:51–58.

PROTECTION OF WOMEN WORKERS
AND THE COURTS:
A LEGAL CASE HISTORY

ANN CORINNE HILL

The issue of protective labor legislation for women has been at
the center of many discussions of the proposed Equal Rights Amendment to the United States Constitution. Advocates of the amendment have argued that protective legislation that applies only to
women is discriminatory, that the effect of such laws is too often
to *restrict* women's employment opportunities rather than to "protect" them on the job. In contrast, opponents of the amendment
often take the position that it will fly in the face of a century-long
struggle for the protection of women workers by eliminating labor
laws that are necessary and beneficial.[1]

The current debate over protective legislation has faltered because
both sides have argued their positions in an historical vacuum. This
essay is an attempt to contribute to a feminist perspective on the
question by examining the largely unknown history of protective
legislation in the United States in one important context, that of
the decisions of the courts and particularly the Supreme Court,
over the last one hundred years on the constitutionality of these
laws. Protective labor legislation owes much of its shape—its very
existence—to the decisions of state and federal courts upholding
its validity.

To understand the decisions of the courts, we must place them
against a background of two dominant and pervasive factors in
American labor history: segregation in jobs and sex-based discrimination in the labor market. Language itself—there are workers,
and then there are *women* workers—underscores this fact. Even
today, as we read of women becoming the "first female" police
officers, bus drivers, firefighters and construction workers in their
locales, federal statistics bring us back to the economic reality that
a woman earns, on average, fifty-seven cents for every dollar earned
by a man. The Equal Pay Act and Title VII notwithstanding, the
two dominant features of the labor market for women still remain

segregation in low-paying, dead-end jobs in traditionally female
occupations and discrimination against those who compete with
men for traditionally male jobs.

It is in this context of sex segregation and discrimination that
we must understand the concept of "protection" of women workers. It is my contention that the courts, in their decisions on protective legislation, have legitimated rather than challenged the
second-class position of women in the American labor force. After
a hundred years of rulings on various aspects of the employment
of women, the courts in general and the United States Supreme
Court in particular, have yet to recognize that women have a *right*
to employment, a right to enter and pursue the occupation of their
choice. The Supreme Court has viewed and continues to view wom-
en as "special," in a class by themselves, when it comes to employment. The courts generally see male workers as the norm and treat
women as "aliens" in the labor force. They have conferred alien
status upon women in the workforce by upholding laws that prohibit them from working in certain occupations; by validating so-
called protective laws for women only that set different employment terms for women than for men (thereby making them unable
to compete on the same terms); and most recently, by limiting
women's fringe benefits to only those benefits required by men.

My analysis will focus on four historical periods. Concentrating
on the implications of specific cases and decisions, I will try to lay
the groundwork to answer what must be, for feminists, the ultimate
question: Can women workers ever seek or accept protection as a
class apart from working men without compromising their struggle
for equality in the labor force? The first period opens with the
decision of the Massachusetts Supreme Court in 1876 to uphold
the first piece of protective legislation for women, and it closes
with a ruling by the Supreme Court in 1923 that struck down a
minimum wage law for women on the grounds of their supposed
equality with men. Decisions in this early period focus on the
constitutionality of protective laws for women only, and include
the landmark *Muller* v. *Oregon* decision by the Supreme Court in
1908, which continues to have the most far-reaching effects on the
treatment of working women by the courts. The second period,
1935 to 1948, encompasses the Great Depression and World War
II. The exigencies of massive unemployment initially led to decisions which for the first time recognized the validity of protection
for men and women alike; later, the contradictions of thousands
of women taking so-called men's jobs during the war raised new
questions of equality in the labor force for consideration by the
courts. The third period, 1964 to 1971, was a time when unpre-

cedented numbers of women entered the work force, aided by the first fair employment laws and an expanding war-time economy. For the first time, working women, rather than their employers, challenged protective legislation. The last section is devoted to the present, the last five years, during which the Supreme Court has ruled more often on cases charging sex discrimination against women workers than at any other time in its history.

"Protection" is still central to the debate in the recent cases; yet women workers are not seeking "special" protection for themselves as a class apart from men, but rather protection *equal* to that already afforded men. Furthermore, they are seeking protection against old and new forms of employment discrimination and occupational segregation by sex. Whether and to what extent the Supreme Court understands the nature of the new protection sought by working women is the focus of my conclusion.

Before turning to specific cases, a few remarks and qualifications are in order about the nature and efficacy of protective legislation. At the same time we analyze its effects, legally and socially, on limiting women's employment, we must still keep in mind the limited area in which it has operated. Protective labor legislation for women has never covered all women workers. These laws were originally enacted for the protection of women working in factories. In some states, they were later extended to saleswomen and to women in laundries, restaurants, and canneries. There have never been laws enacted to protect the vast number of female domestic workers or women in agriculture; rarely have professional women, such as nurses, teachers, and clerical workers, been included. At the peak of the protective labor legislation movement in 1930, only one-third of the eight and one-half million women working were covered by regulation of their working hours.

The scope of protective legislation has also been limited by difficulties in enforcing such laws. Each state has its own bundle of protective laws, and its own procedure for enforcement. Some of the laws are weakened at the outset by exceptions explicitly made for certain industries. For example, for years, many maximum hours laws excepted canneries during the months designated as "rush" season, which—in this seasonal industry—covered most of the months of employment. Other laws, although rigid in content, are not enforceable as, for example, those that require chairs for women workers. Finally, the penalties for violating many protective laws are so low that they do not act as a deterrent.[2]

3

THE FIRST COURT DECISIONS: 1876-1923

This period was marked by the struggle in the legislatures and courts for acceptance of the idea that workers, especially women and children, needed protection against their employers. By 1920 the legal, economic, and social bases for protective labor legislation for women, albeit *not* for men, were well established. A vocal minority of feminists, however, supporters of an Equal Rights Amendment, had begun to challenge the wisdom of protective labor legislation that covered women only. For this reason certain factions of the movement for social reform in industry in this period called for protective measures for all workers, regardless of sex. But the first protective law, adopted in 1874, was Massachusetts' maximum hours law for women and children in the textile industry. Why were men excluded from this legislation? To answer this, we must first look at the laissez-faire notion of freedom of contract. The theoretical right of *men* freely to enter into employment contracts—workers with capitalists, capitalists with workers—was considered the cornerstone of the American economy. Employees (males, that is) were, in theory, on an equal footing with their employers (also male), and had a right as citizens to be free of interference in their affairs, even if that interference took the form of "protection."

Women, however, still years away from the basic right to vote, were hardly able to be freely contracting citizens. Thus, like children, they were seen as fit subjects for regulation. In 1870, their legal position was still derived from the common law notion that a woman, on marrying, became a part of her husband. Until marriage, young women were considered wards of the state; marriage simply transferred their wardship to their husbands. State laws limiting the property rights of married women by conferring the right of property management to their husbands were one manifestation of this wardship. The idea that women, married or single, had the right to engage in any lawful occupation of their choosing also ran counter to the common law tradition. In 1872, the Supreme Court upheld the decision of an Illinois court to deny a woman the right to practice law; and twenty years later it upheld another state court decision that denied women the right to practice law in state courts.[3] This exclusion from certain occupations applied only to women; there were no instances in which men were forbidden from engaging in a particular occupation open to women. Of course, few men would have wanted the kind of work—and wages—available to women. In sum, then, if the law could exclude women entirely from some occupations, it could certainly "protect" them in others. And so, in 1876 the Massachusetts Supreme Court, in *Commonwealth* v. *Hamilton Mfg. Co.*,[4] upheld the first maximum hours law for women and children as a valid health measure.

There were, indeed, points at which the exclusion of men from protection was questioned. In *Holden* v. *Hardy*, in 1898,[5] the Supreme Court upheld a maximum hours law for miners, as it had for female textile workers in Massachusetts, on the grounds that it was a valid health measure in such a hazardous and unhealthy occupation. But in 1905 it returned to a strict view of protection for men as interfering with their freedom of contract. In *Lochner* v. *New York*,[6] the Court ruled against a maximum hours law for bakers on the grounds that it was not a valid health measure and thus unnecessarily interfered with the right of bakers to make contracts freely determining their working hours. In an opinion rife with laissez-faire ideology, the majority stated, "There is no contention that bakers as a class are not equal in intelligence and capacity to men in other trades or manual occupations, or that they are not able to assert their rights and care for themselves without the protecting arm of the State interfering with their independence of judgment and of action. They are in no sense wards of the state."[7] In effect, the majority had engaged in a game of intellectual dishonesty, elevating liberty of contract as an absolute right guaranteed by the Constitution, although as the dissenting Justice Holmes correctly pointed out, reasonable restrictions on this "liberty," such as those recognized in *Holden* v. *Hardy*, had been consistently upheld by the Supreme Court. Holmes charged the majority with riding roughshod over the right of the citizens of New York to adopt laws which protected the health of their workers. Considerable evidence had indeed been submitted to the Supreme Court that bakers' work was grueling and unhealthy—no less so in its own way, in fact, than that of miners. Bakers suffered from inflammation of the lungs, running eyes, rheumatism, cramps and swollen legs, and had a shorter life span than that of other workers, according to studies placed before the Court. The majority, however, ignored the impressive studies and reports submitted and stated firmly that "to the common understanding, the trade of a baker has never been regarded as an unhealthy one."[8]

Throughout the majority opinion, it is clear that the five justices dreaded creeping social welfarism. All the scientific data were supplanted by their "common understanding" that bakers' work was not dangerous and that bakers were not in need of protection. While they could not overrule *Holden* v. *Hardy* (three of them

5

were in the majority in that case), they intended to insure that miners were the only exception to the rule that men needed and wanted no legislative infringement on their "right to contract." It should be noted that the plaintiff in *Lochner*, as in *Holden* v. *Hardy*, was an *employer* who had been indicted for violating the maximum hours provision. Yet, in a twist of chicanery, the decision championed the right of the *employees* to freedom of contract.

All protective labor legislation was fair game for constitutional challenges after the *Lochner* decision. Two years later, New York's highest court invalidated a protective law that prohibited the employment of women at night because it was "discriminative against female citizens, in denying to them equal rights with men in the same pursuit."[9] In *Lochner*, advocates of protection had gone for the whole loaf—protection of all workers—and lost. Determined to salvage the protective labor legislation movement in the face of these adverse decisions, its leaders joined forces to win back one-half the loaf—protection for women—in *Muller* v. *Oregon* (1908).[10]

It should be noted that protective labor legislation for women was, at the time, much less than one-half the loaf, because women comprised less than 20 percent of the work force and were concentrated in their own "women's industries." Thus a ruling favorable to women stood little chance of affecting the majority of American workers—men. It was because of the inventiveness of the leaders of the protective labor legislation movement, most of whom were women, that even laissez-faire judges could be convinced that the regulation of female workers posed no real threat.

The *Lochner* Court had worried out loud that if (male) bakers could be regulated in their hours of work, so could (male) law clerks, (male) bank clerks, and other men employed by the professions. But because women were neither law clerks nor bank clerks, let alone lawyers or bankers, the creeping welfare state problem did not present itself with protective measures for them.

Still, there remained the problem of making legal sense of invalidating protection for men while retaining it for women. A very capable group of reformers, led by Josephine Goldmark of the National Consumer's League and Louis Brandeis, an attorney, showed the Supreme Court how to reconcile *Lochner* with a decision upholding the constitutionality of a maximum hours law for women in *Muller*. The "Brandeis Brief" argued that women were entitled to special protection on their jobs because, as mothers of the future generation, their health was a matter of public concern. Furthermore, women *required* such protection because "scientific studies" showed that women were not physically constituted to withstand long hours of industrial labor, whatever the industry. These arguments, supported by hundreds of pages of "scientific evidence" assembled by Josephine Goldmark, won the day for protection for women only in *Muller.*[10]

Acknowledging the impact of the Brandeis brief on its ruling, the unanimous Court concurred with the "widespread belief that woman's physical structure, and the functions she performs in consequence thereof, justify special legislation restricting or qualifying the conditions under which she should be permitted to toil." The Court's further remarks on the "nature" of woman are worth quoting at length:

> That woman's physical structure and the performance of maternal functions place her at a disadvantage in the struggle for subsistence is obvious. This is especially true when the burdens of motherhood are upon her. Even when they are not, by abundant testimony of the medical fraternity continuance for a long time on her feet at work, repeating this from day to day, tends to injurious effects upon the body, and as healthy mothers are essential to vigorous offspring, the physical well-being of woman becomes an object of public interest and care in order to preserve the strength and vigor of the race.

The Court went on to observations about the innate dependence of the female sex:

> Still again, history discloses the fact that woman has always been dependent upon man. He established his control at the outset by superior strength, and this control in various forms, with diminishing intensity, has continued to the present. . . . Doubtless there are individual exceptions, and there are many respects in which she has an advantage over him; but looking at it from the viewpoint of the effort to maintain an independent position in life, she is not upon an equality. Differentiated by these matters from the other sex, she is properly placed in a class by herself, and legislation designed for her protection may be sustained, even when like legislation is not necessary for men and could not be sustained.[11]

Muller's reasoning, so tailored to the Court's notions about the social role of women, certainly did not advance the cause for men. The Court pointedly did not overrule its decision in *Lochner.* The *Muller* decision did, however, seem to guarantee certain success in the courts for all future protective labor laws for women—unless the very nature of women changed, or the form of the protection posed a threat to the reigning law of laissez-fairism. Yet, in a rather quick turnabout to this logic, nine years later the Supreme Court upheld a maximum hours law for men, in *Bunting* v. *Oregon,*[12] and fifteen years later it struck down a minimum wage law for women only, in *Adkins* v. *Children's Hospital of the District of Columbia.*[13]

The same coalition that prepared *Muller* for the Supreme Court argued the constitutionality of the maximum hours law for men in *Bunting* and won the case. Their arguments are especially interesting in that they were analogous to those applied to women in the so-called Brandeis Brief in *Muller*. Josephine Goldmark and Felix Frankfurter, who replaced Brandeis as attorney, used the same scientific studies and reports from European countries submitted to the *Muller* court to prove that men's health was destroyed by long working hours in the same way that the health of women workers was irreparably impaired. It should be noted, however, that while state courts immediately followed the *Muller* decision, *Bunting* was ignored, and stood alone for years as the only case recognizing that the state could regulate men's hours in industries that were not extrahazardous (as was mining in *Holden* v. *Hardy*).[14]

In *Adkins* v. *Children's Hospital of the District of Columbia* (1923), the strategy that had worked so well in *Muller* and *Bunting* of gaining Court approval of "special protection" for women and then extending this protection to men was a miserable failure. The decision in *Adkins* defied the logic of *Muller* by invalidating a minimum wage law for women. The *Adkins* legacy was serious: not until 1941, nearly twenty years later, was the Supreme Court able to overcome it and uphold as constitutional a minimum wage provision for workers.

Reviewing its past decisions on protective labor laws—*Holden* v. *Hardy, Lochner, Muller,* and *Bunting*—the *Adkins* majority concluded that the *Lochner* dogma of liberty of contract should govern its opinion. The *Adkins* majority did not overrule *Muller*, but claimed that *Muller* was no longer controlling because women had achieved equality with men with the passage of the Nineteenth Amendment and no longer needed special protection in employment. The Court conceded that there were still physical differences between the sexes which could justify special maximum hours laws for women; but these could not be used to justify the new scourge of laissez-faire economics, the minimum wage law.

At times the Court opinion in *Adkins* ironically reads like a feminist tract as it attacks *Muller's* paternalism:

The decision [in *Muller*] proceeded upon the theory that the difference between the sexes may justify a different rule respecting hours of labor in the case of women than in the case of men. It is pointed out that these consist in differences of physical structure, especially in respect of the maternal functions, and also in the fact that historically woman has always been dependent upon man, who has established his control by superior physical strength. . . . In view of the great—not to say revolutionary—changes which have taken place since that utterance, in the contractual, political, and civil status of women, culminating in the Nineteenth Amendment, it is not unreasonable to say that these differences have now come almost, if not quite, to the vanishing point.[15]

Because of these "revolutionary" changes, the *Adkins* Court declared that women's freedom of contract could not be restrained:

To do so would be to ignore all the implications to be drawn from the present-day trend of legislation as well as that of common thought and usage, by which woman is accorded emancipation from the old doctrine that she must be given special protection or be subjected to special restraint in her contractual and civil relationships.[16]

The *Adkins* Court thus recognized that so-called protective measures might actually serve as restraints on women workers when applied only to them and not to their male counterparts. But despite the heady egalitarian language of the Court, its main concern was not guaranteeing the individual plaintiff, who earned thirty-five dollars a month as an elevator operator, the right to compete equally on the job with men; rather, it was to quash the latest attempt at social welfare legislation.

One final note on *Adkins*: there is a distinct quality of what I call "equal-rights-with-a-vengeance" in the Court's majority opinion. On the one hand, the majority agreed with *Muller*'s opinion that women's physical differences still make them physically unequal with men; on the other, the Court found that the Nineteenth Amendment, like magic, gave women instant equality with men in all fields of endeavor. The Court told women that, with the help of the Nineteenth Amendment, they were free to run on the same track with men as equals, as if they were at the same starting point. This insistence on the equality of women provoked a no less adamant insistence by two justices in their dissents that women were not (and never would be) equal because of their physical differences. As one stated succinctly, "It will need more than the Nineteenth Amendment to convince me that there are no differences between men and women, or that legislation cannot take those differences into account."[17]

Neither *Muller* nor *Adkins* addressed the issue crucial to women: whether differential treatment of women and men workers was an invidious and unconstitutional form of discrimination, like race discrimination, which violated the Equal Protection Clause of the Fourteenth Amendment. And so women were forced to choose between decisions like *Muller* that upheld much-needed protective measures at the cost of separate and unequal treatment, or decisions

9

like *Adkins* that espoused a theoretical equality between the sexes
for the limited purpose of invalidating necessary and beneficial
single-sex protective laws as a violation of the even more abstract
"freedom of contract." In the 1920s, most organizations speaking
for women workers—trade union women and reformers—went for
the protection.

The cost of this strategy can be seen in *Radice* v. *New York* just
one year later.[18] The Court upheld a New York criminal statute
prohibiting the employment of women in restaurants between
10 P.M. and 6 A.M., thus excluding many women workers from
night work. The night work prohibition was deemed a valid protective measure because the state legislature had a mass of information showing that night work was harmful to the health of
women. The Court deferred to the legislature's judgment that
the harmful effects of night work bore more heavily against wom-
en than men because women were more "delicate." *Radice* is a
clear-cut instance of sex discrimination in the guise of protection.

The element which unites all the cases in this period is the treatment of women workers as a class in need of special protection.
It was not unreasonable for protective labor law advocates to use
this tack. It could work to the benefit of women *and* men, as the
Bunting decision proved. It was also not entirely unreasonable,
given the sex segregation of the labor force, to view women workers in those years as a class apart from men. What *was* unreasonable was the intellectual basis put forth to justify treatment of
women workers as a separate class. Women were said to be physically weaker, burdened by the responsibilities of motherhood
and therefore dependent on men for their protection. Anatomy,
for women, spelled economic dependency—not just for some wom-
en, but for all women. This, despite the fact that the vast majority
of working women were the sole support of themselves or their
children or families.

In the period when protective legislation was first propounded,
even the staunchest advocates of laws for the protection of women
only recognized that men also needed protection and that, in the
end, the goal was regulation of *industry* for the protection of *all*
workers. As Felix Frankfurter put it:

Once we cease to look upon the regulation of women in industry as excep-
tional, as the law's graciousness to a disabled class, and shift the emphasis
from the fact that they are *women* to the fact that it is *industry* and the relation of industry to the community which is regulated, the whole problem is
seen from a totally different aspect.[19]

Frankfurther also stated that "science has demonstrated that there is no sharp difference in kind as to the effect of labor on men and women."[20] Yet, he still insisted there was a difference in *degree*, that both men and women need protection, but for apparently different reasons. But whether a jurist recognized a difference in *kind* or in *degree* between women's and men's needs for job protection, the result would be the same. Women were lumped right back into that "class by themselves" where by "nature," with a little help from the law in *Muller*, they belonged.

PROTECTION FOR EVERYONE—
EXIGENCIES OF DEPRESSION AND WAR: 1935-1948

In the 1930s, the Great Depression forced millions of women and men out of work. In the 1940s, the demands of wartime industry and the exodus of men to the military allowed thousands of women to enter the industrial labor force. Until the Depression, most labor legislation had emanated from the states—all of the protective labor laws challenged in the *Muller* era were state or local statutes. The national scope of unemployment in the Depression, however, called for a national policy on employment and labor relations. The federal government did not preempt the field of labor law; but from 1932 onward, it was involved with the states in the passage of social welfare legislation for workers.

The major pieces of federal legislation in this period were the Social Security Act of 1935 and the Fair Labor Standards Act of 1938. The Fair Labor Standards Act incorporated the major types of state protective laws into a comprehensive labor law that applied to workers regardless of sex. It provided for minimum wages and maximum hours and increased compensation for overtime for those employees it covered (those engaged in the production of goods for interstate commerce).

The Social Security Act established an entirely new kind of protection for workers. Under this act the federal government set up a system for the *future* protection of workers and their families against job loss through infirmity, disability, and old age. Like the Fair Labor Standards Act, it covered all workers regardless of sex. Nonetheless, many of its provisions discriminated against women by not providing them with the same protection afforded to men. The provisions of the Fair Labor Standards Act, however, did not treat women workers differently than their male counterparts. In providing for maximum hours and minimum wage limitations for men as well as women, Congress had clearly accepted the position that all industry—not just particularly hazardous or unhealthful employments—needed to be regulated for the general welfare.

11

Congress succeeded in passing this law just one year after the Supreme Court had been asked to reconsider its ruling in *Adkins*. With the threat of a court-packing measure over its head, it reversed itself by upholding a state minimum wage law for women in *West Coast Hotel Co. v. Parrish*.[21] The minimum wage law at issue in *Parrish* had been in effect in Washington State since 1913. It had withstood two state court challenges to its constitutionality. Thus, despite the adverse *Adkins* decision, proponents of protective labor laws for workers had kept the battle for minimum wage provisions alive until the time was right to return to the Supreme Court. (It is a testament to the strength of laissez-fair-advocates that in 1937 in the midst of massive unemployment and impoverishment, the Supreme Court could barely muster a five to four majority to uphold the state of Washington's minimum wage law.)

The majority in *Parrish* based its holding in part on the "common knowledge" it had gained from the Depression of workers' needs for protection:

The exploitation of a class of workers who are in an unequal position with respect to bargaining power and are thus relatively defenseless against the denial of a living wage is not only detrimental to their health and well being, but places a direct burden for their support upon the community. What these workers lose in wages the taxpayers are called upon to pay. The bare cost of living must be met. We may take judicial notice of the unparalleled demands for relief which arose during the recent period of depression and still continue to an alarming extent despite the degree of economic recovery which has been achieved.[22]

This would seem to imply that a minimum wage for men as well as women was valid. Unfortunately, the Court turned aside from this implication by reinvoking the spirit of *Muller*. But the decision against a minimum wage in *Adkins* had to be faced, and *Muller* was used to dispose of it:

With full recognition of the earnestness and vigor which characterize the prevailing opinion in the *Adkins* case, we find it impossible to reconcile that ruling with these well-considered declarations. What can be closer to the public interest than the health of women and their protection from unscrupulous and overreaching employers?[23]

Women were "ready victims," the lowest paid class of workers with the least bargaining power. Protecting them was a legitimate exercise of state power.

What about the fact that men were in need of the same protection, and that this law, in covering only women, was sex discriminatory? The Court dismissed this argument as "unavailing," adopting for a whole new generation of jurists the position that protective measures for women only were reasonable under the Due Process Clause of the Fourteenth Amendment. Along with this legal theory came the belief, supported by fact and fiction, that all women workers needed more and special protection than did all men workers: first, women workers as a class were more exploited; second, their health was a matter of *public* interest because of their function as mothers.

After *Parrish*, the pattern of the earlier *Muller* and *Bunting* cases was repeated. Once again the "weaker" class, women, in gaining constitutional acceptance of their need for special protection, prepared the way for general acceptance of not-special protection for men workers. Four years after *Parrish*, the Supreme Court upheld the minimum wage provisions of the Fair Labor Standards Act, which were applicable to men and women alike.[24] Thus the half-loaf/whole-loaf strategy worked well, winning approval of the newest and most potent protective measure—the minimum wage law—for all workers regardless of sex. Perhaps the language and reasoning were different, sometimes repugnant, when the Court ruled on a "women's case," but in the long run did not all workers benefit from the strategy?

The answer is no. And the best (or worst) support for this answer is the outrageous decision of the Supreme Court in *Goesaert* v. *Cleary*,[25] which upheld a Michigan "protective" labor law for women in the bartending business. The concept of "protection" in *Goesaert* is not one of improving work conditions for a class of workers, but rather of "protecting" one class of workers (men) from competition from another class (women). Writing for the Court, Justice Felix Frankfurter, champion of protective labor legislation, upheld a Michigan law that *prohibited* all women from working as bartenders (except the wives and daughters of male bar owners). The words of *Muller* and *Parrish* were perversely used against the women in *Goesaert*, who sought the Court's protection against a law whose sole purpose and effect was to keep them out of a high-paying, male-dominated profession. Michigan women had made some inroads into the profession during World War II; and after the war, Michigan men returned and wanted their bartending jobs back. Their male-dominated union and legislature paved the way with this "protective" measure for women.

Goesaert completely denied a woman's right to employment. No decision before or after *Goesaert* is so clear on the point that a state may absolutely bar women from any given profession. Justice Frankfurter interpreted the Fourteenth Amendment, as did his brothers before and after, to permit sex classifications as

13

long as there was a rational basis—any rational basis—to support doing so. In *Goesaert*, he hypothesized a state interest in protecting the morals of women as the "rational" basis for sex classification.

The American labor force, from the start of the industrial age through the 1930s, was characterized by a high degree of sex segregation by occupation. Only during World I did women make some significant but short-lived breakthroughs into male-dominated industries. Until World War II, however, women by and large did not compete with men for jobs. World War II, which called millions of men away from their jobs for several years, gave women their first opportunity on a large scale to penetrate men's industries, such as the steel, automobile, and defense industries. Women also entered service occupations, like bartending, that had been dominated by men before the war. At the close of World War II, more women were in the labor force in more varied occupations than ever before. Although sex segregation still dominated the labor force, a significant number of men found themselves in occupations in which they had to compete with women for jobs.

As they looked about for ways to win back their jobs, men were helped not only by federal veterans' preference acts, but also by old and new state "protective" laws for women. Such laws for women only, particularly the old maximum hours laws, weight restriction laws, and more recent premium overtime provisions, were enforced (often for the first time), to *remove* women from competition with men. They were turned upside down and applied to keep women out of jobs, rather than to protect them on the job. For example, in many factories promotions came to be based on the amount of overtime a worker put in. If a state had a maximum hours law for women, all women covered by the law were precluded from doing the overtime necessary to win promotions. Employers could claim they were simply obeying the protective law, in "good faith," when they promoted only men. They also could claim to be operating in good faith when they hired only men on the grounds that they needed people who could work overtime. Thus, female "veterans" of World War II in many factories around the country worked for years after the war without promotion. Laws enacted for their protection were perversely used to keep them at the lowest level position in "men's industries." Where the old laws did not do the entire job, states passed new laws like Michigan's *Goesaert* provision.

PRESSURES FOR EQUAL OPPORTUNITY: 1964-1971

Through most of the Eisenhower years the nation was in an economic recession, but in the early 1960s the labor force began to grow again. The largest growth came in the number and proportion of full-time women workers. By 1968, 37 percent of all workers were women. These new workers were considerably older than the women who had worked in the 1920s. While the average age of women workers in 1920 was twenty-five years, the average in 1970 was forty-five years. Women who entered the labor force in the 1950s and 1960s also stayed longer. Two-thirds worked out of dire necessity, either as the sole breadwinner or to help support a family with an annual income below $7,000.[26]

Although their economic needs were the same as those of men, women workers were rarely able to earn as much. At one point in the 1960s, women's wages, on average, had climbed to 60 percent of men's wages, but since then the gap has widened again. Spurred by women's growing demands for wage parity and better job opportunities, Congress adopted two important pieces of "protective" legislation. The Equal Pay Act of 1963 provided that women and men should get equal pay for the same or similar jobs. Furthermore, in situations in which men earned more than their female coworkers, employers could not lower the men's salaries to meet the provisions of the new law; they had to raise women's wages to the level of men's.

The Equal Pay Act was limited in its usefulness to integrated situations in which women worked side by side with men. Title VII of the Civil Rights Act of 1964 was a much more comprehensive fair employment law. It prohibited discrimination in employment on the basis of sex, race, color, religion, and national origin. Title VII also called for affirmative efforts by employers to provide equal employment opportunities to groups like blacks and women who had suffered from discrimination in the past.

Title VII gave women a powerful legal tool to help dismantle the outdated network of state protective labor laws that too often were used against them to protect men's jobs. It explicitly prohibited employers from classifying employees "in any way which would deprive or tend to deprive any individual of employment opportunities or otherwise adversely affect his status as an employee, because of such individual's . . . sex." The strength and simplicity of its prohibition of both sex discrimination and sex segregation, however, were diluted by another provision of Title VII. The section, known as the bona fide occupational qualification (BFOQ) defense, reads: that it is not unlawful to hire on the basis of sex

15

"in those certain instances where . . . sex, . . . is a bona fide occupational qualification reasonably necessary to the normal operation
of that particular business or enterprise. . . ."[27] It is important to
note that there is no bona fide occupational qualification defense
against race discrimination in Title VII. Title VII's enforcement
agency, the Equal Employment Opportunity Commission (EEOC),
did make it clear that the BFOQ exception was to be narrowly construed. Today, in fact, many Title VII scholars think the BFOQ
defense has been narrowed down into total disuse.[28] But in the
early days of Title VII interpretation, the EEOC, under a great
deal of pressure from unions and employers alike, stated in its
guidelines that certain state protective labor legislation for women
only would be valid as a BFOQ exception. In 1969, the EEOC
took the position that "the Commission does not believe that
Congress intended to disturb such laws and regulations which
are intended to, and have the effect of, protecting women against
exploitation and hazard. Accordingly, the Commission will consider qualifications set by such state laws or regulations to be bona
fide occupational qualifications."[29] This guideline appeared to be
limited to laws that provided real, not sham, protection against
"exploitation and hazard." But who was to determine which were
real and which were sham, especially in light of the Supreme Court's
ruling in *Goesaert*, upholding a sham protective law as though it
were real?

Women workers themselves took on the task of challenging sham
laws as violating Title VII. After some initial setbacks, they won a
major part of the legal battle in two federal circuit court decisions,
Weeks v. *Southern Bell Telephone and Telegraph Company* and
Rosenfeld v. *Southern Pacific Company.*[30]

In *Weeks,* the plaintiff sought the job of "switchman" in the
phone company and was denied it on the pretext that it was "strenuous." Southern Bell claimed that women were not able to perform the switchman job because it required weight lifting and
strenuous physical exertion. Southern Bell could not contend
that the state mandated that women *should not* do strenuous work
because the one Georgia law prohibiting women workers from lifting over thirty pounds had just been superseded by an amendment
that made this law sex-neutral. Consequently, the *Weeks* court
held that Southern Bell had to prove that women actually *could
not* do the job. The Court concluded that the telephone company
failed to so prove:

They introduced no evidence concerning the lifting abilities of women. Rather,
they would have us "assume," on the basis of a "stereotyped characterization"

that few or no women can safely lift 30 pounds, while all men are treated as if they can. While one might accept, *arguendo*, that men are stronger on the average than women, it is not clear that any conclusions about relative lifting ability would follow. . . . What does seem clear is that using these class stereotypes denies desirable positions to a great many women perfectly capable of performing the duties involved.[31]

Fully aware of women's growing presence in the labor force and their demands for men's jobs hitherto denied them, the *Weeks* court closed with a refreshing breath of reality: "Men have always had the right to determine whether the incremental increase in remuneration for strenuous, dangerous, obnoxious, boring or unromantic tasks is worth the candle. The promise of Title VII is that women are now to be on equal footing."[32] Thus, according to the *Weeks* court, Title VII would not tolerate the type of sex classification permitted by the Supreme Court in *Goesaert* in which it was used against individual women who were willing and able to do "men's work."

Two years later, the Ninth Circuit Court of Appeals tackled head-on the conflict between Title VII and protective labor laws for women in *Rosenfeld* v. *Southern Pacific Company*.[33] The plaintiff, Leah Rosenfeld, wanted to be an agent-telegrapher. Southern Pacific denied her the job on two grounds: first, that women were not physically or "biologically" suited for such work; second, that giving the plaintiff the job would violate California's maximum hours and weight restriction laws for women. In the interim between *Weeks* and *Rosenfeld*, the EEOC formulated a new guideline on protective labor laws:

The Commission believes that such state laws and regulations, although originally promulgated for the purpose of protecting females, have ceased to be relevant to our technology or to the expanding role of the female worker in our economy. The Commission has found that such laws and regulations do not take into account the capacities, preferences and abilities of individual females and tend to discriminate rather than protect. Accordingly, the Commission has concluded that such laws and regulations conflict with Title VII of the Civil Rights Act of 1964. . . .[34]

The *Rosenfeld* court deferred to this interpretation of Title VII. It rejected Southern Pacific's claim that protective laws provided a bona fide occupational qualification defense to the exclusion of Leah Rosenfeld and other women. As to the argument that women as a class were not suited for the work, the *Rosenfeld* court said that individual women, like individual men, had to be given the opportunity to show that they were physically qualified for a job:

"This alone accords with the Congressional purpose to eliminate subjective assumptions and traditional stereotyped conceptions regarding the physical ability of women to do particular work."[35] The *Rosenfeld* court clearly enunciated Title VII's mandate that women workers be treated and judged as individuals, not lumped into a class by themselves—a class defined by assumptions and stereotypes of the generic woman. It was not as clear nor as helpful in hastening the demise of sham protective labor laws for women. In a very important aspect of the case, the court recognized that Southern Pacific had used a weight restriction law to keep women out of desirable jobs, but concluded nonetheless that the company had relied in good faith on the law and therefore owed Rosenfeld no damages for its discrimination. The court stated tersely that, "an employer can hardly be faulted for following the explicit provisions of applicable state law."[36]

Consequently, to this day employers can continue to rely on protective labor laws, wherever they still exist, to exclude women from jobs. If caught, they are told to stop and the law is struck down; but the good faith reliance doctrine, as set forth in *Rosenfeld*, has consistently been used to deny women any damages for the employer's past discrimination.[37] Without an effective deterrent such as large back pay awards, women workers must continually bring lawsuits to challenge their particular employers and their states' particular "protective" laws.

The first Title VII case involving sex discrimination decided by the Supreme Court was *Phillips* v. *Martin-Marietta.*[38] It did not involve the conflict between Title VII and protective laws for women. Instead, the plaintiff in *Phillips* claimed that she had been denied a job because she had preschool age children, while men with preschool age children were hired for the same job. The Supreme Court dealt with the issue of whether this differential treatment constituted sex discrimination under Title VII. The lower court in the case had said that while sex may have been a factor in the employer's decision, it was not the only factor. The main reason for denying Phillips the job, the lower court had decided, was not that she was female, but that she had children for whom she had to care.[39] Title VII, the lower court stated, did not prohibit discrimination based on sex *plus* another factor, a legitimate factor. There was no pure male-female discrimination; rather, there was discrimination between certain women workers, those with preschool age children, and all other workers, male and female.

The Supreme Court did not agree with the lower court's analysis and gave women workers a tentative but important victory in *Phillips.* It referred the case back to the lower federal court for "facts" on whether the burdens of motherhood were greater than the burdens of fatherhood in terms of employee absenteeism. But it stated that the policy, at first glance, of hiring men with pre-school age children and not hiring women similarly situated appeared to violate Title VII. For that reason the Court placed the burden on the employer to defend its policy either as a business necessity or as a legitimate BFOQ exception.

Protection was not a visible issue in *Phillips*. But the same general assumptions about women that sustained protective measures for women over the years were at play. The first protective laws were passed so that women workers would be strong enough to become mothers with healthy children; the plaintiff in *Phillips* was a mother of young children. Left unspoken was the further assumption that, with motherhood, a woman should leave the work force for her "rightful place" in the home. While many women did leave the labor force when they became mothers, or even earlier when they learned of their pregnancies, many others could not afford to leave their jobs for motherhood or any other reason. Ida Phillips was working as a waitress on the all-night shift when she applied for the much higher-paying daytime position with Martin-Marietta. The day job would have given her the chance to be with her children before school and in the evenings, and it would have given Phillips and her children much better protection in terms of job security, medical coverage, and pension benefits. Yet she was denied this employment opportunity in the name of motherhood and her responsibilities to her children.

THE FIGHT FOR EQUAL PROTECTION IN THE SEVENTIES

For the past five years working women have kept the Supreme Court very busy by challenging laws and policies that deny them the same employment rights as men and equal protection on the job with men. There are two major lines of cases, the pregnancy cases and the dependency cases, that have evolved in this short period.

In the pregnancy cases, women plaintiffs put forth arguments supporting their fundamental right to employment and, as part of that right, the right to equal benefits with their male coworkers. The first of these cases, *Cleveland Board of Education* v. *LaFleur*,[40] challenged the compulsory maternity leave policy of the Cleveland Board of Education which forced women teachers who became pregnant to leave their jobs at the end of their fifth month of pregnancy. *LaFleur* was the first case at the Supreme Court level to isolate one of many long-standing policies used to get women out of the work force once the "burdens of motherhood" approached.

As I have noted, pregnancy and motherhood were rationales as far back as *Muller* for giving women more protection than men. Such protection, like maximum hours laws, was designed to keep women healthy until they left their jobs for their *real* function in life, motherhood. Employers, legislators, and judges had assumed for years that working women, at the point of pregnancy, would voluntarily leave the labor force. When women did not conform to this assumption, employers such as the Cleveland Board of Education wrote policies to force them to leave. Compulsory maternity leaves were in fact terminations, but because of men's assumptions about pregnancy, they were called "personal leaves" rather than medical or sick leave; and women were generally not only terminated but, because they were no longer considered employees, were also denied medical and pregnancy disability benefits.

When *LaFleur* was argued before the Supreme Court, all states had a series of laws and policies that were adopted to force women out of the work force on the grounds of pregnancy and to keep them out—well beyond the period of convalescence following childbirth. These laws ranged from the *LaFleur*-type compulsory maternity leave to the denial of unemployment compensation to pregnant women workers to requirements that women with children, in order to collect unemployment insurance, show proof of their childcare arrangements. *LaFleur* was the first case before the Supreme Court to challenge this pervasive and systematic discrimination on the grounds of pregnancy as a denial of equal protection to women workers. Justice Stewart, writing the opinion for the Court, did not follow the lower court's lead and treat the case as an employment discrimination case. Nor did he agree with the lower court that women were denied equal protection with respect to their employment rights. Instead, he struck down the policy on forced maternity leave as an arbitrary and unreasonable interference with a woman's *personal right to privacy in matters of childbearing*:

This Court has long recognized that freedom of personal choice in matters of marriage and family life is one of the liberties protected by the Due Process Clause of the Fourteenth Amendment. . . . By acting to penalize the pregnant teacher for deciding to bear a child, overly restrictive maternity leave regulations can constitute a heavy burden on the exercise of these protected freedoms.[41]

Justice Stewart totally ignored the equal protection issue raised by the plaintiff and adopted by the lower court, that the forced leave policy was sex discriminatory. Stewart's decision clearly demonstrates that the Court could not get beyond its assumption that pregnancy is a *personal* matter, not an employment concern as well. The Court made no acknowledgment of a woman's right to work, pregnant or otherwise. In fact, it found fault with the forced leave policy only on the grounds that it was so restrictive; it unduly penalized women for getting pregnant. Thus the door was still left open for *less* restrictive forced leave policies.

LaFleur also left the door open for other forms of discrimination against women in the name of pregnancy. Employers who terminated women on the grounds of pregnancy also excluded them from medical and disability coverage. The reasoning was clear: once a pregnant woman was forced to leave work, the employer had no more responsibility to her because the employer intended and expected that her leave be permanent. The reality, however, was different. Even though women were forced to leave at some point in pregnancy, they expected to return to work, if only to pay off the medical expenses of pregnancy and childbirth. The reality was that women needed to work as much as men, and for the same economic reasons. Women plaintiffs placed this reality before the Supreme Court in *Geduldig v. Aiello* and *General Electric Co. v. Gilbert.*[42] The policy challenged in *Aiello* and *Gilbert* was that of excluding disabilities related to pregnancy and childbirth from health and disability insurance plans.

In *Aiello*, women employees challenged such a plan as unconstitutional under the Equal Protection Clause of the Fourteenth Amendment. The Supreme Court, evoking the spirit of *Goesaert*, held that a plan was rational that covered all disabilities known to man except disabilities related to childbirth (which, of course, are known to man, but only experienced by women). But the *Aiello* decision went one important step beyond *Goesaert's* finding that sex discrimination was rational so long as the Court could find any basis for the gender-related classification. The *Aiello* court insisted there *was* no sex discrimination in pregnancy discrimination:

[T]he California insurance program does not exclude anyone from benefit eligibility because of gender but merely removes one physical condition—pregnancy—from the list of compensable disabilities. While it is true that only women can become pregnant, it does not follow that every legislative classification concerning pregnancy is a sex-based classification. . . .[43]

This reasoning was based on the "sex-plus" doctrine which the Supreme Court ostensibly rejected in *Phillips.* The logic of the lower federal court in *Phillips* was that it was nondiscriminatory to deny a woman a job because of her sex *plus* the fact that she

had small children. Similarly, the Supreme Court in *Aiello* argued
that it was nondiscriminatory to deny a woman job protection in
the form of disability payments because of her sex *plus* the fact
that she was pregnant. While it is true that not all women workers
are pregnant, as the Court in *Aiello* (and later in *Gilbert*) so percep-
tively noted, it is also true that not all women workers have pre-
school age children. The Supreme Court, however, failed to see
the conflict between its reasoning in *Aiello* and its decision in
Phillips.

In *General Electric Co.* v. *Gilbert*, the Court reviewed a disability
income insurance plan under Title VII. The decision in *Gilbert* is
the best example of intellectual dishonesty masquerading as adherence to "established constitutional principles" since *Lochner*
(*Goesaert* runs a close second). *Gilbert* cannot be analyzed in a
logical way because it defies logic. The Supreme Court majority
in *Gilbert*, for instance, claimed that because "discrimination" was
nowhere defined in Title VII, the Court must look to the Fourteenth Amendment and cases decided thereunder for the definition
of "sex discrimination." The Court could have looked to *Weeks*
or to its own opinion in *Phillips*—in short, to the whole line of sex
discrimination cases decided under Title VII, but it did not. It
could have looked to the guidelines of the EEOC, Title VII's enforcement agency, for its definition of discrimination, but it did
not. In sum, as a dissenting justice pointed out in his opinion, the
majority created a conceptual framework that made inevitable its
conclusion that the exclusion of pregnancy-related disabilities from
comprehensive disability plans did not violate Title VII's prohibition against sex discrimination.

In these three cases, *LaFleur, Aiello* and *Gilbert*, women workers
asked the Supreme Court to provide them with a measure of *real*
protection on the job—protection against job loss, loss of income,
and other economic hardship during a period of temporary disability after childbirth. Unlike their sisters in *Muller*, they were not
asking for special protection or for more protection than men.
They were, indeed, asking for protection that would have cost
employers some money, but as men workers have learned, most
real protection does cost money. While the Court in *LaFleur* was
ready to allow women to continue working beyond the fifth month
of pregnancy, it was not ready to shed the notion that pregnancy
and childbirth are personal concerns for individual women rather
than a legitimate employment concern which all employers of
women must take into account. One gets the distinct impression
that the Court saw a man in the background in every case, with
an income and health insurance to cover his working wife's expen-

22

ses during her childbearing leave. While that may have been the ideal of the Court, it is not the real situation (or the ideal one) for most women.

Women workers have fared much better to date in the dependency cases. These cases have had the common theme that women were presumed to be dependent on men for their support, while men were presumed *not* to be dependent on women for their support. Here again, the theme was as old as *Muller*; and it has had some basis in fact, given the pervasive discrimination against women in employment that results in the segregation of women into low-paying clerical and service jobs, and the large gap between women's and men's earnings. But the factual basis could also be used to conjure up time-worn fictions about women. In *Kahn v. Shevin*,[44] for example, the "poor old widow lady" was revived to sustain a magnanimous $500 tax exemption for widows (but not for widowers) in Florida on the grounds that the legislature *might have intended* that the exemption be one-way to eliminate the effects of past discrimination against women. Such reasoning would have been most welcome in *Aiello* and *Gilbert* in which the protection sought was real. But in *Kahn v. Shevin*, in which the protection was minimal, it was another variation on the *Goesaert* theme that sex classifications will be upheld, no matter how discriminatory, so long as a Court can find some basis in reason, no matter how hypothetical.

In contrast, the Court's decisions in *Frontiero v. Richardson, Weinberger v. Wiesenfeld*, and *Califano v. Goldfarb*[45] took account of actualities in working women's lives. In all three cases, the Court treated women as individuals entitled to the same protection as men; and furthermore, it recognized that their contributions to their family's support were as significant as the contributions of men. In *Frontiero*, a four-judge plurality held that sex should be treated as a suspect classification just like race under the Fourteenth Amendment. The Court struck down a military provision that required women, but not men, to prove that their spouses were actually dependent on them in order to get a dependency allowance added to their salary.

Both *Wiesenfeld* and *Goldfarb* involved provisions of the Social Security Act of 1935 that denied husbands of deceased women workers the same survivors' benefits granted to wives of deceased male workers. *Wiesenfeld*'s provision was an absolute denial, while *Goldfarb*'s required proof of actual dependency similar to that required by the military provision in *Frontiero*. Both were based on the "generally accepted presumption that a man is responsible for the support of his wife and children"[46] while a woman is not responsible for her husband. Justice Brennan dealt with these general presumptions about men and women with a directness that is encouraging:

Obviously, the notion that men are more likely than women to be the primary supporters of their spouses and children is not entirely without empirical support. . . . But such a gender-based generalization cannot suffice to justify the denigration of the efforts of women who do work and whose earnings contribute significantly to their families' support.[47]

The difference between the *Wiesenfeld* decision and *Aiello* can certainly be expressed in legal terms. The major difference in constitutional interpretation is that *Wiesenfeld* treated sex discrimination as race discrimination under the Fourteenth Amendment and *Aiello* did not. The Court that does not treat sex discrimination as invidious and that uses irrational arguments to deny its very existence is still operating with a *Muller* mentality about women workers. Thus, the Court in *Aiello* and *Gilbert* continued to treat women as fit *subjects* for different treatment and regulation by employers and state legislatures alike, without inquiry into the motives and effects of such differential treatment and regulation. In contrast, the Court in *Frontiero, Wiesenfeld,* and *Goldfarb* treated women as they would treat men, as individuals entitled to equal treatment in employment, as in every other field of endeavor. The two lines of cases cannot be reconciled. The *Aiello-Gilbert* Court still saw women as "the problem," while the *Wiesenfeld* Court finally viewed the issue as the regulation of employers for the protection and benefit of all workers equally.

CONCLUSION

Sixteen-hour days have given way to eight-hour days, but workers still need protection. The movement for protective labor legislation never encompassed some of the most exploited workers. Groups like farmworkers and household workers, mainly black and Hispanic, are still fighting for maximum hours, a minimum wage, and basic fringe benefits.

The most exploited workers have never been all male or all female, although they have usually been racial and ethnic minorities. Just as the law lets both rich and poor sleep under bridges at night, it lets both women and men be exploited by their employers. But just as more of the poor sleep under bridges than the rich, more women have been treated worse by their employers than have men. What is wrong, then, with adopting a protective law to cover *all* women on the basis that many women actually need the protection?

What is wrong, I contend, is that some women do *not* need the protection, and that many *men* who do need the protection are left out. Above all, as the historic practice of courts and employers shows, sex-defined protective laws too easily become a basis for exclusion.

Protection of workers along sex lines, while politically necessary in the past, is at this point harmful to both the movement for protection and the movement for equality for all workers. Neither women nor men can afford to be in a class by themselves when a real need exists for protection on a particular job. If, for example, lead poses a health hazard to women of childbearing age, protective measures should be aimed at eliminating the hazard, not at removing all women as a class from jobs involving lead. Furthermore, hazards to men of childbearing age should not be overlooked by employers who express zealous concern for their women employees' health. Perhaps the danger is to the reproductive system of both women and men and the employer will have to spend money to eliminate the danger, rather than to "over-protect" women out of their jobs and "under-protect" men on the job.

For women, class protection has been more often a curse than a blessing. In order to support class legislation protecting women, courts have consistently gone far beyond legal theories to rely on "widespread beliefs" (*Muller*) and "common knowledge" (*Parrish*) about the generic Woman. They have spun a web of myths about all women—all women are weaker than men, all women are dependent on men, all women will leave the labor force and become mothers. And this web has too often ensnared women workers and held them back from their goal of equality with men in the labor force. All women *are* entitled to equal employment opportunity and equal protection on the job, but the way to achieve this is not through class legislation that singles out women for some sort of "special" treatment. Rather, the way to achieve equality is to recognize that women are in the labor force to stay; that their needs are the needs of all workers; and that policies or laws—or disability insurance plans—that do not take this into account deny them their right to equal protection in employment. Women do not want to be "special"; they want to be equal.

NOTES

This paper integrates parts of an earlier paper written by the author, entitled "Protective Labor Legislation for Women: Its Origin and Effect." The integration and extensive editing of the two papers were done by Christine Stansell. The editors of *Feminist Studie* and the author wish to thank Chris for her careful and valuable work. The research, theories and conclusions are those of the author alone.

25

[1] See the 1970 debate on the Equal Rights Amendment on the floor of the House of Representatives for a presentation of the controversy over protective labor legislation. 116 *Congressional Record* 137 (91st Congress, 2nd Session), pp. H-7947–H-7985 (August 10, 1970).

[2] For a detailed historical account of the weaknesses inherent in protective legislation, see Elizabeth Baker, *Protective Labor Legislation* (New York: Columbia University Press, 1925), pp. 278-350. See also, Barbara Babcock et al., *Sex Discrimination and the Law* (Boston: Little, Brown, 1975).

[3] Bradwell v. the State, 16 Wall. 130, 141 (1872); *Ex Parte* Lockwood, 156 U.S. 116 (1893).

[4] 120 Mass. 383 (1876).

[5] 169 U.S. 366 (1898).

[6] 198 U.S. 45 (1905).

[7] Ibid., p. 57.

[8] Ibid., p. 59.

[9] People v. Williams, 189 N.Y. 131 (1907).

[10] Muller v. Oregon, 208 U.S. 412 (1908).

[11] Ibid., pp. 420-22.

[12] 243 U.S. 426 (1917).

[13] 261 U.S. 525 (1923).

[14] Note also that the two decisions (in *Bunting* and *Muller*) do not view men and women in exactly the same way: in *Bunting* the court was concerned that overworked men would not be good *citizens*, while in *Muller* the court was concerned that overworked women would not be good *mothers* and *wives*.

[15] Ibid., pp. 552-53.

[16] Ibid.

[17] Ibid., pp. 569-70.

[18] 264 U.S. 292 (1924).

[19] "Hours of Labor and Realism in Constitutional Law," 29 *Harvard Law Review* 353 (February 1916): 367.

[20] Ibid.

[21] 300 U.S. 379 (1937).

[22] Ibid., p. 399.

[23] Ibid., p. 398.

[24] U.S. v. Darby, 312 U.S. 100 (1941).

[25] 335 U.S. 464 (1948).

[26] The labor statistics which I cite in this paper are derived from publications of the Women's Bureau and the Bureau of Labor Statistics of the U.S. Department of Labor. Most of the same statistics are cited in Babcock et al., pp. 191-229.

[27] 42 U.S.C. 2000e-2(e)(1).

[28] See, for example, Kathleen Lucas-Wallace, "Women's Employment and Suspected Health Hazards" (paper delivered at Smith College Conference on Protective Legislation and Women's Jobs, November 3-5, 1977), pp. 6-7, where the author indicates that the 'critical" Title VII defense at this point is business necessity.

[29] Section 1604.1(3) of Guidelines of Equal Employment Opportunity Commission, '9 C.F.R. 1604.1(3).

[30] Weeks v. Southern Bell Telephone and Telegraph Company, 408 F. 2d 228 (5th Cir. 1969); Rosenfeld v. Southern Pacific Company, 444 F. 2d 1219 (9th Cir. 1971).

[31] 408 F. 2d 228, p. 235 (5th Cir. 1969).

[32] Ibid., p. 236.

[33] 444 F. 2d 1219 (9th Cir. 1971).

[34] 29 C.F.R. 1604.1(b) (August 19, 1969).

[35] 444 F. 2d 1219, p. 1225.

[36] Ibid., p. 1227.

[37] Cf. Roxanne Barton Conlin, "Equal Protection Versus Equal Rights Amendment—Where Are We Now?" *Drake University Law Review* 24, no. 1 (Winter 1975): 294-300. Conlin reviews all the states in which protective laws for women are still on the books, in some cases even *after* they have been held unconstitutional by the courts. See also Charles E. Guerrier, "State Protective Legislation: Good Faith Compliance or Convenient Discrimination," *Employee Relations Law Journal* 1, no. 3. Guerrier presents cogent arguments for awarding damages to Title VII plaintiffs in cases in which employers have claimed to rely "in good faith" on protective labor laws in discriminating against women workers.

[38] 400 U.S. 542 (1971).

[39] Phillips v. Martin Marietta Corp., 416 F. 2d 1257 (5th Cir. 1969).

[40] 414 U.S. 632 (1974).

[41] Ibid., pp. 639-40.

[42] Geduldig v. Aiello, 417 U.S. 484 (1974); General Electric Co. v. Gilbert, 97 S.Ct. 401 (1976).

[43] 417 U.S. 484, pp. 496-97.

[44] 416 U.S. 351 (1974).

[45] Frontiero v. Richardson, 411 U.S. 677 (1973); Weinberger v. Wiesenfeld, 420 U.S. 636 (1975); Califano v. Goldfarb, 430 U.S. 199 (1977).

[46] 420 U.S. 636, p. 644.

[47] Ibid., p. 645.

SEXUAL HARASSMENT AND RACE: A LEGAL ANALYSIS OF DISCRIMINATION

Judy Trent Ellis*

INTRODUCTION

The American workplace is highly sexualized, mirroring a society where sexual bantering and flirtation are commonplace. The problem of sexual harassment, however, goes far beyond such mutually agreeable contacts to situations where a woman is subjected to repeated and unwelcome sexual advances, derogatory statements based on her sex, or sexually demeaning gestures or acts. She is often made to feel degraded, ridiculed, or humiliated while she is working or threatened with adverse job consequences if she does not yield to sexual advances. The harassment takes an emotional, physical, and economic toll: women placed in this situation do not perform well on the job and often quit rather than continue to work in a threatening environment.

Although sexual harassment has existed in the workplace since women entered the work force, it is only now coming into public view as a significant legal problem. The identification of sexual harassment as an important issue coincides with the rapid increase of women in the work force and a concomitant upsurge of feminist activities throughout the country. Women are feeling less powerless and are encouraging each other not to accept the harassment previously considered an unavoidable part of a woman's worklife.

There has been an increasing awareness of sexual harassment in the workplace and growing testimony to its seriousness. Every United States Circuit Court of Appeals presented with this issue has held that sexual harassment violates Title VII of the 1964 Civil Rights Act.[1] In 1979 the Subcommittee on Investigations of the House Committee on Post Office and Civil Service held hearings on sexual harassment in the federal government. At the conclusion of the hearings, the subcommit-

---

*   Attorney, Appellate Division, and former Special Assistant to the General Counsel of the Equal Employment Opportunity Commission. B.A., Oberlin College, 1962; M.A., Middlebury College, 1967; J.D., Northwestern University School of Law, 1972.

The author wishes to thank Dr. Nancy C. M. Hartsock, Barbara A. Bush, Esq., Joan Vermeulen, Esq., and Dr. Peggy Crull for their encouragement and their helpful comments on earlier drafts of this article.

This article was written by Ms. Ellis in her private capacity. No official support or endorsement by the United States Equal Employment Opportunity Commission or any other agency of the United States Government is intended or should be inferred.

1.   Barnes v. Costle, 561 F.2d 983 (D.C. Cir. 1977); Tomkins v. Public Service Electric & Gas Co., 568 F.2d 1044 (3d Cir. 1977); Garber v. Saxon Business Products, 552 F.2d 1032 (4th Cir. 1977); *cf.* Miller v. Bank of America, 600 F.2d 211 (9th Cir. 1979) (court accepts defendant's concession that a complaint of sexual harassment can state a cause of action under Title VII).

tee requested that the Office of Personnel Management issue a policy statement defining sexual harassment and declaring it a prohibited personnel practice. The subcommittee also requested that the Merit Systems Protection Board conduct a study of the scope of sexual harassment in the federal employment sector and that the Equal Employment Opportunity Commission (EEOC) improve its processing of sexual harassment complaints.[2] As a result of this new visibility, practices previously viewed as acceptable behavior are being redefined as unacceptable. The issue now has a name, and the parameters of what constitutes sexual harassment are being defined.

Sexual harassment is less an expression of sexuality than of power, whether real or desired. In this respect, it is analogous to rape and exemplifies the same "conscious process of intimidation."[3] There are several reasons why this expression of power is possible in the workplace. Continued job segregation and employment discrimination maintain a profile of the work force in which men are in positions of power and in positions to exploit that power. Women remain concentrated in the lower-paying, traditionally female occupations, comprising 80% of the country's clericals, 63% of the service workers, and 64% of retail sales workers.[4]

Although women comprised two-fifths of the work force in 1979, the median weekly earnings of female wage-earning and salaried workers was approximately 62% that of male workers.[5] In spite of civil rights legislation and the prominence of affirmative action, this differential has remained essentially unchanged since 1961.[6] Even within the same occupation groups, women's earnings rarely approach the earnings of men.[7] This disparity can be attributed, in part, to the record influx of women into the work force, many at entry-level, and to their decisions to choose traditionally female jobs. The fact remains that female earnings are low. The few statistics that exist concerning sexual harassment reveal that a large portion of the harassment that women experience is caused by their male supervisors.[8] The structure of the

---

2. *Sexual Harassment in the Federal Government: Hearings Before the Subcomm. on Investigations, House Comm. on Post Office and Civil Service*, 96th Cong., 2d Sess. 1 (1980) [hereinafter cited as *1980 Hearings*]. In September 1980, the agencies reported back to the House Committee regarding their compliance with those requests. *See* note 8 *infra*.

3. S. BROWNMILLER, AGAINST OUR WILLS: MEN, WOMEN AND RAPE 15 (1975).

4. WOMEN'S BUREAU, U.S. DEP'T OF LABOR, TWENTY FACTS ON WOMEN WORKERS 1 (1979) [hereinafter cited as TWENTY FACTS].

5. WOMEN'S BUREAU, U.S. DEP'T OF LABOR, EMPLOYMENT GOALS OF THE WORLD PLAN OF ·ACTION: DEVELOPMENTS AND ISSUES IN THE UNITED STATES 3, 10 (1980) [hereinafter cited as EMPLOYMENT GOALS].

6. WOMEN'S BUREAU, U.S. DEP'T OF LABOR, THE EARNINGS GAP BETWEEN MEN AND WOMEN 1 (1979) [hereinafter cited as EARNINGS GAP].

7. EMPLOYMENT GOALS, *supra* note 5, at 10.

8. MERIT SYSTEMS PROTECTION BOARD, SUMMARY OF PRELIMINARY FINDINGS ON SEXUAL HARASSMENT IN THE FEDERAL WORK FORCE, 96th Cong., 2d Sess. 11 (1980) (submitted to the Subcommittee on Investigations of the House Committee on Post Office and Civil Service).

work force reflects male dominance in society and puts men in a position to exploit that dominance.

Women are also harassed by male colleagues. Although not in positions of power in the employment context, they view themselves, as men, as having power *at least* over women; that power often is expressed through harassing behavior. This situation has been exacerbated by the extraordinary increase during the 1970's in the number of women in the work force.[9] At the same time, some men in the work force are experiencing personal pressure from the women in their families who are reacting in many different ways to the current surge of feminism. Often, the anger and frustration that they feel toward women cannot be expressed in their personal relationships and is displayed in the employment context. Incidents of harassment are thus likely to increase in the coming years.

Discussions of sexual harassment often advert to racial harassment cases and the general principles expressed in those cases. The references are, however, confusing and contradictory, and analogies are unclear. For example, there is a statement in the EEOC Guidelines on sexual harassment to the effect that the principles in the guidelines will also apply to cases of racial harassment.[10] On the other hand, in *Barnes v. Costle*, the court noted that sexual harassment cases differ from racial harassment cases.[11] The fact remains that although racial and sexual harassment cases are similar, they are also distinguishable. The relationship between the two, however, has not been carefully explored.

This article will examine both forms of harassment and attempt to clarify the nexus between them in order that sexual harassment issues be better understood. In particular, it will suggest that there are two analytical models for sexual harassment cases: (a) a *generalized harassment* model, which parallels racial harassment, and (b) a *sexual exploitation* model, which is analogous to rape. After discussing this analysis, the article focuses on sexual harassment as it applies to black women, a group that is uniquely vulnerable to sexual harassment, and that is caught in the interstices between sex and race. The article will further argue for the recognition of the category of sex-race discrimination, a recognition that will aid in the analysis and proof of cases of discrimination against black women.

SEXUAL HARASSMENT AND RACIAL HARASSMENT

As both racial and sexual harassment are both an expression of dominance and control by one group over another and a process of intimidation to maintain a certain social structure, they have the same

9. In 1975, there were 37 million women in the labor force; by 1979, the number had jumped to 43 million, greatly outpacing male gains in the labor force. EMPLOYMENT GOALS, *supra* note 5, at 3.
10. 29 C.F.R. § 1604.11(a) (1980).
11. 561 F.2d 963, 1001 (D.C. Cir. 1977).

underpinnings. The two forms of harassment are sometimes manifested in the same power statement: racial harassment often takes on sexual overtones, and sexual harassment often takes on racial overtones.[12] Sexual harassment has been carried to its extreme in the rape of black and white women; racial harassment has been carried to its extreme in the lynching and castration of black men. Power in society is demonstrated by who has sexual power over whom.[13]

Although both racial and sexual harassment stem from the exercise of power, there are important differences. The unique history of black-white relationships in this country and the unique character of male-female relationships have led to differing perceptions of discrimination. The history of enslavement has put black oppression into an easily identifiable and understandable category. For example, one outgrowth of the slave history was the passage of the Thirteenth, Fourteenth, and Fifteenth Amendments, which prohibited slavery, granted former slaves the right to vote, and guaranteed protection from state denials of due process or equal protection of the laws. While concerns over race discrimination have found expression in the Constitution, the Equal Rights Amendment still awaits ratification.

The opinions issued by the Supreme Court reflect society's divergent perceptions of racial and sexual discrimination. Classifications based on race are inherently suspect and subject to strict judicial scrutiny under the equal protection clauses of the Fifth and Fourteenth Amendments. Classifications based on sex, however, are not considered inherently suspect.[14] For example, Justice Powell, writing for the majority in *Bakke v. Regents of the University of California*,[15] explained the differences in the levels of scrutiny.

> [T]he perception of racial classifications as inherently odious stems from a lengthy and tragic history that gender-based classifications do not share. . . . [T]he Court has never viewed such classifications as inherently suspect or as comparable to racial and ethnic classifications for the purpose of equal protection analysis.[16]

As the Court noted in *Personnel Administrator of Massachusetts v. Feeney*,[17] when "classifications . . . in themselves supply a reason to infer antipathy, [r]ace is the paradigm."[18] To the extent that historical and

---

12. *See, e.g.*, DeGrace v. Rumsfeld, 614 F.2d 796, 800 (1st Cir. 1980), where one of the threatening notes left for a male worker stated, "Hey boy get your Black ass out before you don't have one"; for a discussion of the sexual harassment of black women, *see also* section of text entitled SEXUAL HARASSMENT OF BLACK WOMEN *infra*.

13. For further discussion of this point, *see* S. BROWNMILLER, *supra* note 3; A. HIGGINBOTHAM, JR., IN THE MATTER OF COLOR (1978); W. JORDAN, WHITE OVER BLACK: AMERICAN ATTITUDES TOWARDS THE NEGRO, 1550-1812 (1968).

14. Classifications according to race, alienage, and ancestry are inherently suspect. Only a showing of a compelling state interest will justify such a classification. *See generally* Mass. Bd. of Retirement v. Murgia, 427 U.S. 307 (1976).

15. 438 U.S. 265 (1978).

16. *Id.* at 303.

17. 442 U.S. 256 (1979).

18. *Id.* at 272.

social perceptions of sexual discrimination differ from perceptions of racial discrimination, sexual discrimination will not be viewed by the courts with the same degree of concern.

"Proximity," the degree of distance which can be maintained within the two groups, also has an important bearing on society's perception of discrimination. Race and power can sometimes be dealt with in an abstract manner: one can be insulated from racial tensions by geography, social position, or wealth. Sex and power, however, are daily issues that are always perceived in an intimate and personal way. As a result, it is in the best interest of the dominant class in society that the magnitude of the sex-power problem remain obscure in order to maintain the status quo.

CATEGORIZATION OF HARASSMENT CASES

Because sexual and racial discrimination have underpinnings that are both different and the same, it is not surprising that the two forms of harassment are manifested in ways that are both similar and dissimilar. The categorization of harassment into a *generalized harassment* model and an *exploitative-harassment* model facilitates the analysis of racial and sexual harassment issues. *Equal Employment Opportunity Commission v. Murphy Motor Freight* [19] exemplifies the generalized harassment model in a racial discrimination case. Racial epithets were written on the walls of the plant, the black employee was isolated by his coworkers in the company lunch area, and his car tires were slashed. The district court found the company's working environment to be permeated with racial harassment and intimidation. *Brown v. City of Guthrie*, [20] on the other hand, presents a case of generalized sexual harassment. In that case, plaintiff's supervisor and colleagues (all police officers) subjected her to lewd comments and gestures, displayed pornographic pictures and made comparisons with her body, and replayed and commented upon video tapes of strip searches of female prisoners. A variation of this generalized harassment model occurs when an employer subjects a female employee to harassment by others who do not work with her. For example, in *Equal Employment Opportunity Commission v. Sage Realty Corp.*, [21] the female employee was discharged for refusing to wear a provocative and revealing costume during her employment as an elevator operator. The court held that this job requirement, which subjected the complaining employee to harassment by the public, constituted a term or condition of employment made unlawful by Title VII.

The pattern of generalized harassment which usually appears in all racial harassment cases does not appear in all sexual harassment cases.

---

19.   488 F. Supp. 381 (D. Minn. 1980).
20.   22 Fair Empl. Prac. Cas. 1627 (W.D. Okla. 1980).
21.   [1981] 4 EMPL. PRAC. GUIDE (CCH) (24 Empl. Prac. Dec.) 19, 163 (S.D.N.Y. Jan. 29, 1981).

There is a model of harassment unique to sexual harassment, the exploitation-harassment model. This model involves pressure upon a woman for sexual favors with an implicit or explicit statement that noncompliance will jeopardize her employment situation.

This form of sexual harassment presents two basic problems in the public mind. One difficulty with the exploitation cases is that they lack a ready framework for analysis. The generalized sexual harassment cases can be dealt with much like the racial harassment cases. Women making an analogy to racial harassment can "bootstrap" claims of sex discrimination onto the racial analysis. Those claims might receive, therefore, the greater consideration that is given racial discrimination in the legal system.

Another problem is that the line between flirtation and sexual exploitation may be a subtle one. Exploitation is sometimes difficult for even women to recognize and more difficult to demonstrate to others. In the generalized harassment cases, either racial or sexual, a cause of action arises when an employee has been ridiculed, intimidated, or degraded because of his or her sexual or racial identity. In the exploitation cases, however, the normalcy of male-female sexual interaction and the "normalcy" of male aggression and dominance cloud the issue; courts are unsure if a cause of action is present. As the district court noted in *Barnes v. Costle*, plaintiff introduced evidence of an "inharmonious personal relationship" but not of a Title VII violation.[22] The exploitation cases also raise the fear that men engaged in harmless flirtation will somehow find themselves in violation of the law, victims of character assassination. It has been suggested, therefore, that charges of exploitation harassment be corroborated.[23]

The concerns raised about the legitimacy of sexual harassment complaints are similar to those raised about rape charges: (1) a fear of malicious prosecution and a concomitant need for corroboration; (2) a generalized feeling that sexual encounters are a "natural phenomenon" and that it is inappropriate to invoke the law to deal with them; and (3) the view that women somehow invite the unwanted sexual attention.[24] Therefore, in order to understand the fears and evidentiary problems raised by these similar issues, it is better to analogize exploitation cases to rape, rather than to the generalized harassment cases. It is useful to examine the well-reasoned decision in *Heelan v. Johns-Manville Corp.*,[25] an exploitation-harassment case, to see how the trial judge scrutinized the evidence in the case, assessing the credibility of the witnesses. The court held that "sexual harassment of female employees is

---

22. *See* note 1 *supra*.
23. *Sexual Harassment in the Federal Government: Hearings Before the Subcomm. on Investigation of the House Comm. on Post Office and Civil Service*, 96th Cong., 1st Sess. 11, 67, 110, 122-24 (1979).
24. C. MacKennon, Sexual Harassment in the Workplace 47-48 (1979).
25. 451 F. Supp. 1382 (D. Colo. 1978).

gender-based discrimination which can violate Title VII."[26] The opinion is significant because it illustrates that sexual exploitation cases can be presented within the framework of Title VII.

Categorization of sexual harassment cases into a generalized model or an exploitation model facilitates legal analysis by providing a clearer understanding of the analytic relationship between sexual and racial discrimination cases. One can determine when legal analogies will be relevant and helpful. The following principles, developed in racial harassment cases, have been applied appropriately to both types of sexual harassment: (1) one incident of harassment generally does not rise to the level of a Title VII violation;[27] (2) harassment which is harmful to plaintiff's working environment may constitute a violation of Title VII.[28] Another principle that emerged in a broad-based sexual discrimination case holds that the existence of sexual harassment is probative on the existence of other kinds of sexual discrimination.[29] This last principle should be followed in all harassment cases.

Another developing concept is that when only one person complains of harassment, plaintiff's case is weakened.[30] The courts seem to be searching for a statistical pattern to support the individual claim of harassment. Repeated incidents of harassment are more probative in generalized harassment cases, where it seems unlikely that only one of a group would be singled out for harassment. Statistical evidence, however, is of limited value in the exploitation-harassment cases, where the selection of one female as a sex partner is not at all unlikely. As the Court of Appeals for the District of Columbia noted in *Barnes v. Costle*, a cause of action for sexual discrimination can be maintained under Title VII, even though no other individual of the same gender

---

26. *Id.* at 1388.
27. EEOC v. Murphy Motor Freight, 488 F. Supp. 381 (D. Minn. 1980) (racial harassment); Brown v. City of Guthrie, 22 Fair Empl. Prac. Cas. 1627 (W.D. Okla. 1980) (sexual harrassment).

    Where the harassment is of an extreme nature, however, more than one incident should not be required before the victim can seek the protection offered by Title VII. *See* Taub, *Keeping Women in Their Place: Stereotyping Per Se as a Form of Employment Discrimination*, 21 B.C.L. Rev. 345, 375-77 (1980).
28. Rogers v. EEOC, 454 F.2d 234 (5th Cir. 1971), *cert. denied*, 406 U.S. 957 (1971) (racial harassment); Brown v. City of Guthrie, 22 Fair Empl. Prac. Cas. 1627 (W.D. Okla. 1980) (sexual harassment).

    See also Bundy v. Jackson, — F.2d —, 24 Fair Empl. Prac. Cas. 1155 (D.C. Cir. 1981). The D.C. Circuit applied the *Rogers* "work environment" theory to a case of sexual harassment, holding that plaintiff need not prove that the harassment caused a tangible loss of job benefits to make out a Title VII violation, where the employer created or condoned a discriminatory work environment.
29. Dacus v. S. College of Optometry, 22 Fair Empl. Prac. Cas. 963 (D. Tenn. 1979); *see also* Bundy v. Jackson, — F.2d —, 24 Fair Empl. Prac. Cas. 1155 (D.C. Cir. 1981), where the court eased plaintiff's burden of proof on her claim of discriminatory denial of a promotion, as she had already proved that she was the victim of sexual harassment. *Id.* at 1165-68.
30. Edwards v. Foucar, Ray & Simon, Inc., 23 Fair Empl. Prac. Cas. 1644 (N.D. Cal. 1980) (racial harassment); Munford v. Barnes & Co., 441 F. Supp. 459 (E.D. Mich. 1977) (sexual harassment); Vinson v. Taylor, 23 Fair Empl. Prac. Cas. 37 (D.D.C. 1980) (sexual harassment).

was mistreated in the same way.[31] Finally, another principle concerns the duration of the harassment before a complaint was lodged. When generalized harassment occurs over a long period of time, the court will permit, for purposes of liability, an inference that the employer knew or should have known of the harassment.[32] When, on the other hand, harassment of the exploitation type continues over a long period of time without notice to the employer, the courts will not infer notice. They presume that they are being presented with either a personal relationship that has soured or a mere annoyance.[33] Although both inferences seem appropriate to the kind of harassment presented, it is important to recognize that even when dealing with a personal relationship that has soured, a woman can be sexually harassed by someone with whom she has had a mutually desired relationship. If courts analyze the kind of sexual harassment with which they are confronted, they will be better able to apply the appropriate principles developed in both racial and sexual harassment cases.

REMEDIES FOR SEXUAL AND RACIAL HARASSMENT

Remedies for harassment must be developed to provide better protection to both women and minority men. No matter what kind of harassment they experience, it is rare that plaintiffs will be made whole, even though the courts have been granted full equitable powers under Title VII to fashion complete relief.[34] Some of the racial harassment cases present a unique pattern: a black male, who has been harassed over a period of time, physically attacks his tormentors in retaliation and is fired. Courts have uniformly held that an employer does not violate Title VII by discharging the black worker without discharging those who harassed him.[35] A comparable situation exists in sexual harassment cases, where the court finds discriminatory harassment, but refuses to reinstate the plaintiff due to the tensions and hostilities generated by the situation.[36] Two questions must be asked, however:

---

31. 561 F.2d at 993.
32. Croker v. Boeing, 437 F. Supp. 1138, 1194 (E.D. Penn. 1977). *But see* Miller v. Bank of America, 600 F.2d 211 (9th Cir. 1979) (strict liability imposed on employer where supervisor harassed employee without knowledge of the employer); EEOC Guidelines, 29 C.F.R. § 1604.11(c) (1980) (employer is liable for acts of its agents whether acts were authorized or forbidden by the employer and whether the employer knew or should have known of those acts).

    See also J. VERMEULEN, EMPLOYER LIABILITY UNDER TITLE VII FOR SEXUAL HARASSMENT BY SUPERVISORY EMPLOYEES (1981) (to be reprinted in 10 CAP. U. L. REV. — (1981)). Ms. Vermeulen argues that the elements of proof required for employer liability in a sexual harassment case under Title VII should not be more stringent than those in other Title VII cases and that the addition of tort concepts such as notice are not only unwarranted but unnecessary.
33. Bundy v. Jackson, 19 Fair Empl. Prac. Cas. 828 (D.D.C. 1980), *rev'd*, 24 Fair Empl. Prac. Cas. 1155 (D.C. Cir. 1981); *see* notes 28-29 *supra*. *See also* Vinson v. Taylor, 23 Fair Empl. Prac. Cas. 37 (D.D.C. 1980).
34. *See* Albemarle v. Moody, 422 U.S. 405, 418-21 (1975).
35. *See, e.g.*, Edwards v. Foucar, Ray & Simon, Inc., 23 Fair Empl. Prac. Cas. 1644 (N.D. Cal. 1980).
36. *See, e.g.*, Brown v. City of Guthrie, 22 Fair Empl. Prac. Cas. 1627 (W.D. Okla. 1980).

(1) Who generated the tensions and hostilities?; and (2) Who is being asked to pay for the creation of the tense situation with loss of employment? These two situations are not identical. Clearly, physical attacks cannot be tolerated on the job; however, in both situations, the person who was harassed pays for defending his or her rights by losing a job. Our courts should structure a more equitable outcome.

Cases of racial or sexual harassment inevitably generate enormous amounts of anger and tension; reinstatement could always be denied for that reason. This outcome, however, is basically unfair. The person discriminated against loses a job, while the person who violated the law remains employed. A backpay award is often inadequate to recompense a plaintiff or to deter future harassment. Especially in recessionary times, workers will not dare to complain about harassment, if they fear they will win on the principle but lose employment. The best remedy is to reinstate the discriminatee at his or her previous job in a non-harassing situation.[37] If this is not possible due to an unavoidable, close working relationship with the harassing individual, then the harassing individual should be moved to a different part of the company. If transfer of the harassing individual is not possible, then the discriminatee should be offered a comparable job in another part of the company. Finally, if for some reason (for example, size of the company) reinstatement is not possible at all, the employer should be required to give "front pay" to the discriminatee. Front pay, a sum of money sufficient to provide time for him or her to find comparable employment,[38] should be added to the backpay award. Its payment would come closer to compensating the discriminatee for loss of a job and would create more incentive for the employer to eliminate harassment from his work force.

In racial harassment actions there have been several cases in which the employer disciplined or fired the harasser because of his conduct.[39] Comparable action by employers is appropriate and necessary in cases of sexual harassment. Aggressive use of the court's equitable powers is

---

37. *See, e.g.*, Kyriazi v. Western Electric Co., 476 F. Supp. 335 (D.N.J. 1979), where the court ordered reinstatement in spite of intense sexual harassment and protracted litigation.

38. *See* Fitzgerald v. Sirloin Stockade, — F.2d —, 22 Fair Empl. Prac. Cas. 262 (10th Cir. 1980) (front pay appropriate remedy where reinstatement is impractical due to hostility between parties); EEOC v. Kallir, Phillips, Ross, Inc., 420 F. Supp. 919 (S.D.N.Y. 1976), *aff'd*, 559 F.2d 1203 (2d Cir. 1977), *cert. denied*, 434 U.S. 920 (1977) (plaintiff denied reinstatement due to erosion of necessary trust and confidence, but granted one year's salary as front pay to give her time to find comparable employment). *But cf.* Burton v. Cascade School Dist., 512 F.2d 850 (9th Cir. 1975), *cert. denied*, 423 U.S. 839 (1975) (Lumbard, J., dissenting) (front pay inadequate remedy for unconstitutional discharge of homosexual teacher; only reinstatement is sufficient to vindicate her rights and deter future unconstitutional action).

39. Harberson v. Monsanto Textiles Co., 17 Fair Empl. Prac. Cas. 99 (D.S.C. 1976) (employer discharged white Ku Klux Klan member for making racially derogatory remarks); Howard v. National Cash Register Co., 388 F. Supp. 603 (S.D. Ohio 1975) (employer suspended white employee for saying "nigger"). In Continental Can v. Minnesota, — Minn. —, 297 N.W.2d 241 (1980), although the employer in a sexual harassment case did suspend the harassing employee for six weeks, this action was taken only after the Urban League threatened to boycott the company.

also required. In a recent racial discrimination case,[40] for example, the court found that although the employer had failed to renew plaintiff's contract because of her race, there was no point in reinstating her in a hostile work environment pervaded with racism. At that point, the court determined that the plaintiff had standing "not only to seek reinstatement, but to seek to be reinstated in a workplace where all people are treated with decency and respect."[41] Instead of denying plaintiff reinstatement, the court imposed a race-conscious hiring goal on the employer. This was based on its finding that "as the environment approaches a fairer racial representation, the degree of racism tends to diminish."[42] This creative use of the court's powers gives meaning to the equitable concept of "complete justice."

Without adequate remedies, it will be impossible to eliminate discrimination or to protect those who complain about harassment. In the area of judicial remedies, the law of racial harassment and sexual harassment should develop in tandem.

SEXUAL HARASSMENT OF BLACK WOMEN

Sociological and Mythological Bases of Harassment

Black women have a unique position in American history and mythology which makes them extremely vulnerable to sexual harassment. That position has been defined by the history of slavery and by the social and psychological framework that made slavery possible. The sexual exploitation of black women began during slavery, when they were available to white men as sex objects and unable to seek protection from black men. They were both sexually accessible and unprotected. Exploitation continued during the post-slavery era. Part of the mythology created to support this exploitation portrayed the black woman as "loose," exemplifying promiscuity and sexual abandon.[43] Black women are still perceived as more promiscuous than white women. The white man who makes sexual demands on a black woman often sees his power aggrandized by associating the sexual exploitation to a period in history where a master-slave relationship was possible.[44] Black men, who are still forbidden to defend themselves actively,[45] are also forbidden to come to the defense of black women who are being harassed.[46] Black women, thus, are denied both the real and the sym-

---

40. Taylor v. Jones, 495 F. Supp. 1285 (E.D. Ark. 1980).
41. *Id.* at 1294.
42. *Id.*
43. G. LERNER, BLACK WOMEN IN WHITE AMERICA 149-50, 163-64 (1972).
44. In *Continental Can*, one harasser of a black woman co-worker made frequent references to a movie about slavery and told her that "he wished slavery days would return so that he could sexually train her and she would be his bitch." Continental Can v. Minnesota, — Minn. —, 297 N.W.2d at 246.
45. *See* text accompanying note 35 *supra*.
46. The court noted in Continental Can v. Minnesota, — Minn. —, 297 N.W.2d 241 (1980), that it was denying plaintiff reinstatement and reducing her backpay by half due to two incidents

bolic protection of black men. The history of slavery still marks black women as sexually available, sexually promiscuous, and unprotected by black men.

The second factor that makes black women susceptible to harassment also emanates from the history of slavery and oppression: it is the economic vulnerability of black women. Fifty-three percent of all black women are in the work force. Compared to white men and women and black men, their median salary is the lowest.[47] In 1978, approximately one out of eight female workers was a head of a family; yet, one quarter of all black women workers were heads of households.[48]

More than half of the families headed by black women had incomes below the poverty level in 1977 (58%).[49] In addition, one-third of all black children under the age of eighteen are living in families headed by black women that are below the poverty level.[50] The highest unemployment rate for any group is for black female teenagers (41% in 1978); the highest unemployment rate for all adults is black women (11.1% in 1978).[51] Taken all together, these statistics portray a situation of despair and economic vulnerability. They indicate that black women are largely either looking for work or employed in marginal jobs, earning low wages. At the same time black women are very often the sole support of the family.[52] Sexual harassment takes on an even more sinister tone when the threat of losing a job is seen against this desperate background.

Statistics on the sexual harassment of black women are scarce. The one large-scale study of sexual harassment which asked questions relating to race was conducted by the Merit Systems Protection Board. In its initial report, the Board concluded that black and white women in the federal government suffer sexual harassment to approximately the same degree.[53] While this may be true in the federal sector, it should not be expanded to a general proposition covering the work force as a whole. The federal sector is unique in terms of the safeguards built into the system to protect the rights of the employees. For black wo-

---

which added to tensions and racial hostilities. *Id.* at 1816. Both incidents involved plaintiff's husband, a black man, when he took an active role in defending his wife.

Black women are also frequently sexually harassed by black men. To the extent that there are several groups of men who have power over black women, black women will be sexually vulnerable to all of them. Attitudes towards black women, attitudes which are shaped by the thoughts and behavior of the dominant group (white males), will come to be attitudes accepted by the culture as a whole. *Cf.* W. JORDAN, *supra* note 13, at 150.

47. TWENTY FACTS, *supra* note 4, at 1; EARNINGS GAP, *supra* note 6, at 20.
48. WOMEN'S BUREAU, U.S. DEP'T OF LABOR, FACTS ABOUT WOMEN OF HOUSEHOLDS AND HEADS OF FAMILIES (Dec. 1979); TWENTY FACTS, *supra* note 4, at 2.
49. WOMEN'S BUREAU, *supra* note 48, at 8.
50. U.S. BUREAU OF THE CENSUS, CURRENT POPULATION REPORTS: CONSUMER INCOME, Ser. P-60, No. 124, Table 9 (1980).
51. TWENTY FACTS, *supra* note 4, at 8.
52. For further discussion of the unique situation of black women workers, *see* P. WALLACE, BLACK WOMEN IN THE LABOR FORCE (1980).
53. MERIT SYSTEMS PROTECTION BOARD, *supra* note 8, at 9.

men, these jobs are probably the best that they can find. In the private sector, black women, of all groups studied, were found to have the highest chance of working for the minimum wage or less.[54] Whereas the largest number of white working women are in clerical jobs, the largest number of black women are in service jobs. More than half of the household workers in the country are black.[55] Many service occupations, such as that of household worker, place black women in isolated, invisible jobs which have few, if any, built-in protections, jobs in which they are neither entitled to nor dare to ask for the minimum wage. These are positions in which women are vulnerable to both economic and sexual exploitation. In fact, a recent article in the *Washington Post* concerning the movement to professionalize household workers revealed that sexual harassment is chronic and commonplace.[56] Sexual harassment, like incidents of rape, is underreported due to the victim's feelings of embarrassment and impotence and also to the realities of her economic vulnerability.[57] To the extent that black women are even less powerful and more economically vulnerable than white women, the incidence of sexual harassment against black women will show gross underreporting.[58]

Legal Analysis

Courts, when confronted with an allegation of sexual harassment raised by a black women, often have grappled with the question of whether they were dealing with sex discrimination or race discrimination. This confusion is not surprising, as the legislative history of Title VII shows Congress' uncertainty with regard to treating black women as blacks or as women for purposes of the Act.[59] In *Miller v. Bank of America*,[60] plaintiff alleged that she was fired because she refused her supervisor's demand for sexual favors from a "black chick." Plaintiff alleged racial and sexual discrimination and filed suit under both Title VII and section 1981. The district court, however, dismissed the section

---

54. Minimum Wage Study Comm'n, A Demographic Profile of Minimum Wage Workers 10 (Sept. 1980).
55. Women's Bureau, U.S. Dep't of Labor, Women Private Household Workers: A Statistical and Legislative Profile (1978).
56. Wiener, *Careers: Standing Up for Household Technicians*, Washington Post, Sept. 30, 1980, at B-5.
57. *1980 Hearings*, *supra* note 2, at 96, 166 (testimony of Eleanor H. Norton and Ruth T. Prokop).
58. Many black women, nonetheless, have been active in protecting themselves against sexual harassment. It is interesting to note that although relatively few sexual harassment cases have been appealed through the courts, three of the five Circuit Courts of Appeals cases on sexual harassment were brought by black women; in several lower court decisions, the plaintiffs are identified as black. This activism is probably due both to the greater or more severe harassment visited upon black women and the black woman's long familiarity with discrimination and willingness to seek redress through the courts.
59. The legislative history of Titles VII and IX of the Civil Rights Act of 1964 can be found in H.R. Rep. No. 914, 88th Cong., 2d Sess., *reprinted in* [1964] U.S. Code Cong. & Ad. News 2355, 2401, 2408; S. Rep. No. 872, 88th Cong., 2d Sess., *reprinted in* [1964] U.S. Code Cong. & Ad. News 2355, 2401, 2408.
60. 600 F.2d 211 (9th Cir. 1979).

1981 claim, stating that it was not a racial discrimination case and that plaintiff had conceded that only sexual discrimination was involved.[61] On appeal, the court found that plaintiff had made no such concession and reinstated her claim of racial discrimination.[62] In *Munford v. James T. Barnes & Co.*,[63] plaintiff alleged both sexual and racial discrimination, arguing that sociological studies showed that she was more likely to be a victim of sexual harassment because she was black. The district court granted a motion for summary judgment on the racial discrimination claim, allowing only the sexual discrimination claim to remain in the case.[64] In the *Continental Can* case,[65] although plaintiff alleged only sexual discrimination, the verbal abuse showed clear racial overtones. Finally, there is some indication that employees of agencies who investigate charges of harassment mislead black women on how to file their charges, based on the perception that one must choose either sex or race as a basis for the complaint.[66]

Because black women are often harassed due to both race and sex, they should not be foreclosed from defining discrimination against them in such terms. A representative of the Working Women's Institute, an independent resource and research center that is in the forefront of work on sexual harassment, stated that the majority of black women who come to the Institute with complaints of sexual harassment suspect that they are dealing with instances of sex-race discrimination. This is manifested either implicitly, so that the woman is unsure whether the harassment is racially or sexually motivated, or explicitly, where the harasser expressed his sexual interest in terms of her race.[67]

One district court has held that black women who filed a class action suit under both Title VII and section 1981 are not a special subcategory entitled to protection and that "they should not be allowed to combine statutory remedies to create a new 'super-remedy' which would give them relief beyond what the drafters of the relevant statutes intended."[68] On appeal, the Eighth Circuit noted in dicta that it did not subscribe entirely with the district court's reasoning in rejecting the sex-race claim.[69]

---

61. 418 F. Supp. 233, 234 (N.D. Cal. 1976).
62. 600 F.2d at 212.
63. 441 F. Supp. 459 (E.D. Mich. 1977).
64. *Id.* at 466-67.
65. — Minn. —, 297 N.W.2d 241 (1980).
66. *See, e.g.*, Barnes v. Costle, 561 F.2d 983 (D.C. Cir. 1977), where the agency EEO officer advised plaintiff to file on the basis of race only.
67. Interview with Peggy Crull, Research Director of the Working Women's Institute, in New York City (Nov. 11, 1980).
68. Degraffenreid v. General Motors Corp., 413 F. Supp. 142 (E.D. Mo. 1976), *aff'd in part, rev'd in part*, 558 F.2d 480 (8th Cir. 1977). The EEOC participated as *amicus curiae* in the *Degraffenreid* case on appeal, and argued that Title VII is available to eliminate all discriminatory practices in whatever form they appear, including race and sex discrimination against black women. The Commission has long supported the concept of sex-race discrimination. *See, e.g.*, EEOC Dec. No. 72-0679, [1971] EEOC Dec. (CCH) ¶ 6,324; EEOC Dec. No. 72-0320, [1971] EEOC Dec. (CCH) ¶ 6,294.
69. Degraffenreid v. General Motors Corp., 558 F.2d at 484.

The Fifth Circuit, on the other hand, has recognized the unique legal predicament of black women. Its opinion in *Jeffries v. Harris County Community Action Association*[70] states in part that "[r]ecognition of black females as a distinct protected subgroup for purposes of the prima facie case and proof of pretext is the only way to identify and remedy discrimination directed toward black females."[71] The court based its decision on the language of the statute and the legislative history, yet found its decision mandated by the holdings of the Supreme Court in the "sex plus" cases.

The "sex plus" cases involve employment policies that single out certain subclasses of women for discriminatory treatment, for example, women with children, married women, and pregnant women. The court reasoned that it would be illogical to hold that although an employer could not discriminate against a "sex plus" subgroup, he would be free to discriminate against the black female subgroup. As the court stated, "[t]his would be a particularly illogical result, since the 'plus' factors in the former categories are ostensibly 'neutral' factors, while race itself is prohibited as a criterion for employment."[72]

Judge Randall differed from the majority of the panel on what she called "combination discrimination." She stated first of all that there was no legal authority to support a "combination discrimination" claim.[73] Nevertheless, one can find several examples in which courts have found a cause of action for combination discrimination.[74] Secondly, Judge Randall argued that the factual differences between sex-plus discrimination and combination discrimination preclude the use of the "sex plus" analysis in combination cases.[75] The "sex plus" analysis is helpful, however, for it requires that courts carefully examine Congress' proscriptions and give full credit to those proscriptions. Congress did not say explicitly that discrimination on the basis of "sex plus," for example, marital status, would violate Title VII, but courts have developed a "sex plus" theory of discrimination that has found widespread acceptance. What Congress did say, however, and quite explicitly, is that neither discrimination on the basis of race nor on the basis of sex will be allowed. Courts must heed this mandate and must eliminate

---

70. 615 F.2d 1025 (5th Cir. 1980).
71. *Id.* at 1034.
72. *Id.*
73. *Id.* at 1034-35 n.7.
74. Payne v. Travenol Laboratories, 416 F. Supp. 248 (N.D. Miss. 1976), *rev'd and vacated in part on other grounds, aff'd in part*, 565 F.2d 895 (5th Cir. 1978), *cert. denied*, 439 U.S. 835 (1978) (certification of class of black females alleging sex-race discrimination); Griffiths v. Hampton, — F. Supp. — (D.D.C. 1976) (court has authority to fashion appropriate relief to black female who alleged sex-race discrimination); Logan v. St. Luke's Hospital, 428 F. Supp. 127 (S.D.N.Y. 1977) (black female established prima facie case of racial and/or sexual discrimination); Collins v. City of Los Angeles, 18 Fair Empl. Prac. Cas. 594 (C.D. Cal. 1978) (statistics are insufficient to show that black female was terminated because of racial and/or sexual discrimination); Vuyanich v. Republic National Bank of Dallas, 409 F. Supp. 1083 (N.D. Tex. 1976) (court suggests evidence of termination of black female "smacks of sexual as well as racial discrimination," *id.* at 1089).
75. 615 F.2d at 1033-34.

these kinds of discrimination whether they appear as an individual claim or in a combined form.[76]

Another example clarifies the issue. Title VII has been interpreted to prohibit discrimination on the basis of "sex plus" age, for example, in the airline stewardess cases.[77] As age discrimination is no longer a "plus," but has its own statutory basis in the Age Discrimination in Employment Act,[78] discrimination on the basis of sex-age is now combination discrimination just as is sex-race discrimination. Could one now argue that sex-age cases are entitled to less protection than before? Such a conclusion would make a mockery of Congressional intent to accord age discrimination even greater protection. Judge Randall's view of sex-race claims would do the same. Finally, Judge Randall cites the evidentiary problems involved in proving discrimination against a subgroup of females.[79] However, forcing a plaintiff to choose between sexual or racial discrimination ensures that the evidence selected will be both inappropriate and insufficient to prove the case. Once the nature of the discrimination has been analyzed properly, proving discrimination against black women as a group should be no more difficult than proving discrimination against women with children or women over forty.

It is important for courts and practitioners to understand that black women often experience discrimination because of sex-race; it is even more important that black women understand this fact. Without a clear understanding of the underlying cause of whatever discrimination is taking place, the discriminatee will not be able to focus attention and investigation in a helpful way. Black women are in a unique position: they may face discrimination based on race, sex, or sex-race. A clearer understanding of the existence of black women as a discrete group and acceptance of this third category as a real possibility will make discrimination against black women easier to identify and eliminate.

CONCLUSION

This article has attempted to clarify the nature of sexual harassment by looking at it through the lens of race. In the process, the article has shown that although sexual and racial harassment share many of the same psychological and sociological underpinnings, the unique nature

---

76. In Franks v. Bowman, 424 U.S. 747 (1976), the Supreme Court noted that "in enacting Title VII of the Civil Rights Act of 1964, Congress intended to *prohibit all practices in whatever form* which create inequality in employment opportunity due to discrimination on the basis of race, religion, sex, or national origin . . . ." *Id.* at 763 (emphasis added).
77. EEOC Dec. No. 66-5762, [1968] EEOC Dec. (CCH) ¶ 6,001 (violation of Title VII to require stewardesses to resign or accept reassignment at age 32); EEOC Dec. No. 70-38, 2 Fair Empl. Prac. Cas. 165 (1969) (violation of Title VII to require discharge of motorbus hostesses who reach age 32); EEOC Dec. No. 70-167, [1969] EEOC Dec. (CCH) ¶ 6,076 (requiring stewardesses to resign at age 32 violates Title VII).
78. 29 U.S.C. §§ 621-634 (1976), *as amended by* the Age Discrimination in Employment Act Amendments of 1978, Pub. L. 95-256, 92 Stat. 189.
79. 615 F.2d at 1034-35, 1035 n.7.

of the male-female interaction makes sexual harassment a more complicated issue. To the extent that these similarities and differences are understood, a clearer picture of the nature of sexual harassment emerges. In order to provide clarity, the article has discussed two analytical models for sexual harassment cases: (a) a generalized harassment model that is analogous to racial harassment, and (b) a sexual exploitation model that is analogous to rape. By adopting these suggested models, courts will be able to identify more clearly relevant evidentiary matters, legal issues, and appropriate remedies.

Finally, this study has explored the unique situation of black women facing sexual harassment in the work force and has shown that they are often exploited because of their sex and race. Recognition that black women are a distinct group in American society and that sex-race discrimination in employment exists is the first step in eradicating that discrimination.

Discrimination in this country takes subtle, varied, and changing forms. It is all, however, a totality. To the extent that we can grasp the essence of discrimination, we can identify and eliminate its many manifestations.

Comparable Worth:
Is This A Theory For Black Workers?

*JUDY SCALES-TRENT**

I. INTRODUCTION

Comparable worth is a theory which moves beyond the general proposition that people should be paid the same when they are performing equal work, and argues that they should be paid the same when they are performing work of comparable value to the employer. Its proponents believe that because minorities and women have been channelled into certain job categories, their jobs have been devalued—and their wages depressed—solely because of their race or sex. The comparable worth theory seeks to attack these depressed wages as discrimination compensable under Title VII of the Civil Rights Act of 1964. For example, proponents of this theory argue that not only should janitors and cleaning women who are performing essentially the same work be paid equally, but that secretaries and carpenters should be paid the same where those jobs are judged to be of comparable worth to the employer.

In the past several years, the comparable worth issue has been gaining support, and drawing a round of debate. Articles have been written,[1] cases have been brought,[2] and unions and public interest groups have organized to further the cause. Comparable worth is a means of attacking wage discrimination where jobs are segregated and devalued because of the identity of those who hold the jobs. As such, the theory is equally applicable whether the jobs are segregated and devalued due to the race, or the sex, of the job holder.[3] The Third Circuit has strongly suggested that the comparable worth theory is available to all protected groups, not only women.[4] And, in fact, the first "wage comparability" case was a race case.[5] Nonetheless, the wage comparability issue is widely perceived as a women's issue,[6] and by many, as a white women's

---

* Judy Scales-Trent recently joined the law school faculty at SUNY-Buffalo as an associate professor of law. She was formerly an appellate attorney with the Equal Employment Opportunity Commission.

1. See, e.g., Note, *Equal Pay, Comparable Work, and Job Evaluation*, 90 YALE L. J. 657 (1981); Nelson, Opton & Wilson, *Wage Discrimination and the "Comparable Worth" Theory in Perspective*, 13 U. MICH. J. L. REF. 231 (1980) [hereinafter cited as Nelson, Opton & Wilson]; and Blumrosen, *Wage Discrimination, Job Segregation, and Title VII of the Civil Rights Act of 1964*, 12 U. MICH. J.L. REF. 397 (1979) [hereinafter cited as Blumrosen].

2. See, e.g., AFSCME v. State of Washington, 578 F. Supp.

846 (W.D. Wash. 1983); Plemer v. Parsons-Gilbane, 713 F.2d 1127 (5th Cir. 1983); Lemons v. City and County of Denver, 620 F.2d 228 (10th Cir.), *cert. denied*, 449 U.S. 888 (1980); Christensen v. Iowa, 563 F.2d 353 (8th Cir. 1977).

3. The Civil Rights Act of 1964, 42 U.S.C. § 2000e (1976). Title VII § 703(a) of the Act provides, in pertinent part:

It shall be unlawful employment practice for an employer (1) to...discriminate against any individual with respect to his compensation...because of such individual's *race*, color, religion, *sex*, or national origin; or (2) to...classify his employees...in any way which would deprive or tend to deprive any individual of employment opportunities or otherwise adversely affect his status as an employee, because of such individual's *race*, color, religion, *sex*, or national origin. (Emphasis added.)

See Blumrosen, *supra* note 1 at 309-401; *see also* D. TREIMAN & H. HARTMANN, WOMEN, WORK AND WAGES: EQUAL PAY FOR JOBS OF EQUAL VALUE 9, 13-17 (1981) [hereinafter cited as TREIMAN & HARTMANN].

4. See IUE v. Westinghouse Elec. Corp., 631 F.2d 1094, 1097, 1100 (3rd Cir. 1980), *cert denied* 452 U.S. 967 (1981) (narrow interpretation of Bennett Amendment would mean that comparable worth theory would be available to all protected groups except women).

5. See Quarles v. Phillip Morris, Inc., 279 F. Supp. 505 (E. D. Va. 1968).

6. See, e.g., B. SCHLEI & P. GROSSMAN, EMPLOYMENT DISCRIMINATION LAW, 477 n.142 (2d ed. 1983).

[Women's Rights Law Reporter, Volume 8, Number 1-2, Winter 1984]
© *1984 by Women's Rights Law Reporter, Rutgers—The State University*
0085-8269/80/0908

issue.[7] The question which will be explored in this article is "why?" Is this theory in reality only available to women? To white women? And if not, why have black workers—both men and women—not taken up the cause of comparable worth to improve their employment situation? What forces are at play that lead to the perception that this is an issue for white women only? This article will also explore the related question of whether comparable worth will benefit white women workers at the expense of black workers.

It is the thesis of this article that groups which suffer employment discrimination in this country suffer in different ways, and that a particular group will use whatever legal theory will ameliorate its distinct employment problem. Thus, because of the peculiar discrimination faced by white women today—and to some extent, the problems of black and white women overlap—this is the group for which a wage comparability theory is most useful. Also, although legally and analytically wage comparability is available to challenge wage discrimination based on race, the major employment problems facing black men today are not pure wage issues, but unemployment and underemployment. It is therefore unlikely that the theory will be widely utilized in a pure race context in the near future. Finally, this article rejects the simplistic notion that a legal theory which benefits white women automatically harms black workers, and discusses ways in which wage discrimination against one group of workers can be remedied without harming the employment opportunities of others.

II. ANALYSIS

Because one's position in the work force determines what she will do to improve that position—and therefore, which legal theories will be helpful—the first step in this analysis is to look separately at the employment problems of white women, black women, and black men, in order to understand what group can best profit from a wage comparability theory at this time.

A. Employment Situation of White Women

Unemployment is not a major employment issue for white women.[8] Their major employment

problem is that they are concentrated in a limited number of occupations with low pay. For example, they are secretaries, nurses, dieticians, and elementary and secondary school teachers.[9] Thus, for white women to improve their employment picture, they have two choices: they can move into traditionally male jobs, which are higher paying, or they can stay in what are traditionally women's jobs and seek higher pay for those jobs by, for example, raising comparable worth claims.

Although it is easy to argue that white women should just change jobs if they want more money, in fact such a massive dislocation is not likely to occur in the near future.[10] Many pressures coalesce to make such a job shift unlikely, including discrimination against women in non-traditional jobs, and the training investment which many women have made in the traditional female jobs.[11] Also, because of early childhood socialization, many women choose female ("helping") roles at work.[12] Continuity between the woman's role at home and at work is deemed important. Therefore, many of the traditional female jobs—nurse, teacher, secretary—while carrying a certain amount of status for women, also fulfill some aspect of their socialization.[13] Finally, studies have shown that in certain settings, women can lose rank in an organization by crossing over to male jobs.[14] There are thus strong incentives for white women to stay in the traditional female jobs,

---

UNDEREMPLOYMENT BLACKS, HISPANICS, AND WOMEN, 14, 56 (1982) [hereinafter cited as U.S. COMM'N ON CIVIL RIGHTS]. In 1980, the unemployment rate for white females was 5.6% as compared to 6.0% for white males, and 13.0% for black males and females. *Id.* at 5. This low unemployment rate reflects their concentration in high demand occupations, as well as the fact that they tend to leave the workplace when work is unavailable. *Id.* at 14.

9. *Id.* at 6.

10. As of 1970, 44% of white women would have had to shift their jobs in order to attain the identical job distribution as white men. TREIMAN & HARTMANN, *supra* note 3 at 25. Because women are still majoring in traditionally women's fields in college, and still moving into traditional female occupations DAILY LAB REP. (BNA) No. 197, at A-7 (Oct. 11, 1983), this percentage has probably not declined over the past decade.

11. TREIMAN & HARTMANN, *supra* note 3 at 2, 55, 67.

12. Madden, *Discrimination—A Manifestation of Male Market Power?* at 163-164, and Lloyd, *The Division of Labor Between the Sexes*, at 15-18, in SEX, DISCRIMINATION, AND THE DIVISION OF LABOR: A REVIEW (C. Lloyd ed. 1975); Schrank & Riley, *Women in Work Organizations*, in WOMEN AND THE AMERICAN ECONOMY 94, (J. Kreps ed. 1976) [hereinafter cited as Schrank & Riley].

13. TREIMAN & HARTMANN, *supra* note 3 at 53-54. See also Schrank & Riley, *supra* note 12 at 92-94.

14. Schrank & Riley, *supra* note 93.

---

7. *See, e.g.,* statement by M. Horowitz, counsel to the Director of the Office of Management and Budget. N.Y. Times, Jan. 22, 1984, § 1, at 15, col. 5-6, reproduced infra in text accompanying note 45.

8. U.S. COMM'N ON CIVIL RIGHTS, UNEMPLOYMENT AND

and to seek better pay for them: wage comparability is the perfect theory in that situation.

B. Employment Problems Facing Black Workers

The employment problems facing black workers are very different from those white women confront. The major problems for both black men and women is simply getting a job. They have the highest unemployment rates of any other group in the country—twice the unemployment rate of whites.[15] The second major problem faced by blacks is keeping full-time work once they get a job. Black men have an exceptionally high rate of intermittent employment—that is, they experience significant amounts of unemployment on a yearly basis.[16] Black women have a very high rate of involuntary part-time work—that is, they have jobs, but work less than a full week due to factors beyond their control.[17]

The third major problem facing black workers involves the kinds of jobs they have. Black women are grossly overrepresented in marginal jobs,[18] working as cashiers, maids, messengers, child care workers, etc. In 1980, 21.6 percent of all black women workers held such jobs.[19] Black men are also overrepresented in marginal jobs,[20] but the more crucial aspect of their underemployment is that they are by and large unable to translate their education into better jobs. In 1980, over one-third of black men (37 percent) were in jobs which required substantially less education than they had attained.[21] Given this general picture, one can begin to see why a legal theory which is aimed at wage

discrimination alone will not be of immediate interest to large groups of black workers.

C. Employment Picture of Black Women

The employment picture of black women, however, deserves a closer look. Despite the fact that black women suffer employment problems which white women do not (unemployment, overrepresentation in marginal jobs), one of the major employment changes in the post-'60's period has been the "increased convergence" in the job structure of black and white women.[22] Black women now make almost the same as white women in white-collar jobs, and over 90 percent of the earnings of white women in blue-collar jobs.[23] They have narrowed this earnings gap, however, because they have moved into the same jobs in which white women are concentrated—the low-paying jobs which are traditionally easier for blacks to enter. In 1980, 36 percent of all white women and 29.3 percent of all black women were employed as clericals.[24] Black women are also concentrated in the same low-paying professions as white women—elementary school teaching, social work, and nursing.[25] As the United States Commission on Civil Rights has pointed out, inequitable pay for women—be they white, black, or hispanic—is the largest employment problem experienced by *any* group.[26]

Given this convergence of job structure, there is every reason to believe that black women will become more interested in wage comparability and will join in suits and non-litigation strategies with white women, as they have in suits brought under the Equal Pay Act. This interest is already beginning to manifest itself. For example, black women are involved, along with white women, whenever the American Federation of State, County and Municipal Employees (AFSCME) institutes a wage comparability action. In fact, one of the named plaintiffs in *AFSCME v. State of Washington*, was a black woman.[27] Black economists have noted that

---

15. U.S. COMM'N ON CIVIL RIGHTS, *supra* note 8 at 14-16. In January 1984, the unemployment rate for blacks was 16.7%, and for whites, 6.9%. N.Y. Times, Feb. 4, 1984 § 1, at 4, col. 1. The unemployment rate for black teenagers is approximately 50%. *Id.* at 1, col. 4.

16. U.S. COMM'N ON CIVIL RIGHTS, *supra* note 8 at 16-19. In addition to the impact on earnings, intermittent employment causes hardship because of the inability to obtain seniority, and the creation of an unstable work record. Black men suffer intermittent employment at twice the rate of white men, in part because they are more likely to be employed in industries which have frequent layoffs. *Id.* at 17-18.

17. *Id.* at 7.

18. *Id.* at 7-9, 20-21. "Marginal jobs" are those with poor working conditions, low wages, and high labor turnover; they neither require nor offer any training. *Id.* at 7-8. Marginal jobs constitute a form of underemployment because although the jobs offer full-time work, they offer little chance for advancement or economic reward. *Id.*

19. *Id.* at 8-9.

20. *Id.*

21. *Id.* at 10, 23-26.

22. P. WALLACE, BLACK WOMEN IN THE LABOR FORCE 8 (1980) [hereinafter cited as WALLACE].

23. Westcott, *Blacks in the 1970's: Did they Scale the Job Ladder?* MONTHLY LABOR REVIEW, June 1982 at 29, 36.

24. *Id.* at 30.

25. Kilson, *Black Women in the Professions, 1890-1970,* MONTHLY LABOR REVIEW, May 1977 at 38, 40.

26. U.S. COMM'N ON CIVIL RIGHTS, *supra* note 8, at 45.

27. Telephone conversation with Winn Newman, special council for AFSCME, who represented the union in *AFSCME v. State of Washington*, 578 F. Supp. 846 (W. D. Wash. 1983). *See also Pay Equity,* ESSENCE, Apr. 1984, at 20

black women will benefit from successful wage comparability claims.[28] And, finally, two Washington-based public interest groups, The National Institute for Pay Equity and The National Institute for Women of Color, have joined forces to highlight the importance of the wage comparability issue for all minority women with their joint publication, *Women of Color and Pay Equity.*

Black women's interest in comparable worth may nonetheless not be widespread due to the general suspicion and distrust with which most black women view the "white woman's movement," and issues which emanate from it.[29] Another possible explanation for the lack of interest is the time lag which inevitably occurs when black women confront discrimination in the workforce. They must first overcome the race barrier in order to get into the kinds of jobs held by white women; as a second step, they will express their concern about inequitable wages in those jobs. However, despite any lack of interest, there can be no doubt that black women will benefit from any gains white women make with comparable worth strategies.

D. Comparable Worth and Black Men

As it is clear that black women can profit from the wage comparability theory where they are in jobs which are devalued due to sex, the question remains, "what of a 'pure' race case?" Is pay equity an issue only for women, regardless of the race of the woman? Surely, there can be no doubt that jobs are segregated and devalued due to the race of the jobholder, and that the comparable worth theory can analytically and legally be applied to race cases. Why hasn't it been?

One way to answer this question is to set out the elements that are presumably present in a classic wage comparability situation, and see whether black men, in their current employment situation, fit within that paradigm. These elements are:
- having a job
- job stability
- job segregation by class membership

- low wages
- job with intrinsic value to job holder
- investment in training for job.[30]

It is immediately clear that in their current employment situation black men simply do not fit within this paradigm. They have significant difficulty in getting a job, and in keeping a job. And the jobs that they have are not, by and large, jobs they would want to keep. As noted above, they are still over-represented in marginal jobs (e.g., cab drivers, dishwashers, office 'boys,' messengers, garage workers).[31] These are not jobs, like teaching or nursing, for which they have invested in training. Also, as noted above, more than one-third of all black men should be in higher level jobs than the ones they have, by virtue of their education.[32] Finally, there is no chance that black men, like women, might lose status by moving into the higher-paying white male jobs. Thus, while one set of cultural values coalesces to keep women in traditional "female" jobs, a different set of values leads black men to want to move out of their jobs, and into the high-paying, prestigious jobs held by white men. Nonetheless, the comparable worth theory is fully available to black workers alleging race discrimination, and has been used by black workers.[33] It should be considered again when an appropriate case presents itself.

In order to determine whether wages in job categories with a high percentage of minorities are lower than wages for comparable jobs which are predominantly white, black workers should pressure their employers to conduct a job evaluation study, which might provide the basis for a pay equity suit. Unions and women's groups have been organizing for years around this issue with much success.[34] Also, when women employees are pressuring the employer to conduct an evaluation study of

---

(black women leading librarians in Virginia in fight for pay equity).

28. *Black America is in a State of Crisis,* BLACK ENTERPRISE, Jan. 1984 at 33.

29. *See, e.g.,* G. JOSEPH & J. LEWIS, COMMON DIFFERENCES: CONFLICTS IN BLACK AND WHITE FEMINIST PERSPECTIVES 276-77 (1981); and L.R. WALUM, THE DYNAMICS OF SEX AND GENDER: A SOCIOLOGICAL PERSPECTIVE 212-15 (1977).

30. See discussion of employment situation of white women, *supra* text accompanying notes 8-14 for elements of wage comparability paradigm.

31. *See supra* text accompanying notes 20 & 21 and U.S. COMM'N ON CIVIL RIGHTS, *supra* note 8 at 61.

32. *See supra* text accompanying note 21.

33. *See, e.g.,* Kirby v. Colony Furniture Co., 613 F.2d 696 (8th Cir. 1980) (black employees allege classification system enables employer to pay whites more than blacks for comparable work). Needless to say, a comparable worth case could also be present where black men *and* women are concentrated in a job category which is devalued due to their race.

34. *Pay Equity: Equal Pay for Work of Comparable Value, 1982: Hearing Before the Subcomm. on Civil Service, Subcomm. on Human Resources, and Subcomm. on Compensation and*

the work force to determine if certain jobs are being undervalued and underpaid due to the sex of the job holder, blacks should insist that the study also include an analysis of job categories by race. An employer who performs a job evaluation study for female workers but not for similarly situated black male workers, violates Title VII, and risks a suit brought by black workers for injunctive relief.[35]

In the public sector, although there has been much legislative activity concerning the implementation of pay equity in various civil service systems, the emphasis is on male/female wage differentials, and not on race. For example, although eighteen states are presently conducting job evaluation studies of their civil service systems as a basis for wage comparability analyses, only one of these states, New York, is studying its civil service system by race, as well as by sex.[36] On the federal level, four bills and two concurrent resolutions which seek to promote pay equity in both the federal and private sectors are currently pending before Congress. Whereas all the bills introduced in 1983[37] saw the pay equity issue solely in terms of sex discrimination,[38] those introduced this year all have as their stated purpose the elimination of discrimination based on *sex, race,* or *ethnicity* through

pay equity.[39] Although this apears to be good news for black workers, it is nonetheless apparent that even in the 1984 proposals, "race" was added as an afterthought, as it is not integrated into the bills in any meaningful fashion.[40] As presently drafted, these bills are ineffective legal tools for black workers. Because of the large representation of blacks in the federal work force, congressional initiatives which propose to look at the civil service system in terms of promoting pay equity for black workers deserve the careful attention of black citizens and legislators, in order to determine whether these proposals meet black interests. If not, it might be appropriate to deny the initiatives black support.

When a special committee of the National Academy of Sciences undertook a study of wage comparability on behalf of the Equal Employment Opportunity Commission, it stated that it concentrated on the inequalities between male and female jobholders, instead of those between blacks and whites, for three reasons: (1) the difference between the earnings of men and women is greater than the difference between the earnings of blacks and whites, and is growing; (2) the extent of occupational segregation is greater by sex than by race; and (3) most of the research on wage comparability focuses on sex, not race.[41] What the Committee said, in effect, was that it decided to concentrate on the most egregious case, and the case with the most data already available. Although it emphasized that

---

Employee Benefits, 97th Cong., 2d Sess. 7 (1982) (Statement of Nancy Perlman, Chairperson, National Committee on Pay Equity).

For a concise description of the importance of job evaluation studies and how they can be used, see Note, *Equal Pay, Comparable Work and Job Evaluation,* 90 YALE L. J. 657, 673-77 (1981).

35. The refusal to perform a study for black workers which was performed for white workers would constitue disparate treatment under Title VII, which commands that benefits of employment must be granted equally to all similarly situated workers. *See* Newport News Shipbldg. & Dry Dock Co. v. EEOC, 103 S. Ct. 2622 (1983).

36. Telephone conversation with Joy Ann Grune, Executive Director, National Committee on Pay Equity, Washington D.C. (May 1, 1984). *See also Pay Equity: Equal Pay for Work of Comparable Value, 1982: Hearings Before the Subcomm. on Civil Service, Subcomm. on Human Resources, and Subcomm. on Compensation and Employee Benefits,* 97th Cong., 2d Sess. (1982) (Statement of Ronnie Steinberg, Research Director, Center for Women in Government, State University of New York at Albany).

37. S. 1900, 98th Cong., 1st Sess. (1983) (bill to require executive branch to enforce laws which promote pay equity); H.R. 4237, 98th Cong., 1st Sess. (1983) (bill to guarantee pay equity to federal employees); S. Con. Res. 83, 98th Cong., 1st Sess. (1983) (resolution to establish a commission to study pay equity in the legislative agencies).

38. Although S. 1900, *supra* note 37, has as its stated purpose the elimination of "Wage-setting practices which discriminate on the basis of sex, race, ethnicity," the *Statement of*

Findings and Purpose discusses only the male/female wage differential. *See* § 2(a)(1)-(5). Furthermore, it defines "discriminatory wage-setting practices" solely in terms of how wages are set for female workers. *Definitions,* § 3 (4).

39. H.R. 4599, 98th Cong., 2d Sess. (1984) (bill to promote pay equity in federal civil service system); H.R. 5092, 98th Cong., 2d Sess. (1984) (bill requiring periodic reports by EEOC, the Attorney General, and the Secretary of Labor on their actions to promote pay equity); H. Con. Res. 239, 98th Cong., 2d Sess. (1984) (resolution to establish a commission to study pay equity).

40. The congressional findings in H.R. 4599, *supra* note 39, mention only sex discrimination. Further, that bill also defines "discriminatory wage-setting practices" solely in terms of sex. *Definitions,* § 3(2). In H.R. 5092, *supra* note 40, the first five findings are devoted to sex discrimination; race and ethnicity are added only in the sixth finding. Rep. Oakar, who introduced both H.R. 4599 and H.R. 5092, has repeatedly stated that this legislation is aimed at eliminating the wage gap between *men* and *women. See* DAILY LAB. REP. (BNA) No. 19 at A-5 (Jan. 30, 1984); DAILY LAB. REP. (BNA) No. 65 at A-2 (Apr. 4, 1984).

41. TREIMAN & HARTMANN, *supra* note 3 at 16. Note, however, that even by the Committee's own data, the extent of occupational segregation by race is very high. *Id.* at 27 and Table 7.

"its analysis is applicable whenever substantial job segregation between different groups exists and whenever particular jobs are dominated by particular groups"[42] its study—significantly entitled *Women, Work and Wages*—has nonetheless contributed to the dominant viewpoint that pay equity is only a woman's issue. This narrow interpretation must be laid to rest.

III. IS COMPARABLE WORTH A THEORY WHICH WILL HARM BLACK WORKERS?

A final issue that must be addressed in this discussion of black workers and comparable worth is whether pay equity will ultimately harm black workers at the same time that it benefits white women. One highly placed administration official has criticized the comparable worth theory, stating that "it would help middle-class white women at the expense of blacks."[43] He added:

> There is nothing the Reagan Administration has done that holds as much long-term threat to the black community as comparable worth. The maintenance man will be paid less so the librarian can be paid more.[44]

It is important to note that those who raise the specter of white female gains wiping out black gains are playing on a very real and very old source of tension between the black movement and the women's movement. Although this tension is real, one should not be carried away by hyperbole, but look carefully at this argument to see if it withstands scrutiny.

As one can see, those who foresee this dire result do not really articulate how it might come to pass. It is difficult to respond to unarticulated hypotheticals. It should be noted initially, however, that those who claim that they can see how pay equity claims will play out in the long run are being disingenuous. They are not basing their conclusions on long-term studies of organizations which have implemented comparable worth remedies; they are not factoring into their analysis action which will be taken by other protected groups to vindicate their rights. And what about the imponderables: if female jobs begin to pay well, will they become more attractive to males, including minority males? Or consider this: a "female-dominated" job category for purposes of a wage comparability claim is one which is 70 percent or more female.[45] What about the other 30 percent? What percentage of the remainder is minority men, who will win increased wages along with the women?[46] It is simply too difficult to track a straight line from legislation or agreements mandating wage shifts into the future. Who would have expected, for example, that as a result of the passage of the Pregnancy Discrimination Act, men could successfully sue their employer for increased medical benefits, as they did in *Newport News Shipbuilding & Dry Dock Co., v. EEOC?*[47]

Furthermore, those who argue that pay equity will harm black workers fail to recognize that to the extent that black women benefit from wage comparability, the black family and black community will also be enriched: approximately one out of every three black families is headed by a woman,[48] and earnings by black wives make up a large part of the income of black families.[49]

The administration official quoted suggested that the "maintenance man" (presumably black) would be paid less so that the "librarian" (presumably white female) could be paid more, without explaining how this would take place. And, indeed, it is hornbook law that an employer may not *lower* the wages of a group of employees in order to equalize a discriminatory wage differential: the wages of the lower paid group must be *raised* in order to come into compliance with the law.[50] Black workers need not fear, therefore, that their wages will automatically be lowered if the employer is forced to remedy a pay equity claim, just as black workers' wages have not been lowered to enable employers to pay claims brought under the Equal Pay Act.

One could argue, however, that due to a pay equity claim, an employer might have such a large

42. *Id.* at 16.

43. Statement by M. Horowitz, counsel to the Director of the Office of Management and Budget, N.Y. Times, Jan. 22, 1984, § 1, at 15, col. 5-6.

44. *Id. See also* Nelson, Opton & Wilson, *supra* note 1, at 236.

45. Blumrosen, *supra* note 1 at 461 & n.236.

46. *Id.* at 498-99.

47. 103 S. Ct. 2622 (1983).

48. WALLACE, *supra* note 22, at 80.

49. *Id.* at 64-65.

50. Under the Equal Pay Act, the only way a violation can be remedied is for the lower wages to be raised to the higher. 29 U.S.C. § 206(d)(1) (1976); Corning Glass Works v. Brennan, 417 U.S. 188, 207 (1974). Several courts have held that the same rationale must be followed under Title VII. *See, e.g.,* Rosen v. Pub. Serv. Elec. & Gas Co., 477 F.2d 90 (3rd Cir. 1973), and Hays v. Potlatch Forests Inc., 465 F.2d 1081 (8th Cir. 1972).

liability that it might have to resort to layoffs—which would harm black employees—or that it might be unable to meet its affirmative action hiring commitments. In reality, though, many pay equity claims will involve limited job categories,[51] and limited relief. Also, where wage equalization will require large payments, those payments need not take place at one time. Labor and civil rights leaders have pointed out that expenses can be held down if the parties avoid litigation, and negotiate settlements which will phase in the pay raise over a three to four-year period.[52] All workers have a strong interest in maintaining the economic well-being of the organization for which they work. This is especially true for workers who file pay equity claims, for they are working for improved wages in a job they intend to keep.

Nonetheless, in a situation where an employer is faced with a huge liability, one must remember that the courts have shown a willingness to exercise their inherent equitable authority to limit the relief so as not to unduly harm the interests of other protected parties, or of innocent parties. For example, in *Romasanta v. United Air Lines*,[53] the court refused to award complete retroactive seniority to identified white female discriminatees, in part, to enable the employer to meet its affirmative action obligation to hire blacks under a consent decree.[54] Of course, employers faced with huge liability need not automatically lay off workers to save money: private companies could limit their profit margin, and government entities could cut back on services or raise taxes to cover the cost of remedying the wage discrimination. Companies could consider money-saving devices such as work-sharing or early retirement programs.[55] It is up to black workers to

use unions, the courts, and political pressure to ensure that employers think creatively about how they might meet their financial obligation without limiting the employment situation of blacks. White workers and unions who want black support would do well to participate in this creative enterprise.

In conclusion, whenever commentators bemoan the fact that opportunities for white women may be closing doors on black men, they trigger longstanding tension between the black movement and the women's movement. They pit black men and white women in a struggle for limited employment opportunities in an economic system that has a clear hierarchy by race and sex, and at the same time, they ignore the needs of black women workers. More importantly, these commentators divert attention from the fundamental questions: Why does such an employment hierarchy exist at all? And how can it be eliminated? Instead of following the agenda of those who suggest that black men engage in a struggle with white women for limited employment opportunities, it seems more appropriate for black men and women to set their own agendas, directing their action at these more fundamental questions.

IV. CONCLUSION

This analysis of the employment situations of different groups shows that because of the specific employment situation of white women today—high job segregation and low wages—wage comparability is, for the moment, primarily a theory for white women. As black and other minority women merge into that job structure, however—and as they become aware of their common position with respect to wages—their interest in wage comparability is likely to grow. This analysis also shows that because it is unlikely that black men would want to stay in "traditional" black male jobs, and because the other employment problems of black men are so pressing, wage comparability is not a theory which will find wide appeal among black male workers.

It is important to remember, nonetheless, that wage comparability can be a race issue. Black workers should be watching with interest for the re-

---

51. *See, e.g.*, Lemons v. City and County of Denver, 620 F.2d 228 (10th Cir.), *cert. denied*, 449 U.S. 888 (1980) (nurses); Christensen v. Iowa, 563 F.2d 353 (8th Cir. 1977) (clericals); TREIMAN & HARTMANN, *supra* note 3 at 2 (university librarians).

52. *See* comments by Eleanor Holmes Norton, former Chair of the Equal Employment Opportunity Commission DAILY LAB. REP. (BNA), No. 50 at A-6 (March 14, 1984). *See also Battle of the Sexes over Comparable Worth*, NEWSWEEK, Feb. 20, 1984, at 74.

53. Romasanta v. United Airlines, Inc., 717 F.2d 1140, *cert. denied sub nom*, McDonald v. United Airlines, Inc., 104 S. Ct. 1928 (1984).

54. *Cf.* Arizona Governing Comm. v. Norris, 103 S. Ct. 3492 (1983) (retroactive monetary relief denied to identified discriminatees where contrary ruling would jeopardize pension fund).

55. *See, e.g.*, Stotts v. Memphis Fire Dep't., 679 F.2d 541,

563 (6th Cir. 1982), *reversed sub nom* Firefighters Local Union No. 1784 v. Stotts, 104 S. Ct. 2576 (1984) (district court order enjoining layoffs which interfered with affirmative action requirements under consent decree overturned by Supreme Court, district court had emphasized that city had alternative methods to meet its economic crisis without adversely affecting decree).

sults of the New York State job evaluation study. These findings could indicate how fruitful the same inquiry might be in other states with a large number of black employees in the civil service, and might pinpoint specific job categories for careful study. Black workers in other large organizations should insist that race be studied whenever a job evaluation study of possible sex discrimination is being considered. They should also look carefully at the legislation pending before Congress, and inform their representatives that race must be an integral part of the pay equity bills, especially those bills regarding federal workers.

Finally, this article suggests that those who maintain that compensating women for wage inequities will harm the black community, are using a "red herring" to divert attention from the fundamental issues which underlie the massive employment inequities in this country. Black workers should be aware that wage comparability might well be a theory for them, and should plan their strategies and alliances accordingly.

Sexual Harassment:
Its First Decade in Court
(1986)

S exual harassment, the event, is not new to women. It is the law of injuries that it is new to. Sexual pressure imposed on someone who is not in an economic position to refuse it became sex discrimination in the midseventies,[1] and in education soon afterward.[2] It became possible to do something legal about sexual harassment because some women took women's experience of violation seriously enough to design a law around it, as if what happens to women matters. This was apparently such a startling way of proceeding that sexual harassment was protested as a feminist invention. Sexual harassment, the event, was not invented by feminists; the perpetrators did that with no help from us. Sexual harassment, the legal claim—the idea that the law should see it the way its victims see it—is definitely a feminist invention. Feminists first took women's experience seriously enough to uncover this problem and conceptualize it and pursue it legally. That legal claim is just beginning to produce more than a handful of reported cases. Ten years later, "[i]t may well be that sex harassment is the hottest present day Title VII issue."[3] It is time for a down-the-road assessment of this departure.

The law against sexual harassment is a practical attempt to stop a form of exploitation. It is also one test of sexual politics as feminist jurisprudence, of possibilities for social change for women through law. The existence of a law against sexual harassment has affected both the context of meaning within which social life is lived and the concrete delivery of rights through the legal system. The sexually

The original version of this speech was part of a panel on sexual harassment shared with Karen Haney, Pamela Price, and Peggy McGuiness at Stanford University, Stanford, California, Apr. 12, 1983. It thereafter became an address to the Equal Employment Opportunities Section of the American Bar Association, New Orleans, Louisiana, May 3, 1984 and to a workshop for the national conference of the National Organization for Women, Denver, Colorado, June 14, 1986. The ideas developed further when I represented Mechelle Vinson as co-counsel in her U.S. Supreme Court case in the spring of 1986. I owe a great deal to my conversations with Valerie Heller.

103

harassed have been given a name for their suffering and an analysis that connects it with gender. They have been given a forum, legitimacy to speak, authority to make claims, and an avenue for possible relief. Before, what happened to them was all right. Now it is not.

This matters. Sexual abuse mutes victims socially through the violation itself. Often the abuser enforces secrecy and silence; secrecy and silence may be part of what is so sexy about sexual abuse. When the state also forecloses a validated space for denouncing and rectifying the victimization, it seals this secrecy and reenforces this silence. The harm of this process, a process that utterly precludes speech, then becomes all of a piece. If there is no right place to go to say, this hurt me, then a woman is simply the one who can be treated this way, and no harm, as they say, is done.

In point of fact, I would prefer not to have to spend all this energy getting the law to recognize wrongs to women as wrong. But it seems to be necessary to legitimize our injuries as injuries in order to delegitimize our victimization by them, without which it is difficult to move in more positive ways. The legal claim for sexual harassment made the events of sexual harassment illegitimate socially as well as legally for the first time. Let me know if you figure out a better way to do that.

At this interface between law and society, we need to remember that the legitimacy courts give they can also take. Compared with a possibility of relief where no possibility of relief existed, since women started out with nothing in this area, this worry seems a bit fancy. Whether the possibility of relief alters the terms of power that gives rise to sexual harassment itself, which makes getting away with it possible, is a different problem. Sexual harassment, the legal claim, is a demand that state authority stand behind women's refusal of sexual access in certain situations that previously were a masculine prerogative. With sexism, there is always a risk that our demand for self-determination will be taken as a demand for paternal protection and will therefore strengthen male power rather than undermine it. This seems a particularly valid concern because the law of sexual harassment began as case law, without legislative guidance or definition.

Institutional support for sexual self-determination is a victory; institutional paternalism reinforces our lack of self-determination. The problem is, the state has never in fact protected women's dignity or bodily integrity. It just says it does. Its protections have been both condescending *and* unreal, in effect strengthening the protector's

104

choice to violate the protected at will, whether the protector is the individual perpetrator or the state. This does not seem to me a reason not to have a law against sexual harassment. It is a reason to demand that the promise of "equal protection of the laws" be *delivered upon* for us, as it is when real people are violated. It is also part of a larger political struggle to value women more than the male pleasure of using us is valued. Ultimately, though, the question of whether the use of the state for women helps or hurts can be answered only in practice, because so little real protection of the laws has ever been delivered.

The legal claim for sexual harassment marks the first time in history, to my knowledge, that women have defined women's injuries in a law. Consider what has happened with rape. We have never defined the injury of rape; men define it. The men who define it, define what they take to be this violation of women according to, among other things, what they think they don't do. In this way rape becomes an act of a stranger (they mean Black) committed upon a woman (white) whom he has never seen before. Most rapes are intraracial and are committed by men the women know.[4] Ask a woman if she has ever been raped, and often she says, "Well . . . not really." In that silence between the well and the not really, she just measured what happened to her against every rape case she ever heard about and decided she would lose in court. Especially when you are part of a subordinated group, your own definition of your injuries is powerfully shaped by your assessment of whether you could get anyone to do anything about it, including anything official. You are realistic by necessity, and the voice of law is the voice in power. When the design of a legal wrong does not fit the wrong as it happens to you, as is the case with rape, that law can undermine your social and political as well as legal legitimacy in saying that what happened was an injury at all—even to yourself.

It is never too soon to worry about this, but it may be too soon to know whether the law against sexual harassment will be taken away from us or turn into nothing or turn ugly in our hands. The fact is, this law is working surprisingly well for women by any standards, particularly when compared with the rest of sex discrimination law. If the question is whether a law designed from women's standpoint and administered through this legal system can do anything for women—which always seems to me to be a good question—this experience so far gives a qualified and limited yes.

It is hard to unthink what you know, but there was a time when

105

the facts that amount to sexual harassment did not amount to sexual harassment. It is a bit like the injuries of pornography until recently. The facts amounting to the harm did not socially "exist," had no shape, no cognitive coherence; far less did they state a legal claim. It just happened to you. To the women to whom it happened, it wasn't part of anything, much less something big or shared like gender. It fit no known pattern. It was neither a regularity nor an irregularity. Even social scientists didn't study it, and they study anything that moves. When law recognized sexual harassment as a practice of sex discrimination, it moved it from the realm of "and then he . . . and then he . . . ," the primitive language in which sexual abuse lives inside a woman, into an experience with a form, an etiology, a cumulativeness—as well as a club.

The shape, the positioning, and the club—each is equally crucial politically. Once it became possible to do something about sexual harassment, it became possible to know more about it, because it became possible for its victims to speak about it. Now we know, as we did not when it first became illegal, that this problem is commonplace. We know this not just because it has to be true, but as documented fact. Between a quarter and a third of women in the federal workforce report having been sexually harassed, many physically, at least once in the last two years.[5] Projected, that becomes 85 percent of all women at some point in their working lives. This figure is based on asking women "Have you ever been sexually harassed?"—the conclusion—not "has this fact happened? has that fact happened?" which usually produces more. The figures for sexual harassment of students are comparable.[6]

When faced with individual incidents of sexual harassment, the legal system's first question was, is it a personal episode? Legally, this was a way the courts inquired into whether the incidents were based on sex, as they had to be to be sex discrimination. Politically, it was a move to isolate victims by stigmatizing them as deviant. It also seemed odd to me that a relationship was either personal or gendered, meaning that one is not a woman personally. Statistical frequency alone does not make an event not personal, of course, but the presumption that sexual pressure in contexts of unequal power is an isolated idiosyncrasy to unique individual victims has been undermined both by the numbers and by their division by gender. Overwhelmingly, it is men who sexually harass women, a lot of them. Actually, it is even more accurate to say that men do this than to say

106

that women have this done to them. This is a description of the perpetrators' behavior, not of the statisticians' feminism.

Sexual harassment has also emerged as a creature of hierarchy. It inhabits what I call hierarchies among men: arrangements in which some men are below other men, as in employer/employee and teacher/student. In workplaces, sexual harassment by supervisors of subordinates is common; in education, by administrators of lower-level administrators, by faculty of students. But it also happens among coworkers, from third parties, even by subordinates in the workplace, men who are women's hierarchical inferiors or peers. Basically, it is done by men to women regardless of relative position on the formal hierarchy. I believe that the reason sexual harassment was first established as an injury of the systematic abuse of power in hierarchies among men is that this is power men recognize. They comprehend from ·personal experience that something is held over your head if you do not comply. The lateral or reverse hierarchical examples[7] suggest something beyond this, something men don't understand from personal experience because they take its advantages for granted: gender is also a hierarchy. The courts do not use this analysis, but some act as though they understand it.[8]

Sex discrimination law had to adjust a bit to accommodate the realities of sexual harassment. Like many other injuries of gender, it wasn't written for this. For something to be based on gender in the legal sense means it happens to a woman as a woman, not as an individual. Membership in a gender is understood as the opposite of, rather than part of, individuality. Clearly, sexual harassment is one of the last situations in which a woman is treated without regard to her sex; it is because of her sex that it happens. But the social meaning attributed to women as a class, in which women are defined as gender female by sexual accessibility to men, is not what courts have considered before when they have determined whether a given incident occurred because of sex.

Sex discrimination law typically conceives that something happens because of sex when it happens to one sex but not the other. The initial procedure is arithmetic: draw a gender line and count how many of each are on each side in the context at issue, or, alternatively, take the line drawn by the practice or policy and see if it also divides the sexes. One by-product of this head-counting method is what I call the bisexual defense.[9] Say a man is accused of sexually harassing a woman. He can argue that the harassment is not sex-based because

107

he harasses both sexes equally, indiscriminately as it were. Originally it was argued that sexual harassment was not a proper gender claim because someone could harass both sexes. We argued that this was an issue of fact to be pleaded and proven, an issue of did he do this, rather than an issue of law, of whether he could have. The courts accepted that, creating this kamikaze defense. To my knowledge, no one has used the bisexual defense since.[10] As this example suggests, head counting can provide a quick topography of the terrain, but it has proved too blunt to distinguish treatment whose meaning is based on gender from treatment that has other social hermeneutics, especially when only two individuals are involved.

Once sexual harassment was established as bigger than personal, the courts' next legal question was whether it was smaller than biological. To say that sexual harassment was biological seemed to me a very negative thing to say about men, but defendants seemed to think it precluded liability. Plaintiffs argued that sexual harassment is not biological in that men who don't do it have nothing wrong with their testosterone levels. Besides, if murder were found to have biological correlates, it would still be a crime. Thus, although the question purported to be whether the acts were based on sex, the implicit issue seemed to be whether the source of the impetus for doing the acts was relevant to their harmfulness.

Similarly structured was the charge that women who resented sexual harassment were oversensitive. Not that the acts did not occur, but rather that it was unreasonable to experience them as harmful. Such a harm would be based not on sex but on individual hysteria. Again shifting the inquiry away from whether the acts are based on sex in the guise of pursuing it, away from whether they occurred to whether it should matter if they did, the question became whether the acts were properly harmful. Only this time it was not the perpetrator's drives that made him not liable but the target's sensitivity that made the acts not a harm at all. It was pointed out that too many people are victimized by sexual harassment to consider them all hysterics. Besides, in other individual injury law, victims are not blamed; perpetrators are required to take victims as they find them, so long as they are not supposed to be doing what they are doing.

Once these excuses were rejected, then it was said that sexual harassment was not really an employment-related problem. That became hard to maintain when it was her job the woman lost. If it was, in fact, a personal relationship, it apparently did not start and stop there, although this is also a question of proof, leaving the true mean-

108

ing of the events to trial. The perpetrator may have thought it was all affectionate or friendly or fun, but the victim experienced it as hateful, dangerous, and damaging. Results in such cases have been mixed. Some judges have accepted the perpetrator's view; for instance, one judge held queries by the defendant such as "What am I going to get for this?" and repeated importunings to "go out" to be "susceptible of innocent interpretation."[11] Other judges, on virtually identical facts, for example, "When are you going to do something nice for me?"[12] have held for the plaintiff. For what it's worth, the judge in the first case was a man, in the second a woman.

That sexual harassment is sex-based discrimination seems to be legally established, at least for now.[13] In one of the few recent cases that reported litigating the issue of sex basis, defendants argued that a sex-based claim was not stated when a woman worker complained of terms of abuse directed at her at work such as "slut," "bitch," and "fucking cunt" and "many sexually oriented drawings posted on pillars and at other conspicuous places around the warehouse" with plaintiffs' initials on them, presenting her having sex with an animal.[14] The court said: "[T]he sexually offensive conduct and language used would have been almost irrelevant and would have failed entirely in its crude purpose had the plaintiff been a man. I do not hesitate to find that but for her sex, the plaintiff would not have been subjected to the harassment she suffered."[15] "Obvious" or "patently obvious" they often call it.[16] I guess this is what it looks like to have proven a point.

Sexual harassment was first recognized as an injury of gender in what I called incidents of quid pro quo. Sometimes people think that harassment has to be constant. It doesn't; it's a term of art in which once can be enough. Typically, an advance is made, rejected, and a loss follows.[17] For a while it looked as if this three-step occurrence was in danger of going from one form in which sexual harassment can occur into a series of required hurdles. In many situations the woman is forced to submit instead of being able to reject the advance. The problem has become whether, say, being forced into intercourse at work will be seen as a failed quid pro quo or as an instance of sexual harassment in which the forced sex constitutes the injury.

I know of one reported case in employment and one in education in which women who were forced to submit to the sex brought a sexual harassment claim against the perpetrator; so far only the education case has won on the facts.[18] The employment case that lost on the facts was reversed on appeal. The pressures for sex were seen to

109

state a claim without respect to the fact that the woman was not able to avoid complying.[19] It is unclear if the unwanted advances constitute a claim, separate and apart from whether or not they are able to be resisted, which they should; or if the acts of forced sex would also constitute an environmental claim separate from any quid pro quo, as it seems to me they also should. In the education case, the case of Paul Mann, the students were allowed to recover punitive damages for the forced sex.[20] If sexual harassment is not to be defined only as sexual attention imposed upon someone who is not in a position to refuse it, who refuses it, women who are forced to submit to sex must be understood as harmed not less, but as much or more, than those who are able to make their refusals effective.

Getting recoveries for women who have actually been sexually violated by the defendant will probably be a major battle. Women being compensated in money for sex they *had* violates male metaphysics because in that system sex is what a woman is for. As one judge concluded, "[T]here does not seem to be any issue that the plaintiff did not desire to have relations with [the defendant], but it is also altogether apparent that she willingly had sex with him."[21] Now what do you make of that? The woman was not physically forced at the moment of penetration, and since it is sex she must have willed it, is about all you can make of it. The sexual politics of the situation is that men do not see a woman who has had sex as victimized, whatever the conditions. One dimension of this problem involves whether a woman who has been violated through sex has any credibility. Credibility is difficult to separate from the definition of the injury, since an injury in which the victim is not believed to have been injured *because she has been injured* is not a real injury, legally speaking.

The question seems to be whether a woman is valuable enough to hurt, so that what is done to her is a harm. Once a woman has had sex, voluntarily or by force—it doesn't matter—she is regarded as too damaged to be further damageable, or something. Many women who have been raped in the course of sexual harassment have been advised by their lawyers not to mention the rape because it would destroy their credibility! The fact that abuse is long term has suggested to some finders of fact that it must have been tolerated or even wanted, although sexual harassment that becomes a condition of work has also been established as a legal claim in its own right.[22] I once was talking with a judge about a case he was sitting on in which Black teenage girls alleged that some procedures at their school violated their privacy. He told me that with their sexual habits they had

110

no privacy to lose. It seemed he knew what their sexual habits were from evidence in the case, examples of the privacy violations.

The more aggravated an injury becomes, the more it ceases to exist. Why is incomprehensible to me, but how it functions is not. Our most powerful moment is on paper, in complaints we frame, and our worst is in the flesh in court. Although it isn't much, we have the most credibility when we are only the idea of us and our violation in their minds. In our allegations we construct reality to some extent; face to face, their angle of vision frames us irrevocably. In court we have breasts, we are Black, we are (in a word) women. Not that we are ever free of that, but the moment we physically embody our complaint, and they can see us, the pornography of the process starts in earnest.

I have begun to think that a major reason that many women do not bring sexual harassment complaints is that they know this. They cannot bear to have their personal account of sexual abuse reduced to a fantasy they invented, used to define them and to pleasure the finders of fact and the public. I think they have a very real sense that their accounts are enjoyed, that others are getting pleasure from the first-person recounting of their pain, and that is the content of their humiliation at these rituals. When rape victims say they feel raped again on the stand, and victims of sexual harassment say they feel sexually harassed in the adjudication, it is not exactly metaphor. I hear that they—in being publicly sexually humiliated by the legal system, as by the perpetrator—are pornography. The first time it happens, it is called freedom; the second time, it is called justice.

If a woman is sexually defined—meaning all women fundamentally, intensified by previous sexual abuse or identification as lesbian, indelible if a prostitute—her chances of recovery for sexual abuse are correspondingly reduced. I'm still waiting for a woman to win at trial against a man who forced her to comply with the sex. Suppose the male plaintiff in one sexual harassment case who rented the motel room in which the single sexual encounter took place had been a woman, and the perpetrator had been a man. When the relationship later went bad, it was apparently not a credibility problem for *him* at trial that he had rented the motel room. Nor was *his* sexual history apparently an issue. Nor, apparently, was it said when he complained he was fired because the relationship went bad, that he had "asked for" the relationship. That case was reversed on appeal on legal grounds, but he did win at trial.[23] The best one can say about women in such cases is that women who have had sex but not with the ac-

111

cused may have some chance. In one case the judge did not believe the plaintiff's denial of an affair with another coworker, but did believe that she had been sexually harassed by the defendant.[24] In another, the woman plaintiff actually had "linguistic intimacy" with another man at work, yet when she said that what happened to her with the defendant was sexual harassment, she was believed.[25] These are miraculous. A woman's word on these matters is usually indivisible. In another case a woman accused two men of sexual harassment. She had resisted and refused one man to whom she had previously submitted under pressure for a long time. He was in the process of eliminating her from her job when the second man raped her. The first man's defense was that it went on so long, she must have liked it. The second man's defense was that he had heard that she had had sexual relations with the first man, so he felt this was something she was open to.[26] This piggyback defense is premised on the class definition of woman as whore, by which I mean what men mean: one who exists to be sexually done to, to be sexually available on men's terms, that is, a woman. If this definition of women is accepted, it means that if a woman has ever had sex, forced or voluntary, she can't be sexually violated.

A woman can be seen in these terms by being a former rape victim or by the way she uses language. One case holds that the evidence shows "the allegedly harassing conduct was substantially welcomed and encouraged by plaintiff. She actively contributed to the distasteful working environment by her own profane and sexually suggestive conduct."[27] She swore, apparently, and participated in conversations about sex. This effectively made her harassment-proof. Many women joke about sex to try to defuse men's sexual aggression, to try to be one of the boys in hopes they will be treated like one. This is to discourage sexual advances, not to encourage them. In other cases, judges have understood that "the plaintiffs did not appreciate the remarks and . . . many of the other women did not either."[28]

The extent to which a woman's job is sexualized is also a factor. If a woman's work is not to sell sex, and her employer requires her to wear a sexually suggestive uniform, if she is repeatedly sexually harassed by the clientele, she may have a claim against her employer.[29] Similarly, although "there may well be a limited category of jobs (such as adult entertainment) in which sexual harassment may be a rational consequence of such employment," one court was "simply not prepared to say that a female who goes to work in what is apparently a predominantly male workplace should reasonably ex-

112

pect sexual harassment as part of her job."[30] There may be trouble at some point over what jobs are selling sex, given the sexualization of anything a woman does.

Sexual credibility, that strange amalgam of whether your word counts with whether or how much you were hurt, also comes packaged in a variety of technical rules in the sexual harassment cases: evidence, discovery, and burden of proof. In 1982 the EEOC held that if a victim was sexually harassed without a corroborating witness, proof was inadequate as a matter of law.[31] (Those of you who wonder about the relevance of pornography, get this: if nobody watched, it didn't happen.) A woman's word, even if believed, was legally insufficient, even if the man had nothing to put against it other than his word and the plaintiff's burden of proof. Much like women who have been raped, women who have experienced sexual harassment say, "But I couldn't prove it." They mean they have nothing but their word. Proof is when what you say counts against what someone else says—for which it must first be believed. To say as a matter of law that the woman's word is per se legally insufficient is to assume that, with sexual violations uniquely, the defendant's denial is dispositive, is proof. To say a woman's word is no proof amounts to saying a woman's word is worthless. Usually all the man has is his denial. In 1983 the EEOC found sexual harassment on a woman's word alone. It said it was enough, without distinguishing or overruling the prior case.[32] Perhaps they recognized that women don't choose to be sexually harassed in the presence of witnesses.

The question of prior sexual history is one area in which the issue of sexual credibility is directly posed. Evidence of the defendant's sexual harassment of other women in the same institutional relation or setting is increasingly being considered admissible, and it should be.[33] The other side of the question is whether evidence of a victim's prior sexual history should be discoverable or admissible, and it seems to me it should not be. Perpetrators often seek out victims with common qualities or circumstances or situations—we are fungible to them so long as we are similarly accessible—but victims do not seek out victimization at all, and their nonvictimized sexual behavior is no more relevant to an allegation of sexual force than is the perpetrator's consensual sex life, such as it may be.

So far the leading case, consistent with the direction of rape law,[34] has found that the victim's sexual history with other individuals is not relevant, although consensual history with the individual perpetrator may be. With sexual harassment law, we are having to de-

113

institutionalize sexual misogyny step by step. Some defendants' counsel have even demanded that plaintiffs submit to an unlimited psychiatric examination,[35] which could have a major practical impact on victims' effective access to relief. How much sexual denigration will victims have to face to secure their right to be free from sexual denigration? A major part of the harm of sexual harassment is the public and private sexualization of a woman against her will. Forcing her to speak about her sexuality is a common part of this process, subjection to which leads women to seek relief through the courts. Victims who choose to complain know they will have to endure repeated verbalizations of the specific sexual abuse they complain about. They undertake this even though most experience it as an exacerbation, however unavoidable, of the original abuse. For others, the necessity to repeat over and over the verbal insults, innuendos, and propositions to which they have been subjected leads them to decide that justice is not worth such indignity.

Most victims of sexual harassment, if the incidence data are correct, never file complaints. Many who are viciously violated are so ashamed to make that violation public that they submit in silence, although it devastates their self-respect and often their health, or they leave the job without complaint, although it threatens their survival and that of their families. If, on top of the cost of making the violation known, which is painful enough, they know that the entire range of their sexual experiences, attitudes, preferences, and practices are to be discoverable, few such actions will be brought, no matter how badly the victims are hurt. Faced with a choice between forced sex in their jobs or schools on the one hand and forced sexual disclosure for the public record on the other, few will choose the latter. This cruel paradox would effectively eliminate much progress in this area.[36]

Put another way, part of the power held by perpetrators of sexual harassment is the threat of making the sexual abuse public knowledge. This functions like blackmail in silencing the victim and allowing the abuse to continue. It is a fact that public knowledge of sexual abuse is often worse for the abused than the abuser, and victims who choose to complain have the courage to take that on. To add to their burden the potential of making public their entire personal life, information that has no relation to the fact or severity of the incidents complained of, is to make the law of this area implicitly complicit in the blackmail that keeps victims from exercising their rights and to enhance the impunity of perpetrators. In effect, it means open season

114

on anyone who does not want her entire intimate life available to public scrutiny. In other contexts such private information has been found intrusive, irrelevant, and more prejudicial than probative.[37] To allow it to be discovered in the sexual harassment area amounts to a requirement that women be further violated in order to be permitted to seek relief for having been violated. I also will never understand why a violation's severity, or even its likelihood of occurrence, is measured according to the character of the violated, rather than by what was done to them.

In most reported sexual harassment cases, especially rulings on law more than on facts, the trend is almost uniformly favorable to the development of this claim. At least, so far. This almost certainly does not represent social reality. It may not even reflect most cases in litigation.[38] And there may be conflicts building, for example, between those who value speech in the abstract more than they value people in the concrete. Much of sexual harassment is words. Women are called "cunt," "pussy," "tits";[39] they are invited to a company party with "bring your own bathing suits (women, either half)";[40] they confront their tormenter in front of their manager with, "You have called me a fucking bitch," only to be answered, "No, I didn't. I called you a fucking cunt."[41] One court issued an injunction against inquiries such as "Did you get any over the weekend?"[42] One case holds that where "a person in a position to grant or withhold employment opportunities uses that authority to attempt to induce workers and job seekers to submit to sexual advances, prostitution, and pornographic entertainment, and boasts of an ability to intimidate those who displease him," sexual harassment (and intentional infliction of emotional distress) are pleaded.[43] Sexual harassment can also include pictures; visual as well as verbal pornography is commonly used as part of the abuse. Yet one judge found, apparently as a matter of law, that the pervasive presence of pornography in the workplace did not constitute an unreasonable work environment because, "For better or worse, modern America features open displays of written and pictorial erotica. Shopping centers, candy stores and prime time television regularly display naked bodies and erotic real or simulated sex acts. Living in this milieu, the average American should not be legally offended by sexually explicit posters."[44] She did not say she was offended, she said she was discriminated against based on her sex. If the pervasiveness of an abuse makes it nonactionable, no inequality sufficiently institutionalized to merit a law against it would be actionable.

115

Applications

Further examples of this internecine conflict have arisen in education. At the Massachusetts Institute of Technology pornography used to be shown every year during registration.[45] Is this *not* sexual harassment in education, as a group of women complained it was, because attendance is voluntary, both sexes go, it is screened in groups rather than individually, nobody is directly propositioned, and it is pictures and words? Or is it sexual harassment because the status and treatment of women, supposedly secured from sex-differential harm, are damaged, including that of those who do not attend, which harms individuals and undermines sex equality; therefore pictures and words are the media through which the sex discrimination is accomplished?

For feminist jurisprudence, the sexual harassment attempt suggests that if a legal initiative is set up right from the beginning, meaning if it is designed from women's real experience of violation, it can make some difference. To a degree women's experience can be written into law, even in some tension with the current doctrinal framework. Women who want to resist their victimization with legal terms that imagine it is not inevitable can be given some chance, which is more than they had before. Law is not everything in this respect, but it is not nothing either.[46] Perhaps the most important lesson is that the mountain can be moved. When we started, there was absolutely no judicial precedent for allowing a sex discrimination suit for sexual harassment. Sometimes even the law does something for the first time.

116

66

9. Sexual Harassment

1. The first case to hold this was Williams v. Saxbe, 413 F. Supp. 654 (D. D.C. 1976), followed by Barnes v. Costle, 561 F.2d 983 (D.C. Cir. 1977).

2. Alexander v. Yale University, 459 F. Supp. 1 (D. Conn. 1977), *aff'd*, 631 F.2d 178 (2d Cir. 1980).

3. Rabidue v. Osceola Refining, 584 F. Supp. 419, 427 n.29 (E.D. Mich. 1984).

4. See data at "Rally against Rape," notes 1–3.

5. U.S. Merit System Protection Board, *Sexual Harassment in the Federal Workplace: Is It a Problem?* (1981).

6. National Advisory Council on Women's Education Programs, Department of Education, *Sexual Harassment: A Report on the Sexual Harassment of*

251

Students (1980); Joseph DiNunzio and Christina Spaulding, Radcliffe Union of Students, *Sexual Harassment Survey (Harvard/Radcliffe)* 20–29 (1984): 32 percent of tenured female faculty, 49 percent of nontenured female faculty, 42 percent of female graduate students, and 34 percent of female undergraduate students report some incident of sexual harassment from a person with authority over them; one-fifth of undergraduate women report being forced into unwanted sexual activity at some point in their lives. The Sexual Harassment Survey Committee, *A Survey of Sexual Harassment at UCLA* (185), finds 11 percent of female faculty (N = 86), 7 percent of female staff (N = 650), and 7 percent of female students (N = 933) report being sexually harassed at UCLA.

7. If a superior sexually harasses a subordinate, the company and the supervisor are responsible if the victim can prove it happened. 29 C.F.R. 1604.11(c). With coworkers, if the employer can be shown to have known about it or should have known about it, the employer can be held responsible. 29 C.F.R. 1604.11(d). Sexual harassment by clients or other third parties is decided on the specific facts. *See* 29 C.F.R. 1604.11(e).

8. The EEOC's requirement that the employer must receive notice in coworker cases suggests that they do not understand this point. 29 C.F.R. 1604.11(d). One reasonable rationale for such a rule, however, is that a coworker situation does not become hierarchical, hence actionable as *employment* discrimination, until it is reported to the workplace hierarchy and condoned through adverse action or inaction.

In one inferior-to-superior case, staff was alleged to have sexually harassed a woman manager because of an interracial relationship. Moffett v. Gene B. Glick Co., Inc., 621 F. Supp. 244 (D. Ind. 1985). An example of a third-party case that failed of "positive proof" involved a nurse bringing a sex discrimination claim alleging she was denied a promotion that went to a less qualified female nurse because that other nurse had a sexual relationship with the doctor who promoted her. King v. Palmer, 598 F. Supp. 65, 69 (D.D.C. 1984). The difficulty of proving "an explicit sexual relationship between [plaintiff] and [defendant], each of whom vigorously deny it exists or even occurred," id., is obvious.

9. Catharine A. MacKinnon, *Sexual Harassment of Working Women* 203 (1979).

10. Dissenters from the denial of rehearing en banc in Vinson v. Taylor attempted a revival, however. *Vinson v. Taylor,* 760 F.2d 1330, 1333 n.7 (Circuit Judges Bork, Scalia, and Starr).

11. Scott v. Sears & Roebuck, 605 F. Supp. 1047, 1051, 1055 (N.D. Ill. 1985).

12. Coley v. Consolidated Rail, 561 F. Supp. 647, 648 (1982).

13. Meritor Savings Bank, FSB v. Vinson, 106 S.Ct. 2399 (1986); Horn v. Duke Homes, 755 F.2d 599 (7th Cir. 1985); Crimm v. Missouri Pacific R.R. Co., 750 F.2d 703 (8th Cir. 1984); Simmons v. Lyons, 746 F.2d 265 (5th Cir. 1984); Craig v. Y & Y Snacks, 721 F.2d 77 (3d Cir. 1983); Katz v. Dole, 709 F.2d 251 (4th Cir. 1983); Miller v. Bank of America, 600 F.2d 211 (9th Cir. 1979); Tomkins v. Public Service Electric & Gas Co., 568 F.2d 1044 (3d Cir. 1977); Barnes v. Costle, 561 F.2d 983 (D.C. Cir. 1977); Bundy v. Jackson, 641

252

F.2d 934 (D.C. Cir. 1981); Henson v. City of Dundee, 682 F.2d 897 (11th Cir. 1982) (sexual harassment, whether quid pro quo or condition of work, is sex discrimination under Title VII). The court in *Rabidue* was particularly explicit on the rootedness of sexual harassment in the text of Title VII. Rabidue v. Osceola Refining, 584 F. Supp. 419, 427–29 (E.D. Mich. 1984). Woerner v. Brzeczek, 519 F. Supp. 517 (E.D. Ill. 1981) exemplifies the same view under the equal protection clause. Gender has also been found to create a class for a 42 U.S.C. § 1985(3) claim if the injury is covered by the Fourteenth Amendment. Scott v. City of Overland Park, 595 F. Supp. 520, 527–529 (D. Kansas 1984). *See also* Skadegaard v. Farrell, 578 F. Supp. 1209 (D.N.J. 1984). An additional question has been whether sexual harassment is intentional discrimination. Courts have been unimpressed with intent-related defenses like, he did it but "it was his way of communicating." French v. Mead Corporation, 333 FEP Cases 635, 638 (1983). Or, I did all of those things, but I am just a touchy person. Professor Sid Peck, in connection with the sexual harassment action brought against him by Ximena Bunster and other women at Clark University, reportedly stated that he exchanged embraces and kisses as greetings and to establish a feeling of safety and equality. *Worcester Magazine,* Dec. 3, 1980, at 3; *Boston Phoenix,* Feb. 24, 1981, at 6. *But see* Norton v. Vartanian, where Judge Zobel finds, inter alia, that the overtures were never sexually intended, so no sexual harassment occurred. 31 FEP Cases 1260 (D. Mass. 1983). The implicit view, I guess, is that the perpetrator's intent is beside the point of the harm, that so long as the allegations meet other requirements, the perpetrator does not need to intend that the sexual advances be discriminatory or even sex-based for them to constitute sex discrimination. Katz v. Dole holds that a showing of "sustained verbal sexual abuse" is sufficient to prove "the intentional nature of the harassment." 709 F. 2d, 255–56 esp. 256 n.7. As I understand it, this means that so long as the harassment is not credibly inadvertent, acts of this nature are facially discriminatory. Intentionality is inferred from the acts; the acts themselves, repeated after indications of disinclination and nonreceptivity, show the mental animus of bias. In short, the acts may not be intentionally discriminatory, yet still constitute intentional discrimination. The upshot seems to be that sexual harassment allegations are essentially treated as facial discrimination.

14. Zabkowicz v. West Bend Co., 589 F. Supp. 780, 782–83 (E.D. Wisc. 1984).

15. 589 F. Supp., 784.

16. Henson v. City of Dundee, 29 FEP Cases 787, 793 (11th Cir. 1983). In Huebschen v. Dept. of Health, 32 FEP Cases 1582 (7th Cir. 1983), the facts were found not gender-based on a doctrinally dubious rationale. There a man was found to have been sexually harassed by his female superior. This result was reversed on the partial basis that it did not present a valid gender claim. Basically the court said that the case wasn't gender-based because it was individual. I remember this argument: the events were individual, not gender-based, because there was no employment problem until the relationship went sour. In my view, if the defendant is a hierarchical superior and the

253

plaintiff is damaged in employment for reasons of sexual pressure vis à vis that superior, especially if they are a woman and a man, a claim is stated. It is one thing to recognize that men as a gender have more power in sexual relations in ways that may cross-cut employment hierarchies. This is not what the court said here. This case may have been, on its facts, a personal relationship that went bad, having nothing to do with gender. But these are not the facts as found at trial. The Court of Appeals did suggest that this plaintiff was hurt as an individual, not as a man, because the employment situation was fine so long as the sexual situation was fine—that is, until it wasn't. After which, because of which, the man was fired. Maybe men always stay individuals, even when women retaliate against them through their jobs for sexual refusals. But, doctrinally, I do not understand why this treatment does not state a gender-based claim. Not to, seems to allow employment opportunities to be conditional on the *continuing* existence of an undesired sexual relationship, where those opportunities would never be allowed to be conditioned on such a relationship's *initial* existence. Women have at times been gender female personally: "As Walter Scott acknowledges, he 'was attracted to her as a woman, on a personal basis. Her femaleness was a matter of attraction.'" Estate of Scott v. deLeon, 37 FEP Cases 563, 566 (1985).

17. *Barnes v. Costle* is the classic case. All of the cases in note 13 above are quid pro cases except *Vinson, Katz, Bundy,* and *Henson.* Note that the distinction is actually two poles of a continuum. A constructive discharge, in which a woman leaves the job because of a constant condition of sexual harassment, is an environmental situation that becomes quid pro quo.

18. In Vinson v. Taylor, 23 FEP Cases 37 (D.D.C. 1980), plaintiff accused defendant supervisor of forced sex; the trial court found, "If the plaintiff and Taylor did engage in an intimate or sexual relationship . . .[it] was a voluntary one by plaintiff." At 42. Vinson won a right to a new trial for environmental sexual harassment. Meritor Savings Bank, FSB v. Vinson, 106 S. Ct. 2399 (1986). *See also* Cummings v. Walsh Construction Co., 561 F. Supp. 872 (S.D. Ga. 1983) (victim accused perpetrator of consummated sex); Micari v. Mann, 481 N.Y.S.2d 967 (Sup. Ct. 1984) (students accused professor of forced sex as part of acting training; won and awarded damages).

19. Vinson v. Taylor, 753 F.2d 141 (D.C. Cir. 1985), *aff'd* 106 S. Ct. 2399 (1983).

20. Micari v. Mann, 481 N.Y.S.2d 967 (Sup. Ct. 1984).

21. Cummings v. Walsh Construction Co., 31 FEP Cases 930, 938 (S. D. Ga. 1983).

22. *Bundy* and *Henson,* note 13 above, establish environmental sexual harassment as a legal claim. Both that claim and the plaintiff's credibility in asserting it, since she was abused for such a long time, were raised in Vinson v. Taylor before the U.S. Supreme Court.

23. Huebschen v. Department of Health, 547 F. Supp. 1168 (W.D. Wisc. 1982).

24. Heelan v. Johns-Manville, 451 F. Supp. 1382 (D. Colo. 1978). *See also* Sensibello v. Globe Security Systems, 34 FEP Cases 1357 (E.D. Pa. 1964).

254

70

25. Katz v. Dole, 709 F.2d 251, 254 n.3 (4th Cir. 1983) ("A person's private and consensual sexual activities do not constitute a waiver of his or her legal protections against unwelcome and unsolicited sexual harassment").

26. An attorney discussed this case with me in a confidential conversation.

27. Gan v. Kepro Circuit Systems, 28 FEP Cases 639, 641 (E.D. Mo. 1982). *See also* Reichman v. Bureau of Affirmative Action, 536 F. Supp. 1149, 1177 (M.D. Penn. 1982).

28. Morgan v. Hertz Corp., 542 F. Supp. 123, 128 (W.D. Tenn. 1981).

29. EEOC v. Sage Realty, 507 F. Supp. 599 (S.D.N.Y. 1981).

30. Pryor v. U.S. Gypsum Co., 585 F. Supp. 311, 316 n.3 (W.D. Mo. 1984). The issue here was whether the injuries could be brought under worker's compensation. The suggestion is that women who work in adult entertainment might be covered under that law for sexual harassment on their jobs.

31. EEOC Decision 82-13, 29 FEP Cases 1855 (1982).

32. Commission Decision 83-1, EEOC Decisions (CCH) 6834 (1983).

33. Koster v. Chase Manhattan, 93 F.R.D. 471 (S.D.N.Y. 1982).

34. Priest v. Rotary, 32 FEP Cases 1065 (N.D. Cal. 1983) is consistent with congressional actions in criminal rape, Fed. R. Evid., Rule 412, 124 *Cong. Rec.* H11944–11945 (daily ed. Oct. 10, 1978) and 124 *Cong. Rec.* S18580 (daily ed. Oct. 12, 1978) (evidence of prior consensual sex, unless with defendant, is inadmissible in rape cases) and with developments in civil rape cases. Fults v. Superior Court, 88 Cal. App. 3d 899 (1979).

35. Vinson v. Superior Court, Calif. Sup. SF 24932 (rev. granted, Sept. 1985).

36. A further possibility—more political fantasy than practical—might be to insist that if the plaintiff's entire sexual history is open to inspection, the defendant's should be also: all the rapes, peeping at his sister, patronizing of prostitutes, locker-room jokes, use of pornography, masturbation fantasies, adolescent experimentation with boyfriends, fetishes, and so on.

37. *See, e.g.*, U.S. v. Kasto, 584 F.2d 268, 271–72 (8th Cir. 1978), *cert. denied*, 440 U.S. 930 (1979); State v. Bernier, 491 A.2d 1000, 1004 (R.I. 1985).

38. Another reason women do not bring claims is fear of countersuit. The relationship between sexual harassment and defamation is currently unsettled on many fronts. *See, e.g.*, Walker v. Gibson, 604 F. Supp. 916 (N.D. Ill. 1985) (action for violation of First Amendment will not lie against employer Army for hearing on unwarranted sexual harassment charge); Spisak v. McDole, 472 N.E.2d 347 (Ohio 1984) (defamation claim can be added to sexual harassment claim); Equal Employment Opportunity Commission v. Levi Strauss & Co., 515 F. Supp. 640 (N.D. Ill. 1981) (defamation action brought allegedly in response to employee allegation of sexual harassment is not necessarily retaliatory, if brought in good faith to vindicate reputation); Arenas v. Ladish Co., 619 F. Supp. 1304 (E.D. Wisc. 1985) (defamation claim may be brought for sexual harassment in the presence of others, not barred by exclusivity provision of worker's compensation law); Ross v. Comsat, 34 FEP Cases 261 (D. Md. 1984) (man sues company for retaliation in discharge following his complaint against woman at company for sexual harassment).

255

Educational institutions have been sued for acting when, after investigation, they find the complaints to be true. Barnes v. Oody, 28 FEP Cases 816 (E.D. Tenn. 1981) (summary judgment granted that arbitrators' holding for women who brought sexual harassment claim collaterally estops defamation action by sexual harassment defendant; immunity applies to statements in official investigation). Although it is much more difficult to prove defamation than to defeat a sexual harassment claim, threats of countersuit have intimidated many victims.

39. Rabidue v. Osceola Refining, 584 F. Supp. 423 (E.D. Mich. 1984).

40. Cobb v. Dufresne-Henry, 603 F. Supp. 1048, 1050 (D. Vt. 1985).

41. McNabb v. Cub Foods, 352 N.W. 2d 378, 381 (Minn. 1984).

42. Morgan v. Hertz Corp., 27 FEP Cases at 994.

43. Seratis v. Lane, 30 FEP 423, 425 (Cal. Super. 1980).

44. Rabidue v. Osceola Refining, 584 F. Supp. 419, 435 (E.D. Mich. 1984). This went to whether the treatment was sex-based. Note that the plaintiff did not say that she was offended but that she was discriminated against.

45. Women students at MIT filed a sexual harassment claim under Title IX, which was dismissed for lack of jurisdiction. Baker v. M.I.T., U.S. Dept. Education Office of Civil Rights #01-85-2013 (Sept. 20, 1985).

46. Particularly given the formative contribution to the women's movement of the struggles against racial and religious stigma, persecution, and violence, it is heartening to find a Jewish man and a Black man recovering for religious and racial harassment, respectively, based on sexual harassment precedents. Weiss v. U.S., 595 F. Supp. 1050 (E.D. Va. 1984) (pattern of anti-Semitic verbal abuse actionable based on *Katz* and *Henson*); Taylor v. Jones, 653 F.2d 1193, 1199 (8th Cir. 1981) (*Bundy* cited as basis for actionability of environmental racial harassment under Title VII).

256

COMPARABLE WORTH: THE PARADOX OF TECHNOCRATIC REFORM

SARA M. EVANS and BARBARA J. NELSON

Comparable worth, the policy Eleanor Holmes Norton labeled "the issue of the 1980s,"[1] is poised at the juncture of an inequitable past and a feminist vision of the future in a way that may clarify some of the problems and paradoxes we face as we struggle to move from one to the other. It evolved as a conscious strategy in the 1970s (although its roots were much older) as people recognized how deeply the history of discrimination is embedded in our economic institutions. Neither affirmative action nor equal pay for equal work had proved sufficient to address the inequities of a labor force segregated by gender, race, and ethnicity.

There is no need to belabor the structural and historic realities that prompted the development of comparable worth as a strategy for change. Work in all industrialized economies is segregated by sex, race, and ethnicity; women and minorities are concentrated in the lowest paid jobs with fewest opportunities for advancement.[2] Comparable worth challenges not so much the distribution of workers among jobs as the valuation of the work itself. As the National Academy of Sciences recently found, "in many instances . . . jobs held mainly by women and minorities pay less at least in part because they are held mainly by women and minorities."[3]

Comparable worth is a strategy intended to remove the negative weight of a history that devalued women, minorities, and the work they do. It holds the promise of a future in which wages are more equitably distributed, with all the side effects that could have for the independence and autonomy of women and people of color. But between the heaviness of the past and our vision of the future, we face the immediate realities of specific changes that bear unforeseen fruits. Although most discussions of comparable

---

Feminist Studies 15, no. 1 (Spring 1989). © 1989 by Feminist Studies, Inc.

worth have focused either on analyses of labor force segregation and discrimination — establishing that there is indeed a problem requiring such a policy — on economists' predictions of long-range consequences for employment, or on the techniques of implementation,[4] we propose to discuss the concrete realities involved in the implementation of comparable worth in state and local jurisdictions. Our objective is to deepen the discussion by examining how the process of winning and implementing comparable worth affect its possibilities for social transformation.

Our analysis focuses on the experience of the state of Minnesota and twenty-two localities in that state (four counties, ten cities, and eight school districts).[5] Minnesota's state employees are covered by the 1982 State Employees Pay Equity Act, which was fully implemented by 30 June 1987.[6] Local employees are covered by the 1984 Local Government Pay Equity Act, a piece of comparable worth legislation mandating that all local jurisdictions conduct comparable worth studies; report their findings to the state Department of Employee Relations for transmission to the legislature; and develop plans to remedy any inequities found between male, female, and balanced job classes. To understand these laws and the policies they created we need to begin with some definitions.

DEFINING COMPARABLE WORTH

Comparable worth is a wage policy designed to correct historically discriminatory wages of female- and minority-dominated jobs. Although there are many possible ways to identify and correct such discrimination, by the late 1970s most definitions of comparable worth presumed the use of job evaluation technology. In this framework, comparable worth is a wage policy requiring equal pay within a jurisdiction or firm for male- and female-, majority- and minority-dominated job classifications that are valued equally in terms of skill, effort, responsibility, and working conditions.[7]

The single job evaluation system measures in *detail* the skill, effort, responsibility, and working conditions of every job classification and combines the scores in each area to produce a single overall score for every classification. Job classifications with equal overall scores are considered to have equal value to the jurisdiction or firm.

A large number of studies have shown that if two job classifications have the same value according to the job evaluation system,
but one is held primarily (i.e., 80 percent or more) by men and the
other held primarily (i.e., 70 percent or more) by women, the job
held by men usually pays more.[8] Under a comparable worth wage
policy, classifications with the same scores – regardless of whether
they are dominated by women, minorities, or white men – should
be paid equivalently. However, all individuals holding jobs within
equal classifications would not be paid the same wages, because
seniority, merit, and the quantity or quality of work done would
continue to differentiate individuals' wages within equivalent
classifications.

Theory and practice do not always coincide when comparable
worth is implemented. In theory, at any one time, comparable
worth compares male or white jobs and female or minority jobs
within a workplace without reference to wage rates outside the
firm. This is because market rates reflect the historic undervaluation of the work done by women and people of color. Essentially,
the market is viewed as setting wages nondiscriminatorily only for
white men, and even then only under certain conditions.[9] If wage
rates for female- and minority-dominated jobs are compared with
existing market rates, some of the undervaluation of female and
minority jobs is reintroduced into wage setting.

The state of Minnesota closely conformed to comparable worth
theory, comparing female-dominated positions to equally valued
male-dominated positions but not to current wages for these positions outside Minnesota. State implementation of comparable
worth was "distributive," offering a remedy to historically low
wages through an "add-on."[10] In budgetary and legislative terms,
distributive policies frequently have unorganized oppositions and
are thought, by supporters at least, to be desirable to society as a
whole and not likely to be adopted without government intervention.[11]

Unlike the state, most local jurisdictions in Minnesota did not
implement comparable worth in this manner. Like the settlement
of the San Jose, California, comparable worth strike and the final
results of the comparable worth dispute in the state of Washington, most Minnesota local jurisdictions adopted some sort of pay-
for-points policy, often comparing the salaries of equally valued
jobs to the average salary of all jobs having that value and to

market rates for those positions.[12] In many Minnesota localities, like Hennepin County which employs 8,000 workers, comparable worth means that if two jobs have the same job evaluation score, the salary and benefits in the highly paid (usually male-dominated) position will grow more slowly than in the less well paid (usually female-dominated) position. Local implementation often was a legislatively and budgetarily redistributive policy, rearranging the wage bill more than adding to it. In general, politicians do not like redistributive policies, and they often try to make them more distributive. This was sometimes achieved in Minnesota local governments by making all "underpaid" positions, regardless of what sex of workers predominated in them, eligible for wage increases. Some localities also made all "overpaid" classes vulnerable to slower wage growth. These practices rely on definitions of fairness that do not take into account the historical undervaluation of female labor.

Examining the workings of a specific job evaluation system helps to demystify what is meant by "jobs of equal value." The state of Minnesota contracted with a management consultant firm,

COMPARISON OF MONTHLY SALARIES

Zookeeper	$967	Painter	$1,368
Human Services Technician	$783	Social Worker	$1,103

Poultry Improvement Specialist	$1,227
Human Services Specialist	$ 912

Police Training Director	$1,841	General Maintenance Worker	$1,027
Director of Nurses	$1,583	Administrative Secretary	$ 912

Fig. 1. Comparison of wages in equally valued jobs for 1981 (source: Minnesota Department of Employee Relations).

Hay Associates, to conduct a job evaluation study that was completed and adopted in 1979. Subsequently, in 1981, the state Council on the Economic Status of Women appointed a Pay Equity Task Force to reanalyze the Hay study by sorting out and comparing the wages of male, female, and balanced job classes. The Task Force study revealed systematic discrepancies between male- and female-dominated jobs similar to those found in studies of other large employers and governmental jurisdictions.[13] For example, according to the state of Minnesota's job evaluation system, a zookeeper's job and a human services technician's job (e.g., caring for the mentally retarded in a state hospital) received approximately the same number of points. The predominantly male zookeepers earned $967 per month, however, compared with $783 for human services technicians (see fig. 1). Similarly, equivalently rated jobs such as vocational education teacher (male) and registered nurse (female) differed dramatically in pay. The result of such disparities is a dual wage system, illustrated most effectively with a scattergram that plots male- and female-dominated jobs on a graph that has job evaluation points along the horizontal axis and wages along the vertical axis (see fig. 2).

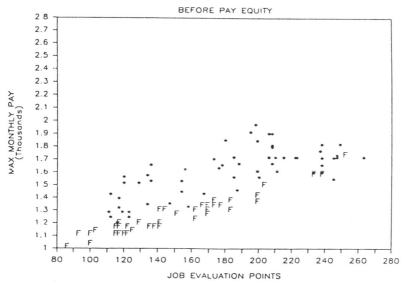

Fig. 2. Job classes by Hay point and salary (source: Commission on the Economic Status of Women, 1985). * = male-dominated job classes (80 percent or more male incumbents); F = female-dominated job classes (70 percent or more female incumbents).

A scattergram is the most graphic, and the most common, method of illustrating the fact that most employers operate on a dual wage scale, a higher one for male-dominated jobs and a lower one for female-dominated jobs. The regression line drawn through the male jobs shows the mathematical average, or trend line, for those jobs, and a similar line could be drawn through the female jobs at a lower level. In the state of Minnesota, not a single female-dominated job could be found at or above the male wage trend line. This same method could be used to plot white- and minority-dominated jobs to discover racially based wage discrimination. However, because only 3.8 percent of Minnesota's state labor force are minorities (a figure slightly above the proportion of minorities in the population as a whole) an analysis by race and ethnicity is not possible from these data.

As discussed above, under a pure comparable worth policy, the wages of female- and minority-dominated jobs would be raised so that all jobs scatter around the male or white male wage line. In Minnesota, after four years during which members of female-dominated job classes have received special salary increments, the male- and female-dominated jobs now fall along a single line (see fig. 3). However, comparisons are made only between equivalently valued positions. Therefore, comparable worth would not compare the salaries of, for example, secretaries and physicians, because a sound job evaluation system would not rate them as essentially equal in skill, effort, responsibility, and working conditions. Thus, while comparable worth works to achieve horizontal equity among equally valued jobs, it is not a strategy that addresses hierarchical relationships in the workplace. On the contrary, the technology of comparable worth – job evaluation – valorizes existing vertical status and pay arrangements.

Any close examination of the actual implementation of comparable worth reveals that it is a highly technical reform. The concepts and values that underlie comparable worth are clear and easy to grasp. But the technique of job evaluation evolved in the twentieth century to rationalize the workplace and facilitate the work of managers, not to remedy historical discrimination and inequity. The result is a series of paradoxes that we would like to explore.

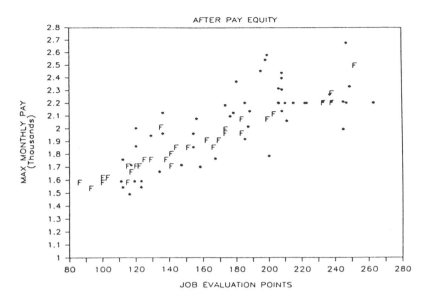

Fig. 3. Job classes by Hay point and salary (source: Commission on the Economic Status of Women, 1985). * = male-dominated job classes (80 percent or more male incumbents); F = female-dominated job classes (70 percent or more female incumbents).

PARADOXES OF TECHNOLOGICAL CHANGE

We should begin by pointing out that comparable worth is one of many strategies for challenging inequity in a world organized by color and gender. Comparable worth is not in competition with but rather complements affirmative action and workplace organizing efforts. Like these other approaches, comparable worth is a long-term strategy for wage justice that requires constant political attention. But unlike other strategies, comparable worth requires long-term attention to the technocratic aspects of determining job worth and assigning wages to jobs with specific evaluation scores. Although there are many methods of raising wages for low-paid workers, currently *there is no nontechnocratic method for implementing comparable worth.*[14] In this regard, comparable worth is like the Occupational Safety and Health Act (OSHA) or various types of water and air pollution prevention legislation. Because of these complexities, comparable worth is neither a single utopian answer to wage inequity nor is it dismissible because it does not do everything.

Problems arise from the fact that comparable worth, because it is technocratic in practice, intersects with and sometimes contradicts other democratic and egalitarian changes. Too often we forget that in solving one problem we may create others. Only by looking unflinchingly at possible conflicts may we think clearly about long-range consequences and future strategies. The three issues we will discuss are democracy, hierarchy, and jobs.

Democracy. In the first place, workplaces are not democratic, and comparable worth is not going to make them so. The extensive use of technical experts to implement comparable worth exacts a high cost both literally and figuratively. The price that concerns us here, however, is the erosion of an ideal of democratic and participatory decision making and the empowerment of the individual. Toward that end, many of us have worked to demystify "experts" in many fields (healthcare, for example, with the self-help movement, or nuclear power). With comparable worth we find ourselves arguing for and relying on experts and also struggling to demystify their expertise. Organizing for comparable worth *can* be both democratic and empowering as women and minorities rethink the value of their own work and challenge the hierarchy of values enshrined in the wage scale. Once employees win a commitment to comparable worth, however, the choice of technicians often remains in the hands of employers, and the process becomes management-dominated.

At the state level, Minnesota implemented comparable worth with amazing ease and little or no disruption of established bargaining relationships. This occurred for two reasons, the first of which was wholly accidental but proved crucial. The state had completed its job evaluation several years before it established its pay equity policy and distributed the first pay equity raises. Because of this, pay equity was not tied to the often painful and disruptive process of establishing job hierarchies. A second important condition was that all the important leaders in the implementation process understood in great detail the arguments supporters made about the structural origins of women's low wages. Most leaders in the American Federation of State, County, and Municipal Employees (AFSCME) and the Department of Employee Relations wholeheartedly believed that jobs held primarily by women had low wages in part because women usually held those jobs. The commitment of these leaders to the underlying rationale of equal pay for jobs of equal value led to their decision to use the male pay practices line as the standard against which female-dominated jobs would be compared. When Commissioner of Employee Relations Nina Rothchild was asked why the state did not merely compute the pay practice line for all jobs and compare salaries in female-dominated jobs to it, she responded, "I was a math major at Smith College. I know enough not to include the salaries of women's jobs, which have been held down by discrimination, in my standard for nondiscriminatory wages."[15]

Neither of these conditions obtained at the local level. Local jurisdictions usually had no job evaluation system, or even in many cases a job classification system, only a proliferation of job titles. In addition, because comparable worth was a state mandate, those most closely involved with implementation, both managers and employee representatives, were not strongly committed to the concept as had been the case with the state. Thus, issues of management prerogative and the process of job evaluation itself became central to local perceptions of comparable worth.

Advocates of comparable worth frequently recommend that job evaluation systems be jointly chosen and overseen by labor and management.[16] Minnesota laws, however, clearly defined the choice of system as a management prerogative not subject to collective bargaining. In a few instances, such as in the cities of Minneapolis and St. Paul, strong unions won some right to participate in this choice, but most managers chose simply to "meet and confer" with employee representatives, informing them of decisions already made.

The issue of employee participation becomes far more complex, however, once a job evaluation method has been selected. Many methods require a substantial amount of employee participation—filling out questionnaires, serving on committees to evaluate jobs, or, as in the case of the University of Minnesota, even developing the factors and weights themselves. But the interpretation of results is wholly managerial, and subsequent wage setting is, at best, negotiated. The final product of summed scores and redesigned job classes is often confusing and upsetting even to employees active in the process.[17] Regression lines, the definition of "male-," "female-," and "minority-" dominated classes with a fairly arbitrary mathematical cutoff, tend to leave people intimidated and confused. This places a special and continuing burden on proponents of comparable worth, who must constantly explain both the policy and the method in order to maintain credibility, to respond to opponents, and to allow constituents to interact critically and knowledgeably with whatever system is in use. The fact that many local managers and politicians have chosen to use the "all jobs" pay line as their comparable worth standard signals both budgetary constraints and a lack of acceptance of the underlying premise of a comparable worth policy.

Hierarchy. Job evaluation, as a method, also exacts a price, and that price is hierarchy. Job evaluation systems evolved out of the movement to make management more rational and scientific in the early twentieth century. They presume hierarchy by providing a "scientific" method for ranking jobs from least to most valuable for the purpose of distributing pay. The factors used to rate jobs on skill, responsibility, effort, and working conditions are referred to in the literature as "compensable factors." Thus, on our way to equality, we find ourselves validating and even entrenching hierarchy as long as it is not biased by race, ethnicity, or sex. Comparable worth policies should ensure that nurses and pharmacists are paid equivalently, but they do not raise the question of whether and how much more physicians should be paid than nurses.

Although any labor-management policy in effect accepts a hierarchical wage structure, the genuine pain experienced by many employees in the process of job evaluation and comparable worth analysis derives largely from the fact that such an analysis makes hierarchies explicit and rearranges them. Because the state of Minnesota separated these two processes, employees experienced far less disruption. But, at the local level, comparable worth essentially "took the blame" for a variety of status concerns and anxieties raised by job evaluation. In part, these concerns clarify the fundamental nature of gender in workplace hierarchies. In tiny Princeton, Minnesota, police at first refused to sign a contract when they learned about the substantial raises three clerical workers were slated to receive as a result of a comparable worth study. According to Police Association head Jules Zimmer, "we weren't aware of the large increases given to the female employees."[18] In St. Paul, firefighters joked bitterly that "it's very dangerous to be a librarian. Everyone knows a book could fall on your head at any time."[19]

Two years later, however, St. Paul firefighters were far more upset that the comparable worth process had resulted in the loss of parity with the police. One informant told us, warning of the key status issues at stake, that "the police hate women and the firefighters hate the police." The bitterness of firefighters when police received a "comparable worth" (really, pay-for-points) raise echoed that observation. When the city council refused to restore firefighters to parity with the police, the local firefighters' association president told them: "We will not go away. We'll be a wound that won't heal."[20]

Such issues arise in part because the technocratic nature of comparable worth reform makes it easy to attach other, unrelated agendas to its implementation. Managers frequently see a demand for comparable worth as an opportunity to rationalize their job classification and wage system by doing an entire overhaul. They, of course, are as eager to find "overpaid" as "underpaid" classes and can, if they wish, use comparable worth to generate serious conflict in an already fragmented labor force by arguing that comparable worth really means "pay for points," a technocratic and meritocratic definition of fairness that avoids historical arguments or responsibilities.

The definition of comparable worth as pay for points not only fails to acknowledge the structural undervaluation of female and minority labor, but it also reflects the strength of opposition to any wholly or partially redistributive policy. Because redistributive policies *transfer* valued resources – establishing what is often viewed by participants as real, long-term winners and losers – politicians are pressured to reconfigure policies in a more distributive manner, where a greater number of people benefit, but often without targeting those most in need. The lack of commitment of many local managers to the goals of comparable worth, the necessity to invent the mechanisms to achieve the policy, and the dependence on outside technical experts allow these redistributive actions to take place.

Unions that encompass both female and male units can do much to educate their members about what is going on, as can managers who support the policy, but there is much room also for "divide-and-conquer" strategies that pit employees against one another. AFSCME, which represents 62 percent of Minnesota state employees, was in a position to control employee responses and keep comparable worth on track. Educational meetings emphasized that the policy was fair, a long-overdue issue of pay equity. But AFSCME conveyed this message about comparable worth far more vigorously to female-dominated units than to male-dominated units. Where male- and female-dominated jobs are represented by different unions, competition over scarce resources can easily undermine the original purpose of comparable worth, that is, the elimination of sex- and race-based wage discrimination. Some, such as the St. Paul police, have loudly and successfully demanded their "comparable worth" based on job evaluation studies, upsetting other male-dominated groups that could not do the same.

Jobs. The market may also exact a price in the loss and transformation of jobs if we are not alert. Comparable worth is designed in part to modify wage setting on the assumption that current market wages incorporate into them past discrimination. Economist Heidi I. Hartmann argues that comparable worth helps to correct a flaw in the market.[21] Yet she and other economists also recognize that labor has always been rationed in industrial society, either through the market or through other mechanisms. Comparable worth joins a host of other policies designed to ration labor in ways the market would not. Immigration laws, for example, either encourage or discourage the flow of workers into the country. In the latter case, the purpose is primarily to protect the jobs of workers who are already here. Similarly, debates over tariffs and trade protection are, from labor's point of view, about retaining jobs in this country rather than allowing them to be exported. Plant closing laws, the minimum wage, and child labor laws all place constraints on "free market" decisions, protecting some jobs at the expense of others. In this sense, comparable worth is neither so new nor so radical as opponents would have us believe. But like these other policies it also will interact in a crowded arena with outcomes we can only partially anticipate.

Neoclassical economists predict that comparable worth will generate significant unemployment among women as employers either substitute male for female workers or simply eliminate jobs. However, studies of Australia, where comparable worth was implemented for the entire economy in the space of a couple of years, have shown that the costs in terms of unemployment for women were quite minimal, in large part because the labor force remains gender-segregated, with few men competing for jobs traditionally held by women.[22] When two economists simulated the impact of comparable worth policies on employment in U.S. state and local governments, they found the possible decline in female employment to be a "surprisingly small" 2 to 3 percent even though "our personal priors were that we would find larger estimates of potential job loss for females."[23] (Indeed, even these unemployment estimates may be high because they are not predicted on firm-level decision making about hiring and retention.)

At the state level in Minnesota, Commissioner Rothchild reported there has been no loss of jobs due to comparable worth.[24] But there may be pressures to reduce the size of work forces in some Minnesota localities, pressures that may be real or may be invented as threats in the bargaining process. Nationwide, the trends for part-time work and contracting out in the public sector have increased in the last decade. As David Lewin reported, 22 percent of state and local public employees were employed part-time in 1982, and only 7.9 percent of part-time public employees were unionized.[25]

Where might these pressures be felt? School boards have a number of programs that are often required to be self-supporting, like latch-key programs or food preparation. Some school personnel, like a number in Stillwater, Minnesota, have indicated that they fear these programs might be eliminated or modified if the (mostly) women who worked in them were paid higher wages. Similarly, city and county officials, like those in Olmstead County, have remarked that home health workers might be vulnerable to personnel cuts or contracting out.[26] What is telling about these comments, whether they presage actual change or set the tone for labor negotiations, is that they refer to programs that have begun to respond to the changing status of women, especially the necessity for many families, however they are composed, to balance paid work and childrearing. In other words, local governments are reacting to comparable worth with threats to renege on the emerging social commitment to policies addressing what have been traditionally defined as *women's* problems. Well-unionized localities would be better able to meet these threats (if they materialize) than would those without employee representation.

Many unions have faced these problems before in regard to janitorial work and garbage collection, mostly men's work. This time it is possible, however, for comparable worth raises whose beneficiaries are mostly women to become the scapegoat for unpopular management decisions to shrink the size of the labor force.

THE CASE FOR COMPARABLE WORTH

Some of the problems described above simply clarify the limits of comparable worth as a reform and in fact are problematic only if one expects comparable worth to solve problems it was never designed to address. The significance of any of these problems depends on the conditions under which a particular comparable worth policy is implemented. In Minnesota, for example, there has been a dramatic contrast between the apparent simplicity and ease of implementation at the state level and the technocratic complexities and conflicts in many local jurisdictions. An examination of the differences may clarify more of the strategic concerns that must inform any comparable worth campaign.

The state of Minnesota passed a law in 1982 establishing comparable worth as a policy for state employees. Special appropriations in 1983 and 1985 provided funds for "pay equity increments" which were allocated through the process of collective bargaining. By 30 June 1987, the process was complete and a scattergram of female- and male-dominated job classes clustered neatly around what had formerly been the male wage line, as figure 3 shows. Several conditions contributed to this smooth process.

First, the state had a job evaluation system in place, completed by Hay Associates in 1979. Comparable worth advocates made a strategic decision that despite that system's biases (which tend to underrate typically female jobs), they would use it in their analysis and as the basis for changes in salaries. Thus, they avoided the disruption of job evaluation and the addition of managerial agendas having to do with reclassification and rationalization of personnel policies. Comparable worth in such a setting seems "cleaner," less likely to take the blame for other discontents.

Second, both managers and union representatives strongly supported the policy and accepted the view that comparable worth was a necessary remedy for historic discrimination against traditionally female jobs. Rothchild had been one of the prime movers behind the original legislation in her former role as director of the state Council on the Economic Status of Women. And AFSCME had been the most powerful lobby in its behalf. This basic commitment meant that neither side used comparable worth divisively. No wages were lowered or frozen. Indeed, the separate appropriation of comparable worth funds left the impression that this was *additional* money that would not otherwise have been allocated to salaries. And the collective bargaining process remained the central mechanism for allocating those funds within the established guidelines.

Finally, both sides downplayed the comparable worth process, seeking to avoid division and hostility. This was, of course, a double-edged policy. It succeeded in its purpose and was probably necessary. Yet, in a systematic telephone survey of state employees conducted in 1985, we found that 43 percent of employees who actually received comparable worth raises were unaware of that fact, a finding with complicated implications for comparable worth as a policy of social transformation.[27] What is the role of changed consciousness in social transformation? Are there different long-term results in the autonomy and power of individuals who knew the origins of their comparable worth raises as well as spent them, in comparison with individuals who merely spent them?

At the local level, there was significant conflict over comparable worth. Of the 1,597 local jurisdictions in Minnesota, approximately one-half used a simple job match with the state's Hay system. But most larger jurisdictions instituted new job evaluation systems. In many cases, managers, concerned with satisfying the letter of the law but unwilling to accept the underlying premise that women's historic wages are discriminatory, seized the opportunity for rationalization and found ways to redistribute raises rather than augment pay levels.[28] Constant discussion, with confusing and incomplete information, about a technology that even managers did not fully understand also fed employees' fears and led to conflict.

Nevertheless, comparable worth does extract a price from patriarchy which makes it a strategy worthy of our best efforts. At the bottom line, comparable worth puts money in the hands and pockets of women and minorities who are at the lowest end of the pay scale. For example, the comparable worth analysis undertaken in Minnesota showed that the lowest-paid position in the state was Clerk 1. The implementation of comparable worth dramatically changed the compensation for this job. If comparable worth had not been implemented, the base pay of an entry-level Clerk 1 in contract year 1983-84 would have been $11,922. If, four years later, the position had received its general pay raises of $1,753 but had not received pay equity raises, the base pay of an entry-level Clerk 1 would have increased to $13,675. With comparable worth, entry-level base pay for the Clerk 1 position actually rose to $15,931 in contract year 1986-87, the year that comparable worth was fully implemented. Of the $4,009 increase in base salary, $1,753 came from regularly negotiated raises, and $2,256 came from comparable worth raises.

Another perspective on these raises can be seen by comparing entry-level salaries for the Clerk 1 position to the poverty line for a family of four. In 1983, the poverty line for a family of four was $10,178, and the base salary for an entry-level Clerk 1 (before comparable worth increments were added) was $11,922 or 117 percent of the poverty line. If over the next four years this position had only received the pay raises negotiated between the union and the state, the base salary of $13,675 would have been 122 percent of the poverty line (which was $11,203). The actual salary of $15,931 – the salary that included the completed implementation of comparable worth raises as well as general salary raises – was 142 percent of the poverty line. Of course, not every Clerk 1 was the sole support of a family of four, but the salary change indicated the change in the capacity of people working as Clerk 1's to support or help to support families.

The process of providing comparable worth raises is far from complete in Minnesota's local jurisdictions. Already it is clear that the financial benefit to workers in female-dominated classes will be muted by policies designed to contain costs. For example, in the Minneapolis School District the decision to use the pay line based on all jobs rather than one based on male-dominated jobs, combined with an "equity corridor" which claims that salaries within 7.5 percent above or below the line will be considered equitable, reduced the potential cost to the district by a factor of ten. At the same time, preliminary figures from a suburban school district illustrate the very real impact comparable worth policies can have. A Health Associate, in 1985-86, earned an entering salary of $6.21 per hour. If the associate worked full-time (forty hours per week for thirty-nine weeks), which many did not, the salary would be $9,687.60 for the year or 86 percent of the poverty line. Following the guidelines of its job evaluation and reclassification study, the district proposed that the minimum salary for health associates in 1986-87 be $7.75 per hour. That would raise a full-time associate's yearly salary to $12,090 or 108 percent of the poverty line for a family of four.

The point of our essay is that comparable worth is a long-term strategy, whose consequences, both good and troublesome, we will have to wrestle with for the foreseeable future. Comparable worth is a *procedural* reform – not the same as creating new individual rights and leaving individuals to enforce them in the courts. Like environmental protection, where we can never stop testing air quality regardless of specific victories, comparable worth will require constant vigilance. If it validates hierarchy, we need to be thinking about other, simultaneous ways to press for participation and power. If comparable worth is incorporated in other political agendas, we need to understand the implications of those agendas and fight or ally with them consciously. If it means possible unemployment, particularly in women's occupations, we must debate among ourselves how the social costs of childcare and other traditional women's responsibilities should be borne. If comparable worth legislation strengthens the hands of public managers, then seeking comparable worth directly through collective bargaining may offer a different set of possibilities.

This prescription for vigilance, however, raises questions about how crowded the feminist agenda is and how we can gird ourselves to persevere when issues like comparable worth leave the front pages and the legislative hearing rooms. In Minnesota, the police and firefighter unions went to the legislature in the spring of 1985 to challenge and weaken the comparable worth law affecting local governments. At that time, the women's organizations that had backed the original legislation were absorbed in other issues on the presumption that the comparable worth battle had been "won." Suddenly, two committees approved the police and firefighters' bill, and women's groups found themselves on the defensive. Only strenuous efforts headed by the League of Women

Voters and other women's groups saved the day. Comparable worth is not an issue that can be won as policy and forgotten in implementation.

NOTES

We would like to thank Nancy Johnson for research assistance. This research was supported by grants from the Northwest Area Foundation, the National Academy of Sciences, and the University of Minnesota. University support included grants from the Center for Urban and Regional Affairs, the Office of the Academic Vice-President, the Graduate School, the Hewlett Center on Conflict Resolution, and the Hubert H. Humphrey Institute of Public Affairs.

1. Eleanor Holmes Norton, quoted in Leslie Bennett's "The Equal Pay Issue," *New York Times,* 26 Oct. 1979, 20.
2. William T. Bielby and James N. Baron, "Undoing Discrimination: Job Integration and Comparable Worth," in *Ingredients for Women's Employment Policy,* ed. Christine Bose and Glenna Spitze (Albany: State University of New York Press, 1987), 211-29. See also Barbara F. Reskin, ed., *Sex Segregation in the Workplace: Trends, Explanations, Remedies* (Washington, D.C.: National Academy Press, 1984).
3. Donald Treiman and Heidi I. Hartmann, *Women, Work, and Wages* (Washington, D.C.: National Academy Press, 1981), 93.
4. See ibid.; U.S. Commission on Civil Rights, *Comparable Worth: Issues for the Eighties,* vol. 1 (Washington, D.C.: U.S. Commission on Civil Rights, 1984); Helen Remick, ed., *Comparable Worth and Wage Discrimination: Technical Possibilities and Political Realities* (Philadelphia: Temple University Press, 1984); Michael Evan Gold, *A Dialogue on Comparable Worth* (Ithaca, N.Y.: ILR Press, 1983); Mark Aldrich and Robert Buchele, *The Economics of Comparable Worth* (Cambridge, Mass.: Ballinger Publishing Co., 1986); Phyllis Schlafly, ed., *Equal Pay for Unequal Work* (Washington, D.C.: Women's Research and Education Institute, 1984); *Gender at Work: Perspectives on Occupational Segregation and Comparable Worth* (Washington, D.C.: Women's Research and Education Institute, 1984); and Elaine Johansen, *Comparable Worth: The Myth and the Movement* (Boulder: Westview Press, 1984).
5. Using a natural experiment methodology, we chose local jurisdictions for careful examination on the basis of type, size, and geographic locations. The University of Minnesota's Comparable Worth Research Project collected data from local media, public documents, and interviews with key managers, elected officials, union leaders, and other employees. We also interviewed officials in the major jurisdictional professional associations (the Association of Minnesota Counties, the Minnesota League of Cities, and the Minnesota School Boards Association) to determine their influence on policy making. See Sara M. Evans and Barbara J. Nelson, "Mandating Local Change in Minnesota: State Required Implementation of Comparable Worth by Local Jurisdictions," in *Comparable Worth: A View from the States,* ed. Ronnie Steinberg (Philadelphia: Temple University Press, forthcoming, 1989).
6. For a discussion of the passage of these laws, see Sara M. Evans and Barbara J. Nelson, "Initiating a Comparable Worth Wage Policy in Minnesota: Notes from the Field," *Policy Studies Review* 5 (May 1986): 849-62; Sara M. Evans and Barbara J. Nelson, "Comparable Worth for Public Employees: Implementing a New Wage Policy in Min-

nesota," in *Comparable Worth, Pay Equity, and Public Policy*, eds. Rita Mae Kelly and Jane Bayes (Westport, Conn.: Greenwood Press, 1988), 191-212.

7. This definition of comparable worth draws on Treiman and Hartmann, chaps. 4 and 5; Helen Remick, "Beyond Equal Pay for Equal Work: Comparable Worth in the State of Washington," in *Equal Employment Policy for Women*, ed. Ronnie Steinberg-Ratner (Philadelphia: Temple University Press, 1980), 405-48; Ronnie J. Steinberg, "A Want of Harmony: Perspectives on Wage Discrimination and Comparable Worth," in Remick, *Comparable Worth and Wage Discrimination*, 3-27; and Barbara J. Nelson, "Comparable Worth: A Brief Review of History, Practice, and Theory," *Minnesota Law Review* 69 (May 1985): 1199-2000.

8. Aldrich and Buchele (p. 130 n. 3) derive the criteria for female- and male-dominated jobs in the following manner:

In 1980 civilian non-agricultural employment was 43.2 percent female. An occupation in which women were represented in proportion to their numbers in total employment would therefore employ 432 women for every 1,000 employees or 432 women for every 568 men. If women are *over-represented* by a factor of three [the typical measure of overrepresentation], there would be 3 × 432 = 1,296 women for very 568 men – that is, the occupation would be 1,296/(1,296 + 568) = 70 percent female. Likewise, an occupation in which men were overrepresented by a factor of three would contain 3 × 568 = 1,704 men for every 432 women – that is, it would be 1,704/(1,704 + 432) = 80 percent male.

For research on the underpayment of equally valued jobs, see Treiman and Hartmann, 59-62; Ronnie J. Steinberg, "Identifying Wage Discrimination and Implementing Pay Equity Adjustments," in *Comparable Worth: Issues for the Eighties*, 99-116.

9. Heidi I. Hartmann, "The Political Economy of Comparable Worth" (Paper presented at the Conference on Alternative Approaches to the Labor Market, University of Utah, Salt Lake City, 12-13 Oct. 1985).

10. Randall Ripley and Grace A. Franklin, *Policy Implementation and Bureaucracy*, 2d ed. (Chicago: Dorsey Press, 1986), 95-101, 115; Raymond A. Bauer, Ithiel de Sola Pool, and Lewis Anthony Dexter, *American Business and Public Policy: The Politics of Foreign Trade* (New York: Atherton, 1963); Theodore J. Lowi, "American Business, Public Policy, Case Studies, and Political Theory," *World Politics* 16 (1964): 677-715; Theodore J. Lowi, *The End of Liberalism: Ideology, Policy, and the Crisis of Public Authority* (New York: Norton, 1969); Lewis A. Froman, Jr., "The Categorization of Policy Contents," in *Political Science and Public Policy*, ed. Austin Ranney (Chicago: Markham, 1968), 41-52; E.E. Schattschneider, *Politics, Pressures, and the Tariff: A Study of Free Enterprise in Pressure Politics As Shown in the 1929-1930 Revision of the Tariff* (New York: Prentice-Hall, 1935) and *The Semi-Sovereign People* (New York: Holt, Rinehart & Winston, 1960); Robert H. Salisbury, "An Exchange Theory of Interest Groups," *Midwest Journal of Political Science* 8 (1969): 1-32; Robert H. Salisbury and John P. Heinz, "A Theory of Policy Analysis and Some Preliminary Applications," in *Policy Analysis in Political Science*, ed. Ira Sharkansky (Chicago: Markham, 1970), 39-60; Michael T. Hayes, *Lobbyists and Legislators: A Theory of Political Markets* (New Brunswick, N.J.: Rutgers University Press, 1981), 19-39.

11. Ripley and Franklin, 72-73.

12. Janet A. Flammang, "Effective Implementation: The Case of Comparable Worth in San Jose," *Policy Studies Review* 5 (May 1986): 615-37; Helen Remick, "The Case of Comparable Worth in Washington State," *Policy Studies Review* 5 (May 1986): 838-49.

13. See, for example studies in Remick's *Comparable Worth and Wage Discrimination*; Alice H. Cook, *Comparable Worth: A Case Book of Experiences in States and Localities* (Honolulu: Industrial Relations Center, University of Hawaii at Manoa, 1985); Rita Mae Kelly and Jane Bayes, eds., "Symposium: Implementing Comparable Worth in the Public Sector: Theory and Practice," *Policy Studies Review* 5 (May 1986): 769-870. See also Treiman and Hartmann.

14. The Swedish policy of solidarity wage setting, where lower-paid jobs get higher percentage raises, does address the salary problems of low-wage workers but is silent on the work value problems. See chap. 4 of Sara M. Evans and Barbara J. Nelson, *Wage Justice: Comparable Worth and the Paradox of Technocratic Reform* (Chicago: University of Chicago Press, 1989).

15. Nina Rothchild, Address to the Association of Minnesota Counties, St. Paul, 22 Jan. 1985.

16. See Lisa Portman, Joy Ann Grune, and Eve Johnson, "The Role of Labor," in Remick, *Comparable Worth and Wage Discrimination*, 219-37.

17. This was true in Oregon. See Joan Acker, "Comparable Worth: The Oregon Case," in Steinberg, *Comparable Worth: A View from the States.*

18. Jules Zimmer, quoted in Joel Stottrup "Equal-Pay-for-Equal-Work Idea Part of City Pay Hikes," *Princeton Union Eagle,* 18 Feb. 1984.

19. St. Paul Mayor George Latimer, panel presentation, conference on "New Directions in Comparable Worth: Minnesota and the Nation," Minneapolis, 18 Oct. 1985.

20. Larry Oakes, "St. Paul Firefighters Lose Pay Beef with City Council," Minneapolis *Star and Tribune,* 6 Aug. 1987, 5B.

21. Heidi I. Hartmann, "The Case for Comparable Worth," in Schlafly, 11-24.

22. See R.G. Gregory and R.C. Duncan, "Segmented Labor Market Theories and Australian Experience of Equal Pay for Women," *Journal of Post-Keynesian Economics* 3 (Spring 1981): 403-28; R.G. Gregory and V. Ho, "Equal Pay and Comparable Worth: What Can the U.S. Learn from the Australian Experience?" Centre for Economic Policy Research, Australian National University, Discussion Paper no. 123, July 1985.

23. Ronald G. Ehrenberg and Robert S. Smith, "Comparable Worth in the Public Sector," in *Public Sector Payrolls,* ed. David A. Wise (Chicago: University of Chicago Press, 1987), 279-80.

24. Commission on the Economic Status of Women, *Pay Equity: The Minnesota Experience* (St. Paul: CESW, 1985), 15; also Bonnie Watkins, Pay Equity Coordinator for the State of Minnesota, "Pay Equity: The Minnesota Experience," Remarks to the National Committee on Pay Equity Senate Staff Briefing, Washington, D.C., 14 Mar. 1986.

25. David Lewin, "Public Employee Unionism in the 1980s: An Analysis of Transformation," in *Unions in Transition: Entering the Second Century,* ed. Seymour Martin Lipset (San Francisco: ICS Press, 1986), 246.

26. Jeann Linsley, "Stillwater Schools' Equity Raises May Cost $510,000," *St. Paul Pioneer Press,* 9 Oct. 1985, 3NE; interview with David Griffin, Director of Personnel Services, Olmstead County, 13 Mar. 1987.

27. This figure is based on a random survey of state employees conducted in June 1985 by the University of Minnesota's Comparable Worth Research Project.

28. The latter was done by manipulating the statistical techniques used in a comparable worth analysis. Hennepin County led the way with a policy that would (1) use the "balanced class" pay line rather than the male wage line as their goal, (2) place a 15 percent corridor on either side of that line within which wages would be considered equitable (in other words, wages could differ by 30 percent at the same point and still be "equitable"), and (3) conduct a market survey and pay no more than 10 percent above or 10 percent below the market rate regardless of what their study showed. Many jurisdictions also have frozen wages in higher paid occupations, offering cash bonuses instead of raises in base pay.

Conceptualizing Black Women's Employment Experiences

Cathy Scarborough

> For me to think about racism and sexism meant I had to pull myself together and look at myself as one person under a law that separates me into my woman being and into my Black being.
>
> Kimberlé Crenshaw[1]

Black women[2] in America[3] have always been workers—as slaves, farmers, domestics, skilled and unskilled laborers, and even, in small numbers, as professionals. Their ability to find and retain jobs has usually been essential to the survival of their families.[4] Despite their history of industriousness, Black women have found it impossible to escape racism and sexism in the job market. The very laws designed to eliminate employment discrimination have actually placed new obstacles in front of Black women. In order to challenge employment discrimination, Black women must use legal remedies and strategies that were designed for others. Whenever the legal system has attempted to deal with the problems Black women face in the workplace, it has consistently ignored their social history and failed to truly understand their experiences or address their concerns.

This Note attempts to provide an historical account of how the law has perceived and treated Black women. Title VII of the Civil Rights Act of 1964[5] provides a framework for viewing the interaction between Black women and the law. Section I of this Note examines the experiences of Black women in America from slavery to the present in order to reveal why the experiences of Black women cannot be understood simply as a

---

1. Address by Professor Kimberlé Crenshaw, Women And The Law: A Feminist Jurisprudence (Apr. 2, 1986) [hereinafter Crenshaw].

2. I focus on the experiences of African-American women in the United States from slavery to the present. However, other people protected by Title VII of the Civil Rights Act of 1964, 42 U.S.C. § 2000e-2(a) (1982), may also benefit from my proposal. *See infra* note 123 and accompanying text.

3. The term America in this paper means the United States of America.

4. *See* P. Giddings, When And Where I Enter: The Impact Of Black Women On Race And Sex In America 150-51 (1984).

5. Title VII makes it unlawful for an employer "to fail or refuse to hire or to discharge any individual, or otherwise to discriminate against any individual with respect to his compensation, terms, conditions, or privileges of employment, because of such individual's race, color, religion, sex, or national origin." 42 U.S.C. § 2000e-2(a) (1982).

combination of Black men's and white women's experiences. It is necessary to study Black women's experiences in America in order to understand who they are and how to adequately address their concerns. Section
II examines the legislative history of Title VII as it relates to the employment discrimination concerns of Black women. Section III analyzes how
courts have dealt with the question of whether Black women can be considered a special class protected by Title VII. Finally, Section IV proposes
methods that courts can use to adequately address the employment concerns of Black women—first, by understanding that Black women are not
a subgroup of an ideal "main" group; second, by considering Black
women's perspectives; third, by discarding the "sex-plus" rationale advocated in *Jefferies v. Harris County Community Action Ass'n*[6] and limited
in *Judge v. Marsh*;[7] and lastly, by applying Title VII in a way that encompasses Black women's experiences in their entirety.

I. HISTORICAL EXPERIENCES OF BLACK WOMEN IN THE UNITED STATES

American society has long considered men more valuable than women,
and whites more valuable than Blacks.[8] In addition, Black women have
not been viewed as a separate group with different concerns and experiences from both white women and Black men. The difficulties Black
women face in the American legal system have their roots in a society that
has historically avoided considering Black women as whole persons. Society has tended to use broader terms such as "Blacks" and "women," while
really meaning Black men and white women, and thereby reinforcing the
invisibility of Black women.[9]

Despite the marginalization of their experience in American society,
Black women have played and continue to play an important and unique
role. Yet, because their separate reality has been ignored, it has been difficult for courts and legislatures to devise appropriate legal means to deal
with the composite effects of their "Blackness" and "womanness."

---

6. 615 F.2d 1025 (5th Cir. 1980).

7. 649 F. Supp. 770 (D.D.C. 1986).

8. The common historical belief was expressed in an editorial in a *New York Herald* newspaper:
   How did woman first become subject to man as she now is all over the world? By her nature,
   her sex, just as the negro is and always will be, to the end of time, inferior to the white race,
   and, therefore, doomed to subjection; but happier than she would be in any other condition,
   just because it is the law of her nature. The women themselves would not have this law
   reversed.
   R. GINSBURG, CONSTITUTIONAL ASPECTS OF SEX-BASED DISCRIMINATION 2 (1974) (quoting A.
   KRADITOR, UP FROM THE PEDESTAL: SELECTED WRITING IN THE HISTORY OF AMERICA FEMI-
   NISM 190 (1968)).

9. "No other group in America has so had their identity socialized out of existence as have black
   women. . . . When black people are talked about, the focus tends to be on *black* men; and when
   women are talked about, the focus tends to be on *white* women." B. HOOKS, AIN'T I A WOMAN:
   BLACK WOMEN AND FEMINISM 7 (1981).

A. *Black Women As Slave Workers*

Sojourner Truth once said that Black women suffered by having to work like men without the rights of men, while also having to deal with the agonies of being women with none of the privileges and advantages of white women.[10] During slavery, Black men and Black women were treated as chattels by both federal and state legislatures and courts.[11] The Constitution deprived slaves and white women of the right to vote, thereby perpetuating racism and sexism and protecting the power and property rights of those in control.[12]

In addition, Black women were exploited as only women in their position could be.[13] They were viewed as reproductive servants.[14] Black women, as slaves, could not bring legal claims alleging rape because they had no rights.[15] *Hamilton v. Cragg*[16] illustrates Black women's unique racial and sexual exploitation as a class of slaves. In that case, a Black woman sought to take her child, born to her when she was a slave, with her when she gained freedom. The court held that as a slave, she was Black chattel whose body "issues" and physical and sexual being belonged to her white owner.[17]

---

10. *Quoted in* M. MARABLE, HOW CAPITALISM UNDERDEVELOPED BLACK AMERICA 64 (1983).

11. D. BELL, RACE, RACISM AND AMERICAN LAW 11 (1980) (citing K. STAMPP, THE PECULIAR INSTITUTION 197-236 (1956)); *see also* Dred Scott v. Sanders, 60 U.S. (19 How.) 393 (1857) (Blacks are not citizens within meaning of Constitution). In pre-Civil War cases, Black men and Black women were the objects—the property in dispute—not the plaintiffs or defendants. D. BELL, *supra*, at 11–12.

12. The "Founding Fathers" excluded Black slaves from citizenship, and even personhood, through the force of law. The Constitution established that persons bound in service were to be considered only as three-fifths of a person. U.S. CONST. art. I, § 4, cl. 3. It also denied them the constitutional rights of free men. D. BELL, supra note 11, at 22-23. Black men and Black women were excluded from the constitution as slaves, and white women, who were thought to occupy a separate "feminine" sphere and were considered unequal to men, *see supra* note 8, were also denied the vote by the Constitution's authors. D. BELL, *supra* at 11, 16; R. GINSBURG, *supra* note 8, at 2.

13. *See* A. DAVIS, WOMEN, RACE AND CLASS 6-7 (1981).

14. *Id.* Slave-masters minimized the importance of Black women's role as "mothers" and emphasized their role as breeders. L. RODGERS-ROSE, THE BLACK WOMAN 18 (1980).

15. Black women were thought of as not being "rapable" because of how society viewed them. The white woman was "depicted as goddess rather than sinner; she was virtuous, pure, innocent, not sexual and worldly," B. HOOKS, *supra* note 9, at 31, while the "predominant image [of the Black woman was] that of the "fallen" woman, the whore, the slut, the prostitute." *Id.* at 52. Even today, "Black women['s] . . . unique position in American history and mythology . . . makes them extremely vulnerable to sexual harassment on the job. The mythology and stereotypes, which at one time made Black women unrapable, continue to affect their job opportunities." Black women are still thought of as more sexually available "[a]nd more promiscuous than White women." Ellis, *Sexual Harrassment and Race: A Legal Analysis of Discrimination,* 8 J. LEGIS. 30, 39 (1981).

16. 6 H & J 16 (Md. 1823) (cited in J. WHEELER, A PRACTICAL TREATISE ON THE LAW OF SLAVERY 26 (1837)).

17. The child born to the Black woman while she was as a slave was deemed to be a product belonging to the slave owner. Id. at 26. The court held in *Hamilton* that, as a slave:

> she had no civil rights, and could have pursued no legal remedy against her mistress on any account . . . and was subject to all the disabilities and incapacities incident to a state of slavery. She was a mere chattel, the property of her mistress, who could have sold or transferred her at pleasure.

Hamilton, 6 H & J at 17.

As Manning Marable states, Black women, as slaves, were white people's property, and "[a]s prop-

B. Black Women As "Free" Workers

As "free" workers after Emancipation, Black women as a class continued to suffer the burden of race-sex discrimination. The courts reinforced
the societal invisibility of Black women by referring to women exclusively
in stereotypical terms of white women's experiences. In *Bradwell v.
State*,[18] which allowed states to prohibit women from practicing law, Justice Bradley wrote in his concurrence that "[t]he natural and proper ti-
midity and delicacy which belongs to the female sex evidently unfits it for
many of the occupations of civil life. . . . The paramount destiny and
mission of woman are to fulfill the noble and benign office of wife and
mother. This is the law of the Creator."[19] This stereotypical depiction of
white womanhood[20] contrasts sharply with Black women's experiences,
since Black women were in no way considered timid or delicate.[21] The
Court's words lie in sharp contrast to the resonating challenge of Sojourner Truth:

> Nobody ever helped *me* into carriages, or over mud puddles, or give
> *me* any best place! And ain't *I* a woman? Look at me, look at my
> arm! I have plowed, and planted, and gathered into barns—and no
> man could head me—and ain't *I* a woman? I have born'd five chil-
> dren and seen'em most all sold off into slavery, and when I cried out
> with a mother's grief, none but Jesus heard . . . and ain't *I* a
> woman?[22]

After slavery, Black women had to deal with economic hardship.[23] The

---

erty, Black women were expected to produce wealth for their owners. But as females, Black women
were also constantly subjected to the physical and sexual assault of white males. . . . For the white
male American, the Black woman's vagina was his private property." M. MARABLE, *supra* note 10,
at 72-73.

18.   83 U.S. (16 Wall.) 130 (1872).
19.   *Id.* at 141.
20.   It is doubtful that the *Bradwell* Court accurately described the reality even of most white
women's experiences. *See generally* A. DAVIS, *supra* note 13, at 228-29 (describing experiences of
working class white women and development of "universal" vision of "womanhood").
21.   *See* A. DAVIS, *supra* note 13, at 7-8; J. JONES, LABOR OF LOVE, LABOR OF SORROW:
BLACK WOMEN, WORK, AND THE FAMILY FROM SLAVERY TO THE PRESENT 58-59 (1985); Palmer,
White Women/ Black Women: The Dualism of Female Identity and Experience in the United States,
9 FEMINIST STUDIES 151, 153 (1983).
22.   *Quoted in* M. MARABLE, supra note 10, at 69. In Muller v. Oregon, 208 U.S. 412 (1908),
the Court continued to follow *Bradwell*'s sanctioning of differential treatment of men and women
based upon a stereotypical vision of white womanhood. The Court ruled that an Oregon employment
statute which prohibited women from being employed in any mechanical establishment, factory, or
laundry for more than 10 hours a day was constitutional. *Id.* at 416. The Court justified its decision
by stating that "[t]he two sexes differ in structure of body, in the functions to be performed by each, in
the amount of physical strength, in the capacity for long-continued labor, particularly when done
standing. . . ." *Id.* at 422. The Court believed that women were dependent upon men and that they
needed to be protected from the greed and passion of men. A woman's place was in the home, fulfilling her maternal function and thereby safeguarding the wellbeing of the race. Once again, the
Court's understanding of the condition of "women" clearly did not reflect Black women's experiences
in the United States.
23.   L. RODGERS-ROSE, *supra* note 14, at 22.

majority of Black women in the early 1900s were still working on farms, taking care of white people's homes,[24] or employed as unskilled service laborers.[25] The jobs held by Black women often required them to work well over ten hours per day, even though they may have had children at home or been pregnant. Thus, the Court clearly did not consider Black women in developing its myth of womanhood. Although the term "women" was used in a broad and inclusive manner, the emphasis on the weak physical structure of women and their place in society ignored Black women's historical experiences and contributions.

During World War I, when Black women were allowed to enter into manufacturing and mechanical jobs in limited numbers,[26] unlike their white sisters, who were viewed as being "timid" and "delicate," they were made to perform the most difficult and the dirtiest jobs.[27] Yet, the courts failed to acknowledge the existence of any image of womanhood other than that which they perceived to be experienced by white women, ignoring the reality of the concerns and experiences of many women.

C. *Recent History*

The Civil Rights Movement of the 1950s and 1960s also ignored Black women's separate concerns.[28] The focus and concern of both Black men and Black women was to end the racist segregationist practices that existed in America.[29] The Movement led to the enactment of statutes and administrative practices prohibiting race discrimination.[30] These statutes, which included Title VII, gave Black men and Black women the right to challenge race discrimination in the courts. However, the unique problems Black women faced as a class were not addressed in the new legislation, nor in the cases which followed.[31] Male members of the Black Power Movement, which grew out of the Civil Rights Movement in the late

---

24. Terborg-Penn, *Survival Strategies Among African-American Women Workers: A Continuing Process*, in WOMEN, WORK AND PROTEST: A CENTURY OF U.S. LABOR HISTORY (R. Milkman ed. 1985).

25. J. JONES, supra note 21, at 155–58; S. HARKEY & R. TERBORG-PENN, THE AFRO-AMERICAN WOMAN: STRUGGLES AND IMAGES 10 (1979); L. RODGERS-ROSE, *supra* note 14, at 23.

26. S. HARKEY & R. TERBORG-PENN, *supra* note 25, at 7.

27. P. GIDDINGS, *supra* note 4, at 144 ("The historical stereotypes assigned to Black women were largely responsible for this. For example, because they were thought to be able to withstand more heat, they got the most heat-intense jobs."). However, it was not until World War II that Black women were allowed to work in factories in any significant numbers. *Id.* Once again, when Black women entered these jobs they were paid less than white women for doing the same or a harder job and were required to work in worse conditions than white women. B. HOOKS, *supra* note 9, at 135. For example, Black women were hired to clean, sweep, and fill the hardest and most unpleasant positions, while others used the machines and held supervisory positions. Terborg-Penn, *supra* note 24, at 147.

28. M. MARABLE, *supra* note 10, at 99 ("In theory and practice, the Black protest movement was compromised and gutted by its inability to confront squarely the reality of patriarchy.")

29. P. GIDDINGS, *supra* note 4, at 302.

30. C. & B. WHALEN, THE LONGEST DEBATE: A LEGISLATIVE HISTORY OF THE 1964 CIVIL RIGHTS ACT 222–38 (1983); M. MARABLE, *supra* note 10, at 99.

31. *See infra* Sections II & III.

1960s, presumed that if the Black man advanced, so would the Black woman.[32] Many were only concerned that Black men regain their manhood.[33]

Furthermore, Black women were blamed for the poverty and "backwardness" of the Black race, as evidenced by the conclusions of the Moynihan Report.[34] The Moynihan Report, which reflected American society's patriarchal underpinnings, described Black women as matriarchal figures, incapable of caring for their children and responsible for producing male children unable to deal with the world because they had been weakened by their domineering mothers.[35] The report proposed that Black society mimic the sexual hierarchy of white middle-class society in order to improve its conditions.[36] The report focused on the problems of Black males and paid little attention to Black females.[37] Black women remained invisible, except as a focus for blame.

The Supreme Court's review of women's history in *Frontiero v. Richardson*[38] illustrates contemporary courts' lack of awareness of Black women. Justice Brennan, writing for the plurality, addressed the "long and unfortunate history of sex discrimination"[39] in the United States and acknowledged that this discrimination "was rationalized by an attitude of

---

32. Male pride became the focus, and Black men demanded that Black women support them and stop being "bossy" and "pushy." *See* B. HOOKS, *supra* note 9, at 85; M. MARABLE, *supra* note 10, at 85. Paula Giddings agrees that "a male-conscious motif ran throughout the society . . . ." P. GIDDINGS, *supra* note 4, at 314. Kathleen Cleaver, a Black Panther Party officer, said that her views were often ignored because she was a woman: "[I]f I suggested [ideas], the suggestion might be rejected; if they were suggested by a man the suggestion would be implemented." *Id.* at 317. Angela Davis similarly observes, "I was criticized very heavily especially by male members of (Ron) Karenga's (U.S.) organization for doing a 'man's job'." *Id.* at 316. The male perspective is reflected in the remarks of several of the movement's leaders. Floyd McKissic of Congress Of Racial Equality (CORE) stated that in "[t]he year 1966 . . . we left our imposed status as Negroes, and became Black Men." *Id.* at 315. Stokley Carmichael stated that "in the coming racial war Black People would stand on our feet and die like men, if that's our only act of manhood." *Id.* Similarly, the women's movement, which began in the late 1960s, failed to include Black women. "[I]t was evident that the White women who dominated the movement felt it was 'their' movement, that is, the medium through which a white woman would voice her grievances to society," as opposed to an organization created for all women to voice their grievances. B. HOOKS, *supra* note 9, at 136-37.

33. REID, BLACK WOMEN'S STRUGGLE FOR EQUALITY 3 (1976).

34. OFFICE OF POLICY PLANNING AND RESEARCH, UNITED STATES DEPARTMENT OF LABOR, THE CASE FOR NATIONAL ACTION—THE NEGRO FAMILY, 29, 34 (1985) [hereinafter MOYNIHAN REPORT]. According to this report "negro children without fathers flounder and fail," unlike White children who see the pattern of men working all around them. *Id.* at 1, 35.

35. *Id.*

36. *Id.* at 5, 45.

37. The report said nothing about the employment discrimination experienced by Black women, nor did it cite the unemployment rate of Black women: It was, instead, concerned with their divorce rates, the number of illegitimate children they had, and the *allegedly* negative effect of the Black matriarchal structure on the Black family. The report found fault with the fact that almost as many Black men as Black women attended college, compared to the white ratio in which men clearly outnumbered women, and the fact that more Black women were working than Black men. *Id.* at 31-32. No reference was made to the fact that Black women were paid less than both Black men and white women. *See id.* at 33. This report did not seek to understand the separate concerns of the Black woman or attempt to devise policies that would empower her to help uplift the race.

38. 411 U.S. 677 (1973).

39. *Id.* at 684.

'romantic paternalism,'" which placed "women" upon a pedestal that turned out to be no more than a paternalistic cage.[40] Ignoring Black women's history, the opinion also viewed "Blacks" as a uniform group and observed that Blacks had gotten the right to vote—before women.[41] The Court saw only two categories: Black men, who had the right to vote, and white women, who were imprisoned in a paternalistic cage. Where do Black women fit into this picture? The Court's failure to recognize and articulate the unique experiences of Black women as workers, slave breeders, and "unrapable"[42] women, whose womanhood has continuously been devalued by American society,[43] led it to project the experiences of one class of women onto all women.

D. Current Problems of Black Women

Black women's problems have not vanished. Currently, the effects of racism-sexism limit the opportunities of most Black women. Although Black women have begun to occupy jobs similar to those held by white women, they still fill the least prestigious and lowest paying jobs within that sector, and fill them in far smaller numbers than white women.[44] Black women find that employers discriminate against them in pay and promotions, even though those same employers may not discriminate against Black men or white women.[45]

Historically, the unemployment rate for Black people has always been higher than the rate for white people.[46] As of 1986, Black women had an unemployment rate of 14.2%, compared with 14.8% for Black men.[47] The

---

40. Id.

41. Id. at 685.

42. See supra note 15.

43. B. HOOKS, supra note 8, at 51–86.

44. See Haywood, Can Theories Of Intentional Wage Discrimination And Comparable Worth Help Black People?, 10 NAT'L BLACK L.J. 16, 18–19 (1987).

45. Id. at 27. See also Jefferies v. Harris County Community Action Ass'n, 615 F.2d 1025 (5th Cir. 1980) (discrimination against Black women can exist even in absence of discrimination against Black men or white women).

46. For the unemployment rates of Black women, Black men, white women, and white men for the years 1950–1970, see U.S. DEPARTMENT OF COMMERCE, U.S. BUREAU OF CENSUS, HISTORICAL STATISTICS OF THE U.S.: COLONIAL TIMES TO 1970, table 2, at 84 (1972). For the years 1975–1985, see U.S. DEPARTMENT OF COMMERCE, U.S. BUREAU OF CENSUS, STATISTICAL ABSTRACT (1986).

47. U.S. DEPARTMENT OF COMMERCE, STATISTICAL ABSTRACT OF THE UNITED STATES 1988: No. 611, at 368 (108th ed. 1988) (citing figures from U.S. BUREAU OF LABOR STATISTICS, EMPLOYMENT AND EARNINGS) [hereinafter UNEMPLOYMENT REPORT]; see generally U.S. DEPARTMENT OF COMMERCE, U.S. BUREAU OF CENSUS—HISTORICAL STATISTICS OF THE U.S: COLONIAL TIMES TO 1970: D 87-101 Series, at 134 (historical data).

The unemployment rate for Black women has always been comparable to that of Black men. Hooks argues that historically, Black men have sometimes had a slightly higher rate of unemployment than Black women because "even if white people had been eager to hire Black men in service jobs to work as maids and washermen, such jobs would have been refused because they would have been regarded as an assault on male dignity." B. HOOKS, supra note 9, at 80. While these unemployment rates have shifted back and forth, the "illusion that Black women . . . had achieved parity or had exceeded Black men's earnings was not simply false, but a gross reversal of economic reality." M. MARABLE, supra note 10, at 102. Jones similarly concludes that "[t]he vast majority of black women employees

---

unemployment rate of Black people remains disproportionately high when compared with the rates for white men and white women, which were 6.0%, and 6.1%, respectively.[48]

In addition, Black women as a group have always received the lowest income as year-round, full-time workers when compared to Black and white men and white women.[49] The median earnings of Black women working full-time in 1986 was $12,126 annually, while white women received $13,961. Black and white male year-round, full-time workers received incomes of $15,125 and $22,390, respectively.[50]

Some researchers[51] state that, in some settings, the wages of Black women have recently been approaching those of white women[52] because Black women are employed primarily in occupations which are viewed as "typically female jobs."[53] However, Julianne Malveaux observes that even "within occupational categories . . . there are differences in the status of Black and white women,"[54] for Black women occupy different enclaves of jobs which are typically female jobs. Failure to understand the interaction of racism and sexism in Black women's lives has led to society's non-recognition of what Malveaux terms "Black women crowding."[55] Malveaux observes that "proportionately fewer Black than white women work in management, sales, and professional jobs, while proportionately more Black women work in service, operative (manufacturing), and private household jobs."[56] The jobs into which Black women are

---

at the lower echelons of the work force find employers eager to exploit their labor, because that labor is cheap and easily routinized." J. JONES, *supra* note 21, at 325. But racism and sexism still deprive Black women of a living salary, no matter how hard they work. *Id.* at 199, 383 n.15-17.

48. UNEMPLOYMENT REPORT, *supra* note 47.

49. *See* U.S. DEPARTMENT OF COMMERCE, BUREAU OF CENSUS, CONSUMER INCOME MONEY INCOME OF FAMILIES AND PERSONS IN THE UNITED STATES: 1981 SERIES P-60, No. 137, at 120–22.

50. *Id.*

51. *See generally* Albelda, *"Nice Work If You Can Get It": Segmentation of White and Black Women Workers in the Post-War Period,* 17 REV. RADICAL POL. ECON. 72 (1985).

52. CONSUMER INCOME MONEY INCOME OF FAMILIES AND PERSON IN THE UNITED STATES: 1986 SERIES P-60 No. 159, at 162.

53. This broad term has been used to define jobs into which most "women" are disproportionately concentrated. Malveaux & Wallace, *Minority Women in the Workplace,* in WORKING WOMEN: PAST-PRESENT-FUTURE 265, 279 (K. Koziara, M. Moskow & L. Tanner eds. 1987)

54. Malveaux, *Comparable Worth and Its Impact on Black Women,* in SLIPPING THROUGH THE CRACKS 53 (M. Simms & J. Malveaux eds. 1985).

55. Professor Malveaux created the term "black women crowding" to describe the racial-gender crowding of Black women into "typical black female" jobs. Malveaux, *supra* note 54, at 54. Black women are concentrated in female service and clerical occupations, and even within these job sectors, they are segregated into the lowest pay and lowest status jobs. *Id.* at 53. Professor Williams defines this phenomenon occurance as the "intra-gender racial crowding of black women." R. Williams, Beyond Human Capital: Black Women, Work And Wage—Working Paper No. 183, at 4. (Mar. 1988) (unpublished work available at Wellesley College Center for Research on Women).

56. *Id.* at 53 (citations omitted). For example, Black women are not overrepresented as bank tellers, secretaries/receptionists, and other occupations which are more than 95% female. Malveaux & Wallace, *supra* note 53, at 278. Within each occupational category there is a difference in the status of white and Black women. Black women are, for the most part, crowded into the lowest clerical positions—typists, file clerks, key punch operators, calculating machine operators—and service positions—chambermaids, nurses aids and practical nurses. *Id.*

crowded command less prestige and pay than those of white women[57] and cast doubt on the supposed convergence of the wages of Black women towards those of white women.[58] It is, therefore, not surprising that Black women, as individuals, continue to suffer the highest poverty rate. As of 1986, 34.5% of Black women lived in poverty, compared to 27.3% of Black men. White men and women had a poverty rate of only 12.3% and 9.6%, respectively.[59]

As these statistics indicate, Black women remain at the bottom of the economy.[60] In order to help alleviate some of the particular problems Black women face, methods must be developed that address their historical experiences and current social status.

II. THE LEGISLATIVE HISTORY OF TITLE VII AND BLACK WOMEN

A. Congressional Response

Congressional concern with the problems experienced by Black women in America had little influence on the development and language of Title VII. Despite an awareness of the problems faced by Black women expressed by a few members of Congress, other legislators thought that these problems would be addressed by the race provision.[61]

During the debates on Title VII, the House of Representatives did not consider the problem of sex discrimination until Representative Smith, an opponent of the measure, proposed that "sex" be added to the language of the bill.[62] He hoped to make the bill so controversial that neither the House nor the Senate would pass it.[63]

To counter Smith's surprise attack, Representative Green opposed the inclusion of "sex" in the bill.[64] She believed that a Black woman, when

---

57. *Id.*

58. *Id.*

59. U.S. DEPARTMENT OF COMMERCE, BUREAU OF THE CENSUS, POVERTY IN THE UNITED STATES 1986, SERIES P-60, No. 160, at 30. Although all female heads of households face high poverty rates, Black women have the highest. Black women heads of household with no husband present experience a poverty rate 14.6% greater than white women's rate. Black women heads of household with no husband present had a 51.7% poverty rate as of 1984, compared to 27.1% for similarly situated white women. Male heads of household with no wife present are, however, much better off. Black men in these circumstances showed a poverty rate of 23.8%, compared to 10.4% for white men. U.S. DEPT OF COMMERCE, U.S. BUREAU OF THE CENSUS, STATISTICAL ABSTRACT OF THE U.S. BUREAU OF THE CENSUS, 1985, CURRENT POPULATION REPORTS SERIES P-60, No.146.

60. Professor Ellis' 1978 statement still defines the position of Black women today: "[Taken] all together, these statistics portray a situation of despair and economic vulnerability. They indicate that Black women are largely looking for work or employed in marginal jobs, earning low wages. At the same time Black women are very often the sole supporter of the family." Ellis, *supra* note 15, at 30.

61. *See infra* notes 64–67 and accompanying text.

62. 110 CONG. REC. 2577 (1964); C. & B. WHALEN, *supra* note 30, at 115–16; Scales-Trent, *Black Women and the Constitution: Finding Our Place, Asserting Our Rights*, 24 HARV. C.R.-C.L. L. REV. 9, 10–11 (1989); Shoben, *Compound Discrimination: The Interaction of Race and Sex in Employment Discrimination*, 55 N.Y.U. L. REV. 793, 796, 797 (1980).

63. C. & B. WHALEN, *supra* note 30, at 116.

64. *See, e.g.*, 110 CONG. REC. 2721 (1964) ("Let us not further weaken . . . any section of the bill but rather let us by our votes make it abundantly clear that this Congress intends to have the

compared to a white woman, "has suffered 10 times that amount of discrimination. She has a double discrimination. She was born as a woman and she was born as a Negro."[65] Therefore, white women should wait for other legislation to advance their cause.[66] Green believed that the aim of the legislation, providing Blacks with jobs and decent wages, would be undermined by irrelevant amendments.[67] In contrast, Representative Bolton pushed the House to address the problems faced by women as a group. She thought that including "sex" in the statute would help all women.[68]

Despite this recognition of Black women's situation, by at least two representatives, there was some discussion that the bill was necessary to protect the rights of white women against Black women. Representative Griffiths argued that white men, in their unwillingness to include "sex" in the statute, were once again putting white women in the same disadvantageous position[69] that they had during Reconstruction on the issue of extending voting rights.[70] She felt that the new bill, without the word "sex," would provide Black women with a remedy and give white women nothing.[71] Others shared this concern.[72]

B. *Ambiguities in the Statutory Language*

In addition to the dispute over the inclusion of "sex," Representative Dowdy sought to have the word "solely" placed into the bill in order to establish that "any discrimination proscribed in the bill must be based *solely* on race, color, religion, sex *or* national origin."[73] It has been suggested that the House's failure to pass the Dowdy proposal indicates that

---

Federal Government exercise its power in ending discrimination against Negroes wherever it is humanly possible.").

65. *Id.* at 2581–82.

66. For all of her insight into Black women's plight, Representative Green nevertheless neglected to see that the race provison standing alone would not fully address Black women's problems.

67. She felt that "[i]n offering amendments in regard to sex . . . [and] in trying to picture this legislation as the Negro woman against the white woman," the passage of the legislation was being jeopardized. *Id.* at 2721.

68. Bolton had the insight to recognize that for "this amendment to include sex as one of the grounds on which there shall be no discrimination affects very deeply Negro women who, perhaps, are at the small end of the horn in a great many of these areas." *Id.* at 2720.

69. *Id.* at 2580.

70. A. DAVIS, *supra* note 13, at 114–15.

71. Griffths argued that if an employer had only white male employees, and a Black woman and white woman applied for the same job and were both rejected, then only the white woman, would lack a remedy. This new law would place "white men in one bracket, [and] . . . take colored men and colored women and give them equal employment rights," leaving white women "at the bottom of the list . . . with no rights at all." *Id.* at 2579.

72. *See, e.g., id.* at 2584 (statement of Representative Gatherings) ("There can be no plausible reason that a white woman should be deprived of an equal opportunity to get a job simply because of her sex and a colored woman obtain that position because of her preferential rights as contained in this bill."). Representative Andrews also supported the inclusion of "sex" in the bill. He felt that "[u]nless this amendment is adopted, the white women of this country would be drastically discriminated against in favor of a Negro woman." *Id.* at 2583.

73. *Id.* at 2728 (emphasis added).

the "or" in the statute should be considered as an additive term rather than as an exclusive one.[74] If "or" were interpreted inclusively, it would mean that the statute would allow suits and protected class status under Title VII to be based on more than one of the listed characteristics;[75] conversely, interpreting the "or" as exclusive would mean that only one of the protected categories could be used by a plaintiff in an employment discrimination case.[76] However, Congress' subsequent failure to incorporate the word "solely" into the final statute is inconclusive. This fact, standing alone does not provide enough information for determining the circumstances and form of claims that may be brought, under Title VII, by those who are the victims of discrimination on the basis of several protected characteristics.

Although Black women were discussed in the Congressional debates leading to the passage of Title VII, the legislative history of the Act does not provide an established policy or even a guideline for addressing their problems. The inconclusiveness of the legislative history also means that courts are not prohibited from developing strategies that fully address Black women's claims and that fulfill the aims and purposes of the statute.[77] Courts should not merely look at particular clauses in a statute, but should also take into consideration the whole statute, including Congressional aims, as reflected by the statute's language, in order to implement the law in accordance with its true meaning and intent.[78]

III. CURRENT JUDICIAL TREATMENT OF BLACK WOMEN'S TITLE VII CLAIMS

Despite the lack of legislative guidance, Black women brought employment discrimination claims under Title VII based upon both race and sex. When confronted with these claims, many courts did not know how to address the issues involved.[79]

---

74. This amendment was also proposed in the Senate by Senator McClellan. *See* 110 CONG. REC. 13,837 (1964). It was defeated by a rule call. *Id.* at 13,838. Although Black women were not discussed at length in the Senate debates, Senator Humphrey's statement that Title VII was designed to help both Black men and women may also be an indication that the "or" is inclusive. 110 CONG. REC. 6547. *See* Oldham, *Questions of Exclusion and Exception Under Title VII—"Sex-Plus" and the BFOQ,* 23 HASTINGS L.J. 55, 61 (1971).

75. *See* Jefferies v. Harris County Community Action Ass'n, 615 F.2d 1025, 1032 (5th Cir. 1980); *infra* notes 91–94 and accompanying text.

76. *See* Degraffenreid v. General Motors Assembly Dir., 413 F.Supp. 142, 143 (E.D. Miss. 1976), *aff'd in part, rev'd in part, and remanded on other grounds,* 558 F.2d 480 (5th Cir, 1977); *see also infra* text accompanying notes 82–86.

77. *See infra* Section IV(A).

78. *See* Brown v. Duchesne, U.S. (19 How.) 183, 194 (1857) (establishing approach for statutory construction); *infra* notes 114–116 and accompanying text.

79. In many Title VII cases brought by Black women in the 1970s, the issue of whether Black women was a class under Title VII was simply not addressed. In Miller v. Bank of Am., 600 F.2d 211, 212 (9th Cir. 1979), for example, the plaintiff alleged that her employment was unlawfully terminated because of her refusal to grant sexual favors to her supervisor, who wanted to have a good time with a "black chick"; the court allowed the sex claim, but dismissed the race claim. *See also*

A. *The Separate Approach: Race or Sex*

Degraffenreid v. General Motors Assembly Division[80] was the first case to consider whether Black women were a protected class under Title VII. In this 1976 case, the plaintiff, a Black woman, brought a combined race and sex discrimination claim alleging that her employer's "last hired-first fired" layoff policy discriminated against Black women and perpetuated past discriminatory practices.[81]

The *Degraffenreid* court addressed the plaintiff's race and sex discrimination claims separately, viewing them as two distinct and separate causes of action. The court feared that deciding a Black woman's claim based upon the interaction of race and sex would create a "super remedy" for Black women that "would give them relief beyond what the drafters of the relevant statutes intended."[82] In the court's view, Title VII did not designate Black women as a "special class."[83] Therefore, Black women should not be treated any differently from white women or Black men. They must choose to bring either a race action or a sex action in order to avoid the creation of an unauthorized class which would give Black women greater standing and relief.[84] In addition, the court insisted that allowing Black women to combine their claims and create a new class "clearly raises the prospect of opening the hackneyed Pandora's box,"[85] making Title VII unmanageable, since members of other groups then could bring their own individual claims of "special" discrimination.[86]

The absurdity of the position taken by the *Degraffenreid* court becomes apparent upon examination of the analysis used to evaluate claims brought by other groups. Courts have never divided white women into whites and women, or Black men into Blacks and men. Their claims have not been treated as divided because the term "Blacks" has been understood to mean Black men, and "women" to mean white women.[87]

The *Degraffenreid* court did not see Black women as complete persons,

---

Munford v. James T. Barnes & Co., 441 F.Supp. 459 (E.D. Mich. 1977) (dismissing plaintiff's race discrimination claim and allowing sex discrimination claim to stand). Other institutions have also been limited in their ability to address Black women's concerns. *See* Barnes v. Costle, 561 F.2d 983 (D.C. Cir. 1977) (EEOC officer misled plaintiff into bringing gender claim only).

Some courts found causes of action for Black women alleging sex and race claims. Yet, these courts did not state whether Black women are a protected class under Title VII, nor did they explain their analytic approach to Black women's claims. *See* Vuyanich v. Republic Bank of Dallas, 409 F. Supp. 1083, 1089 (N.D. Tex. 1976) (termination of Black woman's employment "smacks of sexual as well as racial discrimination"); Logan v. St. Luke's Hosp., 428 F. Supp. 127 (S.D.N.Y. 1977) (Black woman allowed to bring race and sex claim); *see also* Ellis, *supra* note 15, at 70 (discussing how these courts dealt with Black women's claims).

80. 413 F. Supp. 142 (E.D. Miss. 1976).
81. *Id.* at 143.
82. *Id.*
83. *Id.*
84. *Id.*
85. *Id.* at 145.
86. *Id.*
87. *See supra* note 9.

protected as a class under Title VII because it did not grasp the fact that all people have both a race and a gender, regardless of whether white women or Black men allege both of these factors in their claims. Black women could not fit into the *Degraffenreid* court's analysis because, as Professor Crenshaw explains, Black women are two steps removed from the legal norm, which "is not neutral but is white male."[88]

B. *Sex Plus: An Attempt to Account for Black Women*

In *Jefferies v. Harris Community Action Ass'n,*[89] the Fifth Circuit rejected the *Degraffenreid* approach. Analogizing the race-sex discrimination faced by Black women to "sex-plus" discrimination,[90] the court struck down the district court's order forcing the plaintiff, a Black woman,

---

88. Crenshaw, *supra* note 1, at 30; Minow, *The Supreme Court 1986 Term—Foreword: Justice Engendered*, 101 HARV. L. REV. 1, 13 (1987).

89. 615 F.2d 1025 (5th Cir. 1980)

90. "Sex-plus" analysis is applied to situations where an employer discriminates against an employee on the basis of her/his sex and some additional characteristic or factor related to her/his sex. B. SCHLEI & P. GROSSMAN, EMPLOYMENT DISCRIMINATION LAW 403 (2d ed. 1983). The sex-plus theory was created by the dissent in Phillips v. Martin Marietta Corp., 416 F.2d 1257 (5th Cir. 1969), *rev'd*, 400 U.S. 542 (1971) (Brown, J., dissenting), a case in which an employer refused to hire mothers, but not fathers, of pre-school-aged children. The employer tried to add a non-protected factor (parenthood of pre-school-aged children) to a protected factor (sex) in order to escape liability under Title VII. Thus, the employer's rule applied only to a subset of women with children. The Supreme Court reversed, holding that the plaintiff would have been hired but for her sex. 400 U.S. at 544. Sex-plus has also been applied to cases in which airline companies placed certain restrictions upon female flight attendants that did not apply to males. *See* Laffey v. Northwest Airlines, Inc., 507 F.2d 429, 456 (D.C. Cir. 1976), *cert. denied*, 434 U.S. 1086 (1978) (employer's policy enforced only against female stewardesses held to violate Title VII); Sprogis v. United Airlines, Inc., 444 F.2d 1194, 1198 (7th Cir. 1971), *cert. denied*, 404 U.S. 991 (employer's rule discriminating against married women violates Title VII); Binder, *Sex Discrimination in the Airline Industry: Title VII Flying High*, 59 CALIF. L. REV. 1091 (1971).

In order to prove a disparate treatment sex-plus discrimination claim, a plaintiff is required to show, under a disparate treatment test, that s/he was intentionally discriminated against because of her/his sex and some additional factor. Phillips v. Martin Marietta Corp., 400 U.S. 542 (1971), *rev'g* 411 F.2d 1 (5th Cir. 1969). In a disparate impact sex-plus claim, a plaintiff must show that an employer's practices had an adverse impact upon those of his or her gender who also share a common characteristic or plus factor. Dothard v. Rawlinson, 433 U.S. 321 (1977). However, if the practice or policy that affects a sex-plus group is reasonably necessary to the normal operation of that particular business or enterprise, a bona fide occupational qualification (BFOQ) exemption may be granted by a court in disparate treatment cases. Section 703(e)(1) of Title VII states:

> [I]t shall not be an unlawful employment practice for an employer to hire and employ employees on the basis of his religion, sex, or national origin in those certain instances where religion, sex, national origin is a bona fide occupational qualification reasonably necessary to the normal operation of that particular business or enterprise.

BFOQ defenses are limited to disparate treatment cases because only in that sort of case is there an admission by an employer that s/he is intentionally using a prohibited Title VII classification as a BFOQ. R. RICHARDS, C. SULLIVAN & M. ZIMMER, EMPLOYMENT DISCRIMINATION 106 (2d ed. 1988). Most courts, however, allow limited scope to the BFOQ exemption. For example, sex would be a valid BFOQ for the job of a wet nurse. Some courts have allowed employers in grooming cases to design rules imposed differentially according to sex. In one sex-plus case, an employer's refusal to hire a male applicant who had long hair, because the image associated with men who had long hair would harm the employer's business, was not viewed as sex discrimination. Willingham v. Macon Tel. Publishing Co., 507 F.2d 1084, 1091-92 (5th Cir. 1975) (en banc). According to the Fifth Circuit, hair length is not an *immutable characteristic* or *fundamental right*, such as the right to marry or to raise children or, presumably, the status of being Black. Indeed, Congress did not allow BFOQs for race or color discrimination.

to choose between her race and sex claims.[91] Using the sex-plus approach, the appellate court recognized that a Black woman could experience discrimination, even though Black men and white women did not, and found Black women to be a protected sub-class under Title VII.[92] The court held that Congress intended the word "or" in Title VII to be additive rather than exclusive because it had refused to insert the word "solely" to modify the word "sex."[93] The Fifth Circuit reasoned that the statute "is not to be diluted because discrimination adversely affects only a portion of the protected class"[94] of women. The court felt it important to provide the plaintiff with some way to obtain a "fair remedy" within the confines of existing Title VII analysis. Noting that Congress provided no clear indication of its intent regarding discrimination directed at Black women, the court nevertheless refused to adopt a result which would leave Black women without a viable Title VII remedy.[95]

The Fifth Circuit first addressed only Jefferies' race claim; it examined her sex allegations separately. Finally, the court examined her claim as that of a woman who, due to a secondary category (race), faced discrimination. The court attempted to rationalize its decision by applying an established theory that used sex as the main method of analysis and in doing so, it subordinated race to the level of a secondary factor.[96]

The *Jefferies* majority, like the *Degraffenreid* court before it, failed to tailor the old remedies or create new ones to deal specifically with groups

---

91. In her complaint, Jefferies alleged she was discriminated against "because she is a woman, up in age and because she is Black." *Jefferies*, 615 F.2d at 1025. She brought a race and sex discrimination action against her employer for failing to promote her and for wrongful discharge. The district court did not explain why Jefferies' age discrimination claim was not continued.

The district court, employing the *Degraffenreid* approach, read the "or" in Title VII disjunctively and followed the judicial trend of addressing Black women's race and sex discrimination claims separately. The plaintiff ultimately lost her race claim because the court held that Blacks were not excluded from positions similar to the ones she applied for—one had previously been held by a Black man. Jefferies v. Harris County Community Action Ass'n, 425 F. Supp. 1208 (S.D. Tex. 1977). The court further ruled that the plaintiff did not prove the existence of sex discrimination because white women, too, had held similar positions in the past. *Id.* at 1213.

92. *Jefferies*, 615 F.2d at 1034.

93. *See supra* Section II(B).

94. 615 F.2d at 1034 (quoting *Sprogis v. United Air Lines, Inc.*, 444 F.2d at 1198).

95. *Id.* at 1032.

96. Why were Black women considered a "sub-class" within a sex-plus rationale? Why didn't the court use race-plus, instead of sex-plus or just devise a "protected category-plus" test? What of Judge Brown's statement in *Phillips* that "[o]f course the 'plus' could not be one of the other statutory categories of race, religion, national origin, etc."? *Phillips*, 416 F.2d at 1260 n.10 (Brown, J., dissenting). Judge Randall felt, as she expressed in a footnote to the Fifth Circuit's opinion in *Jefferies*, that "this court is not in a position to decide the question whether black females are a special Title VII class and the related question concerning the effect recognition of such a subclass would have on the traditional framework of proof in Title VII cases." *Jefferies*, 615 F.2d at 1034 n.7. She believed that a sex-plus analysis should not apply to this case because:

[n]one of the "sex-plus" cases involves the use of two statutorily protected characteristics as the basis of employment discrimination. . . . What effect recognition of a subclass of black females should have on the traditional evidentiary framework governing Title VII litigation is simply not addressed in "sex-plus" cases.

Id. at 1035 n.7.

more than one step removed from the white male norm.[97] The sex-plus methodology forces Black women to choose gender as their principal identification,[98] thereby perpetuating a fundamental misunderstanding of the nature of the discrimination experienced by Black women, most of whom do not consider their race to be secondary to their sex.[99]

Jefferies has had an impact on other courts, which have subsequently adopted the sex-plus rational as a framework for understanding Black women.[100] However, even this incomplete concession to the reality of Black women's whole personhood has been limited by one recent case, *Judge v. Marsh.*[101] The *Jefferies* sex-plus approach to understanding Black women's claims actually set the stage for *Judge*'s limitation upon those claims.

In *Judge*, a Black woman employed by the United States Army alleged a Title VII violation based on race and sex.[102] The court accepted the *Jefferies* holding that "[r]ace discrimination directed solely at women is not less invidious because of its specificity,"[103] and that an employer's actions against a Black woman may violate Title VII. However, the court also criticized the *Jefferies* language as being overbroad. The *Judge* court interpreted and applied the concept of "sex-plus" in a restrictive manner, concluding that "the *Jefferies* analysis is appropriately limited to employment decisions based on one protected, immutable trait or fundamental right, which are directed against individuals sharing a second protected, immutable characteristic."[104] Under this analysis, the *Judge* court allowed the plaintiff to maintain a sex-plus discrimination claim as a woman who possessed a second immutable trait—race—that contributed to her discrimination. In addition, although the plaintiff in the case was not seeking to include other pluses in her claim, the court held that a plaintiff in a Title VII case could claim only one plus,[105] which for Black women would almost invariably be their race. The court sought to ensure that the sub-class would be narrowly defined so that Title VII would "not be splintered beyond use and recognition."[106] Allowing additional plus fac-

---

97. *See infra* notes 111-13 and accompanying text.

98. Palmer, *supra* note 21, at 152-53.

99. *See infra* note 113 and accompanying text.

100. The other cases which have adopted the *Jefferies* explanation for allowing Black women to be considered a Title VII sub-group within a sex-plus framework include Hicks v. Gates Rubber Co., 883 F.2d 1406, 1416 n.2 (10th Cir. 1987); Judge v. Marsh, 649 F. Supp. 770, 780 (D.D.C. 1986); Chambers v. Omaha Girls Club, 629 F. Supp. 925, 944 n.34 (D. Neb. 1986); and Graham v. Bendix Corp., 585 F. Supp. 1036, 1047 (N.D. Ind. 1984).

101. 649 F. Supp. 770 (D.D.C. 1986).

102. Referring to *Jefferies*, the court stated that "[e]xtrapolating from . . . sex-plus cases, the Fifth Circuit has determined that Black women are a distinct sub-group, protected by Title VII." *Judge*, 649 F.Supp. at 780.

103. *Id.*

104. *Id.*

105. *Id.*

106. *Id.*

tors, the court felt, would create a "many-headed Hydra, impossible to contain within Title VII's prohibition."[107] The *Jefferies* court, by viewing Black women within a sex-plus framework, gave the *Judge* court the ability to limit Black women's claims. Had the *Jefferies* court viewed Black women as a distinct class under Title VII, who should be given protection because sex and race are both prohibited categories, the issue of sex-plus and what constitutes a "plus" could have been avoided. Instead, the issue would have been whether persons of "like qualities [are] given employment opportunities irrespective of their sex" *and* race, rather than allowing the focus to shift to arbitrary sex-plus limits.[108]

On a practical level, the requirement of constraining "subgroups" to one plus factor is detrimental to Black women, who must use their race as the plus factor. Forcing Black women to use their single plus factor on race prevents them from fairly addressing other issues that may contribute to their discrimination.[109] For example, if a Black woman wanted to allege another plus factor under Title VII, such as being pregnant, married, or single with children,[110] she would have already exhausted her plus "allowance" with her race allegation. By contrast, a white woman could seek a remedy for discrimination on the basis of any of these characteristics, since her race, unlike that of a Black woman, is generally not considered to be a plus factor because of society's tendency to value "whites" over "Blacks." The more someone deviates from the norm, the more likely s/he is to be the target of discrimination. Ironically, those who need Title VII's protection the most get it the least under *Judge*'s limitation.

Questions should also have been raised about the sex-plus theory's classification of the racial element of Black women's claims as an "other" factor and about the effect of addressing Black women's race and sex discrimination claims in the context of sex discrimination. Professor Shoben states that *Jefferies'* sex-plus (women-plus-Black) rationale is based upon a "single-dimension sex discrimination theory," which requires that the court ask only "if the employer's rule singled out only women among Black persons. The answer might be yes, but then only a sex discrimination claim has been established."[111] Generally, courts have not recognized

---

107. *Id. Cf. supra* text accompanying notes 85–86 (*Degraffenreid* court expressing concern about opening "Pandora's box" by allowing Black women to combine race and sex claims).

108. *See* H. KAY, TEXT, CASES AND MATERIAL ON SEX-BASED DISCRIMINATION 491 (3rd ed. 1988) (discussing Phillips v. Martin Marietta Corp., 400 U.S. 542, 547 (1970)).

109. *See infra* notes 120–22 and accompanying text.

110. *Id.*

111. Shoben, *supra* note 62, at 793, 804. Shoben argues that sex-plus does not ask the question "whether a rule against black women amounts to discrimination against a group known to be protected by [Title VII]." *Id.* Instead, a sex-plus approach asks whether "a rule against *blackness applied only to women* amounts to discrimination against *women*." *Id.* Shoben is also concerned that viewing Black women in a sex-plus framework would allow a BFOQ defense. *Id.* However, she indicates that this is unlikely because there is no BFOQ for race discrimination claims. Shoben contends that "[t]he comparable BFOQ for excluding black women would have to depend on a necessity for excluding blackness for women employees—a defense not permitted by the Act." *Id.* at 805; *see*

the limitations of a sex-plus theory as applied to Black women. Sex-plus fails to conceive of Black women's full experience as a unique group. Conceptualizing Black women's experiences as "racism with sexism hooked into it [and] vice versa"[112] results in an incorrect view of Black women as the sum of two parts, rather than as a whole beings.[113]

IV. BEYOND SEX-PLUS

Given the failure of political, economic, and legal institutions to understand the problems of Black women, it is not surprising that many courts in the 1970s did not know how to handle Black women's claims and that, even today, they have yet to develop an approach that adequately deals with Black women.

A. *The Courts' Power to Interpret: the Scope of Title VII*

Although Black women continue to be inadequately protected by Title VII, the primary purpose of the statute, as revealed by both its legislative history and subsequent court decisions, is to eradicate "all aspects of discrimination."[114] Courts have elaborated on this goal by stating that "Title VII is a remedial statute to be liberally construed in favor of the victim of discrimination."[115] Courts have broad discretionary powers to interpret and apply Title VII.[116]

---

generally C. MacKinnon, *Sexual Harassment of Working Women* 190–91 (1979) (commenting on sex-plus doctrine).

112. Crenshaw, *supra* note 1, at 19. This additive approach to discrimination:
  treats the oppression of a Black woman in a sexist and racist society as if it were a *further* burden than her oppression in a sexist but non-racist society, when, in fact, it is a different burden . . . [since] [t]he additive analysis also suggests that a woman's 'racial' identity can be 'subtracted' from her combined sexual and 'racial' identity.
Spelman, *Theories of Race & Gender—The Erasure of Black Women*, 5 QUEST 36, 43, 46 (1982); R. Austin, Sapphire Bound 2 (Oct. 26, 1988) (unpublished draft) (on file with Professor Austin at University of Pennsylvania).

113. A consideration of the experiences of Black women shows that they do not experience their discrimination merely as two discrete units "piled upon each other." The starting point should be that a Black woman, as a whole being—a member of a distinct class—can allege that she is being discriminated against as a "Black woman." She should not be limited to only one plus factor, especially when that factor itself explicitly falls under Title VII's protection.

114. S. REP. No. 867, 88th Cong., 2d Sess. 10 (1964).

115. Robinson v. Adams, 830 F.2d 128, 132 (9th Cir. 1987) (citing Mahroom v. Hook, 563 F.2d 1369, 1375 (9th Cir. 1977), *cert. denied*, 436 U.S. 904 (1978)). Griggs v. Duke Power Co., 401 U.S. 424 (1971), shaped "the statutory concept of 'discrimination' in light of the social and economic facts of our society . . . [by applying a] sensitive, liberal interpretation of [T]itle VII." Blumrosen, *Stranger in Paradise: Griggs v. Duke Power Co. and the Concept of Employment Discrimination*, 71 MICH. L. REV. 59, 62–63 (1972). *Griggs* stated that Congress, in passing Title VII, required courts to remove all artificial, arbitrary, and unnecessary barriers to employment "that operate invidiously to discriminate on the basis of racial or other impermissible classifications." 401 U.S. at 431.

116. Blumrosen, *supra* note 115, at 73. Congress sought "to provide a legal solution to a complex problem and uniformly left many problems including the definitional problems" to the agencies and courts. *Id.* at 67.

B. *Acknowledging Competing Visions of Reality*

The history of Black women, the current levels of poverty and unemployment which they experience, and the special problems they encounter in the workplace indicate that they occupy a unique position in American society. To resolve the inequities that confront Black women, courts must first correctly conceptualize them as "Black women," a distinct class protected by Title VII. Courts should reject the *Jefferies* conception of Black women as a "sub-class" under either a "sex-plus" or "race-plus" analysis because neither adequately encompasses Black women's experiences.

Once Black women are conceptualized correctly, courts must also become sensitive to Black women's unique historical, social, and economic experiences in the United States.[117] Courts should draw upon Black women's experiences and perspectives when reaching decisions concerning Black women.[118] Black women's history and point of view must also become documented in judges' decisions; these decisions should reflect an understanding of the law's impact on Black women, just as the experiences of white women and Black men were acknowledged in the Supreme

---

117. Employment discrimination is harder to prove today because it is more subtle and sophisticated, taking the form in many cases not of intentionally discriminatory acts, but appearing in "well established practices and customs." Haywood, *supra* note 44, at 19, 33. For example, certain promotion systems, career ceilings, stereotyping, job assignment plans, and examinations seem fair in form, but in practice they encourage discrimination. *Id.*; B. RESKIN & H. HARTMANN, WOMEN'S WORK, MEN'S WORK—SEX SEGREGATION ON THE JOB (1986) (discussing subtle types of discrimination faced by women); R. FARLEY, BLACKS AND WHITES: NARROWING THE GAP 57-81, 198 (1984) (addressing discrimination Blacks face and its impact on wage differential between Blacks and whites in America).

Studies analyzing the effects of subtle and sophisticated employment discrimination on Black women are scarce; courts are not the only ones who have thought of Black women as being dealt with under the broad terms of "Blacks" and "women." However, one can begin to understand the effect of race-sex discrimination on Black women by examining the small existing literature concerning Black women. Professor Ellis describes the effect of race-sex discrimination against Black women in sexual harassment cases. Ellis, *supra* note 15, at 39. Malveaux and Wallace describe the existence of "black women crowding" and explain the position of black women in society, revealing that black women are subject to race-sex discrimination which effects them differently than Black men and white women. Malveaux & Wallace, *supra* note 53.

Courts must expand the scope of Title VII to address the concerns of Black women. For example, an extension of Title VII disparate impact theory to pay discrimination claims would address the specific problems of Black women who are crowded into the lowest paying and lowest status jobs. *See supra* notes 49-59 and accompanying text. While the statutory language does not specify that wage differential claims can be brought under Title VII, allowing such claims would be consistent with the broad scope courts have given to Title VII. Title VII "was intended to be broadly inclusive, proscribing, not only overt discrimination but also practices that are fair in form, but discriminatory in operation." Haywood, *supra* note 44, at 34 n.99.

118. *See generally* J. Culp, A Black Perspective on the Law and Economics of Title VII: Judicial Discretion and Discrimination 1 (1989) (unpublished manuscript) (on file with Professor Culp at Duke University). According to Professor Culp, all "judicial interpretation requires some framework that judges use in reaching their decisions." *Id.* at 11. However, the problem with the current legal interpretation is that Black people's perspectives have not been used by judges in making their decisions. *Id.* at 12. Professor Culp argues that "race matters in American legal discussion," *id.* at 14, and that judges must recognize competing visions of reality in order for all people to be able to obtain justice: "For [a] society that lets the 'haves' define all of the choices is only fair if our initial distribution of rights and goods are in fact appropriate from a social justice standpoint." *Id.* at 50; Minow, *supra* note 88, 10-11.

Court's *Frontiero* opinion.[119] This documentation will make the experience of Black women in the American legal system visible, in addition to revealing the importance of viewing Black women as a class "of and unto themselves," who face different problems, often having distinct concerns requiring solutions different from those prescribed for Black men and white women.

C. *"Black Women" and Non-Statutory Factors*

One of the potential harms that Black women face as a result of the *Jefferies* decision is that some courts may be persuaded by the *Judge v. Marsh* interpretation of the *Jefferies* sex-plus approach and allow Black women to use their race as the only "plus" factor.[120] However, under the approach proposed by this Note, if a Black woman with children or a foreign accent brought a race-sex discrimination claim, her race would not be seen as a plus factor; in fact, no category explicitly protected by Title VII could be considered a plus factor. She would be thought of as a Black woman, a member of a separate class fully covered by Title VII. If any factor were to be considered a "plus," it would be her status as, for example, a parent. Thus, this Note proposes, in order to ensure that employers are not allowed to discriminate against people because they are married, have children, or speak with an accent, that the "plus" concept be used by

---

119. *See supra* text accompanying notes 38-39.

120. *See supra* notes 102-07 and accompanying text. *But see Chambers v. Omaha Girls Club*, 629 F. Supp. 925, 944 n.34 (D. Neb. 1986), decided before *Judge*, in which a court upheld the firing of an unmarried pregnant Black woman because she was setting a negative role model for the Girls Club teenage members. The court allowed a "sub-class" of women—Black women—to bring a claim that alleged that their "sub-group" would be discriminated against because of an employer's rule which prohibited unmarried women from becoming pregnant. *Id.* at 943. The court was able to handle three factors without falling victim to the "many-headed Hydra impossible to contain within Title VII's prohibition" and so feared by the *Judge* court. *Judge*, 649 F. Supp. at 780. Despite the negative outcome of *Chambers*, this decision indicates that if a court is able to handle two protected characteristics and an additional plus factor it can handle three or more characteristics protected by Title VII in multi-factor employment discrimination claims, provided that there is an adequate population to make a disparate impact determination possible.

Despite its attempt at managing several factors, the *Chambers* court failed to take into consideration the realities of Black women's perspectives. When it assessed the employer's concerns, it utilized a particular value system without recognizing the effect that such a decision would have upon Black women. As Professor Austin states in *Sapphire Bound*, the *Chambers* court failed to take into consideration the perspective of Black women and instead applied its "white and middle class values" to the case. *See* Austin, *supra* note 112, at 28. In Austin's views the bottom line of this case is that "unmarried black women who have babies are essentially being accused of carrying on like modern-day Jezebels when they should be acting like good revisionist Mammies." *Id.* at 50. The Club's policy of firing a pregnant Black woman because she is unmarried had negative economic effects on her. The decision imposed "a marriage requirement as a condition for working with black youngsters [which] adds to the burden that single black pregnant women and mothers already bear in the name of patriarchy, *i.e.*, the supremacy of the male as the head of the family unit," and penalized Black women economically if they failed to adhere to such requirements. *Id.* at 44.

It is not enough for courts only to change how they view Black women. As Minow states, judges must be aware that their perspectives are only one of many competing views. Minow, *supra* note 88, at 33. Title VII should be utilized by judges in a manner which is free of them imposing their own perspective to the exclusion of others. They must also recognize their own tendencies toward racial and sexual stereotyping.

courts to take into consideration discrimination based upon factors which are not explicitly protected by Title VII.[121] This category-plus approach[122] aims to ensure that Title VII is applied to Black women in the same way that it has been applied to "Blacks" and "women."

D. *Title VII Multi-Factor Claims—A Holistic Approach*

Clearly, recognizing Black women as a protected class under a multi-factor Title VII approach will have implications for other groups facing discrimination, including "Asian women," "Puerto Rican men," and "Ethiopian Jewish women." These groups may have distinct histories, socio-economic situations, and/or a unique current workplace experience, all of which should be recognized by the law so that each group concerns can be understood based upon their own experiences, rather than based upon how much they deviate from the white male norm.[123] Courts that are willing to allow other groups' race-sex claims, based upon the same principles as Black women's race-sex claims, may be uncomfortable recognizing that Title VII claims can be based upon as many as three, four, or five of the protected categories—race, color, religion, sex, and national origin. Professor Minow observes that when those in the mainstream attempt to deal with people who are "many steps away from the norm," the complexity of the situation "seems both overwhelming and incapacitating" because "[b]y bearing into complexity rather than turning away from it, by listening to the variety of voices implicated in our problems, we may lose a sense of ready solutions and steady certainties."[124] Some courts may argue that adopting a multi-factor approach is tantamount to special treatment for Black women and may result in the creation of a "many headed-

---

121. *See* Morris, *Stereotypic Alchemy: Transformative Stereotyping and Anti-discrimination Law* 6 YALE L. REV. & POL'Y REV. __ (forthcoming 1989) (addressing claims brought by overweight people, people with accents, etc.).

122. The category can be any of Title VII's listed factors. *See supra* note 5.

123. Such an approach might also have implications for Black men. One court denied a Black man's claim that he was being discriminated against as a Black man. In *Robinson v. Adams*, 830 F.2d 128 (9th Cir. 1987), the plaintiff alleged that he was discriminated against as a Black man. The defendant, Orange County, did not have any Black male employees. However, Black female employees comprised 1.7% of the Superior Court workforce and 2.7% of both the "Professional" and "Official/Administration" positions in Orange County. *Id.* at 131. The court held:

> Obviously, since Blacks are not statistically underrepresented in the Orange County Superior Court's work force, Robinson cannot plausibly maintain that the Court's hiring practices have a racially discriminatory impact on Blacks as a whole. . . . His showing that Black males are statistically underrepresented cannot, standing alone, show a racially discriminatory impact . . . on Blacks as a whole. The only relevant statistic concerning Blacks, the protected class of which Robinson is a member, indicates that 1.7% of the Superior Court employees were black.

Id. at 131.

Judge Pregerson dissented, stating that "Robinson has raised a genuine issue of material fact on whether blacks and particulary black males are proportionally represented in the court's work force." *Id.* at 133. The *Robinson* majority simply could not see how race and sex could interact to produce a plurality of stereotypes and concomitant patterns of discrimination against Black men. Thus, Black men could also benefit from a more holistic approach to Title VII claims.

124. Minow, *supra* note 88, at 82.

Hydra."[125] For the sake of simplicity, some may argue, the concerns of individuals who face discrimination based on more than two of the listed characteristics must be sacrificed because such people are too "weird," or too far removed from the white-male-Christian norm. Should the experiences of a Jamaican Black woman who faces discrimination as a result of her nationality, race, and sex be ignored because of *Judge*'s arbitrary and artificial limitations? Courts should not be satisfied with extending Title VII's protection only to American-born Black women, but should also reach out to Jamaican Black women. In addition, a Black woman with dark skin, who is being discriminated against because of her race, sex and color, could not bring this type of discrimination claim because she would exceed her plus allowance. Should this person's concerns be ignored? Evidentiary and administrative complications cannot justify such a limitation. *Judge*'s artificial limitations make no sense, particularly in light of the *Chambers* decision, where the court allowed an unmarried pregnant Black woman to bring a discrimination claim, and the clear aim of Title VII.[126]

Courts should also rethink how much justice they are willing to sacrifice for the sake of simplicity. Society "needs a setting in which to engage in the clash of realities that breaks us out of settled and complacent meaning and creates opportunities for insight and growth. This is the special burden and opportunity for the court: to enact and preside over the dialogue through which we remake the normative endowment that shapes current understanding."[127] Even when considering multi-factor cases brought by individuals, for whom there may not be a statistically relevant comparison group (*e.g.,* Ethiopian Jewish Black women), courts must ask whether the present application of the discriminatory impact/intent theories is the only acceptable approach for recognizing discrimination.[128]

---

125. *See supra* text accompanying note 107.

126. *See supra* note 120. In addition, *Judge*'s interpretation of the sex-plus test created by the dissent in *Phillips v. Martin Marietta* is incorrect. The focus should be on whether an individual was treated differently from other persons because of any characteristic protected by Title VII, not whether the plaintiff has exceeded her arbitrarily imposed sex-plus allowance. Clearly, if a plaintiff can prove discriminatory intent, based upon any of Title VII's protected factors, s/he should not be denied relief because a showing of clear intent would make denial of such a claim illogical. Some may argue that although an individual's multi-factor claim under an intent theory might be viable, a multi-factor claim cannot be considered under a discriminatory impact theory if an individual is part of a group that is statistically so small that no valid comparison can be made. However, this is not always the case. If a Jamaican Black woman sought to bring a discrimination case based upon her race, sex, and nationality in the New York City area, where her group forms a sizable population, there would be no reason to prohibit her from bringing a multi-factor claim if that claim indeed reflected the discrimination she had experienced.

127. Lawrence, *The Id, The Ego, And Equal Protection: Reckoning With Unconscious Racism,* 39 STAN. L. REV. 317, 386 (1987). Professor Lawrence also points out that the "victim's perspectives" must be heard so that courts can become a legitimate forum for normative debate. Similarly, Minow argues that judges must recognize that their opinions are only one point of view, and that other points of view and realities exist. Minow, *supra* note 88, at 15, 81.

128. Professor Lawrence has proposed a "cultural meaning" test to be used by judges in equal protection cases to help them recognize race-based discriminatory acts—especially unconscious racially discriminatory acts. Lawrence, *supra* note 127, at 324, 331–39, 387. This approach would require courts—like cultural anthropologists—to consider historical and social context in order to determine

Courts must reconsider whether it is "just" to ignore these people's pains, concerns, and voices—their realities—particularly since the aim of Title VII is to eliminate all forms of discrimination based on race, color, sex, religion or national origin.

V. CONCLUSION

As Black women's historical, social, and economic experiences illustrate, courts must begin to adopt fairer and more consistent anti-discrimination policies—ones that view people within the true context of their present realities and historical experiences and allow their claims to be effectively addressed. By conceptually redefining Black women and adopting a liberal interpretation of Title VII, courts will more properly fulfill Congress' mandate to eliminate employment discrimination and will begin to grant Black women and others the legal recognition they have historically been denied.[129]

---

whether they should apply heightened scrutiny. *Id.* at 356.

129. Despite this Note's proposal, Title VII is still limited in that it only helps Black women who have jobs or who can make discriminatory hiring claims. Therefore, Black women must continue, despite the negative climate, to push for aggressive affirmative action policies, comparable worth, and other "broader affirmative action tactics to address all of the concerns of black women." Malveaux, *supra* note 54, at 60. *See* C. Rutherford, Employment—Redressing the Oversight, Address given at The First Conference on Women of Color and the Law, sponsored by The Collective on Women of Color and the Law at Yale (Apr. 16, 1988); *see generally* Panel, Employment: Empowerment in the Workforce, Address given at the Second Conference on Women of Color and the Law, sponsored by the *NYU Review of Law and Social Change* (Nov. 1, 1988).

Pluralist Myths and Powerless Men: The Ideology of Reasonableness in Sexual Harassment Law

This Article examines the role of the reasonableness standard in "hostile work environment" sexual harassment cases under title VII.[1] My primary purpose is to offer an explanation for how the reasonable person test

† Assistant Professor of Law, University of Denver College of Law. B.A. 1974, Yale University; J.D. 1979, University of Virginia; L.L.M. 1982, University of Virginia.

I would like to thank Richard Bonnie, Michael Klarman, Robert Scott, and Christopher Slobogin for their helpful comments on earlier drafts of this article. Gary Peller not only gave generously of his time and insight, but also introduced me to much of the work that inspired and informed this effort. Finally, Charlie Piot contributed countless hours and, as usual, invaluable support.

1. 42 U.S.C. §§ 2000e-2, 2000e-16 (1982 & Supp. 1987). Two types of sexual harassment claims have been recognized under title VII. The first, termed a quid pro quo cause of action, alleges that the employer has explicitly conditioned a job benefit on acquiescence to sexual demands—or threatened a detriment if demands are rejected. The second, a hostile environment claim, alleges that being subjected to offensive treatment has been made an implicit condition of employment. *See generally* C. MacKinnon, Sexual Harassment of Working Women 32-47 (1979) (describing these two types of claims). Specifically, a plaintiff in a hostile work environment case must prove that the conditions of work to which she was subjected unreasonably interfered with her ability to work or rendered her environment unreasonably offensive. 29 C.F.R. § 1604.11(a)(3) (1989).

retains its legitimacy in the face of numerous analytical weaknesses. Why, for example, in the context of antidiscrimination statutes designed to reform society, is a standard that is explicitly tied to the status quo[2] thought to be a proper vehicle for identifying discriminatory behavior? Why, despite recent scholarship revealing that judicial definitions of reasonableness often reflect the values and assumptions of a narrow elite,[3] is the "objective test" seen as an accurate reflection of societal norms at all? In short, why is it that the test is still seen as the prototypical expression of the law's fairness and objectivity[4] rather than, for example, as a mechanism for facilitating the coercive exercise of social power?

Examining the ideological content of the role of reasonableness in antidiscrimination law,[5] this Article concludes that (unfounded) pluralist assumptions support the courts' use of the reasonable person concept to define discrimination in the sexual harassment setting. Such assumptions allow reasonableness to be seen as mediating a fundamental contradiction between liberty and security in liberal legal thought—a contradiction expressed in this context as the conflict between our desire to promote social diversity by providing autonomy to individual groups and our need to protect vulnerable groups from discrimination by coercing a certain amount

---

2. *See, e.g.*, W. KEETON, D. DOBBS, R. KEETON & D. OWEN, PROSSER & KEETON ON THE LAW OF TORTS 175 (5th ed. 1984) (describing reasonable person of negligence law as "a personification of a community ideal of reasonable behavior").

3. *See* Estrich, *Rape*, 95 YALE L.J. 1087, 1105-21 (1986) ("reasonable resistance" necessary to establish rape is often defined as requiring physical forcefulness that would be more typical of—and effective for—a man than a woman); Donovan & Wildman, *Is the Reasonable Man Obsolete? A Critical Perspective on Self-Defense and Provocation*, 14 LOY. L.A.L. REV. 435, 462-67 (1981) (legal abstractions like reasonable man standard both hide and perpetuate existing social inequities by ignoring social reality of individual judged); Schneider, *Equal Rights to Trial for Women: Sex Bias in the Law of Self-Defense*, 15 HARV. C.R.-C.L. L. REV. 623, 631-32 (1980) (reasonableness standard in self-defense law under which use of deadly weapon is barred unless attacker is armed ignores that many women are, or perceive themselves to be, unable to defend themselves without weapons against men). For a general discussion of the danger that the reasonableness standard might exclude the viewpoints of powerless groups, see G. CALABRESI, IDEALS, BELIEFS, ATTITUDES, AND THE LAW 21-44 (1985).

4. As a broad standard, rather than a narrow rule, the reasonableness test is thought both to allow contextualized judgments in individual cases and to be able to reflect changing societal mores. Despite its supposed flexibility, however, the test is also seen as an objective standard—as sufficiently determinate to impose the same constraints on everyone, and to prevent political decision-making by limiting the discretion of the judge. *See* W. KEETON, D. DOBBS, R. KEETON & D. OWEN, *supra* note 2, at 173-75. For general discussions of the reasonable person standard, see Collins, *Language, History and the Legal Process: A Profile of the 'Reasonable Man'*, 8 RUT.-CAM. L.J. 311 (1977), Reynolds, *The Reasonable Man of Negligence Law: A Health Report on the 'Odious Creature'*, 23 OKLA. L. REV. 410 (1970), and Seavey, *Negligence—Subjective or Objective?*, 41 HARV. L. REV. 1 (1927).

5. In focusing on the ideological content of the reasonableness construct, I draw on a growing body of literature that explores how the ideological messages underlying legal doctrine both hide and justify the substantive content of judicial decisions and thereby contribute to the legitimacy of the legal system itself. *See, e.g.*, Kennedy, *The Structure of Blackstone's Commentaries*, 28 BUFFALO L. REV. 205 (1979); MacKinnon, *Feminism, Marxism, Method, and the State: An Agenda for Theory*, 7 SIGNS 515 (1982); Olsen, *The Family and the Market: A Study of Ideology and Legal Reform*, 96 HARV. L. REV. 1497 (1983); Peller, *The Metaphysics of American Law*, 73 CAL. L. REV. 1151, 1189-90 (1985); Singer, *The Player and the Cards: Nihilism and Legal Theory*, 94 YALE L.J. 1 (1984).

of conformity to general standards of conduct.[6] Through a close reading of a hostile work environment case, the Article illustrates how the ideology of pluralism and the ideology of reasonableness reinforce each other in the sexual harassment context, thereby lending credence to both.

Part I describes the ways in which pluralist ideology informs the traditional "equal opportunity" model of discrimination,[7] making mediation of the contradiction between diversity (the autonomy of individual groups) and conformity (the security of the collective society) seem possible. For this discussion I draw heavily on existing analyses of the operation of liberal individualist assumptions in private law,[8] concluding that similar liberal pluralist assumptions can be found in the antidiscrimination context,[9] and that those assumptions reinforce the use of an "objective" test to define discrimination in sexual harassment cases.

Part II of the Article examines the reasonable person standard as it operates in *Rabidue v. Osceola Refining Company*,[10] a recent hostile work environment case in which the United States Court of Appeals for the Sixth Circuit held that the environment in the defendant's workplace was not unreasonably offensive and had not unreasonably interfered with the plaintiff's ability to work. I argue that the constructs relied upon by the majority in reaching this conclusion—the concept of societal consensus and the abstract principle of tolerance for diversity—fail to surmount the contradiction between the individual group and the collectivity that the reasonableness standard is supposed to mediate. Moreover, the court's pluralist discourse not only supports the use of those constructs but also conceals the fact that its opinion actually reflects and reinforces elitist, nonpluralist attitudes.

Part III explores the implications of this critique of reasonableness. In particular, I evaluate the argument proffered by the dissent in *Rabidue* that a reasonable woman standard, rather than the traditional reasonable person test, should be employed in hostile environment cases. At a more general level, this Part also addresses the efficacy of doctrinal change as a means of legal reform and the limits of pluralism as a normative ideal. I argue that our vision of pluralism needs to be transformed in order to

---

6. In focusing on the mediation of contradictions in legal ideology, I am employing a structuralist methodology developed in the legal context by writers such as Duncan Kennedy, who was the first to identify the core contradiction between liberty and security that recurs throughout liberal legal thought. Kennedy, *supra* note 5, at 205–21, 257–65, 294–98; *see also* Kennedy, *Form and Substance in Private Law Adjudication*, 89 HARV. L. REV. 1685 (1976). For Kennedy's subsequent critique of his own analysis, see Gabel & Kennedy, *Roll Over Beethoven*, 36 STAN. L. REV. 1, 14–18 (1984).

7. The equal opportunity model is the familiar model of formal equality, which dictates that the law should be color-blind, sex-blind, etc., neither imposing burdens on nor providing benefits to an individual on the basis of race, sex, or other illegitimate grounds. *See, e.g.*, Brest, *The Supreme Court, 1975 Term—Foreword: In Defense of the Antidiscrimination Principle*, 90 HARV. L. REV. 1, 1, 21 (1976).

8. *See* Kennedy, *supra* note 5, at 205–21, 257–65, 294–98; Singer, *supra* note 5, at 40–45.

9. *See infra* notes 49–56 and accompanying text.

10. 805 F.2d 611 (6th Cir. 1986), *cert. denied*, 481 U.S. 1041 (1987).

acknowledge the existence of conflict among groups and the unavoidability of choices among them.

I. INDIVIDUALISM, PLURALISM, AND REASONABLENESS

This Part examines the role of reasonableness in liberal legal thought by comparing its role in a particular private law context—negligence—with its role in antidiscrimination law.[11] Identifying both an individualist and a group-based vision in each of these two areas of the law, I will argue that in both areas both of these visions are informed by a common conceptual framework. Because understanding how that framework operates in negligence law will help elucidate its operation in antidiscrimination law, I will discuss the negligence context first.

A. Reasonableness in Negligence Law

There are at least two different visions of the appropriate role of negligence law: a corrective justice vision that sees the law as a mechanism for protecting individual choice and restricting culpable conduct, and an instrumentalist vision that sees the law as a means of implementing general social policies through the resolution of legal disputes.[12] The first approach, of course, focuses on individuals, while the second is more concerned with fairness to different status groups and with the well-being of society as a whole. While both visions find expression in current negligence case law and scholarship, the individualist approach to negligence was at its height in the nineteenth century, while the instrumentalist approach has dominated since the time of the Legal Realists. In the description that follows, I will briefly outline two underlying similarities in the ways that both of these approaches conceptualize negligence law: (1) they both rely upon a dichotomy between public and private, and (2) they both treat negligence law in general and the reasonable person construct in particular as mediating a central contradiction between the individual and the group.

1. The Individualist Vision of Negligence

a. The Public/Private Dichotomy

The traditional, nineteenth-century view of negligence relies upon a vision of the world as divided into two separate spheres, a private sphere of freely-willed interpersonal interactions, and a public sphere of regulation

---

11. The comparison is summarized in three charts on page 1193.
12. See generally H. STEINER, MORAL ARGUMENT AND SOCIAL VISION IN THE COURTS: A STUDY OF TORT ACCIDENT LAW 8, 108–24 (1987) (describing several aspects of shift from first vision to second).

designed to preserve and protect such interactions.[13] Freedom of contract and unfettered competition are considered the norm; governmental interference with private orderings through tort law is justified only when someone has engaged in anti-competitive behavior that distorts the "natural" operation of the market or faulty conduct from which courts can infer consent to be held liable if harm results. Because negligent conduct harms an individual without her consent, its regulation does not constitute interference with the actor's freedom, for the right to liberty extends only to conduct that does not harm others.[14] In regulating such behavior, however—that is, in distinguishing between protected liberty and regulable negligence—the government must not favor either side, for otherwise it will be interfering with, rather than facilitating, the free operation of the private sphere.[15]

To avoid such favoritism (this approach contends), courts should rely upon prevailing social norms for their definition of reasonable behavior. Assuming that, as part of the social contract, individuals implicitly agree to conform their conduct to community standards (in return for others' doing the same), the individualist approach thus defines unreasonableness as a violation of those standards. So defined, the reasonable person test, by serving as a mechanism for importing a pre-existing societal consensus into the law, is thought to constrain judicial decision-making by providing determinate grounds from which to derive results.

b. *Reasonableness as Mediator*

Under the individualist view, to the extent that the reasonableness test is seen as enabling courts to draw a neutral line between the private and the public spheres, it seems to mediate a fundamental contradiction between our desire for freedom and our desire not to be harmed by others.[16] Singer describes this contradiction as follows:

> Liberalism is the invitation to act in a self-interested manner, without impediment from other people, as long as what we do does not harm them. This political theory is founded on a contradiction. We want freedom to engage in the pursuit of happiness. Yet we also want security from harm. The more freedom of action we allow, the

---

13.   On the public/private dichotomy in private law, see Horwitz, *The History of the Public/Private Distinction*, 130 U. PA. L. REV. 1423 (1982) (describing distinction in legal thought).

14.   And, "[s]ince liberal citizens are motivated by self-interest, the only way to achieve security is to give power to the state to limit freedom of action." Singer, *The Legal Rights Debate in Analytical Jurisprudence from Bentham to Hohfeld*, 1982 WIS. L. REV. 975, 980. Individuals are assumed to have implicitly agreed to that exercise of state power as part of the social contract. *See* Peller, *supra* note 5, at 1256.

15.   If a court fails to act neutrally when it intervenes in the private sphere, it corrupts the operation of that sphere, in effect delegating the coercive power of the state to private individuals. *See* Peller, *supra* note 5, at 1202-03, 1222-23.

16.   *See* Kennedy, *supra* note 5, at 211-13, 372-82; Peller, *supra* note 5, at 1201-04.

more vulnerable we are to damage inflicted by others. Thus, the contradiction is between the principle that individuals may legitimately act in their own interest . . . and the principle that they have a duty to look out for others and to refrain from acts that hurt them. Since liberal citizens are motivated by self-interest, the only way to achieve security is to give power to the state to limit freedom of action. The contradiction between freedom . . . and security therefore translates into the contradiction between individual rights and state powers. We must determine the extent to which individual freedom of action may legitimately be limited by collective coercion over the individual in the name of security.[17]

By seemingly allowing individuals to pursue their self-interest unless and until they interfere with the interest of others, the reasonable person standard in negligence law seems to overcome this conflict between the individual and the group, protecting collective security without threatening individual freedom.

2. The Instrumentalist Vision of Negligence

a. The Public/Private Dichotomy

Like the individualist vision, modern instrumentalist analysis still sees negligence law as determining under what circumstances the state should intervene in the operation of the private sphere. However, this vision relies upon a different conception of the inadequacies of the private sphere that justify intervention. For example, rather than being concerned with coercion that overcomes the individual's will (violations of norms, involuntary assumption of risks, fraudulent misrepresentations, etc.), this approach is concerned with such things as "market failure"—imperfections in the functioning of the market that prevent it from producing results that would benefit all of society (such as the "efficient" allocation of resources).[18]

Thus, under this approach, the liberty interests at stake are more likely to be seen not as the free exercise of choice but rather as the ability to reach agreements through perfectly efficient bargaining.[19] Similarly, the threat to security interests that justifies governmental intervention is transformed from the overcoming of individual will to the existence of positive transaction costs that prevent people from reaching beneficial bargains.

Finally, while the same belief that regulation of the private sphere must

---

17. Singer, *supra* note 14, at 980 (citations omitted).

18. While efficiency analysis is not the only form that an instrumentalist approach can take, it is the most prevalent instrumentalist theory in negligence law—and, for simplicity's sake, the one upon which I will focus in this discussion.

19. For example, bargaining conducted in a situation of zero transaction costs, in which nothing would prevent parties who might be benefitted by reaching bargains from doing so. A. M. POLINSKY, AN INTRODUCTION TO LAW AND ECONOMICS 11–12 (1989).

be conducted neutrally characterizes this approach as well, that belief tends to be expressed in terms of neutrality towards groups. Thus, neutrality tends to be seen here as the refusal to take sides between different categories of individuals—employers and employees, landlords and tenants, producers and consumers—rather than as evenhandedness between individual litigants.[20] Moreover, the courts' efforts to use the reasonableness test to draw a neutral line between private freedom and public regulation are no longer thought to be grounded upon some amorphous concept of societal norms, but instead upon an approach that seemingly offers a much more concrete mechanism for identifying the community interest—efficiency analysis.[21] Because that analysis is an even more neutral and determinate indicator of social needs than the concept of societal consensus (so the argument goes), judges who employ it—as long as they do not exceed their proper institutional competency—are that much more certain not to have violated the stricture that the public must be neutral to the private.

b.   *Reasonableness as Mediator*

As just described, while the instrumentalist vision still conceives of negligence rules in general and the reasonable person standard in particular as mechanisms for mediating the contradiction between individual liberty and collective security, it recasts those terms. Thus, reasonableness becomes a vehicle for importing a cost/benefit analysis into the law, a method for distinguishing risk-creating conduct that social groups are free to engage in from conduct that, because it threatens collective security, requires regulation through tort law. In the instrumentalist view, as in the individualist approach, the reasonable person test seems to allow courts to draw these distinctions without limiting either freedom or security. By facilitating the operation of the free market, it protects groups' rights to

---

20. *See* H. STEINER, *supra* note 12, at 115–18.

21. Recognizing that doctrinal analysis is inherently indeterminate, that doctrinal terms like "due care" and "reasonableness" do not "correlate to elements of the real world," Singer, *supra* note 14, at 1016, instrumentalist theory rejects the formalist faith in judges' abilities to categorize conduct as either consensual or coerced, generally accepted or deviant, that characterized the individualist approach. Thus, the instrumentalist sees the definition of reasonableness not as merely a question of logic (of placing behavior into analytically discrete and separate categories) but rather as one of politics (of weighing competing interests). Peller, *supra* note 5, at 1198–99.

Nevertheless, while seeing the choice between two interests in a case as a value choice, this view holds that the *impact* of a particular rule is susceptible to rational determination. Therefore, once the court knows the general policy that should be furthered, it can logically choose the appropriate rule to be used. Under this view, the role of the courts is to draw the line between due care and negligence to serve social needs, needs which the courts must neutrally derive, either from legislative enactments or from other social indicators.

Despite the prescription that social needs must be neutrally derived, however, instrumentalist analysts sometimes just assume that certain things—such as the promotion of economic development and growth, or the efficient use of resources—are generally accepted as being in the interest of society. *Cf.* R. POSNER, THE ECONOMICS OF JUSTICE 67–68 (1981) (arguing that it makes sense to assume general consent to wealth maximization as moral principle).

bargain with each other, while by regulating that market when it functions inadequately, it assures the collective interest in efficient results.

B. *Reasonableness in Antidiscrimination Law*

In the sexual harassment context—specifically, in hostile environment cases—the reasonable person standard serves a similar function of identifying regulable behavior. Under title VII, conduct that unreasonably interferes with the plaintiff's ability to work constitutes prohibited discrimination.[22] For this reason, a discussion of the role of the reasonableness test in sexual harassment law necessarily devolves into a discussion of the role of the concept of discrimination in antidiscrimination law more generally.[23] By examining that role, it can be seen that the concepts of discrimination in general, and the reasonable person standard in particular, perform the same function in antidiscrimination law as the reasonableness test does in negligence law. Before exploring the parallels between the two, however, it is necessary to describe in more detail the ideology underlying antidiscrimination law.

1. *Two Sides of the Traditional Model of Discrimination*

In the following sections, I will discuss the concept of discrimination as it is traditionally understood in American ideology.[24] As noted above,[25] that model, which has dominated judicial decisions for decades,[26] considers actions based on factors such as race or sex to be presumptively illegitimate. Although the model is primarily concerned with protecting the interests of the individual, I will argue here that it also expresses a commitment to group-based pluralism—to a society which preserves the diversity of social groups, and a government that gives no group preferential treat-

---

22. *See* Meritor Sav. Bank v. Vinson, 477 U.S. 57 (1986).

23. That is, since the act of creating (or allowing) a hostile work environment is considered to be discrimination, the way that the reasonable person standard is used to define unreasonable environments will be related to the way that discrimination is conceptualized.

24. While I realize that some subtleties inevitably will be lost as a result, in this Section I will draw on discussions of both race and sex discrimination to make my points. Although there are important differences between the life situations and legal treatment of women, on the one hand, and racial minorities on the other (not to mention the further differences in the experiences of minority women), the various conceptions of discrimination present in each area of thought are nevertheless sufficiently similar to be treated together for this brief description of antidiscrimination ideology.

In describing that ideology, I will focus primarily on examples from political and legal ideology, but it is part of my position—and, indeed, part of the problem I seek to address—that the assumptions I will be discussing are prevalent in the general culture (that is, are held, consciously or not, by many but not necessarily all Americans) as well.

25. *See supra* note 7 and accompanying text.

26. Freeman, *Racism, Rights and the Quest for Equality of Opportunity: A Critical Legal Essay*, 23 HARV. C.R.-C.L. L. REV. 295, 363-64 (1988) (race discrimination); Williams, *Equality's Riddle: Pregnancy and the Equal Treatment/Special Treatment Debate*, 13 N.Y.U. REV. L. & SOC. CHANGE 325 (1984) (sex discrimination). For a description of an alternative model of discrimination that is frequently advocated in the literature and sometimes arises in case law and statutes as well, see *infra* notes 37-38 and accompanying text.

ment.[27] It is this latter, group-based dimension of the traditional concept of discrimination that will be the focus of my concern here.

a. *Protecting the Individual*

It has often been noted that the traditional model of discrimination, sometimes called the equality of opportunity model, focuses on the individual rather than the group.[28] Concerned with protecting the individual from treatment based on group stereotypes, it views the role of the law as assuring that all people are judged on their own merits, free from consideration of their group affiliations. The assumption is that once society is freed of group-based bias, each individual's progress in the world will reflect nothing more or less than her own abilities and effort.[29]

b. *Protecting the Group*

In contrast to the individual-oriented notion of rewarding personal merit is the other side of the traditional model—a concern with protecting groups and perpetuating cultural and political diversity. I will call this concern the pluralist view of discrimination.[30]

The fact that an allegation of membership in a protected group is a prerequisite to a successful discrimination claim under both title VII[31] and the equal protection clause[32] suggests that the preservation of groups has always been one concern underlying antidiscrimination efforts. If protecting individuals from irrational prejudice were the only purpose that such efforts were designed to serve, then someone fired because of the length of

---

27. For discussions of the various ways in which concerns for individuals and groups have been expressed in the case law, see Fiss, *Groups and the Equal Protection Clause*, 5 PHIL. & PUB. AFF. 107 (1976); Freeman, *Legitimizing Racial Discrimination Through Antidiscrimination Law: A Critical Review of Supreme Court Doctrine*, 62 MINN. L. REV. 1049 (1978); Fallon & Weiler, Firefighters v. Stotts: *Conflicting Models of Racial Justice*, 1984 SUP. CT. REV. 1.

28. *See, e.g.,* Fiss, *supra* note 27, at 118; Fallon & Weiler, *supra* note 27, at 13; Freeman, *supra* note 26, at 363.

29. Freeman, *supra* note 26, at 367–85. Because it draws a sharp distinction between the individual and the group, this view sees little or no connection between a person's group membership and his or her personal traits. *See* Fallon & Weiler, *supra* note 27, at 18 (describing this distinction and critiquing it on the grounds that "current talents and abilities correlate closely with educational and cultural background; the lone individual does not stand independent of history as he or she confronts the meritocratic world."); Freeman, *supra* note 26, at 380–85 (criticizing equality of opportunity theory's concept of "natural" talent).

30. As I will discuss more fully below, *see infra*, pp. 1188–89, this pluralist view of discrimination is based in part on the conviction that the success of a democratic system of government depends upon its ability to maintain a pluralist culture. In that respect, like the group-based negligence analysis, it reflects an instrumentalist view of law; it sees antidiscrimination law as a mechanism for attaining general social ends.

31. 42 U.S.C. § 2000e-2 (1982 & Supp. 1987).

32. This notion is basic in equal protection clause jurisprudence. *See* United States v. Carolene Prods. Co., 304 U.S. 144, 153 n.4 (1938) ("[P]rejudice against discrete and insular minorities may be a special condition, which tends seriously to curtail the operation of those political processes ordinarily to be relied upon to protect minorities, and which may call for a correspondingly more searching judicial inquiry.").

his hair or the manner in which he dressed would have a viable claim of discrimination. The fact that such claims do not succeed[33] (unless the trait possessed can be proven to be a proxy for some forbidden category) suggests that American ideology sees something particularly pernicious about discrimination that affects certain groups.[34]

Of course, the concern with protecting groups could still reflect an ultimately individualist purpose. That is, it could reflect a desire to protect individual members of such groups from the loss of self-esteem produced by an awareness of both the discrimination experienced by others in the group (because of their group membership) and the general low status of the group itself. However, I would suggest that this concern also reflects a pluralist purpose of maintaining the diversity of American society, as well as a conviction that government, in attempting to accomplish that purpose, must avoid favoring one group over another.[35] As I will discuss in more detail below,[36] this principle of abstract neutrality towards groups—with its emphasis on keeping the private sphere free from illegitimate governmental intrusion—is analogous to the principle of abstract neutrality towards status groups that animates instrumentalist negligence law. (It is also, of course, parallel to the principle of neutral treatment of individuals that informs the individualist approach in each area.)

It should be apparent at this point that the concern with group protection represented in this pluralist view of discrimination is somewhat dif-

---

33. *See* Fagan v. National Cash Register Co., 481 F.2d 1115, 1125 (D.C. Cir. 1973) (hair length is neither statutorily nor constitutionally protected); *see also* Kelley v. Johnson, 425 U.S. 238 (1976) (applying rational basis test to hold that hair length regulations do not violate due process clause); Willingham v. Macon Tel. Publishing Co., 507 F.2d 1084 (5th Cir. 1975) (hair length rules applied only to men do not violate title VII because hair length is not immutable characteristic).

34. *See* Fiss, *supra* note 27, at 123-26 (describing "groupism" in traditional equal protection theory).

35. The importance of preventing the subjugation of groups and maintaining cultural and racial diversity is a recurrent theme in antidiscrimination law, starting with the famous *Carolene Products* footnote itself. *See supra* note 32; *see also* L. TRIBE, AMERICAN CONSTITUTIONAL LAW §§ 16-21, 16-22 (2d ed. 1988) (citing cases to support contention that avoiding establishment of caste society and assuring diversity are important concerns in antidiscrimination ideology); Fiss, *supra* note 27, at 123-26 (describing elements of equal protection doctrine that are not individualistic); *cf.* Regents of the Univ. of Cal. v. Bakke, 438 U.S. 265, 311-14 (1978) (Powell, J.) (race is legitimate consideration in medical school admissions if part of overall attempt to promote diversity within student body and medical profession); Sunstein, *Interest Groups in American Public Law*, 38 STAN. L. REV. 29, 33 (1985) (noting that establishment of individual right against discrimination is one way to protect against factional domination of legislative process and thus preserve bargaining and compromise among groups that is essence of pluralism). *But see* Brest, *supra* note 7, at 48 ("[G]roup membership is always a proxy for the individual's right not to be discriminated against. Similarly, remedies for race-specific harms recognize the sociological consequences of group identification and affiliation only to assure justice for individual members . . . .").

In rejecting the defendant's argument in *Bakke* that "benign" discrimination against the majority should not be "suspect," Justice Powell emphasized the importance of judicial neutrality towards groups: "It is far too late to argue that the guarantee of equal protection to *all* persons permits the recognition of special wards entitled to a degree of protection greater than that accorded others. . . . There is no principled basis for deciding which groups would merit 'heightened judicial solicitude' and which would not." 438 U.S. at 295-96 (1978) (Powell, J.) (emphasis in original).

36. *See infra* notes 53-55 and accompanying text.

ferent from the group focus found in the "equality of result" model of discrimination that is often advocated in the scholarly literature.[37] Under the latter model, which has not been widely followed by the courts, the concern is neither with protecting individuals from specific acts of discrimination (although it would bar such acts) nor with assuring the neutral governmental treatment of groups themselves, but rather with eliminating the conditions of inequality under which groups exist. In contrast, the traditional ideology lacks this concern with assuring equality of results and does not conceive of discrimination as the perpetuation of structures of inequality.[38]

To better understand the pluralist view of discrimination—to understand why a positive value would attach to the idea of preserving groups per se, why judicial neutrality would seem to be required to attain such preservation, and how such neutrality could nevertheless still be thought of as an effective tool for the elimination of inequality—it will be helpful

---

37. Terminology can be confusing here. In the race discrimination context, group-based and individual-based models have been variously described as the "equality as result" view and the "equality as process" view, Crenshaw, *Race, Reform, and Retrenchment: Transformation and Legitimation in Antidiscrimination Law*, 101 HARV. L. REV. 1331, 1341-42 (1988); the "victim perspective" and the "perpetrator perspective," Freeman, *supra* note 27, at 1052-53; and the "equal opportunity" and "equal treatment" approaches, Belton, *Discrimination and Affirmative Action: An Analysis of Competing Theories of Equality* and Weber, 59 N.C.L. REV. 531, 539-41 (1981); *see also* Fallon & Weiler, *supra* note 27, at 12-26 (describing difference as between model of group justice and model of individual justice); Fiss, *supra* note 27, at 108 (group-disadvantaging principle versus antidiscrimination principle). Although most of the group-based approaches in this literature define discrimination as the failure to eliminate conditions of subordination, there are important differences among them (for example, in the extent to which they believe in the possibility of judicial neutrality).

Within feminist theory, the model that is usually identified as focusing on groups is called the "special treatment" approach; the contrasting, individual-oriented position is called the "equal treatment" approach. *See generally* Williams, *supra* note 26 (describing both approaches and advocating latter); Krieger & Cooney, *The Miller-Wohl Controversy: Equal Treatment, Positive Action and the Meaning of Women's Equality*, 13 GOLDEN GATE U.L. REV. 513 (1983) (advocating group focus); Finley, *Transcending Equality Theory: A Way Out of the Maternity and the Workplace Debate*, 86 COLUM. L. REV. 1118, 1142-63 (1986) (critiquing both positions). However, the "inequality" analysis advocated by Catharine MacKinnon—which rejects the traditional framework within which both equal and special treatment arguments are articulated, defining discrimination as the perpetuation of conditions of inequality—also focuses on groups. C. MACKINNON, *supra* note 1, at 4-5. Thus, like the literature on racial discrimination, feminist writings advocating a group focus vary in the extent to which they reject the goal of abstract neutrality. *See generally* Finley, *supra* (discussing assumption of neutrality in equal and special treatment analyses).

It is not my concern here, however, to categorize existing approaches. Rather, I simply want to call attention to the fact that group-based concerns can and do arise under the narrower definition of discrimination as well as within the more transformative visions. *See also infra* note 38.

38. As the existence of these two different group-based conceptions of discrimination suggests, a concern for groups can lead to either a broad or a narrow definition of discrimination, depending upon which traits of an individual are associated with his or her group status and which ones are thought to be the product of individual choice, ability, and effort. Under the traditional, pluralist discrimination model, few individual traits are attributed to group membership; under equality-of-result models, things such as educational achievement, individual abilities, and even the meaning of the concept of merit itself are seen as the product of historical and structural factors. Some of the equality-of-result advocates recognize that the choice between these two conceptions of the individual is itself indeterminate, and is therefore a political question. *See, e.g.*, Freeman, *supra* note 26, at 381-85 (critiquing "intelligence" tests).

to describe briefly the ideology of political and cultural pluralism underlying that view.

2. *Pluralist Ideology*[39]

Pluralism is based on the assumption that the success of a democratic society depends upon its ability to sustain a relativistic culture—one "that denie[s] absolute truths, remain[s] intellectually flexible and critical, value[s] diversity, and [draws] strength from innumerable competing subgroups."[40] Under this view, pluralistic tolerance of diversity protects a nation from the absolutist ideas that lead to totalitarianism. Rather than being viewed as a dangerous, nihilistic belief system that prevents us from judging others,[41] cultural relativism is seen as a positive good, a guaranty of democracy.

Furthermore, in pluralist ideology, not only is tolerance of groups necessary to democracy, but diversity *itself* improves the success of a democratic society.[42] The existence of a variety of competing viewpoints works as a set of social checks and balances, preventing any one perspective from gaining dominance, and thereby curbing any tendencies toward absolutist thought and totalitarian government.[43] Just as the marketplace of ideas in the social arena and voluntary competition in the economic realm are equated with (and thought to guaranty) individual freedom in liberal individualist thought, so the unencumbered interplay of different perspectives and the competing demands of different interest groups are associated with democracy in pluralist thought.[44]

Finally, cultural relativism is not solely thought of as a prescriptive

---

39. While I will be arguing that the group-based visions within negligence and antidiscrimination law are analogous, I do not mean to suggest that the pluralist ideology described in this Section underlies the instrumentalist approach to negligence as well. It would seem that the ideology underlying negligence, a private law field, is more closely related to economic analysis, while the ideology of antidiscrimination law, a public law field, has greater affinities with political theory. However, a detailed analysis of the ideological underpinnings of negligence law is beyond the scope of this paper.

40. E. PURCELL, THE CRISIS OF DEMOCRATIC THEORY 211 (1973).

41. During the first part of the twentieth century, ethical relativism was attacked as leading to totalitarianism, *id.* at 200, but by the mid-1940's that view had been replaced by an "equation between intellectual relativism and democracy." *Id.* at 209. In response to the rise of extremist ideologies like Nazism and, later, Stalinism, any kind of absolutist faith in a particular belief, whatever its content, came to be seen as dangerous to democracy. *Id.* at 210-11.

42. *Id.* at 214.

43. *See* R. DAHL, PLURALIST DEMOCRACY IN THE UNITED STATES: CONFLICT AND CONSENT 24 (1967).

44. As Horwitz states:

In reaction to the spread of totalitarianism after World War II, progressivism capitulated to the argument that any substantive conception of the public interest was simply the first step on the road to totalitarism. The idea of a public interest thus came to be formulated in the purely proceduralist terms of interest-group pluralism—simply as whatever was the outcome of competition among interest groups. This was, it should be emphasized, a twentieth-century return to a market theory of the public interest—but this time the competitors were groups and the market was the political process.

Horwitz, *supra* note 13, at 1427 (citations omitted).

ideal; it is also seen as a descriptive reality—as an accurate depiction of existing American society. What holds the widely diverse American populace together, it is thought, is a universally held pluralism, a spirit of open-minded debate and tolerance for diversity that crosses all ethnic boundaries.[45] Thus, pluralism functions as a solution to the group/individual contradiction, now expressed at the group level. The heterogeneity of the population poses the possibility of conflict among groups (just as self-interestedness potentially produces conflict among individuals in the individualist vision), but an overarching culture (and practice) of pluralism mediates that conflict within the private sphere (just as economic competition and growth do in the other model).[46]

The role of government, therefore, is to refrain from interfering in the private world of interest-group politics, unless someone uses illegitimate tactics to undermine a group's ability to participate, thereby threatening the public interest.[47] Instances justifying intervention are thought to be the exception rather than the rule, not only because the democratic culture makes intolerant conduct rare, but also because the potential of state power to transform a particular viewpoint into a totalitarian creed means that government itself probably poses the greatest threat to democracy. Thus, it is seen as essential that the government take a relativistic stance to different groups in society, in order to preserve the heterogeneous private sphere that is needed to curb dangerous state power.[48]

---

45. E. PURCELL, *supra* note 40, at 210-11; *see also* Kennedy, *supra* note 5, at 356-57.

46. It is interesting to note that pluralism as a concept thus both affirms and denies diversity, describing our society as heterogeneous while simultaneously claiming that it is united by a common overarching culture.

47.

  Under the pluralist conception, the problem of faction arises from the possibility that one group, or an alliance of groups, will dominate the legislative or executive process and subvert the bargaining and compromise on which the model is based. Factional domination effectively deprives other groups of the opportunity to assert their views. If it were permitted to occur, the political process would be undermined and freedom would be at risk.

Sunstein, *supra* note 35, at 33. While Sunstein talks of the legislative process, I would argue that the concept of pluralism extends beyond that to the notion of a multiplicity of groups participating in intellectual and ethical dialogue within the society as a whole. *See* E. PURCELL, *supra* note 40, at 238.

48. *Cf.* Sunstein, *supra* note 35, at 50-51: "[M]uch of modern constitutional doctrine reflects a single perception of the underlying evil: the distribution of resources or opportunities to one group rather than another solely because those benefitted have exercised the raw power to obtain governmental assistance." Sunstein describes this attitude as a repudiation of pluralism—a rejection of the idea that whatever results from pluralist compromise in the legislative process is legitimate. However, that conclusion is necessary only if one defines pluralism very narrowly—as the belief that interest group struggle inevitably promotes the social welfare and poses no problem of factionalism. Sunstein himself seems simultaneously to adopt that view, *id.* at 33-35, and to reject it. *Id.* at 33 (discussing how problem of faction arises under pluralism and possible responses to it).

I would suggest that it is more accurate to describe contemporary pluralist ideology as including a recognition of the (rare) possibility that interest-group interactions could be subverted by private power, and a belief that, when such subversion occurs, it justifies intervention by the state. Such regulable behavior may be defined in quasi-procedural terms, as the refusal to follow the rules of pragmatic compromise that protect against domination of democratic processes by any one interest. *Cf.* E. PURCELL, *supra* note 40, at 255 (noting that, during heyday of cultural relativism in 1950's, "[b]elief in the primacy of toleration and compromise readily led to the assumption . . . that broad demands for political and economic change were actually irresponsible. The assumption that a 'rea-

For the courts, this relativism translates into neutrality, a refusal to ground judicial decisions on personal preferences for particular perspectives or political judgments about the importance of certain group interests. Only by remaining neutral in the struggle among interest groups can the courts preserve the cultural and political pluralism that is the essence of democracy.

3. Reasonableness in the Pluralist Vision of Antidiscrimination Law

Whether its focus is on individuals or on groups, the traditional, equal opportunity model of discrimination sees antidiscrimination law, like negligence law, as an exercise of governmental power to regulate the private sphere in the interest of the collectivity.[49] It poses the same conflict between the individual and the group, and employs the same public/private dichotomy, as does negligence law. It also, at least in the context of sex discrimination, purports to resolve that conflict by using a reasonableness standard grounded in societal consensus.[50]

Since the traditional model focuses alternately on individuals and on groups, the freedom it seeks to protect in the private sphere can be conceived of as both liberal individualism and interest group pluralism. Thus, when discrimination is characterized as preventing a person from accomplishing whatever she is capable of accomplishing, the liberty of the individual is at stake. On the other hand, when discrimination is thought to threaten society's interest in group diversity and equality—as, for example, in the frequently expressed sentiment that America should not be a caste society[51]—pluralism is the private-sphere freedom that needs to be protected. In both cases, however, the government's role is perceived to be limited to the elimination of minor wrinkles in the otherwise egalitarian operation of that private sphere.

Because the individualist dimension of the traditional model of discrimination has been so thoroughly examined elsewhere,[52] the following discussion will focus on the role of the reasonable person standard within the pluralist view of discrimination.

---

sonable' compromise was always possible . . . made an opposition to established institutions appear politically illegitimate."). Of course, to the extent that pluralism simultaneously recognizes the possibility of factionalism and equates the common good with the results of the political process, it is internally incoherent in the same way that liberal individualism is incoherent when it conceives of individual freedom as both social good and social threat. See supra note 17 and accompanying text.

49. That is, the collective society's interest in preserving private freedom by regulating conduct that threatens such freedom is implicated in both contexts.

50. See Meritor Sav. Bank v. Vinson, 477 U.S. 57, 65 (1986) (defining sexual harassment as conduct that "has the purpose or effect of unreasonably interfering with an individual's work performance or creating an intimidating, hostile, or offensive working environment") (citing 29 C.F.R. § 1604.11(a)(3) (1985)); see also Rabidue v. Osceola Ref. Co., 805 F.2d 611, 622 (6th Cir. 1986) (evaluating sexual harassment charge in context of depictions of women "condone[d]" and "publicly feature[d]" in society), cert. denied, 481 U.S. 1041 (1987).

51. See, e.g., Fiss, supra note 27, at 151.

52. See, e.g., articles cited supra note 27 and sources discussed therein.

a. *The Public/Private Dichotomy*

Antidiscrimination law can be seen as (at least in part) an exercise of government power to regulate the world of interest group pluralism, eliminating both the coercive use of group power and the illegitimate reliance upon group stereotypes that, by disadvantaging the members of the stereotyped groups, impair those groups' abilities to engage in the open dialogue and competitive pursuit of self interest necessary to democracy. Title VII, for example, is designed to secure equal employment opportunity for women and other groups by prohibiting discrimination against them by private employers. In so doing, it assures their effective participation in both the economic and the political realms, thereby furthering not only their interest in equality but the general societal interest in pluralistic democracy (not to mention productivity) as well.

b. *Reasonableness as Mediator*

The role of the courts in this scheme, again comparable to their role in the negligence context, is to determine when conduct has gone beyond the exercise of private freedom and thus imperils the public interest in democratic pluralism. By exerting a countermajoritarian influence, the judiciary is supposed to prevent the tyranny of the majority (or of a minority) that would ultimately threaten the liberty interests of all.[53] But again, in regulating the private sphere it must act neutrally, so that its decisions will not represent merely a delegation of state power to one group or another. Thus, courts should base their decisions on the principle of tolerance for diversity and a concern for the protection of minorities, rather than on the substantive content of the views or needs of different groups.

Here, as in the policy-based negligence vision, the central contradiction between individual liberty and collective security that the courts are supposed to resolve is articulated through groups, not individuals. Thus, in the pluralist view of discrimination, the individual's interests are not of particular concern; rather, it is the contradiction between the liberty and security interests of groups that the legal doctrine must mediate.

And, as in the negligence context, so here doctrinal terms like reasonableness and discrimination are recognized to be indeterminate.[54] Given that indeterminacy, they should be defined (so the argument goes) to implement policy decisions about what types of group-based interests should be protected. The role of the courts, then, is again seen as one of linedrawing—identifying a point along a continuum of conduct that separates (prohibited) discrimination from (protected) freedom—and judges

---

53. *See* L. TRIBE, *supra* note 35, at § 16-12.
54. *See supra* note 21.

are again supposed to perform this task neutrally, deriving the policies that they implement from other, politically legitimate sources.[55]

It is for these reasons that the test for hostile environment sexual harassment can be phrased as that which violates societal norms about how people should be treated in the workplace (and,' implicitly, how groups should be treated in society). Here, as in the negligence law context, the private world of free cultural expression by groups that the courts are seeking to protect is itself seen as providing the solution to the problem of government neutrality. After all, if pluralism both relies upon and reproduces a culture of democracy—a moral consensus voluntarily arrived at and untainted by governmental power—then that culture can provide the neutral standard with which the government can determine when intervention is necessary.[56]

Just as in negligence law, what constitutes reasonable behavior is recognized to be a political question of where to draw the line between group and societal interests—that is, between diversity and conformity—and it is society, not the court, that makes that judgment. Thus, it is not so much that the reasonableness test is itself a neutral standard, but rather that it serves as a vehicle for importing an already-arrived-at (and legitimate) political solution into the law.

In summary (see the chart below), the reasonableness standard, in negligence law and in sexual harassment law, supposedly serves as a mechanism with which courts can distinguish protected exercises of freedom from regulable interferences with collective security. Furthermore, it is thought to allow courts to draw that line neutrally, by basing their decisions on a neutral principle (efficiency, tolerance for diversity) or on a pre-existing policy preference arrived at through freely-willed interactions in the private sphere (societal consensus). However, as my discussion of the *Rabidue* case will illustrate, the reasonable person standard in operation merely contains and suppresses the contradiction between diversity and conformity, rather than overcoming it.

---

55. Pluralism rejects the notion that courts should derive the normative grounds of their opinions from their own ethical reasoning or from some abstract conception of societal welfare. It "treats the republican notion of a separate common good as incoherent, potentially totalitarian, or both. The common good consists of uninhibited bargaining among the various participants . . . ." Sunstein, *supra* note 35, at 32 (footnote omitted).

56. Anecdotal evidence of this reliance upon the private sphere for normative judgments can be seen in a recent incident at a medical school with which I am familiar. When a professor was charged with having made racist comments in the classroom, his defenders argued that the comments could not have been racist since the majority of the (mostly white) class had not found them offensive.

Liberal Individualism in Negligence Law[a] and Sexual Harassment Law[b]

	Political Ideology	Legal Ideology	Negligence Law	Sexual Harassment Law
Private	competiton	free will	due care	merit
Public	anticompetitive behavior	coercion	negligence	discrimination
Mediator	"natural" market	consent/societal consensus	reasonableness	reasonableness

Liberal Instrumentalism in Negligence Law: Efficiency Analysis[c]

	Political Ideology	Legal Ideology	Negligence Law
Private	competition	zero transaction costs	reasonable risk
Public	"market failure"	"positive" transaction costs	unreasonable risk
Mediator	social needs	efficiency	cost/benefit analysis

Liberal Instrumentalism in Sexual Harassment Law: Interest Group Pluralism[d]

	Political Ideology	Legal Ideology	Sexual Harassment Law
Private	pluralist democracy	group freedom (diversity)	cultural expression
Public	absolutism/ intolerance	tyranny of the majority or minority (coerced conformity)	discrimination
Mediator	democratic culture	tolerance/societal consensus	reasonableness

[a]*See supra* pp. 1180–82.
[b]*See supra* p. 1185.
[c]*See supra* pp. 1182–84.
[d]*See supra* pp. 1184–92.

II. RABIDUE V. OSCEOLA REFINING COMPANY: REASONABLENESS IN THE SEXUAL HARASSMENT CONTEXT

This Part examines the role that the reasonable person standard plays in the specific doctrinal context of sexual harassment law. It does so through a close reading of a recent sexual harassment case that applies the reasonable person standard. Before turning to that discussion, however, two points deserve mention. First, in focusing my analysis on one case, I am treating the judicial opinions that comprise that case as a cultural text. That is, I am assuming that the analyses engaged in by the judges were informed by culturally-based notions that can be discovered through a careful reading of those opinions.[57] In addition, I am assuming that an

---

57. In that respect, my approach is analogous to current efforts in many other intellectual fields to use textual analysis as a means of revealing central cultural constructs. *See, e.g.*, C. GEERTZ, LOCAL KNOWLEDGE (1983) (anthropology); C. GEERTZ, THE INTERPRETATION OF CULTURES (1973) (anthropology); J. SCOTT, GENDER AND THE POLITICS OF HISTORY (1988) (social history). On the

exploration of those notions in the context of a particular judicial decision can not only increase one's understanding of that decision but also contribute insights that might be more broadly applicable to other cases and legal contexts. In addition, such an exploration can yield an understanding of law's role in reproducing culture, for the subtle messages residing in a judicial opinion not only reflect existing ideology, but also reinforce, legitimate, and transform it.

Second, in the following discussion I take as given certain things that others might be inclined to debate. Thus, I assume not only that contemporary society is characterized by systematic and significant inequalities—between women and men, lower and upper classes, people of color and whites, etc.—but also that how one perceives a particular social situation or interaction, such as an alleged act of harassment, will be a function both of one's personal psychological makeup and of social factors, such as one's race, sex, class, etc. Thus, while I do not mean to suggest that all women or men think the same way,[58] I do believe that the formidable differences in the material conditions and socialization processes that women and men face will tend to produce broad commonalities of perspective within each sex. (Differences of class, race, sexual orientation and the like, as well as personality factors, will of course cut across and dilute the sex-based similarities.)

Given these assumptions, it should be clear that I would not want to suggest that I am approaching the issue of sexual harassment "objectively." Rather, I believe that anyone dealing with this (or any other) issue will bring to it a particularized perspective, so that a "neutral" assessment is simply not possible. I come to the issue of sexual harassment as a white, upper-middle class woman, and as a feminist—as one who believes both that women are subordinated to men in our society and that the law should be directed towards rectifying that imbalance. I also believe that some men who engage in (what I would call) harassing behavior do so with neither conscious hostility towards women nor an awareness of the effect of their conduct, and I have no doubt that such men would feel personally wronged by judgments declaring their conduct harassment. (Other men, of course, are perfectly aware of what they are doing.)[59]

---

lessons that textual analysis and the resulting recognition that language is indeterminate and relational can provide to legal scholars, see White, *Law & Literature: "No Manifesto"*, 39 MERCER L. REV. 739 (1988).

58. The thought-provoking work of Carol Gilligan, *see, e.g.*, C. GILLIGAN, IN A DIFFERENT VOICE (1982), has greatly improved our understanding of women's situation. It has also, unfortunately, generated much reductionist and essentialist discussion of women's differences from men. Nevertheless, the presence of such crude overgeneralizations about the sexes should not produce the equally crude reaction of totally ignoring the ways in which many women's social and epistemological world—partly because it is *itself* a product of patriarchy—is genuinely different from that of many men.

59. For discussion of some of the possible reasons why men engage in sexual harassment, see *infra* notes 179-92 and accompanying text.

Nevertheless, I am convinced, as will become clear below, that while the elimination of inequality in society inevitably makes some people feel wronged—entailing, as it does, a reduction in the social status and privilege of those on the top of the hierarchy, regardless of whether they harbor personal hostility toward those beneath them—that fact does not justify its perpetuation.

A. *The Case in Brief*

Vivienne Rabidue was an administrative assistant at Osceola Refining Company—the sole woman in a salaried management position in the company.[60] After her discharge in 1977, she filed a sexual harassment claim against her employer,[61] charging that its refusal to stop the display of pornographic posters in private offices and common work areas at the company plant, as well as the stream of anti-female obscenities directed at her and other women by a co-worker in another department,[62] constituted sex discrimination in violation of title VII. She also introduced evidence that she had been denied various managerial privileges accorded to male employees (free lunches and gasoline, entertainment privileges, etc.) and in other ways had been given secondary status in the company.[63]

The conduct of which Rabidue complained was hardly mild or ambiguous. One of the posters displayed at the plant depicted a prone woman with a golf ball on her breasts, straddled by a man holding a golf club and yelling, "Fore."[64] The comments that her co-worker, Douglas Henry, directed at her and her fellow female workers included such epithets as "whores," "cunt," "pussy," "tits," and "fat ass."[65] Henry once remarked of the plaintiff: "All that bitch needs is a good lay."[66] He also engaged in generally uncooperative behavior that impaired Rabidue's ability to perform her job effectively.[67]

Judge Krupansky, writing for the majority of the court and applying the reasonableness standard traditionally used in hostile work environ-

---

60. Rabidue v. Osceola Ref. Co., 805 F.2d 611, 623 (6th Cir. 1986) (Keith, J., dissenting), *cert. denied*, 481 U.S. 1041 (1987).

61. She also filed a discriminatory discharge claim. At the time the claims were filed, Osceola was a division of Texas-American Petrochemicals, Inc., which had acquired Osceola on September 1, 1976. The Sixth Circuit affirmed the district court's ruling that Texas-American could not be held liable for any alleged discriminatory acts that occurred prior to that date, because, given that charges had not been filed with the Equal Employment Opportunity Commission at or before the time of acquisition, Texas-American, as successor, had no notice of contingent charges when it acquired the company. 805 F.2d at 616 (citations omitted). Apparently because at least some of the conduct complained of had occurred after September 1, 1976, the court went on to address the substantive merits of plaintiff's claims. *Id.* at 615, 618.

62. *Id.* at 615.

63. *Id.* at 624 (Keith, J., dissenting).

64. *Id.*

65. *Id.*

66. *Id.*

67. *Id.* at 625.

ment cases,[68] held that the conduct complained of had not unreasonably interfered with Rabidue's ability to work. The court characterized that conduct as a legitimate expression of the cultural norms of workers at the employer's plant and suggested that the prevailing depictions of women in the media indicated that such conduct was not unreasonably offensive in any case. In so doing, the majority treated its solution as promoting pluralism and neutrally reflecting pre-existing norms.[69] In dissent, Judge Keith advocated the use of a reasonable woman (or reasonable victim) standard, rejecting the majority's approach as enforcing an essentially male viewpoint under the guise of universality.[70]

The majority relied upon three distinct arguments in concluding that the conduct at Osceola had not been unreasonably offensive: (1) the plaintiff had "voluntarily" and knowingly entered the Osceola workplace and therefore could not complain about the conditions she encountered there;[71] (2) the court should not interpret title VII as mandating that it transform working class culture, and therefore should not interfere with the Osceola environment (and, implicitly, such noninterference did not constitute discrimination against women because the plaintiff was merely an overly sensitive, aberrational individual);[72] and (3) the Osceola environment was not unreasonably offensive in any case because it was no different from the rest of society.[73] The court presented each of these arguments as a neutral ground for its decision—as a vehicle for distinguishing between legitimate individual or group freedom and illegitimate discrimination. However, as the discussion below will demonstrate, each argument ultimately fails at this enterprise, for each ignores or minimizes the conflict between men's and women's viewpoints that the case presented and thus only "solves" the problem by avoiding it.

---

68. "[A] plaintiff . . . must assert and prove that . . . the charged sexual harassment had the effect of *unreasonably* interfering with the plaintiff's work performance and creating an intimidating, hostile, or offensive working environment . . . ." 805 F.2d at 619 (emphasis added).

69. *See infra* pp. 1201-07.

70. The majority and dissenting opinions in *Rabidue* are analogous to the "equal treatment" and "special treatment" positions, respectively, over which feminist scholars have been debating for years. *See* articles cited *supra* note 37. Thus, the majority seems to assume that applying the same standard to women and men is not problematic, just as equal treatment advocates define justice as the application of completely sex-blind rules. In contrast, the dissent, like special treatment advocates, seems more concerned about validating women's perceptions and achieving concrete gains for women than about complying with a sex-blind ideal of abstract equality.

I do not mean to suggest, however, that equal treatment advocates would have reached the same conclusion as did Judge Krupansky. Indeed, as has been pointed out, one of the problems with the equal treatment approach is that it seems to provide a determinate, neutral principle with which to decide cases but is in fact indeterminate. *See* Finley, *supra* note 37, at 1149-52.

71. *Rabidue*, 805 F.2d at 620 ("the reasonable expectation of the plaintiff upon voluntarily entering [an] environment" pervaded by "a lexicon of obscenity" is relevant factor for court to consider).

72. *Id.* at 620-22.

73. *Id.* at 622.

B. *Reasonableness as Mediator: The Messages Conveyed by the Majority Opinion*

This Section argues that the court's analysis in *Rabidue* draws upon a fundamental set of oppositions that characterizes liberal thought, consistently associating the Osceola situation with freedom, choice, and deference to the private realm, instead of security, coercion, and regulation by the public realm. Moreover, each of the court's three main arguments relies upon one of the traditional mediating constructs used in liberal legal thought to attempt to overcome the contradiction between the poles of these sets of opposition. Thus, the "voluntary entry" point is a classical individualist "free choice" argument; the "working class culture" point invokes the pluralist principle of tolerance for diversity; and the third point, which essentially argues for following societal norms, constitutes a reliance upon consensus as mediator typical of both individualist and instrumentalist discourse.[74] By thus seeming to be the result of the application of neutral abstract principles (choice, tolerance) and independently existing social norms (consensus), the court's conclusions depoliticize what is essentially a political conflict, obscuring the value choices upon which its decision relies.

There are at least two ways to understand the social interaction with which the court grappled in the *Rabidue* case. One way is to see it as posing a fundamental conflict between two unequal groups—men and women—about how they should relate to each other in the workplace, with women saying they should be allowed to be free from (and define) demeaning treatment and men saying they should not.[75] Under such a reading, the court would seem to be faced with no choice but to make a value-laden decision about which group's approach was preferable.[76] Moreover, its rejection of the plaintiff's claim could seem to be nothing

---

74. *See* charts *supra* p. 1193.

75. The posters displayed and conduct engaged in at Osceola can be seen as symptomatic of a more general and "pervasive degradation and exploitation of female sexuality perpetuated in American culture." *Rabidue*, 805 F.2d at 627 (Keith, J., dissenting). Pornography is simply the most obvious example of a whole range of mechanisms through which women are socially constructed as sexual objects. *See, e.g.*, K. MILLETT, SEXUAL POLITICS (1970) (on objectification and degradation of women in works of Henry Miller, Norman Mailer, and others); Cling, *On-Camera Sex Discrimination: A Disparate Impact Suit Against the Television Networks and Major Studios*, 4 LAW & INEQUALITY 509 (1986) (on sex stereotyping of women on television, including their depiction as primarily concerned with their physical attractiveness to men, and negative effects thereof). And the workplace is only one of many contexts in which that construction of women negatively affects their treatment. *See, e.g.*, MacKinnon, *Feminism, Marxism, Method, and the State: Toward Feminist Jurisprudence*, 8 SIGNS 635, 646-55 (1983) (effect of objectification of women on rape law).

76. Once the co-worker's behavior is seen as part and parcel of a general pattern of treatment of women in American society, the question in the case then becomes whether the existing relationship between men and women, in which women are routinely treated as objects to be used for male sexual gratification, should be allowed to persist. In short, should women be allowed to challenge the way sexual relationships are currently constructed (on the grounds that it demeans them and limits their economic opportunities), or should the law reinforce such constructions?

more than judicial enforcement of a powerful group's subordination of the less powerful.

It is also possible, however, to see the case as not involving a conflict between men and women at all. This second vision is the vision that Judge Krupansky's opinion relies upon (and creates). In this section, I examine the rhetorical messages through which such a vision of the case is conveyed. As the discussion will demonstrate, the combined effect of the three aspects of the majority opinion addressed here—its "privatization" of the plaintiff, its recasting of the group conflict in the case, and its equation of reasonableness with consensus—is to make it seem as if Vivienne Rabidue, not Douglas Henry or Osceola Refining Company, was attempting to engage in discrimination, and as if workers and their employers, not women, need the protection of the court.

1. "Privatization" of the Plaintiff: Erasing Group Conflict

Both by describing the plaintiff as an atypical woman and by suggesting that her situation was the product of her own personal choice, the majority opinion conveyed the impression that Vivienne Rabidue's complaint represented a personal, individual claim. Because such a depiction effectively eliminated the plaintiff's group identity (she became an unreasonable, idiosyncratic woman, not a reasonable, typical one), I call it "privatization." This erasing of Rabidue's group membership both allowed the court to avoid visualizing the case as a conflict between men and women, and undermined the legitimacy of the plaintiff's claim by making it seem not to implicate pluralism concerns (since she did not represent the interests of women as a group). Moreover, it legitimated the role of the court in the case, obscuring the value judgments inherent in its application of the "voluntariness" label by making that application seem to be an objective determination of fact.

a. The "Abrasiveness" and Oversensitivity of the Plaintiff

The majority's description of the *Rabidue* situation presented the plaintiff as an overly sensitive, obnoxious woman,[77] incapable of getting along with others,[78] and trivialized the conduct to which she was subjected.[79]

---

77. The court's description of her as "a capable, independent, ambitious, aggressive, intractable and opinionated individual" with "an abrasive, rude, antagonistic, extremely willful, uncooperative, and irascible personality," *Rabidue*, 805 F.2d at 615, effectively obscured the possibility that Rabidue's complaint represented the viewpoint of women in general.

78. Noting that the plaintiff's claim arose primarily out of the "acrimonious working relationship" between her and another employee and concluding that she was fired, in part, because of her "inability to work harmoniously with co-workers and customers," *id.*, the court conveyed the distinct impression that the dispute in the case was primarily attributable to Rabidue's difficult personality.

79. Calling the Osceola posters "calendar type office wall displays," *id.* at 622 n.7, comparing them to "erotica," *id.* at 622, and describing Henry's epithets as "off-color language," *id.* at 622 n.7, Judge Krupansky's opinion trivialized the injury that Rabidue alleged, and thereby suggested that

Through emphasizing the plaintiff's "abrasiveness" and minimizing the harmfulness of the harasser's conduct, the court subtly suggested that something was wrong with Rabidue for having been offended by Henry's behavior.[80] Depicting the case as a situation in which an abnormally sensitive and difficult individual sought to label as sexist what was merely harmless joking,[81] the court reduced Rabidue's complaint from a serious charge of sex discrimination that raised questions of public power[82] and group hierarchy to merely the peevish protest of an unreasonably oversensitive woman.

b. *Her Private "Choice" to Enter the Workplace*

The majority opinion further privatized Rabidue's claim through emphasizing her "voluntary" entry into the workplace. Stating that the factors to be considered in a hostile environment case include "the lexicon of obscenity that pervaded the environment of the workplace both before and after the plaintiff's introduction into its environs, [and] the reasonable expectation of the plaintiff upon voluntarily entering that environment,"[83] Judge Krupansky seemed to suggest that the plaintiff could have avoided the situation had she so desired. In concluding that Vivienne Rabidue essentially had assumed the risk of harassment,[84] the court ignored the possibility that her situation was the product of structural inequities in society that she was powerless to overcome.[85] Treating her situation as the product of individual choice, rather than an instance of group-based discrimination, the court effectively erased Rabidue's group identity, making her seem to be responsible for her own mistreatment.[86]

---

only an unusually sensitive woman would find the conduct at Osceola offensive. His comment that the plaintiff and others were merely "annoyed" by Henry's behavior, *id.* at 615, further suggested that such behavior did not justify Rabidue's supposedly irascible reaction.

80. *See* Finley, *A Break in the Silence: Including Women's Issues in a Torts Course*, 1 YALE J.L. & FEMINISM 41, 60 n.65 (1989). Of course, as the dissent pointed out, the plaintiff's "negative personal traits" were technically irrelevant, for even the possession of such traits would not justify "sex-based disparate treatment" of the sort that she received. *Rabidue*, 805 F.2d at 625 (Keith, J., dissenting). Thus, the majority's apparent conclusion that Vivienne Rabidue's "abrasiveness" was relevant strongly suggests that it saw such abrasiveness as evidence that the plaintiff was not a typical woman—that her reactions to the behavior at Osceola were unreasonable.

81. Sexual harassment is often characterized as harmless joking, but this is not how it feels to women. *See, e.g.,* Collins & Blodgett, *Sexual Harassment . . . Some See It . . . Some Won't*, HARV. BUS. REV., Mar.–Apr. 1981, at 76, 78–80. Several studies confirm that most women find sexual harassment (whether in the form of physical touchings or verbal abuse) an unpleasant, intimidating, and humiliating experience. *See* C. MACKINNON, *supra* note 1, at 47–48 (citing studies by *Redbook Magazine* and Working Women Institute); Collins & Blodgett, *supra*, at 82.

82. It raised questions of public power because, to the extent that the court's decision gave Henry the "right" to engage in his harassing conduct, it constituted government enforcement of such conduct.

83. *Rabidue*, 805 F.2d at 620.

84. I have taken this "assumption of risk" paraphrasing from the dissent. *Id.* at 626 (Keith, J., dissenting); *see also* Finley, *supra* note 80, at 60–61 n.65.

85. *See infra* pp. 1200–01.

86. That is, having already reduced Henry's conduct to trivial proportions, the court transforms Rabidue's objections into matters of personal taste, thereby imposing on her the obligation either to avoid the offensive behavior or to accept it. Moreover, because the court conceptualized discrimination

Moreover, by accepting the trial court's reliance on the "fact" that Rabidue had voluntarily entered the workplace, the court obscured the value choices that such a conclusion required. The idea that individual choice can be used to mark the boundary between protectible exercises of freedom and unprotectible threats to the interests of others, a common refrain in liberal legal analysis,[87] has been widely criticized as circular and incoherent.[88] Judge Krupansky's conclusion that Rabidue "voluntarily" submitted to Henry's verbal abuse is subject to the same criticism. The judge's effort to use private, individual "choice" as his neutral benchmark necessarily assumes that all such choices are themselves freely arrived at—that is, that they are the product of (protected) freedom rather than of (regulable) coercion.

But to decide whether Rabidue's choice was "voluntary," one must decide whether to consider the impact on that choice of current social arrangements—arrangements that severely limit the number and nature of economic opportunities open to women as well as constrain their ability to affect the conditions under which they work.[89] Given current economic realities, Judge Krupansky's conclusion that women can choose between, on the one hand, accepting workplaces where the derogation of women is taken to be humor (my characterization, not his) and, on the other hand, working elsewhere constitutes a decision that women must accept domination by men in order to achieve equal economic opportunity. It "locks the vast majority of working women into workplaces which tolerate anti-female behavior."[90]

---

as bad acts by individuals, *see infra* pp. 1204–05, the privatization of Rabidue also raises the possibility that it is *she* who engaged in discrimination against *Henry*.

87. Thus, for example, consent is said to draw the line between sexual intercourse and rape, *see* Estrich, *supra* note 3, at 1121–32; willing acceptance is thought to distinguish a legal contract from one made under duress. *See* J. CALAMARI & J. PERILLO, THE LAW OF CONTRACTS § 9-2 (3d ed. 1987).

88. To say that the presence or absence of consent determines a judicial result is circular because consent has no meaning separate and apart from what courts say it means. In other words, it is incoherent to argue that consent can help to distinguish between the private and the public, since the act of defining consent itself requires such a distinction. Peller, *supra* note 5, at 1187–91 (critiquing concept of consent in rape law). On the social construction of consent and the indeterminacy of consent-based analysis, see also MacKinnon, *supra* note 75, at 648–55; Olsen, *Statutory Rape: A Feminist Critique of Rights Analysis*, 63 TEX. L. REV. 387, 406–07 (1984) (critiquing concept of autonomy that underlies consent construct).

89. Traditionally, of course, the workplace has been associated with and structured for men, with women's place being in the home. *See generally* Williams, *The Equality Crisis: Some Reflections on Culture, Courts, and Feminism*, 7 WOMEN'S RTS. L. REP. 175, 177–79 (1981–82), and sources cited therein (describing this "separate spheres" ideology). Those jobs open to women have been few in number, and have usually been accorded lower status and significantly lower pay; both of these problems persist today. *See, e.g.,* U.S. BUREAU OF THE CENSUS, STATISTICAL ABSTRACT OF THE UNITED STATES: 1987, at 403 (107th ed. 1986) (median earnings of full-time women workers in 1985 were $15,624, as compared to $24,195 for men).

90. *Rabidue*, 805 F.2d at 627 (Keith, J., dissenting). Having to decide between submitting to sexual harassment and quitting one's job hardly constitutes a choice. In fact, it is exactly this sort of tying of job benefits to sexual demands that the harassment cause of action was designed to prevent. *See* C. MACKINNON, *supra* note 1, at 40–47; *cf. Rabidue*, 805 F.2d at 626 (Keith, J., dissenting) ("In my view, Title VII's precise purpose is to prevent [vulgar] behavior and attitudes from poisoning

Thus, the court's reliance on choice is circular, for it assumes that choice is a pre-existing "thing" in the world that can simply be "identified" by a judge and thus ignores the fact that the definition of that term is itself a subject of controversy between groups. Given that conflict, the court's ruling necessarily reflects a political decision—a decision that the freedom of employers and male workers is more important than the security of women faced with unwelcome and demeaning treatment (or, if they leave work, unemployment). The voluntary entry argument merely reimports the individualism/communalism question into the doctrine at a different level. In relying on choice as a neutral indicator of when individual freedom threatens the collective interest in security, the court has merely restated the problem, not solved it.[91]

2. Tolerance and Consensus as Neutral Grounds for Decision: Minimizing the Choice Between Groups

Although at one level, as described above, the majority opinion in *Rabidue* seems to deny the plaintiff's group status altogether, at another level the court implicitly acknowledges that the case requires a choice between two groups, simultaneously minimizing its own role in making that choice. The act of choice is minimized through the court's reliance upon two seemingly neutral grounds for choosing between groups: the principle of tolerance for diversity and the concept of societal consensus.

a. Tolerance for Diversity: Protecting Minorities as a Neutral Policy

The *Rabidue* court grounded its conclusion about the reasonableness of the behavior at Osceola in the principle of tolerance for diversity, depicting its ruling as a prudent refusal to intrude into private sphere group relations on the side of a powerful group. In refusing to find the conduct engaged in at Osceola unreasonable, the court quoted with approval the following passage from the trial court's opinion:

[I]t cannot seriously be disputed that in some work environments,

---

the work environment of classes protected under the Act."). Since their subordinate position in an employment market that restricts their job opportunities and devalues their work is precisely what makes women vulnerable to harassment in the first place, C. MacKinnon, *supra* note 1, at 41–42, the view that Rabidue's position was voluntarily entered into can be seen as a virtual rejection of the very concept of sexual harassment itself. At a minimum, such a view certainly reflects value judgments about whether and under what circumstances women should be allowed to work in our society. In addition, the recent Supreme Court case of Meritor Sav. Bank v. Vinson, 477 U.S. 57, 68 (1986), which held that unwelcome conduct constitutes harassment even if "consented" to, raises questions about the continued vitality of such reasoning.

91. This discussion illustrates the general problem with using a standard derived from the private sphere as the benchmark for determining when intervention in that sphere is necessary. Unless the private sphere is itself egalitarian and nonhierarchical, a standard derived from it will do nothing but perpetuate inequalities. But, if the private world were so equal that it could generate a standard fair to all, there would be little need for governmental intervention anyway.

humor and language are rough hewn and vulgar. Sexual jokes, sexual conversations and girlie magazines may abound. Title VII was
not meant to—or can [sic]—change this. It must never be forgotten
that Title VII is the federal court mainstay in the struggle for equal
employment opportunity for the female workers of America. But it is
quite different to claim that Title VII was designed to bring about a
magical transformation in the social mores of American workers.[92]

The court thus portrayed the defendant's employees as members of a
prototypically American social class ("American workers") with their own
distinct "social mores" deserving of protection. In so doing, it presented its
decision to allow Henry's conduct as a refusal to enter the private sphere
in order to impose one group's views on another. By emphasizing Henry's
group identity, the court precluded a conclusion that he was a deviant
individual engaging in bad acts,[93] and transformed the case into one of
group conflict in which the court could properly refuse to interfere.

In addition, the court's association of Henry's conduct with the working
class (and its ignoring of his sex) conveyed the impression that its decision
worked to the benefit of a low-status, relatively powerless group. Had the
court presented the plaintiff's claim as challenging *men's* right to express
their "mores," it would of course have highlighted the fact that those mores were being expressed to the disadvantage of women.[94] In short, it
would have drawn attention to the plaintiff's membership in a less powerful group. In contrast, the majority's presentation of the case as one of
socioeconomic rather than sex discrimination (a vision that was supported
by its privatization of Vivienne Rabidue) made its decision seem to be a
defense of the weak against the powerful, a refusal to delegate state power
to private forces of domination. Thus, by redrawing the group lines in the
case, Judge Krupansky's opinion reinforced the impression that the
court's inaction served to preserve the pluralism of the private sphere, protecting a minority rather than enforcing one group's domination of the
other.[95]

Moreover, the majority's redrawing of those group lines obscured the

---

92. *Rabidue*, 805 F.2d at 620–21 (quoting Rabidue v. Osceola Ref. Co., 584 F. Supp. 419, 430
(E.D. Mich. 1984) (Newblatt, J.)).

93. Given that the court conceived of discrimination as bad acts by individuals, *see infra* pp.
1204–05, this depiction mediated against a finding that Henry had discriminated.

94. Of course, many members of the working class are women, but the majority's formulation
renders those people invisible, projecting the image of a homogeneous worker culture consisting only
of the views of working men.

95. On the other hand, one could also argue that, when the court's focus on Henry's economic
class is combined with its privatization of Rabidue, the resulting impression is not that the case represented a judicial refusal to take sides between two groups, but rather that it constituted a judicial act
of protection of a particular group from the hypersensitivities of a single individual. Treating the coworker's conduct as the expression of group mores, the judge elevated that conduct; simultaneously
treating the plaintiff's claim as an idiosyncratic personal reaction (rather than a group-based assertion
of right), he devalued it. Under either interpretation, however, the decision seems to be a defense of a
powerless group.

choices that underlay its ruling. That ruling clearly entailed political judgments, not only about the relative importance of elite and worker values (assuming for the moment that the court's attribution of views to these two groups was accurate),[96] but also—given that the only workers whom the opinion's "class" analysis favored anyway were males—about the relative validity of men's and women's perspectives as well. The majority's reliance upon the principle of tolerance for diversity re-poses the contradiction between individual and group rather than mediating it, and simultaneously obscures the court's choice between the two.

b. Consensus: The Private Sphere as Source of Neutral Grounds

Besides invoking the principle of tolerance of diversity to ground his reasonableness determination, Judge Krupansky also relied upon the notion of societal consensus to provide him with a definition of reasonableness. Like his tolerance of diversity argument, the judge's equating of reasonableness with consensus simultaneously acknowledged the group conflict in the case and minimized the court's role in choosing between the groups.[97]

Concluding that the conduct engaged in at Osceola, "although annoying, [was] not so startling as to have affected seriously the psyches of the plaintiff or other female employees,"[98] Judge Krupansky stated further:

> The sexually oriented poster displays had a de minimis effect on the plaintiff's work environment when considered in the context of a society that condones and publicly features and commercially exploits open displays of written and pictorial erotica at the newsstands, on prime-time television, at the cinema, and in other public places.[99]

In other words, Judge Krupansky seemed to view Rabidue's objections as unreasonable on the grounds that the prevailing consensus in American society is that conduct like Henry's is not offensive.[100] As with the voluntary entry argument, the question was treated as one of fact: either society accepts behavior such as Henry's or it does not. The judge treated societal consensus, like choice, as a pre-existing, neutral mediator, a mechanism for distinguishing between legitimate demands for protection of group interests and illegitimate demands for enforcement of group (or individual)

---

96. *See infra* pp. 1208–09.

97. The court's reliance on consensus also contributed to the privatization of the plaintiff, for it created the impression that Rabidue was just one of a few isolated individuals who did not follow the consensus. *See infra* p. 1204.

98. *Rabidue*, 805 F.2d at 622.

99. *Id.*

100. To give the court the benefit of the doubt, I have not given serious consideration to the other possible interpretation of this quote: that women simply could not be offended by any conduct to which they are frequently subjected.

prejudices. Consensus fails to fulfill that purpose, however, for both the selection and the application of that construct entail value choices.

i. *The Message of Consensus*

Consensus is a particularly powerful symbol of mediation, for it both acknowledges and minimizes difference, and thus both acknowledges and minimizes the coercive potential of a status quo standard. On the one hand, the concept of consensus would have no meaning if everyone were exactly the same. Conveying the idea of voluntarily arrived-at agreement reached after dialogue among diverging views, it implicitly acknowledges the existence of difference.

On the other hand, consensus also conveys the idea of fairly *widespread* agreement,[101] and thus simultaneously minimizes the existence of difference, marginalizing those who do not espouse the viewpoint that has been defined as the societal norm. (After all, if enough people are in sufficient agreement that a "consensus" is produced, then those who do not agree must certainly be few and unimportant, as well as aberrational and possibly even intransigent.)

The notion that the elevation of a particular viewpoint to the status of societal "consensus" results from the operation of individual will also obscures the possibility that the process by which something gets defined as the consensus view is itself characterized by group struggle and hierarchy. Reducing the judicial role in evaluating the reasonableness of conduct to little more than head-counting, the concept of consensus reinforces the message that a judge employing that standard acts objectively, rather than engaging in impermissible state intervention.

In summary, with its overtones of choice, universality, and neutrality, consensus privatizes and depoliticizes those who disagree. And, in so doing, it minimizes the coercive potential in a status quo standard, creating the impression that the government can ensure collective security without limiting individual autonomy, that it can allow all groups to exist yet still protect them from each other, that society can be tolerant of diversity without being destroyed by it. Upon closer examination, however, it can be seen that consensus cannot live up to the mediating message that it conveys.

ii. *Discrimination as Individual Bad Acts*

The court's choice of consensus to give content to the reasonableness standard reflects underlying political judgments about what discrimination itself—the very concept that "consensus" is supposed to be defin-

---

101. *See, e.g.,* THE RANDOM HOUSE DICTIONARY OF THE ENGLISH LANGUAGE 433 (2d ed. 1987) ("consensus . . . 1. majority of opinion . . . . 2. general agreement or concord; harmony").

ing—actually is, and about how discrimination should be eliminated. In equating "reasonableness" with societal consensus (that is, in defining discrimination as deviation from the status quo), the *Rabidue* court (like all courts using this definition of reasonableness) necessarily assumes that the status quo itself is egalitarian, pluralistic, and nondiscriminatory. This in turn shifts the focus to the individual, obscuring the possibility of structural inequalities and creating the impression that only a small number of deviant people fail to conform to society's pluralistic norms (that is, engage in discrimination). Thus, in focusing on whether the particular conduct engaged in by Douglas Henry was generally acceptable (that is, whether it violated social norms) rather than, for example, on whether it perpetuated conditions of inequality,[102] the *Rabidue* majority implicitly assumed that sexual discrimination is merely deviant behavior by individuals, rather than a structural problem inherent in American ideology and institutions. This narrow definition of discrimination favors liberty over security, diversity over conformity, the individual group to society at large (and the powerless groups society seeks to protect).[103]

iii. *The Indeterminacy of the Consensus Standard*

Even if the choice of consensus as a standard could be neutrally made, the construct itself would still not be susceptible of neutral application. Like choice and tolerance, consensus has no inherent meaning, and political decisions must therefore be made in applying it. If popular opinion polls indicate that a majority of Americans espouse a particular viewpoint, is that a consensus? What if only a plurality espouse it? If a majority of national législators vote a certain way, does that reveal a societal consensus? How close do two opinions have to be to be counted together as part of a consensus? In short, what constitutes consensus on a particular norm

---

102 This test is MacKinnon's, and she contrasts it with what she calls the "differences approach" of traditional equal protection jurisprudence, under which the question is whether the plaintiff is similarly situated to, yet treated differently than, members of other groups. C. MacKinnon, *supra* note 1, at 101-02. Like the differences approach, a focus on consensus fails to consider that the supposedly neutral criterion ("real" sex difference, consensus) might be exactly what sex discrimination law should be addressing—that is, might itself be discriminatory. *Id.* at 227 (focusing on sex difference "allow[s] the very factors the law against discrimination exists to prohibit to be the reason not to prohibit them").

103 *Cf.* Freeman, *supra* note 27. Freeman describes two different ways of approaching the concept of racial discrimination. The first, which he identifies with traditional Supreme Court jurisprudence, is the "perpetrator perspective," which "sees racial discrimination not as conditions, but as actions, or series of actions, inflicted on the victim by the perpetrator," *id.* at 1053, and thus views discrimination "not as a social phenomenon, but merely as the misguided conduct of particular actors." *Id.* at 1054. In contrast, the "victim perspective" sees discrimination as

those conditions of actual social existence as a member of a perpetual underclass. This perspective includes both the objective conditions of life—lack of jobs, lack of money, lack of housing—and the consciousness associated with those objective conditions—lack of choice and lack of human individuality in being forever perceived as a member of a group rather than as an individual.

Id. at 1052-53 (footnotes omitted). It recognizes that discrimination will not be eliminated "until the conditions associated with it have been eliminated." *Id.* at 1053.

is no more susceptible of a determinate answer than what constitutes coerced acceptance of a contract offer.[104] Thus, judicial decisions grounded on consensus necessarily contain judgments about what should be taken to be consensus and why—judgments that are generated by a particular political vision of the world.[105]

Consider, for example, the method Judge Krupansky used in *Rabidue* to identify a societal consensus. Emphasizing that such widespread forums of public expression as prime-time television contain the same types of "erotica" as those displayed at Osceola, he essentially equated societal consensus with prevailing social practices.[106] That is, he seemed to conclude that the mere prevalence of pornography suggests general acceptance of the image of women contained within that pornography. There are several problems, however, with equating prevailing media depictions with the viewpoint of most Americans. First, this approach ignores the vast power inequalities between men and women in general, and between antipornography activists and the eight-billion-dollar-a-year pornography industry in particular (not to mention the vastly larger marketing and entertainment industries that also sell their products through the objectification of women). Given the importance of economic and political power to the success of any reform movement, this disparity in resources raises serious questions about the conclusion that the existing practice of depicting women in a degrading and objectifying manner is accepted by the majority of the population. This assumption is especially unwarranted in the context of media depictions, for attempts to reform such practices raise strongly held First Amendment concerns in many people's minds. That is, there are surely many people who, for First Amendment reasons, believe that the publishing and individual consumption of pornography should not be restricted (and would certainly say the same about daytime television) but still find the image of women it projects personally offensive.

In summary, the *Rabidue* majority sees reasonableness as successfully mediating the contradiction between diversity and conformity on the grounds that it merely reflects the working-out of the tension between the

---

104. Or "consent" to intercourse. *See* MacKinnon, *supra* note 75; Peller, *supra* note 5, at 1187–91. For some examples of data courts have considered relevant in determining the content of a societal consensus, *see, e.g.*, Thompson v. Oklahoma, 108 S. Ct. 2687, 2691–97 (1988) (legislative enactments in 19 states, jury determinations, and views expressed by "respected professional organizations" and other Anglo-American nations support conclusion that execution of 15-year-old offender is "generally abhorrent to the conscience of the community"); Bowers v. Hardwick, 478 U.S. 186, 192–94 (1986) (fact that sodomy was criminal offense at common law and was outlawed by all 50 states until 1961 constitutes sufficient evidence upon which to base conclusion that right to engage in consensual homosexual conduct is not " 'deeply rooted in this Nation's history and tradition' ").

105. It is of some relevance here that *Rabidue* was a bench trial, not a jury trial. For example, it is at least arguable that a jury, composed as it usually is of non-elite citizens, would be a better identifier of societal consensus than a judge. However, the problematic nature of the concept of consensus itself, especially the assumption of homogeneity upon which it is based, suggests that many of the shortcomings described here would persist in a case tried by a jury.

106. *Rabidue*, 805 F.2d at 622.

two that has already occurred in the private sphere. But this assumes that the working-out itself was a "free" process, untainted by coercion. For, if the very process by which societal consensus (assuming for the moment that is a meaningful term) is reached is itself characterized by coercion, then to base a finding of reasonableness upon the resulting norm is again merely to delegate the coercive power of the state to certain sectors of the private sphere. Furthermore, there is no way to decide the question of whether the working-out process was coercive without addressing the question of what societal and individual interests justify restricting individuals' freedom. Thus, the entire formulation collapses again, reintroducing rather than resolving the contradiction between diversity and conformity.

3. Hidden Messages: Reinforcing the Status Quo

Despite the fact that its decision superficially seems to be a pluralistic one, refusing to support dominant groups and neutrally enforcing existing societal norms, the *Rabidue* court's opinion is not pluralistic at all. While Judge Krupansky suggests that he disapproves of the harassment of women in the workplace, he nevertheless subtly rejects women's views about such conduct and denies them the means to resist it. And, while the articulated basis for his ruling is deference to worker culture, the rhetoric of the opinion actually derogates that culture. Rather than being pluralistic, the court's opinion privileges one narrow, elite viewpoint and silences others.

a. Disavowing Sexism While Reinforcing Patriarchal Views of Women

Despite the fact that Judge Krupansky seems to condemn Henry's sexist behavior[107] and to endorse equal employment opportunity for all,[108] his discussion reflects very patriarchal attitudes. At the most obvious level, the judge's trivializing of the sexual comments and visual displays at Osceola[109] is consistent with the attitude of many men, who tend to view "milder" forms of harassment, such as suggestive looks, repeated requests for dates, and sexist jokes, as harmless social interactions to which only overly-sensitive women would object.[110] It completely ignores the fact that

---

107. *See infra* notes 119–22 and accompanying text.

108. For example, the judge quotes with approval the trial court's statement that "[i]t must never be forgotten that Title VII is the federal court mainstay in the struggle for equal employment opportunity for the female workers of America." *Rabidue*, 805 F.2d at 621.

109. *See supra* note 79 and accompanying text.

110. *See* Finley, *supra* note 80, at 60; *see also* A. ASTRACHAN, HOW MEN FEEL: THEIR RESPONSE TO WOMEN'S DEMANDS FOR EQUALITY AND POWER 88 (1988) (reporting that many men believe their sexual propositions are just jokes); Collins & Blodgett, *supra* note 81, at 81, 92–93 (noting that three times as many women as men think "eye[ing] the woman up and down" is harassment); Cohen, *What's Harassment? Ask the Woman*, Wash. Post, July 5, 1988, at A19, col. 1 (com-

persistent behavior of this "milder" sort is just as disturbing to many women as is overt quid pro quo harassment.[111]

The judge's assertion that a "proper assessment" of a hostile environment claim will include evidence on "the personality of the plaintiff"[112] suggests that he minimized the conduct involved in *Rabidue* because he shares a common male attitude that the victim of harassment is in some sense to blame for her mistreatment.[113] Many men believe, for example, that women can avoid harassment if they behave properly, and that the tactful registering of a complaint is usually an effective way of dealing with harassment when it occurs.[114] Women, in contrast, harbor no such illusions.[115]

These views about harassment are consistent, of course, with a general distrust of women that has been widely criticized by feminists. Thus, just as rapists' stories have been believed over their victims' on the grounds that women can be expected to "cry rape" in retaliation for the slightest rejection,[116] so too some men worry that female employees will use false harassment allegations as a "smoke screen" to hide poor job performance.[117] Judge Krupansky's focus on the character of the victim echoes these attitudes, belying the "neutrality" of his analysis. While seeming to criticize anti-female behavior, the judge actually expresses and reinforces the very attitudes that produce such behavior. It was these attitudes that led the dissent to criticize the majority for having taken the male viewpoint as the universal norm, and to conclude that "unless the outlook of the reasonable woman is adopted, the defendants as well as the courts are permitted to sustain ingrained notions of reasonable behavior fashioned by the offenders, in this case, men."[118]

---

menting on this tendency of men to trivialize certain forms of harassment).

111. *See* Collins & Blodgett, *supra* note 81, at 78, 80.

112. *Rabidue*, 805 F.2d at 620.

113. Collins and Blodgett, *supra* note 81, at 90.

114. *Id.* Thus, for example, I have heard a university official speaking to a group of women employees about how to prevent sexual harassment urge those women to help matters by making sure that they do not engage in "ambiguous" conduct. One wonders if he also met with male employees to tell them how *they* could help prevent harassment.

115. *Id.* (78% disagree with statement that woman who dresses and behaves properly will not be subjected to harassment). It is a testament to the strength of the male power of naming that even some women do, however, hold the woman responsible. *See, e.g., id.; see also* C. MACKINNON, *supra* note 1, at 47 (many victims of harassment feel guilty and somehow to blame for what happened).

116. *See generally* S. BROWNMILLER, AGAINST OUR WILL: MEN, WOMEN AND RAPE 348, 413 (1975); Estrich, *supra* note 3, at 1132 (describing and criticizing that view of rape victims).

117. Collins & Blodgett, *supra* note 81, at 92. Of course, I am not saying that this would never happen. But such occurrences would be so rare that their possibility simply does not justify failing to condemn the conduct, any more than the same possibility would justify rejecting any other type of discrimination complaint (or legal claim in general, for that matter).

118. *Rabidue*, 805 F.2d at 626 (Keith, J., dissenting) (citation omitted).

b. *Disavowing Elitism while Criticizing Workers as Sexist*

The majority opinion not only reinforces existing male attitudes towards women but also reinforces existing elite attitudes towards the working class. While Judge Krupansky explicitly presents his finding that Douglas Henry's behavior was reasonable as a principled defense of worker culture, a tolerant and pluralistic decision, he simultaneously derogates that culture, devaluing workers' norms while claiming to protect them. Thus, for example, his opinion conveys an attitude of profound disrespect for the working class when it endorses the trial court's description of "some work environments" as the arena of "rough-hewn" "humor."[119] This language reveals a patronizing distaste for such humor, strongly suggesting that it is much inferior to Judge Krupansky's own, more refined variety.[120] Furthermore, as Judge Keith notes in dissent, there is a strong classist dimension to the majority's argument: "[A] disturbing implication of considering defendants' backgrounds [in deciding such cases] is the notion that workplaces with the least sophisticated employees are the most prone to anti-female environments."[121] The majority's implicit message is: "They might be sexist—unlike we civilized people—but boys will be boys!" Thus, Judge Krupansky's effort to be tolerant of workers nevertheless conveys a disparaging attitude towards those not of his own class.[122]

In short, while seeming to follow the neutral principle of tolerance for diversity, the court's opinion in fact reinforces an ideology that disempowers and devalues the very workers of whom it claims to be tolerant. It conveys a specific viewpoint, one that accepts a class hierarchy in which workers are devalued, while simultaneously seeming not to convey any viewpoint at all.

To summarize, by seeming to condemn the harasser's sexist conduct and views at the same time that it both protects and reproduces them, the opinion seems sympathetic to women while actually perpetuating sexist

---

119. *Id.* at 620 (quoting *Rabidue*, 584 F. Supp. at 430 (Newblatt, J.)).

120. The judge also takes great pains to disassociate himself from the conduct he is protecting. Drawing a clear distinction between his positive characterization of Henry's class identity and interests and his own personal condemnation of Henry's viewpoint and conduct, the judge paints a negative picture of the harasser, calling him an "extremely vulgar and crude individual who customarily made obscene comments about women," *id.* at 615, and whose "offensive personality traits" the management had "been unsuccessful in curbing." *Id.*

Of course, this language does not convey a particularly strong indictment of Henry's behavior, reading more like fatherly disapproval of a somewhat frisky and bothersome puppy than like moral condemnation of discriminatory conduct. (The image conveyed also somewhat contradicts the other picture of Henry as not a deviant individual but rather a typical American worker.) Nevertheless, it could hardly be seen as admiring or laudatory treatment. Thus, it reinforces the impression that "worker culture" is not a particularly prestigious or admirable set of beliefs.

121. *Id.* at 627 (Keith, J., dissenting). That attitude is also conveyed in a remark that Henry's supervisor made to him, exhorting him to learn to become more of "an executive type person." *Id.* at 624 (Keith, J., dissenting).

122. Somewhat paradoxically, the judge's disdain might, in turn, reinforce the apparent neutrality of his decision, for it conveys the impression that, because he does not personally endorse Henry's conduct, he was clearly not implementing his own moral vision in reaching his decision.

attitudes and reducing women's power in the workplace.[123] Similarly, by seeming to defend the social class with which the harasser is identified while subtly derogating that class, the majority opinion seems to defend workers while actually reinforcing the existing class hierarchy that devalues and subordinates them.

Moreover, by relying on apparently objective concepts such as choice, consensus, and tolerance for diversity (as well as by disassociating his personal opinions from those of the class and gender groups involved in the case), Judge Krupansky conveys the distinct impression (and might even have believed himself) that he has been able to make the choice between diversity and conformity without resorting to personal political judgments. Transforming the case from one raising questions of gender roles and social hierarchy to one about pluralistic culture and societal consensus, the judge protects male power by treating it as worker powerlessness and reinforces class hierarchy by presenting it as tolerance for diversity. Relying on apparently neutral constructs to resolve the group conflict in the case, the majority's opinion obscures the fact that its ruling actually enforces (and reinforces) a particular, identifiable perspective—that of upperclass men.[124]

C. A Brief Digression on the Reasonable Person Symbol

The discussion thus far has described the liberal vision of reasonableness as a mediating construct and has demonstrated that, at least in the sexual harassment context, that vision is mistaken: the standard fails to mediate between diversity and conformity. This Section presents a brief symbolic analysis of the image often used in negligence literature to give concrete meaning to the idea of reasonableness: "the man who takes the magazines at home and in the evening pushes the lawn mower in his shirt sleeves."[125] This image is in many senses itself a mediating figure, and,

---

123. By making harassment unchallengeable, the court's decision significantly reduces women's power to control the conditions under which they work.

124. Interestingly, because his attempt not to impose an upperclass viewpoint on workers allows their sexist behavior to continue, the judge implicitly presents male workers' interests as contrary to those of female workers. Just as class-focused and sex-focused reform movements are often presented as being in conflict with each other in other contexts (economically, for example, by claims that women's entry into the workplace reduces employment opportunities for men; and theoretically, by arguments about whether class oppression or sex oppression is primary), so here they are also made to seem in conflict with each other, by a legal opinion that treats justice for women as inconsistent with the rights of the working class.

125. See G. CALABRESI, supra note 3, at 23 n.94 (citing Hall v. Brooklands Auto Racing Club, [1933] 1 K.B. 205, 224) (Greer, L.J., quoting unnamed "American author"). For brevity, I will refer to this image as the "man in his shirtsleeves." The English version is "the man on the Clapham omnibus," id. at 23; I have been told that Clapham is a small town, which would suggest that the English symbol conveys the idea of the average citizen, as does the American version. See infra notes 132-33 and accompanying text.

therefore, the messages that it conveys reinforce the reading of *Rabidue* given above.[126]

The symbol of "the man in his shirtsleeves" conveys a message of mediation in two ways. First, it presents the reasonable person standard as an inclusive and tolerant concept, which allows societal diversity without violating societal norms. Second, it (paradoxically) presents that standard as a universal one, expressing and enforcing general norms without threatening diversity. In short, each image conveyed by the symbol simultaneously emphasizes one side of the diversity/conformity dyad while seeming not to exclude the other.

1. *Reasonableness as Tolerance*

Locating the reasonable person in the middle of various continuums, the symbol creates the impression that the role of the objective standard is to mediate between opposing positions. That mediation seems simultaneously to *allow* and to *overcome* the existence of those positions.

In socioeconomic terms, the reasonable person depicted in this image is a member of neither the elite nor the underclass. The T-shirted, grass-smattered, sweaty condition of a man[127] mowing his lawn is not usually associated with a life of wealth and leisure. Nor, on the other hand, does the average service industry worker or welfare mother own a home with a lawn, or have an office at which to receive magazines (receiving them at home instead). The symbol's identification with the middle American thus conveys the idea of mediation and compromise between these two extremes.

A similar message is produced by its gender content. While the central figure of the image is male, it nevertheless carries both masculine and feminine associations. Located at home, in the domestic sphere usually associated with women, the figure is also situated outdoors, in the prototypically male realm of car repairs, sports, and barbecues. The action he is engaged in—lawnmowing—also conveys mixed messages that suggest a mediating role. On the one hand, physical labor is usually associated with male virility. On the other hand, lawnmowing itself is one of those baneful tasks often required (so the ideology goes) of "henpecked" husbands by their wives, and thus could be seen as evidence of emasculation.[128] In short, associating the "man in his shirtsleeves" with the "fe-

---

126. I should emphasize that the analysis presented in this Section is not intended to introduce a detailed examination of the operation of the reasonableness test in negligence law. Instead, it is offered as a speculative reading, the purpose of which is to suggest that the problems that plague the "objective" standard in the sexual harassment context are not unique to that setting, but rather have surfaced in the negligence context as well.

127. It is clearly a male image, in more than just pronouns. *See infra* notes 132-33 and accompanying text.

128. Of course, given that husbands' performance of chores for their wives is often seen as a trivial concession to women in their own sphere, one could argue that the lawnmowing suggests com-

male" world, the symbol feminizes him; associating him with the "male" world, it preserves his masculinity intact. It presents him as a compromise between the effeminized man (or femaleness) and the purely masculine one (or maleness), as a mediator between extremes.

This locating of the "man in his shirtsleeves" at a midpoint between extremes suggests mediation at a more general level as well. By not fully identifying the reasonable person with the high-status term on each continuum (the upper classes, "male" men), the symbol creates the impression that the reasonableness standard is tolerant, inclusive, and flexible, rather than rigidly requiring perfection. In short, it makes the standard seem to allow diversity and facilitate freedom. On the other hand, by not associating the reasonable person with the bottom of each hierarchy either, the symbol simultaneously suggests that the "objective" standard imposes limits on individual behavior, thus fulfilling the societal need for security and coerced conformity as well.

Similarly, the scholarly literature routinely describes the prototypical reasonable person as neither perfect nor wildly careless: While "always up to standard,"[129] he is nevertheless " 'not necessarily a supercautious individual devoid of human frailties' "[130] but rather has "those human shortcomings and weaknesses which the community will tolerate on the occasion."[131] Such imagery constructs the "objective" standard as a mediator of the contradiction between freedom and security, as able to accommodate our desire for careful behavior without unduly coercing human beings who are liable to lapses of care.

2. Reasonableness as Consensus

The "man in his shirtsleeves" symbol depicts the reasonable person standard not only as mediating among diverse positions but also as a neutral and impartial reflection of societal norms. By thus symbolizing societal consensus, the image obscures the existence of diversity and conflict among groups, and thereby emphasizes the security (conformity) side of the liberty/security contradiction.

Although the symbol's message of transcending oppositions conveys the idea of diversity, its message of consensus (paradoxically) conveys the idea of homogeneity. Through the particularized, concrete image that it projects, the symbol obscures the existence of those groups that do not fit that image. By ignoring the existence of people who have no lawn to mow and cannot read or afford to buy magazines—as well as the existence of those who hire someone else to mow the lawn for them—this image pro-

---

passion (and/or appeasement) rather more than emasculation. Either way, however, the image would still be a mixed one.

129. W. KEETON, D. DOBBS, R. KEETON & D. OWEN, *supra* note 2, § 32, at 175.
130. *Id.* § 32, at 175 n.10 (citation omitted).
131. *Id.* § 32, at 175.

motes the illusion that we are all the same, rendering invisible those who differ from the "average" person it creates. Similarly, by gendering its central figure, the symbol also excludes those whose role has never been defined in terms of lawn-mowing and magazine-reading, but rather in terms of cooking, nurturing, and cleaning.[132] In this way, it conceals the possibility that the reasonable person standard might actually exclude some groups' viewpoints, and thus reinforces the message that those who deviate from the norm are just that: deviants.[133]

Thus, this symbol of the reasonable person explicitly sets up middle-class, male values as the source of the "objective" standard, defining "reasonableness" as what a member of that particular group might think. Simultaneously, however, it treats those values as representative of American society, thus rendering other cultural viewpoints invisible. In this way, the symbol conveys the message that only a few discrete individuals are excluded through its use, not entire groups. And, just as Judge Krupansky's privatization of Vivienne Rabidue and reliance on consensus reflect and reinforce the assumption that we can neutrally overcome the contradiction between diversity and conformity, so the "man in his shirt-sleeves" symbol suggests that it is possible to protect all without harming any.

3. Hidden Messages Again

However, like the majority opinion in *Rabidue*, the symbol of the reasonable person simultaneously undercuts its explicit messages, subtly reinforcing the very hierarchies it purports to reject. Thus, while the symbol seems to invoke average, middle-class norms, and norms that establish a compromise between (or combination of) male and female perspectives, it does so by relying upon class and gender hierarchies that derogate those very same norms. For example, the "man in his shirtsleeves" image conveys the idea of tolerance for diversity (that is, allowing fallibility) precisely because the middle-class American depicted by the symbol is traditionally thought to be of lower status than the upper-class American. At the same time, it simultaneously conveys the idea of requiring some con-

---

132. *See* Bender, *A Lawyer's Primer on Feminist Theory and Tort*, 38 J. LEGAL EDUC. 3, 22-23 (1988); Finley, *supra* note 80, at 57-59.

133. This message that those who fail to conform to the societal standard are a few isolated and deviant individuals arises in many scholarly treatments of the reasonable person standard as well. Thus, such people are called "moral defectives," Seavey, *supra* note 4, at 11-12, and their views and conduct are referred to as "individual peculiarities," Reynolds, *supra* note 4, at 425 (quoting O. HOLMES, THE COMMON LAW 108 (1881)), and "personal idiosyncracies," G. CALABRESI, *supra* note 3, at 21. The distinct impression that one gets in reading the literature is that those who fail to comply with a reasonableness standard are aberrational, eccentric, undisciplined, perhaps even selfish. Only Calabresi acknowledges (sometimes) that some failures to conform can be seen as indicative of cultural/normative differences, rather than moral weakness. *Id.* at 28-31 ("Equality, therefore, is based on the capacity of the newly arrived group to learn to behave like the previously dominant group.").

formity (that is, not allowing *total* freedom to be fallible) because that same middle-class American is nevertheless of higher status than the manual laborer.[134] (Thus, "fallibility" is to "perfection" what "lower class" is to "upper class;" and placement between upper and lower classes represents mediation between the extremes of tolerating all diversity and demanding complete conformity.) Only if one accepts the hierarchical relationship among these three classes (workers, middle classes, and upper classes) does one "get" the messages implicit in the symbol.

Similarly, the mixed gender messages associated with the symbol's lawnmowing image work to reinforce the impression that the reasonableness standard assures both freedom (diversity) and security (conformity), precisely because those messages implicitly invoke, and rely upon, the traditional view of the domestic sphere (and women) as less valued than the public sphere (and men), and of manual labor as valued less than nonphysical work. It is only through understanding those hierarchies that one can understand the mediating message conveyed by the gender imagery of the symbol.[135]

In short, while at one level the "man in his shirtsleeves" symbol presents the reasonable person standard as tolerant of societal diversity, at another level it treats that standard as enforcing the consensus of a homogeneous, conflict-free society. Moreover, while the imagery of the symbol suggests that it supports the viewpoint of the average citizen, it simultaneously devalues that viewpoint, validating (and reinforcing) the status (and views) of the elite. Like Judge Krupansky's opinion in *Rabidue*, which undercuts the working class while seeming to support it (and decries sexism while perpetuating it), the symbol is a mystification, subtly elevating men, the public domain, and the upper class.

III. PLURALISM AND THE APPEAL OF REASONABLENESS

This Part argues that the *Rabidue* majority's belief in the reasonable person standard derives, at least in part, from certain pluralist assumptions that underlie its analysis. Moreover, to the extent that the dissent in the case also relied upon the notion of reasonableness, its analysis seems to

---

134. Placing its central figure at a midpoint between the high status term (the upper class) and the low status term (the lower class), the symbol conveys the message that the reasonable person standard requires middle-level conduct from individuals—something between absolute perfection (nonharmful conduct) and utter incompetence (extremely harmful or risky conduct). This makes it seem like a tolerant, flexible standard (and therefore one that allows freedom of conduct), but at the same time like a standard that imposes certain requirements on the citizenry (and therefore demands conformity in the interest of security). Thus, the upperclass-lowerclass dichotomy echoes the conformity-diversity dichotomy, making mediation between the extremes represented by the latter seem possible.

135. Of course, by associating diversity with the lower classes and conformity with the upper classes, the symbol also establishes a hierarchy between diversity and conformity. While I do not believe that hierarchy obtains throughout liberal legal ideology, it makes sense to find it here, in the representation of a legal standard that is thought to impose general societal norms on the individual.

depend upon a comparable belief in pluralist ideology. After briefly describing the dissenting opinion, it will be possible to compare the pluralist assumptions underlying both its and the majority's reasonableness analysis.

A. *The Dissenting Opinion's Reasonable Woman Standard*

Delivering a trenchant critique of the majority opinion, Judge Keith argued in dissent that the court's supposedly neutral analysis actually contained a hidden male perspective. Apparently attributing that problem to the use of the reasonable person test, he concluded that a reasonable woman standard should have been used instead. Because he justified the use of such a standard in terms of the concrete effect of sexual harassment on women, Judge Keith's position illustrates the value of a jurisprudence that directly addresses the intergroup conflicts raised by legal cases. Because of the reasonableness language in which he articulated his position, however, the judge's opinion also illustrates the tenacity of the idea that courts should not engage in explicitly political decision-making.

1. *The Reasonable Woman Standard as a Rejection of the Search for Neutrality*

To Judge Keith, *Rabidue* clearly represented a conflict between the sexes over how they should relate in the workplace, and the Osceola Refining Company was clearly the site of persistent and significant degradation of women by men.[136] Moreover, as far as the dissenter was concerned, all three of the means that Judge Krupansky used to give content to the reasonable person standard were unacceptable. First, the tolerance for diversity argument did not work because the defendant's class was simply irrelevant.[137] Furthermore, the court was wrong to suggest "that such work environments somehow have an innate right to perpetuation."[138] Second, the court's reliance upon plaintiff's "choice" to enter the workplace suggested "that a woman assumes the risk of working in an abusive, anti-female environment."[139] Third, the "society" whose views the majority claimed to be enforcing "must primarily refer to the unenlightened." Wrote Judge Keith, "I hardly believe reasonable women con-

---

136. Judge Keith repeatedly labeled behavior of the type that occurred at Osceola in gender terms—"anti-female obscenity," Rabidue v. Osceola Ref. Co., 805 F.2d 611, 624 (6th Cir. 1986) (Keith, J., dissenting), *cert. denied*, 481 U.S. 1041 (1987), "misogynous language," *id.* at 625, "primitive views of working women," *id.*—and concluded that Rabidue had received "sex-based disparate treatment," *id.*

137. *Id.* at 627.

138. *Id.* at 626.

139. *Id.*

done the pervasive degradation and exploitation of female sexuality perpetuated in American culture."[140]

The dissenter's analysis implicitly rejects the role of courts as neutral
arbiters of disputes. Challenging the idea of a homogeneous consensus in
society, Judge Keith's opinion openly acknowledges that what constitutes
appropriate behavior toward the opposite sex is a subject of dispute between women and men. Moreover, arguing that the reasonableness standard should be based on the viewpoint of the oppressed group, rather than
on that of those doing the oppressing, he implicitly recognizes as well that
the consensus view itself (to the extent that one exists) might simply be
wrong.[141] This recognition implicitly criticizes the idea that discrimination
should or can be defined in terms of an external referent derived from the
private sphere. If societal views about concepts like discrimination, reasonableness, etc., are the product of a discriminatory status quo, then the
private sphere cannot provide a neutral, external definition of those concepts to guide judicial decisions. Judge Keith thus quite explicitly bases
his conclusion about *Rabidue* on a value judgment: "As I believe no woman should be subjected to an environment where her sexual dignity and
reasonable sensibilities are visually, verbally or physically assaulted as a
matter of prevailing male prerogative, I dissent."[142]

2. The Reasonable Woman Standard as a Neutral Mediator

As the discussion above indicates, at one level Judge Keith's opinion
can be read as rejecting the idea that the private sphere can provide a
neutral basis for the definition of discrimination and as offering instead an
explicitly political argument for choosing Rabidue's security over Henry's
freedom. However, his depiction of the reasonable woman standard as itself a neutral construct seems to belie that position. In that respect, Judge
Keith's formulation, like Judge Krupansky's, engages in a futile effort to
overcome the contradiction between diversity and conformity.

In addition to using the traditional "reasonableness" terminology to describe his test, Judge Keith invokes the idea of neutrality in his statement

---

140. *Id.* at 627.
141. "[T]he relevant inquiry at hand is what the reasonable woman would find offensive, not
society, which at one point also condoned slavery." *Id.* Actually, Judge Keith does not make his
position on the question of consensus completely clear. Different statements in his opinion provide
support for each of the following positions: (a) the majority wrongly identified the societal consensus,
which actually favors women (" '[s]ociety' in this scenario must primarily refer to the unenlightened,"
id.); (b) the existing consensus does favor men, but it is wrong ("pervasive societal approval" of
"degradation and exploitation of female sexuality," *id.*); (c) the majority wrongly identified the consensus because there is no consensus; men and women disagree on what constitutes discrimination
("That some men would condone . . . such behavior is not surprising. However, the relevant inquiry
. . . is what the reasonable woman would find offensive, not society . . . ." *Id.*). Either of the last
two positions would be consistent with his advocacy of a reasonable woman standard. The first position, in contrast, would suggest that the reasonable person standard, if properly applied, is perfectly
adequate.
142. *Id.* at 626–27.

that the reasonable woman standard "simultaneously allows courts to consider salient sociological differences as well as shield employers from the neurotic complainant."[143] In short, he seems to believe that the doctrinal construct itself will determine whether a particular woman's complaint is legitimate.[144] Just as the majority conceives of the reasonable person test as a vehicle for identifying where an individual group's right to freedom ends and society's interest in the security of other groups begins, so the dissenter views the reasonable woman test as distinguishing between regulable "neurotic" women and protected "reasonable" women. And just as the majority uses consensus as the neutral mediator between diversity and conformity, so the dissent uses consensus among women as a similar mediator.

This position is subject to a critique similar to that directed at the majority's reasonable person test: Both in deciding to use the reasonable woman standard to begin with[145] and in identifying the consensus view among women that will give it content,[146] a court must necessarily make choices between freedom and security, the individual (or individual group) and the collectivity. The reasonable woman construct itself does not constrain judges' discretion in making these choices.[147] Thus, Judge Keith's

---

143. *Id.* at 626.

144. Of course, it is possible that Judge Keith did not, in fact, believe in the determinacy and neutrality of the reasonable woman construct, but rather packaged his analysis in the discourse of reasonableness because that is the language traditionally used in title VII sexual harassment actions. Neither reformers nor judges can avoid making strategic decisions about how to present their arguments, and the wisdom of retaining traditional terms is hotly disputed. *See infra* notes 195–199 and accompanying text. By criticizing Judge Keith's approach, I do not mean to ignore or minimize the complex and difficult decisions that may have motivated it.

145. A ruling dictating that male/female interactions in the workplace be viewed from the woman's point of view is not merely a pluralistic decision giving women an equal right to be heard and thereby allowing both groups' viewpoints to be accommodated. Because male and female views of acceptable workplace behavior are often diametrically opposed, to enforce those of women is inevitably to reject and/or threaten those of many men. It is an empowering of women and a disempowering of men.

146. For example, imagine a title VII action charging that a lawyer's practice of calling his secretary by her first name while expecting her to call him by his last name constitutes sexual harassment. The secretary alleges that this treatment is degrading and offensive, for it implies that she is inferior to her employer. Furthermore, it has overtones of personal possession and familiarity that stem from a long history of male treatment of women in general, and of secretaries in particular, as sexual property, and it reflects a demeaning view of women as child-like and dependent. Is the plaintiff secretary a reasonable woman, or is she overreacting to what is merely a traditional and nongendered office hierarchy (in which male mailroom workers, for example, are also called by their first names)? Is she a neurotic individual whose complaint should be rejected or a crusader for equal rights for her sex? Should the viewpoint of most secretaries affect the outcome? Of women in general? Should the fact that few secretaries have publicly objected to such practices be relevant?

147. Just as Judge Krupansky concluded that the Osceola workplace is not offensive to the reasonable person, so another judge might easily conclude that the name-use practice described *supra* note 146 is not offensive to the reasonable woman. My point is not that such a decision would be incorrect, although I think it would be, but rather that it would not have been dictated by the doctrinal construct. In fact, the singular failure of the reasonable person standard, itself introduced as a nonsexist alternative to the reasonable man test, to protect women's interests is a striking example of doctrine's inability to constrain judicial decision-making. On the benefits of "reasonable woman" over "reasonable person," however, see *infra* note 153 and accompanying text.

apparent conclusion that substituting his standard for the reasonable person test would assure fairer results for women seems unjustified.[148]

Moreover, in treating the resolution of sexual harassment cases as a matter of neutral decision-making, Judge Keith's approach obscures the fact that his standard, like Judge Krupansky's (or any other standard, for that matter), necessarily requires a court to make substantive judgments about what kind of conduct should be allowed in the workplace. Encouraging a formalistic reliance on doctrine, his reasonable woman test obscures the fact that doctrinal constructs like consensus are merely vehicles for articulating value choices, not determinants of results.

In short, the discourse of reasonableness can create a false sense of security, lulling one into believing that a result is inherently fair regardless of its specific content, and reinforcing the idea that legal analysis can be neutral and objective. For example, to the extent that a reasonable woman standard fails to draw the court's attention to issues of race and class, it may perpetuate existing inequities based on those factors in the same way that the reasonable person standard does when it fails to consider women's point of view.[149]

Of course, one might argue that the result of this critique is an infinite regress, for a "reasonable black woman" standard would still ignore differences of class, a "reasonable lower class black woman" standard would ignore differences of sexual orientation, etc. But that both misses the point and is the point. As one analysis of the use of the reasonableness test in criminal law concluded, "It is the reasonableness part of the standard that is faulty, not merely the sex or class of the mythical person. . . . By emphasizing individual responsibility in the abstract form, the reasonable man standard . . . ignores the social reality of the individual. . . ."[150] As a result, any unequal social conditions that affect an individual's situation are both perpetuated and condoned by such a standard.[151] In short, the goal of employing an "objective" test that is unaffected by the judge's (or any other) world-view and that is sufficiently general to apply to all people is simply an illusory one.[152]

---

148. In fact, Judge Keith's unfortunate choice of terms in which to articulate the role of his standard—that is, his comment that it allows courts to distinguish between "reasonable" and "neurotic" women—suggests that even in his own hands that standard might not always produce desirable results, for women's efforts to articulate their views and object to their disempowerment have often been dismissed as mere neurotic worrying.

149. As Lucinda Finley points out, because the reasonable woman standard merely replaces one stereotype with another, it would still be unfair to any woman who failed to conform to traditionally female standards of conduct, as would be the reasonable person standard to untraditional men. Finley, *supra* note 80, at 63–64. In addition, "substituting a reasonable woman standard to judge the conduct of women, but not going further to question the inclusiveness of the norms informing the reasonable person standard, implies that women's experiences and reactions are something for women only, rather than normal human responses." *Id.* at 64.

150. Donovan & Wildman, *supra* note 3, at 437, 465.

151. *See id.* at 466.

152. Therefore, as I discuss briefly below, *infra* note 201 and accompanying text, it is important

So will you never be satisfied? a reader might ask at this point. Surely the reasonable woman standard is a step in the right direction, for it draws attention to the hidden bias in the reasonable person test and directs the decision-maker to consider the viewpoint of the woman, thus allowing the oppressed to define their own oppression (or at least endorsing the idea that they should be allowed to do so). Moreover, Judge Keith employs a very political tone, justifying his resolution in terms of the concrete effect that it would have on people's daily lives. What more, one might ask, could he have done?

Such objections are not without merit; Judge Keith's formulation is certainly a distinct improvement over the traditional one.[153] However, as I will discuss in the next Section, I am still troubled by the messages that his formulation conveys, and by the assumptions that underlie it.

B. *Pluralism and the Problem of Conflicting Liberties*

How, one might ask, did Judge Keith apparently fall into the same traps that he recognized in the majority opinion? How did he find it so easy to accept (and endorse) Vivienne Rabidue's characterization of the Osceola environment and yet simultaneously believe that he was acting neutrally? Why did he fail to address the impact his ruling might have on the sense of dignity and validity that the men at Osceola might feel? In short, why did he seem not to be concerned with the fact that he was ruling not only for women but against men—that he was making a political choice between groups? The answer, I believe, lies in his implicit acceptance of the ideology of pluralism, in both its descriptive and its normative manifestations. It is to the role of that ideology, and its implications for antidiscrimination law, that I now turn.

1. *Descriptive Pluralism*

Both the majority and dissenting opinions in *Rabidue* reveal a belief, varying considerably in strength between the two opinions, that current American society is pluralistic and egalitarian. Judge Krupansky's belief in a broadly pluralistic society is easy to see; Judge Keith's pluralistic assumptions are narrower and more subtle.

As the above discussion of *Rabidue* illustrates, Judge Krupansky's

---

that judges engage in an analysis that is self-consciously aware both of their own perspectives and of the concrete circumstances and varying viewpoints involved in any dispute. While no judge will be able to completely escape his or her own cultural blinders, such an effort would still be a vast improvement over a purportedly neutral reasonableness analysis that unquestioningly (and often unknowingly) replicates the views of a powerful elite.

153. A facially neutral standard simply makes it too easy for courts to overlook women's viewpoint, creating the false impression that that viewpoint is already subsumed within the general test. In that sense, the switch from reasonable man to reasonable person might have been ill-advised to begin with. *See* Bender, *supra* note 132, at 23.

presentation of his opinion as neutral and apolitical is only convincing if one accepts a pluralistic vision of the world. Equating reasonableness with the status quo, the majority opinion necessarily assumes that American society is not fundamentally hierarchical, and that what gets called the societal consensus represents a truly general view, rather than the viewpoint of a single, powerful group. Relying upon the private sphere for the normative content of his decision, Judge Krupansky must assume that sphere is not itself tainted by illegitimate inequality.[154] Only by believing in the descriptive accuracy of pluralist ideology can he believe in his ability to reach neutral decisions through use of the reasonable person construct.

In contrast, Judge Keith clearly does not conceive of society as a whole as pluralistic, rejecting the reasonable person standard as merely governmental enforcement of the male point of view.[155] However, his reliance upon a reasonable woman test suggests that, at least among women, he assumes equal ability to contribute to the formation of a consensus, ignoring differences of power due to class, race, etc.[156] Indeed, only by ascribing to this partial descriptive pluralism could Judge Keith logically conclude, as he apparently does,[157] that a reasonable woman test would allow courts to reach nonpolitical decisions unaffected by either the judges' own values or existing power differences among women.[158]

2. Normative Pluralism

The judges' shared belief that the reasonableness test can provide an apolitical ground for decision—as well as their apparent conviction that judges should strive for such apolitical grounds—stems also from their acceptance of pluralism as a normative ideal. To reiterate, pluralism basically means diversity, having a culture in which many different groups can peacefully coexist. Implicit in this idea, however, is the need to prohibit conduct that so harms other groups as to destroy pluralism itself—that is, a commitment to protecting minorities. In short, the ideology of pluralism defines group freedom as the freedom to act self-interestedly,

---

154. Cf. Crenshaw, supra note 37, at 1334 (to believe that color-blind policies can ensure "a racially equitable society, one would have to assume . . . that such a racially equitable society already exists"). In contrast, if one views society as an arena of hierarchy and struggle, then the judge's supposedly neutral analysis will seem instead to be value-laden and perspective bound.

155. See supra note 118 and accompanying text.

156. See supra note 149 accompanying text.

157. Although it is possible, as I noted supra note 144, that Judge Keith's reasonable woman standard was merely strategic packaging of his substantive result, in this discussion I will assume that he meant what he said in his opinion.

158. Judge Keith's position also assumes that women exist in a hermetically sealed environment unaffected by male power. That is, his advocacy of a reasonable woman standard ignores the extent to which women's views are themselves constructed by patriarchy. The extent to which "false consciousness" can or should be identified as such is, of course, a huge and difficult issue in feminist thought, but further discussion of it is beyond the scope of this essay.

but only as long as such conduct does not unduly harm other groups (and, implicitly, the societal interest in pluralism).[159] Thus, it implies that it is possible to be tolerant of group diversity and still prohibit discrimination.[160]

Applying this concept to the *Rabidue* case, it can be seen that the majority's emphasis on the need to be tolerant of worker culture and to protect workers against the elite's efforts to impose its own values invokes the ideal of a pluralistic society in which all groups can coexist. Similarly, the dissenter's failure to address the possibility that his desired ruling would have harmed the men at Osceola suggests that he ascribes to the view that women can be accommodated without injuring men—that is, that pluralism is a viable ideal.

This Section argues that the notion that pluralism is an unproblematic goal is logically incoherent and disconsonant with the reality of irresolvable conflicts between groups. As such, that notion discourages courts from recognizing the existence of such conflicts and encourages them to articulate their decisions in the mystifying discourse of neutrality.

a. *Conflicting Liberties*

It is logically incoherent to say that a group is free to pursue its own interest and express its own norms unless that conduct harms other groups. This is so because *all* acts by any one group (or individual) are inevitably harmful to others. One side's freedom can always be seen as the other side's loss of security,[161] one side's equal treatment can seem like the other's unequal treatment, one group's pursuit of its own interest can always be called intolerance of any other group that is affected by that pursuit. In the *Rabidue* situation, for example, either side's conduct can be characterized as discrimination, and, as a result, a ruling either way could be called either governmental regulation *of* discrimination or government engaging *in* discrimination.

Let me expand to illustrate. Assuming for the moment that sexism actually is an important norm among American (male) workers—an important source of their identity and component of their world-view—Douglas Henry's conduct can be seen as an exercise of his group's freedom to fol-

---

159. Individual freedom was similarly defined in classical liberal legal and political ideology. *See* Singer, *supra* note 14; *supra* text accompanying note 14.

160. Thus, the ideal of pluralism assumes an ever-expanding political/legal pie; minorities can get more "rights" without whites losing theirs. This assumption is what animates the "equal opportunity" model's view that "special" treatment of minorities (and women) is both unnecessary and illegitimate. It also at least partially accounts for the ambivalence with which Congress and the courts have often approached the alternative, "equal results" theory of discrimination; to the extent that such a theory seems to require the progress of minorities to be at the expense of whites, courts have been reluctant to endorse it. *See, e.g.*, Crenshaw, *supra* note 37, at 1342 n.52 (describing history of courts' treatment of tension between 1964 Civil Rights Act's goals of eliminating effects of unlawful discrimination and protecting "bona fide" seniority systems).

161. *See generally* Singer, *supra* note 14, at 1050 (discussing this conflict-of-liberties problem).

low its own norms. One way to assess that freedom would be to argue that, since it also harmed Vivienne Rabidue, limiting her freedom to work and subjecting her to public humiliation, it had to be constrained. Under this analysis, Henry's conduct constituted discrimination and can be prohibited by the state.

It makes just as much *logical* sense, however, to say that Rabidue's claim is an attempt to exercise *her* freedom to engage in remunerative employment under conditions she finds acceptable, and that the exercise of her right to freedom harmed Douglas Henry. Under this view, Rabidue's insistence that Henry refrain from displaying pornography would have prevented him from following a fundamental tenet of his group's philosophy and undermined the sense of identity, of maleness, that the act of displaying pornography affirms.[162] Therefore, the argument would go, it was actually Rabidue who tried to discriminate against Henry, not he who discriminated against her.

In other words, although Henry's freedom impinges upon Rabidue's security (and freedom), Rabidue's freedom also reduces Henry's security (and freedom). Each side's liberty is in conflict with the other's. It is impossible for either to act without discriminating, and no matter which side the court rules for, it will be subject to the accusation that it has allowed discrimination against the other side.[163]

One more example might help illustrate the point. Pornographers (and others) attacking the Indianapolis anti-pornography ordinance argued that it violated their right to freedom of expression.[164] Those in favor of the ordinance responded that, without it, their own right to freedom of speech and their right to security from degrading, humiliating, and injurious conduct were threatened.[165] Thus, the court had to decide whether the freedom of one side was worth more or less than the security (and freedom) of the other. A ruling for the pornographers inevitably harmed their opponents; a ruling in favor of the ordinance inevitably harmed the pornographers. The groups' rights were in conflict, and pluralistic tolerance of both was simply impossible.[166]

---

162. This is not as farfetched as it may sound. *See infra* notes 167–73 and accompanying text.

163. To the extent that they recognize that helping one group inevitably entails harming others, those who label affirmative action measures "reverse discrimination" are logically correct (*if* you define discrimination as the exercise of group freedom in a way that harms others). Where they go wrong is in viewing a *refusal* to engage in such programs as neutral, rather than as reinforcing existing inequalities which *also* raise one group over another.

164. *See* American Booksellers Ass'n v. Hudnut, 771 F.2d 323, 325 (7th Cir. 1985), *aff'd per curiam*, 475 U.S. 1001 (1986).

165. *See* MacKinnon, *Pornography, Civil Rights, and Speech*, 20 HARV. C.R.-C.L. L. REV. 1, 22–23 (1985).

166. Allowing the pornographic "speech" would not constitute simply protecting all sides' freedom. To the extent that pornographers are allowed to construct women as objects who enjoy being abused against their wishes, women's protests against such abuse will be all too easy to dismiss, and thus their speech will be restricted. Moreover, women's right to be protected from harm will still be implicated in any case.

b. *The Relational Construction of Groups*

The ideal of pluralism is logically incoherent not only because the concepts of freedom and security are relational (one group's liberty is another's injury), but also because group identities themselves are relationally and hierarchically constructed in current American society. As a result of that construction, individual groups' fates are inextricably linked: One group's benefit will almost always be another's loss.

By saying that group identities are relationally constructed, I mean that groups attain their identity in contrast with other groups, in the same way that words attain their meaning in contrast with other words:

> [T]he meaning generated by linguistic conventions is negative and differential rather than positive and fixed. The meaning of the word "tree" is *artificial* in that it does not flow from anything in the nature of the word itself. Instead the meaning flows from the word's relationship to other words within the socially created representational practice. It acquires its meaning from not being another word, say, "bush" or "woods."[167]

In a similar way, to be "male" is defined in part as to be "not female," "black" attains its meaning in contrast to "white," "rich" in contrast to "poor," and so forth.

Perhaps more importantly, group identities are hierarchized, as feminist scholarship has amply demonstrated. The categories of male and female, for instance, are socially constructed in a relationship of domination and submission, such that what makes a man "masculine" (i.e., truly male) is his ability (and desire) to dominate women and what makes a woman "feminine" (truly female) is her susceptibility to (and apparent desire of) domination by a man.[168] Extending the analysis to a more general level, one could say that maleness is defined, at least in part, as superiority to women, and femaleness as inferiority to men.[169]

The briefest consideration of popular ideology about sex difference confirms this interdependence and hierarchization of male and female identities.[170] Consider, for example, the fact that a man who is "feminine" in demeanor or clothing is considered unmanly (think of how most people would react to a man in a skirt); that the worst epithet to hurl at a male is a charge of homosexuality, that is, of having "female" sexual urges; and that a man who cannot "control" his woman is often considered emasculated. Similarly, to be attractive as a woman is to be pretty (read: pleasing

---

167. Peller, *supra* note 5, at 1164.
168. *See generally* MacKinnon, *supra* note 165, at 19-20 (describing this construction of male and female as existing in relationship of domination and submission).
169. *See* F. Olsen, The Sex of Law (unpublished manuscript on file with author).
170. I take my terminology from Olsen. *Id.* at 2.

as a sexual object) and soft (read: vulnerable, incapable of self-protection), while to be unattractive is to be overly strong, harsh, or aggressive—that is, to be like (and able to resist) a man. And, of course, the worst epithet to fire at a woman is to call her a lesbian (like a man in sexual urges), or, perhaps, ugly (unable to serve as a sex object for men).[171]

Similarly, part of the definition of class identity involves contrasting oneself with other social classes. Suntans indicate wealth precisely because those who work all day lack the leisure time needed to acquire them;[172] unblemished hands mark the professional since laborers' hands get calloused. Part of each group's identity is its awareness of its position in a hierarchy of groups. Because groups are mutually defined in this way, it is simply impossible to accommodate one group without in some way affecting others. And, since one group's gain will virtually inevitably be another's loss, any judicial decision, even one that attempts merely to bring one group up to another's level of power or status, inevitably constitutes a decision that favors one group and harms another.

In this light, it can be seen that the display of pornography in which women are demeaned and threatened reaffirms the male identity of the displayer, underlining his ability to subordinate women. Simultaneously, of course, such displays affirm the construction of women as willing victims. Thus, a judicial decision that bars pornography in the workplace, rejecting the notion that women exist as sexual objects for men, also rejects and undermines a definition of men as beings who can objectify and subordinate women. Because the sexes are mutually defined, Judge Keith's approach would necessarily harm men, just as Judge Krupansky's harms women.[173]

In summary, given that any action by one group produces some sort of harm to others, the ideal of a pluralistic coexistence of all groups is unrealistic, especially within existing social arrangements.[174] Neither the principle of tolerance for diversity nor the concept of societal consensus can provide neutral grounds upon which to resolve cases, for choices

---

171. The fact that women do wear pants, and that feminine beauty has recently been redefined to include (slight) muscularity, whereas male clothing and body styles are still severely constrained, is one of many contrasts that illustrate the fact that the sexes are not only mutually defined but also hierarchically related. Women can adopt some "male" traits (work in the public sphere, for example) because that elevates them. For men to adopt "female" traits (doing housework, for example) is much more unthinkable, because it involves losing status.

172. Contrast current ideals of tanned beauty, for example, with the era when workers worked primarily outside instead of inside, and wealth was indicated by white skin, untouched by the sun.

173. This is not to reject the idea that, ultimately, the elimination of patriarchy would probably benefit both sexes. See infra note 192. But it simply cannot be denied that the transition period would be painful and difficult for many men.

174. Of course, some cultures clearly can (and do) include more groups than others, and I do not mean to say that it is impossible to assess the extent to which a particular society is tolerant of difference. Moreover, I do not mean to suggest that such tolerance is not a laudable goal for a society to have. See infra notes 200–201 and accompanying text. My point is only that to believe tolerance for diversity will assure neutral judicial decisions obscures the fact that some groups are—and must be, given current social arrangements—favored over others through such decisions.

among conflicting groups cannot be avoided. By relying on such concepts, both Judge Krupansky and Judge Keith reached the mistaken conclusion that doctrine could overcome inter-group conflicts—that a reasonableness test could assure fair results to all. In so doing they failed to recognize that liberty is necessarily the freedom *to* harm others,[175] and courts must decide whose liberty wins.[176]

C. *Hierarchies, Helplessness, and Hate: Why Does Douglas Henry Harass?*

Conflict may be inevitable, under current conditions, but that does not mean that progress is impossible. However, in order for efforts at transforming society to be productive, they must recognize and attack the interlocking effects of the various social hierarchies that structure American society. While it is essential that legal decision-makers eschew neutrality in favor of explicit choices, it is equally essential that those working for social change recognize not only the conflicts between different groups but also the connections between the systems that oppress them.

In this Section, I will try to shed some light on those connections by suggesting an explanation for Douglas Henry's behavior towards women. It is not my purpose here to present a thorough or definitive analysis of

---

175. Singer, *supra* note 14, at 986-94, 1049-50 (discussing work of Wesley Hohfeld).

176. Of course, this problem of conflicting liberties only arises if the conflict in a case is between two *groups*. If either the plaintiff or the defendant is not a member of a protected group, then the case will not implicate pluralism concerns and will probably result in a verdict against that individual. While individual freedom might be implicated in such a situation, it would probably lose out to the principle that one's liberty does not extend to the right to harm others. This would seem to be especially true in the area of antidiscrimination law, since group membership is a prerequisite to claiming discrimination. (In fact, the case of an idiosyncratic individual harming a group member is the prototypical case for the deviant-bad-act model of discrimination. *See supra* pp. 1204-05.) The following chart sets out the implications of the parties' group identities in a discrimination case:

	Conduct/Treatment of Plaintiff	
Conduct/Treatment of Defendant	As Individual	As Member of Group
As Individual	(1) no discrimination	(2) discrimination against P[a]
As Member of Group	(3) discrimination against D[b] ("reverse discrimination")	(4) conflict of liberties problem (discrimination, but against whom?)

[a]This could also be characterized as a violation of D's individual right to liberty, but that does not trigger pluralism concerns.

[b]This could also be characterized as a violation of P's individual right to liberty, but that does not trigger pluralism concerns.

The *Rabidue* court's privatization of Vivienne Rabidue—its depiction of her as an idiosyncratic, aberrational woman—narrowed the possible boxes that the case could be identified with to 1 or 3; its class identification of Douglas Henry as a worker placed the case in box 3. In this way, the court avoided the conflict-of-liberties problem that results if the case is situated in box 4. As this case illustrates, the initial characterization of a case as posing group/individual or group/group conflict is yet another place where seemingly value-neutral determinations of fact actually reimport the freedom/security contradiction back into the law.

the causes of sexual harassment[177] or of the effect of feminist reform efforts on men.[178] Rather, I want merely to offer some preliminary observations that will illustrate the need for a complex understanding of how other social hierarchies might affect the genesis of social phenomena like sexual harassment.

In her groundbreaking work, *Sexual Harassment of Working Women*, Catharine MacKinnon provides a powerful account of the dynamics of sexual harassment in the workplace. She argues that women's work role has always been defined as requiring that they be sexually attractive and that they at least *seem* to be sexually available to the men for whom they work.[179] Just as women's role in the home has been defined as providing personal services, sexual pleasure, admiration, and status to their male partners, so female workers are expected to present a "pleasing" appearance and perform "wifely" tasks (getting coffee, keeping the calendar, generally organizing the petty everyday details of the boss's life) in a deferential, loyal, and (preferably) affectionate way.[180] Given the "sexualization of the woman worker as a part of the job,"[181] MacKinnon asserts, sexual harassment should not be seen as individual perversion but rather as merely business as usual—the logical "extension of a gender-defined work role."[182] If men are socialized to think that women should project an image of sexual availability on the job, then it is not that unusual to find women feeling compelled to do so. Nor is it unusual to find men responding to that image, and then blaming women as having "asked for it" when they subsequently complain that they were sexually harassed.[183]

MacKinnon's analysis clearly goes a long way toward explaining the phenomenon of sexual harassment in general and the atmosphere at the Osceola Refining Company in particular. But it does not seem to me to fully capture the dynamics of an interaction like that between Douglas Henry and Vivienne Rabidue. After all, Henry was not Rabidue's superior, and probably had no feelings of being entitled by his position (as opposed to merely by his gender) to deference, sexual availability, or per-

---

177. Much of that task has already been accomplished, of course, by the influential work of Catharine MacKinnon. *See infra* notes 179-83 and accompanying text.

178. That impact is beginning to be explored in a series of recent works that attempt to address the more general issue of the effect of the social construction of gender on men. *See, e.g.*, THE MAKING OF MASCULINITIES: THE NEW MEN'S STUDIES (H. Brod ed. 1987); MEN IN FEMINISM (A. Jardine & P. Smith eds. 1987).

179. C. MACKINNON, *supra* note 1, at 18, 22-23.

180. *Id.* at 18-23.

181. *Id.* at 18.

182. *Id.* at 32; *see also id.* at 18-23. MacKinnon makes a similar argument about rape, suggesting that, because male and female sexual roles are defined in terms of domination and submission, rape is just an exaggerated form of everyday sex. MacKinnon, *supra* note 75, at 647. It would seem, however—and I do not think MacKinnon would necessarily disagree with me here—that even if rape and sex (or harassment and flirting) are variations on the same theme, it is important to differentiate between what a woman experiences as consensual intercourse (or interaction) and what she experiences as violent invasion (or derogation).

183. C. MACKINNON, *supra* note 1, at 21-23.

sonal service from her. Of course, he might very well have felt angered by her managerial status in the company, a status that violated the traditional definition of women's work role that MacKinnon describes. But reading his treatment of Rabidue as nothing more than the aggressive exercise of a male right of sexual access seems to me to ignore the aspects of his situation at Osceola that undercut the image of Henry as someone exerting power, having authority, or feeling a sense of entitlement.

Of course, *Rabidue* does not provide a full-color portrait of Henry's situation at Osceola, but certain details in the case suggest that he was hardly a powerful or high-status member of the managerial staff. Consider, for example, the advice that one of his supervisors gave him, suggesting that he would have better prospects in the company if he learned to become "an executive type person."[184] The patronizing tone of this comment could hardly have made its recipient feel comfortable or respected. Rather, he must have felt painfully aware of his own limited power and nonprofessional status in the company. Labelled as someone who simply did not relate to people or perform his job with the right style, he could not improve by bettering his performance or increasing his productivity; rather, he had to somehow become a different "type." Such feelings of insecurity and inferiority could certainly contribute to a desire to compensate by subordinating women. The behavior that results, then, would seem to be a product of a somewhat different dynamic than just the acting-out of accepted male workplace roles.

A recent analysis of male attitudes towards women in the workplace tends to confirm this conclusion. Anthony Astrachan's study recounts the results of research that included interviews with over 300 men regarding their feelings about the changes women are demanding in society. His description of the way in which feminist demands can threaten men bears quoting at some length:

> The vast majority of men may identify with the powerful, may have explosive fantasies of power, but in reality we have little or no power. We never had . . . . We too, we men, are limited in our choices, dependent on the powerful, and dubious of our ability to change the rules. We find it hard to accept the idea that women are changing the rules themselves. In [Elizabeth] Janeway's words, women are invading the corridors of power, "as if, merely being human, they had a right to be there. But most men have given up that right in return for a quiet life and some sense of security, for government by law as an acceptable bargain between the weak and the powerful. The idea that women are now refusing to accept this bargain acts as a terrifying, a paralyzing challenge to men. Either they too must revolt or they must acknowledge themselves lacking in

---

184. Rabidue v. Osceola Ref. Co., 805 F.2d 611, 624 (6th Cir. 1986) (Keith, J., dissenting), *cert. denied*, 481 U.S. 1041 (1987).

the courage and ambition being shown by their traditionally inferior sisters."[185]

Astrachan's analysis suggests an account of sexual harassment in general, and of the conduct of Douglas Henry in particular, that is somewhat different than, if complementary to, MacKinnon's. It suggests that the subordination of women in the workplace is sometimes related to the sense of disempowerment that male workers feel. If a woman like Rabidue can rise above the position usually reserved for workers of her sex (recall that she was the only woman in a salaried managerial position at Osceola), then a man like Henry, who has accepted his placement in a mid-level, managerial job and the sense of disempowerment he feels as part of a large corporate bureaucracy, should also be able to. His resigned acquiescence is thrown into question, and the sense of superiority to women with which he sustains his self-esteem is shaken. Furthermore, if he compensates for the low status he holds in his company through an exaggerated identification with his own maleness (and, explicitly, with the male social roles of worker and subordinator of women), then the presence of a female co-worker in his workplace, by challenging both of these traditional lines between male and female, will deprive him of an important aspect of his self-identity. Her presence will not only make him feel emasculated, but will also threaten his very sense of self.[186]

If it is true, then, that sexual harassment is partly a reaction to a socioeconomic structure that disempowers and devalues workers at many levels, making them feel inadequate and unable to control their lives, its eradication will be no simple matter.[187] Rather, to the extent that the male worker's acquiescence in the hierarchical and regimented structuring of the capitalist workplace is "bought" by allowing him to retain some sense

---

185. A. ASTRACHAN, *supra* note 110, at 17 (quoting E. JANEWAY, BETWEEN MYTH & MORNING: WOMEN AWAKENING (1975)).

186. *Id.* at 17–18. It is important to point out here that I am emphatically *not* saying that it is the people on the lower end of the socioeconomic and corporate hierarchies who will be the most sexist. While that might at first seem to be the logical conclusion to draw from Astrachan's analysis (and corresponds as well to upper- and middle-class stereotypes), I do not draw it, in part because I believe feelings of powerlessness and inadequacy are not confined to those at the lower strata of the capitalist system. (Astrachan, by the way, also explicitly rejects the conclusion that low-status groups are more sexist. *Id.* at 74.) This is not to deny that those at the top benefit unequally, but only to assert that they feel equally powerless to change the roles they are supposed to play. Nor am I saying that women like Rabidue should not prevail in lawsuits like this one. If we are going to reject traditional gender categories that demean women, relegate them to economic dependency, and hierarchize the relationship between the sexes, then putting up with hostile and humiliating comments and visual displays simply cannot be a condition of work for women seeking to enter, or to remain in, the economic sphere.

187. Another aspect of harassment as a social phenomenon that I have not addressed here is its racial component. The fact that a large proportion of the sexual harassment cases that have been litigated were brought by black plaintiffs begs for explanation. The history of slavery, in which African American women were constructed as "fair game" for the sexual exploits of their white masters, would certainly seem a promising place to start.

of power through subordinating women,[188] sexual harassment will be difficult to stop without changing the workplace structure itself. (And conversely, of course, the harms of capitalism will not be eliminated without addressing the patriarchal system that supports current economic arrangements.[189])

Recognition of the fact that existing economic and gender hierarchies mutually reinforce one another could have a significant impact on efforts to transform society. For instance, understanding the connection between sexual harassment and worker powerlessness might motivate both feminists and labor organizers to work closely with other disempowered employees to more broadly reform the workplace.[190] By encouraging collective action based on a mutual recognition of powerlessness, an analysis that focuses on the interdependence of economic, gender, race, and other hierarchies can help forge alliances among disempowered groups that all too often see themselves as antagonists.[191]

---

188. *Cf.* Crenshaw, *supra* note 37, at 1381 (role of blacks as inferior "other" in race consciousness allows whites to "include themselves in the dominant circle—an arena in which most hold no real power, but only their privileged racial identity"); Davis, *Rape, Racism, and the Myth of the Black Rapist,* in FEMINIST FRAMEWORKS 431 (A. Jaggar & P. Rothenberg eds. 1984) ("When working-class men accept the invitation to rape extended by the ideology of male supremacy, they are accepting a bribe, an illusory compensation for their powerlessness.").

189. The interdependence of capitalism and patriarchy is not a new discovery and is the continuing subject of much provocative work by socialist feminists. *See, e.g.,* Hartmann, *Capitalism, Patriarchy, and Job Segregation by Sex,* in CAPITALIST PATRIARCHY AND THE CASE FOR SOCIALIST FEMINISM 206-47 (Z. Eisenstein ed. 1979) (arguing that men supported development of job segregation by sex in nineteenth century because it preserved their control over women at home by keeping women economically dependent and by retaining their domestic labor); N. HARTSOCK, MONEY, SEX & POWER: TOWARD A FEMINIST HISTORICAL MATERIALISM 259-61 (1983) (discussing question of why certain abstract dualisms—abstract/concrete, mind/body, etc.—are associated with both "abstract masculinity" and exchange).

An important aspect of some socialist feminist work is the recognition that the racial hierarchy in American society is also closely tied to class and gender hierarchies. *See, e.g.,* The Combahee River Collective, *A Black Feminist Statement,* in CAPITALIST PATRIARCHY AND THE CASE FOR SOCIALIST FEMINISM, *supra,* at 362-72. While the discourse of the *Rabidue* case does not easily lend itself to a discussion of the impact of race on the court's analysis (the judicial opinions do not reveal, for example, the races of the individuals involved), I am nevertheless certain that a more complete understanding of that case (and of antidiscrimination ideology in general) would be generated by an exploration of its racial dimensions. To that extent, then, the analysis presented here is incomplete.

190. In fact, the logic behind many feminist reform efforts in the economic sphere would seem to require a radical restructuring of the workplace in any case. Parental leave and comparable worth are two striking examples: the former challenges the traditional management view that workers should be available regardless of family obligations, *see* Finley, *supra* note 37, at 1152-59, 1163, while the latter raises fundamental questions about existing wage hierarchies. *See* Freeman, *The Threat of Comparable Worth,* TIKKUN Jan.-Feb. 1987, at 50. (Of course, feminist theory itself, with its emphasis on including disempowered people and listening to silenced voices, should encourage feminist reformers to be concerned about worker subordination regardless of any perceived connection between capitalism and patriarchy. The women's movement has often, however, been very middle class in its focus and concerns. MacKinnon, *supra* note 5, at 519).

191. This suggestion that both female and male workers could benefit from feminist reforms might make it seem as if conflict among groups is not as inevitable as the discussion thus far has suggested. It does seem clear, for example, that collective action might allow those groups to attain higher degrees of both freedom and security than they currently enjoy. However, *somebody* would still be losing in that scenario: the members of the elite. (Upperclass white women would lose class and race privilege but gain gender equality; workingclass white men would lose gender and race privilege but gain class equality, etc. Only upperclass white men would simply lose.) Thus, I would suggest

Moreover, even without such combined efforts, placing pressure on one system is likely to have an impact on others. Thus, for example, prohibiting sexual harassment might eliminate a safety valve for male workers, forcing them to confront their own dissatisfaction. Seeing women successfully challenge their devalued status might further motivate men to cast a critical eye on both their own position in the class hierarchy and their own assigned gender role, inspiring them to attempt to change their situation as well. Finally, seeing women successfully combine traditionally "male" and "female" traits and escape traditional gender roles might reveal to men the narrow confines of their own gender identities, thus enabling them to see that feminist reforms (ultimately) offer benefits to both sexes.[192]

In short, to ignore the interdependence of capitalism, patriarchy, and other structures of inequality is to guarantee the failure of efforts to eradicate any of them. As the next Section suggests, however, a question still remains as to whether relying upon existing legal constructs to articulate demands for change will eliminate, rather than perpetuate, current social hierarchies.

D. Transforming the Discourse

The discussion thus far suggests that both reasonableness and pluralism are problematic concepts which hide the power struggles behind legal issues and mystify the courts' role in resolving such struggles. Moreover, both Judge Krupansky's and Judge Keith's opinions reveal that the two concepts are mutually enforcing: To protect his conviction that his reasonableness analysis was neutral, each judge had to assume an (at least somewhat) egalitarian, pluralistic society;[193] and, to affirm his vision of an

---

that the appropriate conclusion to draw from my comments here is not that conflict is avoidable, but rather just that the lines of battle should be carefully and appropriately drawn.

Moreover, the extent to which it is important to emphasize the existence of conflict among groups seems to me to depend upon the audience being addressed. Thus, given their penchant for seeing decisions that support the elite as neutral, legal decisionmakers need to be made aware of the conflicts among groups and the choices among them that those decisions often implicitly make. In contrast, those fighting powerlessness do not necessarily need to become more conscious of group conflict per se, but rather to change their focus—to see the commonalities and connections between the conditions of all powerless groups and to recognize the extent to which they are all in conflict with the elite.

192. A. ASTRACHAN, supra note 110, notes not only that men are sometimes envious of women's apparent ability to combine characteristics of both genders, id. at 29, but also that they can feel tremendous relief at any lessening of the burdens of their own sex role, burdens such as having primary responsibility for economic support of the family, being prohibited from expressing emotion or vulnerability, having to project an image of confidence and control at all times, etc., id. at 31-32. This information would suggest that to the extent that men can change their identity—rejecting the hierarchical relationship to women central to its current construction—they will benefit, rather than lose by the elimination of gender hierarchy. Nevertheless, because such a wholesale rejection, especially by those who benefit not only from gender but also from class (and race) hierarchy, seems unlikely to me to happen anytime soon, I believe that it is sufficiently accurate for the time being to say that men must lose for women to gain. (Of course, as I noted supra note 191, the elimination of other overlapping hierarchies would complicate the ultimate tally of wins and losses.)

193. The dissenter had to assume at least equality among women. See supra notes 156-58 and

egalitarian and pluralistic world, each judge had to perceive himself as making nonpolitical, neutral decisions. It is worth exploring briefly, therefore, whether either of these constructs can be salvaged—whether our understanding of either reasonableness or pluralism can be sufficiently transformed to eliminate those constructs' harmful effects and still retain their usefulness.[194]

There are both risks and benefits to retaining and redefining problematic legal and political constructs rather than discarding them altogether.[195] The major risk is that, even when used by the disempowered, the constructs will continue to hide power relationships and thereby legitimate a fundamentally unequal system.[196] Especially if new formulations of old constructs are presented as neutral themselves, the redefined constructs will still merely reinforce and legitimate an unequal status quo. The primary benefit of retaining problematic concepts like reasonableness and pluralism is that their immense symbolic power can serve to legitimate the demands for social transformation that they are used to articulate,[197] while their very vagueness and abstractness can allow them to serve as valuable vehicles for generating dialogue on national values.[198] In this respect, the problem is not with the terms themselves, but with the meanings that we give them.[199] The question, then, becomes essentially one of transition. To the extent that concepts can be infused with new meaning, they can be valuable tools for reform. To the extent that they resist such redefinition, they will continue to legitimate inequality.

1. The Futility of Retaining Reasonableness

In this light, it seems futile to attempt a transformation of the concept of reasonableness. While it might be possible to reconceptualize the reasonable person (or woman) standard as merely shorthand for something

---

accompanying text.

194. Despite their interrelatedness, I think it is both possible and worthwhile to consider the two concepts separately. As Part I indicates, the reasonableness test is used in individualist contexts as well as pluralist ones, and even in group-based analyses it is sometimes more closely tied to economic theories such as efficiency analysis than to political theories such as pluralism. *See supra* pp. 1180–93.

195. There is a growing debate on whether legal constructs like "rights" are valuable or harmful. *See* Crenshaw, *supra* note 37; Freeman, *supra* note 26; Minow, *Interpreting Rights: An Essay for Robert Cover*, 96 YALE L.J. 1860 (1987); Olsen, *supra* note 88; Schneider, *The Dialectic of Rights and Politics: Perspectives from the Women's Movement*, 61 N.Y.U. L. REV. 589 (1986); Williams, *Alchemical Notes: Reconstructing Ideals from Deconstructed Rights*, 22 HARV. C.R.-C.L. L. REV. 401 (1987).

196. For a critique of legal doctrine's reliance upon the concept of rights and an argument that rights discourse should be abandoned in favor of explicitly political, values-focused discussion, see Olsen, *supra* note 88, at 430.

197. For the suggestion that concepts like "legal rights," despite their indeterminacy, are nevertheless valuable, see Crenshaw, *supra* note 37, at 1367 (they allow disempowered groups to elicit concessions by using system's own logic against it); Schneider, *supra* note 195, at 611 (they can help to define goals of political struggle and of community); Williams, *supra* note 195, at 414 (they give such groups feeling of legitimacy and empowerment).

198. *See* Minow, *supra* note 195, at 1871–82.

199. *See* Williams, *supra* note 195, at 432.

like "the judge's considered judgment about the appropriateness of the conduct in question," such a revised vision seems unlikely to succeed. Reasonableness in legal ideology is simply too closely tied to the idea of objectivity—to the notion that the law can resolve legal conflicts without reflecting or reinforcing any personal perspective—to allow for such a transformation. And the homogeneous image of society that results from the traditional equation of reasonableness with societal consensus is simply too harmful, excluding all but the dominant elite, to justify retention.

2. Toward a Transformed Vision of Pluralism

In contrast, the concept of pluralism seems to have the potential for articulating valuable and meaningful ideals. While the idea that judicial decisions can be dictated by a principle of pluralistic tolerance of all groups is unrealistic,[200] this does not mean that the whole notion of a tolerant and diverse nation is bankrupt. Rather than be seen as a guaranty of judicial neutrality, however, pluralism and tolerance for diversity should be viewed as part of an expanded commitment to the true sharing of social power. While it would no doubt be helpful to see pluralism as requiring an in-depth, empathic exploration of social problems,[201] and as mandating that we not ignore the group identification of each individual,[202] these changes in attitude are not enough. It is also essential that we

---

200. It is incoherent to think that the principle of tolerance for diversity can provide the ground for a neutral methodology. See supra notes 161-76 and accompanying text. Pluralism simply cannot provide an external referent that will assure the neutrality of judicial decisions; to ignore that fact is merely to clothe a particularized perspective in the false veneer of objectivity.

201. I have in mind something like Minow's commitment to "the moral relevance of contingent particulars." Minow, The Supreme Court, 1986 Term—Foreword: Justice Engendered, 101 HARV. L. REV. 10, 76 (1987). That is, I believe that we should not think of pluralism as a methodological dictate, as a relativistic refusal to judge; rather, we should think of it instead as a substantive commitment—a dedication, first, to making decisions based on genuine attempts at understanding the perspectives and social circumstances of others, and, second, to reaching results that actually produce the sharing of power with the powerless.

In short, the realization that there is no one "true" perspective should not cause us to eschew choices, but rather lead us to make necessary choices with care and humility. See Kennedy, Distributive and Paternalist Motives in Contract and Tort Law, with Special Reference to Compulsory Terms and Unequal Bargaining Power, 41 MD. L. REV. 563, 646 (1982) ("[W]hat we need when we make decisions affecting the well-being of other people is correct intuition about their needs and an attitude of respect for their autonomy. . . . And even intuition and respect may do no good at all. There isn't any guarantee that you'll get it right, but when it's wrong you're still responsible.").

The recognition that there are multiple perspectives should also, of course, lead us to appreciate that a fundamental restructuring of society is essential, for hierarchical social arrangements, in which decision-makers have little contact with those who are different from them, and virtually no exposure to other social worlds, are not very conducive to the development of empathic understanding.

202. J.R. Pole identifies an individualism that rejects group identification as the basis of the concept of equality throughout most of America's history. See J. POLE, THE PURSUIT OF EQUALITY IN AMERICAN HISTORY 293 (1978). Thus, for example, if an employer considers race, sex, or religion in making a hiring decision—whether positively or negatively—the decision is often considered illegitimate, unless those traits are somehow relevant to job performance. (Of course, "equal results" advocates explicitly reject this principle, and affirmative action is considered an exception to it.) As Pole notes, this definition is closely related to moral individualism: "The individualist principle dissociates people from the context of family, religion, class, or race and when linked with the idea of equality in the most affirmative sense . . . it assumes the co-ordinate principle of interchangeability." Id. at 293.

think more expansively about the need for the redistribution of power, and be willing to accept the hard choices—and losses—that true redistribution would entail. Such expansive thinking and acting is crucial for the success of any effort to eliminate inequality. For as the preceding Section demonstrates, behavior like that of Douglas Henry can be neither understood nor eradicated without addressing the other hierarchies of power and status that contribute to male assertions of dominance over women through harassment, intimidation, and violence.

IV. CONCLUSION

Despite the Statue of Liberty's welcoming arms, American cultural pluralism has always contained an element of coercion. As Guido Calabresi puts it, "The term 'melting pot' implies that equality will not be granted until the group which seeks equality is melted into the pot."[203] Yet American ideology often serves to prevent people from recognizing the limited nature of the society's tolerance for diversity, perpetuating the myth that ours is truly a pluralistic country.

The assimilation of immigrants, for example, tends to be viewed as a gradual process of voluntary adoption of American values, language, and culture, rather than as a forced loss of foreign identities.[204] In addition,

---

By the principle of interchangeability, Pole means the idea that people are fundamentally alike, that it is only through the historical accidents of "social history, oppression, and privilege" that differences are produced, and that those differences are irrelevant to how the person should be treated by the law. *Id.* at 293.

One of the problems with this traditional American view of equality is that it fails to recognize the extent to which what a person *is* is a product of his or her various group memberships. Thus, the argument that those memberships are irrelevant, while at one level an appealing articulation of the concept of tolerance for diversity, at another level strips people of their very identity. *Cf.* Balbus, *Commodity Form and Legal Form: An Essay on the "Relative Autonomy" of the Law,* 11 LAW & SOC'Y REV. 571, 578 (1977) ("'[A legal] form that defines individuals as individuals only insofar as they are severed from the social ties and activities that constitute the real ground of their individuality necessarily fails to contribute to the recognition of genuine individuality.").

This conception of equality also prevents members of devalued groups from ever eliminating negative stereotypes, because their conduct is always seen as that of individuals and therefore as not undermining the validity of the group identification itself. *See, e.g.,* Pole, *supra,* at 340 ("The trouble with making it a policy to stress individual rather than racial achievements [of black people] . . . was that 'the white people will not let you get rid of the idea of race.' ")

203. G. CALABRESI, *supra* note 3, at 28; *see also* Finley, *supra* note 37, at 1153 ("The American melting pot has been a cauldron into which we have put black, brown, red, yellow, and white men and women, in the hope that we will come up with white men."). Who are also Anglo-Saxon Protestant, physically and mentally able, and heterosexual, one might add.

204. Analysts often identify assimilation with choice, *see, e.g.,* Carlin, *Charm and the English Language Amendment,* 101 CHRISTIAN CENTURY 822, 823 (1984) (criticizing English Language Amendment on grounds that it "assumes that compulsion, not attraction, is the best way of spreading a language or a culture"), ignoring the numerous structural barriers to the retention of alien ways. In the area of language, for example, those barriers range from early laws that prohibited the use of languages other than English in public and private schools, Marshall, *The Question of an Official Language: Language Rights and the English Language Amendment,* 60 INT'L J. SOC. LANG. 7, 14 (1986), required English-speaking for naturalization, Leibowicz, *The Proposed English Language Amendment: Shield or Sword?,* 3 YALE L. & POL'Y REV. 519, 537-38 (1985), and even, in some cases, banned the use of other languages in private conversation, *see* FISHMAN, LANGUAGE LOYALTY IN THE UNITED STATES 238 (1966), to the more subtle barriers currently presented by English-only

the prevailing ideology systematically ignores differences among the citizenry as a whole, promoting a homogeneous vision of American society that both excludes those groups who do not fit the accepted American model and elevates a small but powerful elite to the status of universal "type." The history of the exclusion of women and African Americans from American culture and politics[205] is only the most striking example of this pervasive privatization and depoliticization of powerless groups. Rendering such groups invisible by ignoring their differences (or even their existence) and assimilating everyone into a purportedly general type, American ideology conceals the conflict created by those differences and thus allows us to avoid the hard decisions that such conflict requires. Only by denying diversity have we been able to see ourselves as tolerant of it.

The reasonable person standard both reflects and reproduces this mystifying ideology. Perceived as a mediating construct that allows group diversity without sacrificing collective security, it suggests that pluralism is both a descriptively accurate and a normatively viable vision of American society. Creating the impression that judges can rely on abstract tolerance and private orderings to resolve questions of group conflict, it obscures the political decisions that inevitably underlie such resolutions.

Conversely, the concept of pluralism legitimates the reasonable person standard, affirming its message of objectivity. Descriptive pluralism, by presenting contemporary society as egalitarian, affirms that the societal consensus the reasonableness test relies upon is a meaningful concept, reflecting a true and voluntary agreement among groups. Normative pluralism, by suggesting that the coexistence of all groups is not only morally right but also logically possible, validates the idea that the reasonableness test allows courts to avoid political choices between litigants by simply being tolerant of all.

Of course, the concepts of reasonableness and cultural pluralism need not of necessity be vehicles for denying difference and obscuring choices. But as long as reasonableness means abstract neutrality and pluralism means limitless tolerance, each concept will reinforce the other, and both will perpetuate an unequal status quo.

---

education, ballots, governmental forms (such as welfare applications and driving tests), and the like. *See* Leibowicz, *supra*, at 519, 527–28.

Regardless of whether one thinks that bilingual education or other accommodations should be made, to attribute the predominance of English to individual choice makes no more sense than to view Vivienne Rabidue as having voluntarily chosen to be subjected to Douglas Henry's harassment. In language and many other areas, immigrants have become "Americanized", because they were required to do so in order to reap the benefits of American society.

205. On the history of the exclusion of women from culture and politics, see E. FLEXNER, CENTURY OF STRUGGLE (1959), and B. HOOKS, AIN'T I A WOMAN (1981). On the arguably even more severe exclusion of blacks, see E. GENOVESE, ROLL, JORDAN, ROLL: THE WORLD THE SLAVES MADE (1972), T. GOSSESS, RACE: THE HISTORY OF AN IDEA IN AMERICA (1964), B. HOOKS, *supra*, R. KLUGER, SIMPLE JUSTICE (1976), and C. WOODWARD, THE STRANGE CAREER OF JIM CROW (3d ed. 1974).

SEXIST SPEECH IN THE WORKPLACE

Marcy Strauss*

Introduction

Sexist speech in the workplace abounds. A number of surveys conducted in the 1970's and 1980's reveal that a significant proportion of female workers are victims of abusive language, ranging from sexual comments, innuendos or jokes to explicit sexual invitations.[1] Women are called "cunt," "pussy" and "bitch."[2] Men wager on women's virginity and the frequency

* Associate Professor of Law, Loyola Law School. J.D. 1981, Georgetown University Law Center, B.S. 1978, Northwestern University. I wish to thank Martha Chamallis, Jan Costello, Louis Kaplow, Christopher May, Vicki Michel and Sharon Rush for their helpful comments on a previous draft of this manuscript. I am particularly grateful to Erwin Chemerinsky for reading and critiquing the multiple drafts of this Article. Thanks are also owed to Edward Singer for his excellent research assistance.

[1] This Article is concerned with sexist speech directed at women employees by male coworkers or supervisors. Although some sexist speech is directed at men, most harassers are men and most victims are women. In fact, studies indicate that females are nearly three times more likely to be victims of sexual harassment than are males. *See* U.S. Merit Systems Protection Board Office of Policy & Evaluation, Sexual Harassment in the Federal Government: An Update 16 (1988) [hereinafter Merit Systems Study Update] (14% of male federal employees, versus 42% of female employees, complained of being sexually harassed in 1987); Note, *An Equitable Liability Standard for Offensive Work Environment Claims Under Title VII:* Meritor Savings Bank v. Vinson, 29 B.C.L. Rev. 509, 509 n.1 (1988) ("Although women may harass men and persons of the same sex may harass each other, the situations seldom occur.").

In addition, the effects are significantly different when women, rather than men, are the recipients of the speech. Men do not seem to suffer the same deleterious psychological and physical effects that women experience. *See* Sexual Harassment in Employment Project, Help Yourself: A Manual for Dealing with Sexual Harassment 24 (1986) [hereinafter Sexual Harassment in Employment Project] (less than one percent of men have experienced actual negative effects from harassment); *see generally* Taub, *Keeping Women in their Place: Stereotyping Per Se as a Form of Employment Discrimination,* 21 B.C.L. Rev. 345, 365–68 (1980).

Men who are harassed, however, do have a cause of action under Title VII of the Civil Rights Act of 1964, § 2000 (1981), *see* Huebschen v. Department of Health & Social Servs., 547 F. Supp. 1168 (W.D. Wis. 1982), *rev'd on other grounds*, 716 F.2d 1167 (7th Cir. 1983); Williams v. Saxbe, 413 F. Supp. 654 (D.D.C. 1976), *vacated*, 587 F.2d 1240 (D.C. Cir. 1979), and under state tort law.

[2] *See, e.g.,* McNabb v. Cub Foods, 352 N.W.2d 378, 381 (Minn. 1984) (woman called a "fucking cunt"); Rabidue v. Osceola Refining Co., 584 F. Supp. 419, 423 (E.D. Mich. 1984) (woman called "fat ass," "pussy," "cunt" and "tits"); Broderick v. Ruder, 685 F. Supp. 1269 (D.D.C. 1988) (plaintiff subjected to sexually suggestive remarks about her dress and figure).

with which they engage in sexual activity.[3] Millions of women endure whistles, catcalls and references to breast size.

Working women fight offensive speech in a variety of ways. In increasing numbers,[4] women are bringing sexual harassment lawsuits against their employers under both federal[5] and state laws.[6] Courts have held, for example, that "[u]nwelcome sexual advances, requests for sexual favors and other verbal or physical conduct of a sexual nature,"[7] may violate Title VII of the Civil Rights Act of 1964.[8] Women have also alleged that the sexist speech creates a cause of action in tort for intentional infliction of emotional distress.[9] Finally, numerous cities are

---

[3] *See, e.g.,* Downes v. FAA, 775 F.2d 288, 293 (Fed. Cir. 1985).

[4] *See* Coles, *Sexual Harassment: Complainant Definitions and Agency Responses,* 36 Lab. L.J. 369 (1985). Most women, however, still take no legal action against sexist speech. *See* Merit Systems Study Update, *supra* note 1.

[5] *See, e.g.,* Title VII, 42 U.S.C. § 2000 (1981). Lawsuits may also be brought against government employers under 42 U.S.C. § 1983 (1981), claiming violations of the equal protection clause of the fourteenth amendment. *See* Volk v. Coler, 845 F.2d 1422 (7th Cir. 1988) (plaintiff complained, among other things, that her supervisor asked her out after work, made crude remarks and called her "hon," "honey" and "babe"); Skadegaard v. Farrell, 578 F. Supp. 1209, 1212 (D.N.J. 1984) (alleged harassment included embarassing and belittling remarks). A few courts had recognized racial harassment claims under 42 U.S.C. § 1981 (1981). *See* Erebia v. Chrysler Plastic Prods. Corp., 772 F.2d 1250 (6th Cir. 1985); Nieto v. United Auto Workers Local 598, 672 F. Supp. 987 (E.D. Mich. 1987) (claim for racial harassment may be cognizable under § 1981, but facts here—single 15-minute verbal attack—were not sufficient to state a claim). However, in *Patterson v. McLean Credit Union,* 109 S.Ct. 2363 (1989), the Supreme Court held that § 1981 only applies to discrimination in the formation of contracts and rejected § 1981 as a remedy for harassment on the job.

[6] As of June 1987, 33 states had policies against sexual harassment. Michigan adopted the earliest policy in 1979; most state laws were enacted in the early 1980's. *See* Ross & England, *State Government's Sexual Harassment Policy Initiatives,* Pub. Admin. Rev. 259 (May/June 1987).

[7] Guidelines on Discrimination Because of Sex, 29 C.F.R. § 1604.11(a) (1988).

[8] Although Title VII does not explicitly proscribe sexual harassment or abusive speech, it does prohibit sex discrimination in the employment context. In the late 1970's, federal courts began to recognize that the prohibition against sex discrimination included within its ambit the ability to regulate sexual harassment in employment. *See, e.g.,* Bundy v. Jackson, 641 F.2d 934 (D.C. Cir. 1981); Miller v. Bank of Am., 600 F.2d 211 (9th Cir. 1979); Tompkins v. Public Serv. Elec. & Gas Co., 568 F.2d 1044, 1047 (3d Cir. 1977); Barnes v. Costle, 561 F.2d 983, 990–92 (D.C. Cir. 1977). Finally, in 1986, the Supreme Court affirmed that position in Meritor Sav. Bank v. Vinson, 477 U.S. 57 (1986) (harassment creating an abusive, hostile or offensive environment affects the terms and conditions of employment based on sex, and thus violates Title VII).

[9] *See* Dolkart & Malchow, *Sexual Harassment in the Workplace: Expanding Remedies,* 23 Tort & Ins. L.J. 180, 189 (1987) (discussing various state tort remedies for harassment); Swentek v. USAir, 830 F.2d 552, 558–63 (4th Cir. 1987); Bowersox v. P.H. Glatfelter Co., 677 F. Supp. 307 (M.D. Pa. 1988).

This Article focuses on Title VII because state tort claims typically adapt and utilize the requirements of federal law.

considering ordinances and regulations which would ban sexually offensive speech from the workplace.[10]

Although much has been written about the extent and effects of offensive language in the workplace,[11] little attention has been paid to the question of whether speech which harasses deserves some level of first amendment protection. The few courts and commentators that have addressed possible constitutional problems with regulating verbal or written harassment—what I call sexist speech—have done so in a cursory fashion.[12] One court, for example, questioned whether the first amendment permits the judiciary to prohibit people from using offensive, yet not obscene language, but resolved the issue on statutory grounds.[13]

Such inadequate analysis of the first amendment ramifications of regulating sexist speech in the workplace is somewhat surprising, given that a great deal of attention has been devoted

---

[10] Los Angeles recently passed an ordinance regulating sexual harassment. Also, the Los Angeles fire department promulgated its own internal policy, focusing on banning sexually explicit material from the city's firehouse (on file with *Harvard Civil Rights-Civil Liberties Law Review*). Additionally, the Los Angeles Commission on the Status of Women has proposed banning all unwelcome written, verbal or physical contact with suggestive overtones, including suggestive letters, jokes, displays of suggestive objects, pictures, cartoons and posters. *See* L.A. Times, Jan. 12, 1988, § 2, at 1, col. 5. *Cf.* Preventing Sexual Harassment, 73 A.B.A. J., Oct. 1, 1987 at 78 (giving example of private company policy prohibiting repeated, offensive sexual flirtations, advances or propositions; continued or repeated verbal abuse of a sexual nature; graphic verbal commentaries about an individual's body; sexually degrading words used to describe an individual; and the display of sexually suggestive objects or pictures).

[11] *See, e.g.*, L. Farley, Sexual Shakedown: The Sexual Harassment of Women on the Job (1977); C. MacKinnon, Sexual Harassment of Working Women (1979). The topic of sexual harassment has been extensively discussed in movies, television shows, news features and even comic strips. *See, e.g.*, Cohen & Gutek, *Dimensions of Perceptions of Social-Sexual Behavior in a Work Setting*, 13 Sex Roles 317 (1985). Numerous scholarly articles have been written on the subject. *See* Rubinett, *Sex and Economics: The Tie that Binds, Judicial Approaches to Sexual Harassment as a Title VII Violation*, 4 Law & Inequality 245 (1986); Note, *The Harms of Asking: Towards a Comprehensive Treatment of Sexual Harassment*, 55 U. Chi. L. Rev. 328 (1988); Note, *Employer Liability Under Title VII for Sexual Harassment after* Meritor Savings Bank v. Vinson, 87 Colum. L. Rev. 1258 (1987).

[12] *See, e.g.*, Rabidue v. Osceola Refining Co., 584 F. Supp. at 431–32; Attanasio, *Equal Justice Under Chaos: The Developing Law of Sexual Harassment*, 51 U. Cin. L. Rev. 1, 24–25 (1982) (suggesting some first amendment problems with regulating harassing speech under Title VII of the Civil Rights Act); L.A. Times, Jan. 11, 1988, § 2, at 6, col. 1 (editorial criticizing the fire department's regulation of speech in the workplace on first amendment grounds).

[13] Rabidue v. Osceola Refining Co., 584 F. Supp. at 431–32 (vulgar language and posters in workplace not proscribed by Title VII).

in recent years to the constitutional implications of regulating pornographic[14] and racist speech.[15] Government regulation of these areas poses the same fundamental questions as prohibiting sexist speech: should the Constitution protect speech which denigrates, abuses and offends individuals and which perpetuates inequality among groups? How should the values embodied in the right to free speech be balanced against both the desire to prevent offense and the imperative to eliminate inequality?

Professor MacKinnon, after recognizing that much of sexual harassment is verbal, dismissed any first amendment problem with regulating such speech by suggesting that those concerned with free expression "value speech in the abstract more than they value people in the concrete."[16] While I recognize and feel the horror of sexist speech, I cannot minimize the value of free speech for society in general and for feminists in particular. To address these questions, a detailed analysis of the risks posed to freedom of expression by prohibiting sexist speech in the workplace is essential. A solution is needed that protects women in the workplace in a manner consistent with the first amendment.

An examination of the government's interests in regulating sexist speech in the workplace and a careful analysis of the values underlying freedom of expression is required to find that solution. After such an analysis, I conclude that the appropriate form of regulation is not a categorical exclusion of all sexist speech from first amendment protection, but a balancing test to determine whether, in particular circumstances, the state can regulate expression in a manner consistent with the first amendment.

This balancing demonstrates that the state's interests in eradicating sexist speech from the workplace does outweigh,

---

[14] *See* MacKinnon, *Not a Moral Issue*, 2 Yale L. & Pol'y Rev. 321 (1984); MacKinnon, *Pornography, Civil Rights and Speech*, 20 Harv. C.R.-C.L. L. Rev. 1 (1985).

[15] *See, e.g.*, Delgado, *Words that Wound: A Tort Action for Racial Insults, Epithets, and Name Calling*, 17 Harv. C.R.-C.L. L. Rev. 133 (1982); Kretzmer, *Freedom of Speech and Racism*, 8 Cardozo L. Rev. 445 (1987); Lasson, *Group Libel Versus Free Speech: When Big Brother Should Butt In*, 23 Duq. L. Rev. 77 (1984); Rosenfeld, *Extremist Speech and the Paradox of Tolerance*, 100 Harv. L. Rev. 1457 (1987).

[16] C. MacKinnon, Feminism Unmodified 115 (1987).

except in limited circumstances, any free speech concerns. When the offensive speech is directed at a captive audience, or when the speech causes women to be discriminated against in the workplace, the Constitution permits the state to censor sexist speech. When the speech is not directed at a particular woman, however, and is not discriminatory, banning sexist speech violates the first amendment. The final section of this Article offers specific proposals for regulating sexist speech consistent with the Constitution in light of this analysis.

Although sexist speech occurs in a myriad of arenas, the focus of this Article on the workplace is purposeful. Much of the litigation and discussion about sexist speech arises in the context of the workforce. In addition, sexist speech in the employment context has unique and qualitatively different effects than does such speech elsewhere.[17] Women historically have been discriminated against in employment. Even though overt exclusion of women from the job force and unequal pay for women are proscribed by law,[18] ensuring equality in employment requires addressing the more subtle ways in which women are excluded from full participation in the workforce. Sexist speech creates an inhospitable and degrading work environment for women, and thus operates as overt exclusion once did to erect a significant barrier to equality in the workplace.[19]

Furthermore, the employment context raises questions that are not posed by sexist speech in other settings. Employees at work constitute a captive audience, and the state has an interest in protecting these individuals from unwanted and unavoidable exposure to noxious ideas. Additionally, the state interest in eliminating employment discrimination may compel courts to adopt a different first amendment analysis than that which they use for sexist speech in a public forum. While it undoubtedly would be worthwhile to evaluate the regulation of offensive speech generally, this Article has a more focused objective.

---

[17] *See infra* notes 53–55 and accompanying text. Sexual harassment in other areas has recently received a significant degree of attention as well. *See, e.g.*, Schneider, *Sexual Harassment and Higher Education*, 65 Tex. L. Rev. 525 (1987).

[18] *See* Title VII, 42 U.S.C. § 2000 (1981); 29 U.S.C. § 206(d) (1981) (requiring equal pay for men and women performing equal work for the same establishment).

[19] *See infra* notes 53–54 and accompanying text.

I. The Problem of Sexist Speech in the Workplace: The
State's Interest in Regulation

A. A Definition of Sexist Speech

What is sexist speech? The very elusiveness of the term is
revealing. Part of the difficulty in regulating such speech lies in
the amorphousness of defining a category called "sexist
speech."[20] It is possible, however, to formulate a working
definition.

Examining the lawsuits in which women complain of speech
in the workplace is one way to understand what is meant by the
term "sexist speech." These lawsuits indicate that sexist speech
includes a number of different types of speech either directed
at or overheard by an employee in the workplace. For purposes

---

[20] Analogous difficulties exist in defining what constitutes sexual harassment. *See*
Gillespie & Leffler, *The Politics of Research Methodology in Claims-Making Activities:
Social Science and Sexual Harassment*, 34 Soc. Probs. 490, 496 (1987).
According to the Equal Employment Opportunity Commission's Guidelines on
Discrimination Because of Sex:

Unwelcome sexual advances, requests for sexual favors, and other verbal or
physical conduct of a sexual nature constitute sexual harassment when
(1) submission to such conduct is made either explicitly or implicitly a term or
condition of an individual's employment, (2) submission to or rejection of such
conduct by an individual is used as the basis for employment decisions affecting
such individual, or (3) such conduct has the purpose or effect of unreasonably
interfering with an individual's work performance or creating an intimidating,
hostile or offensive working environment.

29 C.F.R. § 1604.11 (1988).
Women Organized Against Sexual Harassment define sexual harassment as

unwanted attention directed at women. This attention can be manifested both
verbally and physically and can range from a sexual remark to rape. The
harasser's intention is irrelevant. The woman's perception of the situation
determines whether or not it's sexual harassment. At its root, sexual harassment is generalized hostility toward women.

Sexual Harassment in Employment Project, *supra* note 1 at 18.
Under California state law, "harassment includes, but is not limited to (A) Verbal
harassment, e.g., epithets, derogatory comments or slurs on a basis enumerated in the
Act; (B) Physical harassment . . . (C) Visual forms of harassment, e.g., derogatory
posters, cartoons or drawings . . . or (D) Sexual favors, e.g., unwanted sexual advances
which condition an employment benefit upon an exchange of favors. . . ." California
Fair Employment and Housing Commission Regulations (on file with *Harvard Civil
Rights-Civil Liberties Law Review*).

of this Article, sexist speech includes the following: (1) speech demanding or requesting sexual relationships; (2) sexually explicit speech directed at the woman; (3) degrading speech directed at the woman; and (4) sexually explicit or degrading speech that the woman employee knows exists in the workplace, even though it is not directed at her.

The first category of sexist speech is speech that requests or demands a sexual relationship. While a request and a demand might be distinct in certain circumstances, as a practical matter a request often acts as a demand. A coworker's sexual invitation may be considered a request when there are no explicit employment consequences and no implied threat of job detriment if the employee ignores or refuses the invitation. When made by a person in a position of authority, however, the invitation should be viewed as a demand. It carries at least an implied threat of repercussion if the employee does not accede, or an implied promise of beneficial treatment if she does. Requests and demands for sex constitute a pervasive form of sexist speech in the workplace.[21]

The second category of sexist speech is sexually explicit speech directed at the woman. Sexually explicit speech includes profanity directed towards a woman about her body or women's bodies in general, and comments about her sexual relations. Remarks about a woman's breasts, buttocks, vagina or her overall figure typify this category of speech.[22] Speculation about a woman's virginity, her choice of sexual partners or positions,

---

[21] *See, e.g.,* Jones v. Wesco Invs., 846 F.2d 1154 (8th Cir. 1988) (employer told plaintiff that someday her breasts would be his and that she should spend more time in the kitchen, where he could see her nipples better in the cool temperature); Ross v. Twenty-Four Collection, Inc., 681 F. Supp. 1547 (S.D. Fla. 1988) (plaintiff complained of repeated requests for sexual relations with her boss); Ford v. Revlon, 153 Ariz. 38, 40, 734 P.2d 580, 582 (1987) (supervisor repeatedly told employee, "I want to fuck you. I am going to fuck you."); Monge v. Superior Ct., 176 Cal. App. 3d 503, 506–07, 222 Cal. Rptr. 64, 65 (1986) (corporate officer sent a message to woman's computer terminal that read, "How about a little head?").

[22] *See supra* note 2. Most epithets relating to females refer to them primarily in sexual terms. "[T]he largest category of words degrading in sexual terms are those for women—especially for loose women. I have located roughly a thousand words and phrases describing women in sexually derogatory ways. There is nothing approaching this multitude for describing men." Schultz, *The Semantic Derogation of Women,* in Language and Sex: Difference and Dominance 64, 71–72 (B. Thorne & N. Henley eds. 1975). *See* R. Lakoff, Language and Woman's Place 24, 36 (1975).

and the frequency with which she engages in sexual relations is included in this category.[23] Pornographic depictions of women, including drawings of particular female employees, are also sexually explicit speech.[24]

The third category of sexist speech is language directed at the woman employee which is degrading to women because of their gender. This category necessarily subsumes speech from the other two categories, but goes further. It includes speech calling the employee "honey" or "dear" as well as "bitch" or "whore."[25] It also encompasses speech which denigrates women as workers by suggesting that women belong at home, rather than in the workplace.[26]

Defining sexist speech becomes increasingly difficult when determining what speech or actions should be considered de-

---

[23] *See, e.g.*, Downes v. FAA, 775 F.2d 288, 293 (Fed. Cir. 1985) (male coworkers speculated on frequency of woman's sexual encounters); Kyriazi v. Western Elec. Co., 476 F. Supp. 335, 340–41 (D.N.J. 1979) (coworkers engaged in "boisterous speculations" about woman's virginity); Morgan v. Hertz Corp., 27 F.E.P. Cases 990, 994 (W.D. Tenn. 1981) (coworkers asked woman, "Did you get any over the weekend?").

[24] *See, e.g.*, Bennett v. Corroon & Black Corp., 845 F.2d 104 (5th Cir. 1988) (employees left obscene cartoons bearing woman employee's name in men's rest room); Shrout v. Black Clawson Co., 689 F. Supp. 774, 779 (S.D. Ohio 1988) (supervisor left magazine entitled *Sex Over Forty* on plaintiff's desk); Mitchell v. OsAir, Inc., 629 F. Supp. 636, 638 (N.D. Ohio 1986) (male coworker left *Playboy* magazine in women's bathroom); Arnold v. City of Seminole, 614 F. Supp. 853, 858 (D.C. Okla. 1985) (coworkers posted pictures of a woman engaged in explicit sex acts and put a woman coworker's name on it); Zabkowicz v. West Bend Co., 589 F. Supp. 780, 782–83 (E.D. Wis. 1984) (in three-year period, 75 sexually explicit drawings posted on pillars and other conspicuous places, including drawings depicting plaintiff engaged in oral sex).

See Abrams, *Gender Discrimination and the Transformation of Workplace Norms*, 42 Vand. L. Rev. 1183, 1212 n.118 (1989) (criticizing the Sixth Circuit's minimization of the effects of pornography in the workplace in Rabidue v. Osceola Refining Co., 805 F.2d 611 (6th Cir. 1986)).

[25] *See, e.g.*, Katz v. Dole, 709 F.2d 251, 254 (4th Cir. 1983) (sexually related epithets were "intensely degrading, deriving their power to wound not only from their meaning but also from 'the disgust and violence they express phonetically'") (quoting C. Miller & K. Smith, Words and Women 109 (1977)). Under Title VII sexual harassment need not be sexual in nature; it is sufficient that the incident would not have occurred if the employee had not been a woman. Hall v. Gus Constr. Co., 842 F.2d 1010, 1014 (8th Cir. 1988); Hicks v. Gates Rubber Co., 833 F.2d 1406, 1415 (10th Cir. 1987); McKinney v. Dole, 765 F.2d 1129, 1138–39 (D.C. Cir. 1985).

[26] *See* Bowersox v. P.H. Glatfelter Co., 677 F. Supp. 307, 308 (M.D. Pa. 1988) (plaintiff complained that, among other things, her supervisor told her that her job was not a woman's job). *Cf.* Middleton, *Judge Reprimanded for Rude Remarks*, Nat'l. L.J., Aug. 24, 1987, at 2 (Judge Arthur Cieslik told a pregnant lawyer that if her husband had kept his hands in his pockets, she would not be in that condition; he asked another lawyer what her husband felt about her being in court, commenting that "ladies should not be lawyers but should be home raising a family").

grading. Is calling a woman "honey" or "sweetie" offensive?[27] What about asking a woman for a date?[28]

Although many women find such comments offensive and destructive of a professional relationship,[29] there is no societal consensus that the terms or requests are degrading. This is partly because these words are widely used in permissible contexts.[30] But even when uttered in an employment setting, and even when the listener objects to being addressed this way, there is significant disagreement about whether these terms are offensive enough to warrant regulation and punishment for their usage.[31]

To a large extent, this question turns on an unresolved issue: whose perspective should be used to determine whether a statement or action is offensive? Recently, Professor Abrams noted that courts apply differing standards:

> [C]ourts strive for a more "objective" viewpoint by subordinating the "subjective" view of the plaintiff to some other standard. Some courts compare the reaction of the plaintiff with the perspective of the "hypothetical reasonable person." Other courts replace the "reasonable person" with the "reasonable woman," yet fail to denominate the difference between the two.[32]

---

[27] *See, e.g.*, Volk v. Coler, 845 F.2d 1422, 1426–27 (7th Cir. 1988) (plaintiff alleged, among other things, that her supervisor called her and other female employees "hon," "honey," "babe" and "tiger").

[28] *See* Yates v. Arco Corp., 819 F.2d 630 (6th Cir. 1987) (supervisor frequently extended unwelcome invitations for drinks).

[29] *See* Walsh, *Confronting Sexual Harassment at Work*, Wash. Post, July 21, 1986, Washington Business, at 1, col. 2 (statement of Claudia Withers, director of employment programs at the Women's Legal Defense Fund) ("When women perceive that things like 'honey' and 'sweetie' make them uncomfortable on the job, it's against the law."). Ironically, 11 female employees in the United States Equal Employment Opportunity Commission, the agency entrusted with overseeing federal civil rights laws, accused the local administrator of sexual harassment, including allegations that he addressed them as "honey." L.A. Times, Nov. 3, 1984, § II, at 4, col. 1.

[30] *Cf.* Heins, *Banning Words: A Comment on "Words that Wound"*, 18 Harv. C.R.-C.L. L. Rev. 585, 591 n.37 (1983) (discussing "acceptable" uses of the word "nigger").

[31] Richard Cohen, a "liberal" *Washington Post* columnist, wrote in his column about an interchange he experienced. He was harshly rebuked by a short-skirted colleague when he told her she had "great legs." Cohen wrote: "[S]exual harassment is now defined so broadly . . . that many men feel like immigrants in their own country. We are not sure any more of what is and what is not permissible . . . . What are the rules?" Cohen, *What's Harassment?*, Wash. Post, July 5, 1988, at A19, col. 1.

[32] Abrams, *supra* note 24, at 1202 (footnote omitted).

Professor Abrams argues that utilizing the ostensibly objective perspective merely entrenches the "male-centered views of harassment that prevail in many workplaces, particularly by excusing verbal sexual abuse or displays of pornography."[33] She advocates a standard that reflects women's perceptions of sexual harassment when determining the necessary elements for liability.[34] Thus, asking a woman for a date or calling her "honey" could be a form of sexist speech if a woman finds such speech degrading and destructive of her ability to function effectively in the work environment.

In the foregoing three categories of sexist speech, the speech is directed at the woman employee; the speaker intends to and actually does convey his message to the woman employee. Sexually explicit and degrading speech, however, can harm women employees even when the speech is not directed. For example, a male employee who posts a picture of a naked woman in his locker may not care if others see it, yet the knowledge that it is there may affect women employees. Alternatively, a man may tell a sexually explicit joke to other employees who are willing listeners. A woman may overhear it, or even avoid hearing the specifics, yet still understand that the story degrades women. Therefore, the fourth category includes sexually explicit or degrading expressions in the workplace that are not directed at any particular woman.[35]

B. The Need for Regulation

An astounding amount of sexist speech occurs in the workplace. While numerous studies reveal varying degrees of harassment, all indicate that a significant number of working women are subjected to harassment on the job. For example, the United States Merit System Protection Board, after a comprehensive study of federal employees, concluded that between 1978 and 1980, forty-two percent of female employees suffered

---

[33] *Id.* at 1206.

[34] *Id.*

[35] The line between directed and nondirected speech is often difficult to draw, but the distinction is critical. This topic is addressed more fully later in this Article. *See infra* notes 183–189 and accompanying text.

some form of sexual harassment.[36] A recent re-examination of these figures by the Merit Board revealed virtually the same number of women complaining of sexual harassment between 1985 and 1987.[37] In sum, "there is little question that sexual harassment is a social problem of pandemic proportion."[38]

Although these studies include in their calculations nonverbal conduct, such as rape and unwanted touching, most complaints of sexual harassment involve at least some allegation of sexist speech, and many involve only verbal abuse. Between twenty and sixty percent of working women experience sexual comments or epithets, while fifty to sixty percent report being the recipient of unwanted flirtatious conduct.[39] Two-thirds of the women in a survey conducted by the Working Women's Institute reported being verbally harassed.[40] Given the tens of millions of women in the workplace, one could reasonably estimate that millions of women endure, to varying degrees, offensive and degrading comments as a condition of employment.

Sexist speech harms both the individual employee and society. This harm provides the state with several reasons for regulating sexist speech: (1) preventing the offense and hurt suffered by victims of sexist speech; (2) protecting a captive audience; (3) promoting sexual equality in the workplace; and (4) ensuring efficiency and productivity in the workplace.

1. Preventing Offense

The well-known children's adage, "sticks and stones may break my bones, but names will never hurt me," is, unfortu-

---

[36] U.S. Merit Systems Protection Board Office of Review and Studies, Sexual Harassment in the Federal Workplace: Is It a Problem? 2–3 (1981). No study has focused exclusively on verbal or written as opposed to physical harassment. Because of this, precise figures detailing the extent and kind of sexist speech in the workplace are unavailable.

[37] Merit Systems Study Update, *supra* note 1.

[38] Thomann & Wiener, *Physical and Psychological Causality as Determinants of Culpability in Sexual Harassment Cases*, 17 Sex Roles 573 (1987).

[39] *See, e.g.*, Brewer, *Further Beyond Nine to Five: An Integration and Future Directions*, 38 J. of Soc. Issues 150 (1987); C. MacKinnon, Feminism Unmodified 115 (1987) (most harassment is verbal); Simross, *Sexual Harassment: The Problem that Won't Go Away*, L.A. Times, Feb. 18, 1988, § 5, at 1, col. 2 (most typical complaint is unwanted verbal attention).

[40] *See* C. MacKinnon, *supra* note 11, at 29.

nately, wrong. It is because speech has the power to hurt that it is protected in the first place.[41] And sexist speech does hurt. It is an affront to individual dignity. Victims of such speech report feelings of personal anguish and powerlessness.[42] Most victims experience isolation, decreased job satisfaction and diminished ambition. Many experience physical manifestations of the emotional harm.[43] Ninety percent of sexual harassment victims in one survey experienced nervousness, fear and anger, while sixty-three percent complained of nausea, headaches and exhaustion.[44] Protecting women from the psychological and physical dysfunction caused by sexist speech is a possible state objective.

2. Protecting a Captive Audience

Distinct from the interest in generally protecting the sensibilities of its citizens, the state may have cause to regulate offensive speech delivered to a captive audience. The captive audience doctrine arises out of concern for individual privacy.[45] It is the counterpart of the right to speak and is justified by the theory that the right of some people to hear what they want to

---

[41] See, e.g., Kretzmer, supra note 15, at 459; A. Bickel, Morality of Consent 70–71 (1975). Cf. Delgado, supra note 15, at 143 ("Mere words, whether racial or otherwise, can cause mental, emotional or even physical harms to their targets, especially if delivered in front of others or by a person in a position of authority.").

[42] Littleton, Feminist Jurisprudence: The Difference Method Makes, 41 Stan. L. Rev. 751, 775 (1989) ("Sexual harassment victims experience powerlessness, humiliation, fear, and loss of self-confidence and self-esteem. No one denies this.").

[43] In one case the employee suffered from anxiety, diarrhea, vomiting, severe nausea and cramping. The doctor diagnosed the illness as due to harassment at work. Zabkowicz v. West Bend Co., 589 F. Supp. at 783. See also Shrout v. Black Clawson Co., 689 F. Supp. 774 (S.D. Ohio 1988) (plaintiff suffered psychological effects, leading to increased absenteeism from work); Ross v. Twenty-Four Collection, Inc., 681 F. Supp. at 1550 (court found that plaintiff's physical and mental health deteriorated markedly due to repeated sexual demands at work). See also Sexual Discrimination in the Workplace: Hearings Before Senate Committee on Labor and Human Resources, 97th Cong., 1st Sess. 518 (1981) (statement of Karen Sawvigni); Sexual Harassment in Employment Project, supra note 1, at 25 (detailing psychological effects of harassment); Bursten, Psychiatric Injury in Women's Workplaces, 14 Bull. Am. Acad. Psychiatry L., 245 (1986) (discussing effects of harassment from psychiatric perspective).

[44] Working Women's Institute, The Impact of Sexual Harassment on the Job: A Profile of the Experiences of 92 Women, Research Series Report No. 3 (1979).

[45] Erznoznik v. Jacksonville, 422 U.S. 205 (1975). See generally Farber, Content Regulation, the First Amendment: A Revisionist View, 68 Geo. L.J. 727, 747 n.71 (1980); Haiman, Speech v. Privacy: Is There a Right Not To Be Spoken To?, 67 Nw. U.L. Rev. 153 (1972).

hear, or to say what they want to say, must at times yield to the right of other people to avoid being forced to hear the speech. Thus, speech is entitled to less first amendment protection when forced upon a captive audience than when directed toward a willing listener. The question then is how to determine when an audience is deemed captive for purposes of employing this doctrine.

Courts have addressed the idea of a captive audience in a variety of contexts, including pedestrians on the streets,[46] commuters on buses,[47] individuals in their homes,[48] and children in a school assembly hall.[49] The finding of captivity in all these circumstances reflects a belief that the recipients of the communication were somehow compelled to hear or see the message. Similarly, women employees sometimes may be forced to endure unwanted messages by virtue of being unable to leave the workplace. If a women really wants to avoid the offensive speech, she may be forced to leave her job.

Certainly a reasonable burden, short of fleeing the workplace, should be placed on the listener to avoid an offensive message. A court's conclusion that an audience is captive necessarily involves a balancing of the free speech concerns against the right of the recipient not to hear. Thus, precise analysis of the application of the captive audience doctrine to women employees will be presented following discussion of the first amendment interests.

3. Promoting Equality in the Workplace

The greatest evil of sexist language may be in the damage it docs to the societal goal of sexual equality in the workplace. Sexist speech, like rape, is not only—and perhaps not at all—about sex.[50] It is about power.[51] It is the way that some men

---

[46] *Erznoznik*, 422 U.S. 205 (1975). *See infra* notes 154–155 and accompanying text.

[47] Lehman v. City of Shaker Heights, 418 U.S. 298 (1974).

[48] *See infra* note 150 and accompanying text.

[49] *See* Bethel School Dist. No. 403 v. Fraser, 478 U.S. 675, 685 (1986) (suggesting that high school students attending a school-sponsored, on-campus assembly were captive because they could not avoid hearing what was said at the assembly).

[50] *See* S. Estrich, Real Rape (1987).

[51] *See* Lafontaine & Tredeau, *The Frequency, Sources and Correlates of Sexual Harassment Among Women in Traditional Male Occupations*, 15 Sex Roles 433, 436

respond to the threat posed by the reality of women in the workplace, especially when women enter a field traditionally occupied by men.[52] In essence, sexist speech reinstitutionalizes barriers in the workplace based on gender. When women subjected to sexist speech leave the job, or persist but with decreased productivity, it serves to perpetuate male dominance in the workplace.[53]

The state's interest in promoting equality in the workplace arguably justifies censoring speech based on two theories. First, the state may want to ban speech because the speech implicitly or explicitly advocates inequality. For example, when a man tells a woman worker that she is a "stupid whore," the speech may be viewed as conveying a message about the subordination of women. Second, the state may want to censor speech because the speech itself discriminates. The message "you're a stupid whore" could compel women to withdraw from the workplace, either by leaving the job or by functioning less productively. Each theory requires separate consideration.

The state may have an interest in suppressing speech that advocates inequality on the ground that such speech leads to discriminatory behavior. Speech has the power to change or reinforce attitudes and therefore influence behavior. Indeed, studies of racist speech reveal the critical role that speech plays

---

(1986). The authors conclude: "The existence of sexual harassment in the workplace comes as no surprise, of course, given the pervasiveness of male sexual dominance in society as a whole . . . . The workplace represents simply one additional arena in which men exercise their general social/sexual power." *See also* Adams, *Sexual Harassment and the Employer-Employee Relationship*, 84 W. Va. L. Rev. 789 (1982); B. Gutek, Sex and the Workplace 10 (1985).

[52] The fact that sexual harassment is an issue of power more than of sex may explain why women in male-dominated occupations experience greater harassment. Lafontaine & Tredeau, *supra* note 51. *See also* Fain & Anderton, *Sexual Harassment: Context and Status*, 17 Sex Roles 291, 308 (1987) (women in traditionally male occupations are seen as a greater threat to male power and privilege). *Cf.* Chicago Tribune, Oct. 8, 1987, § 1A, at 53, col. 1 (25% of Finnish men in traditionally female-dominated occupations complained of women making suggestive remarks, telling sexual jokes and pressuring them for sex).

[53] *See* Roberts v. U.S. Jaycees, 468 U.S. 609, 625 (1984) (recognizing that the stereotypical view of women undercut their full participation in society); Taub, *supra* note 1, at 368 (sexual harassment is one more reason that women do not advance beyond the inferior position they traditionally have held); Bursten, *Psychiatric Injury in Women's Workplaces*, 14 Bull. Am. Acad. Psychiatry L. 245, 247 (1986) (harassment is a barrier to full participation in workforce). *Cf.* American Bookseller Ass'n v. Hudnut, 771 F.2d 323 (7th Cir. 1985), *aff'd*, 475 U.S. 1001 (1986) (depiction of subordination in the context of pornography tends to perpetuate subordination of women).

in increasing the incidence of racial prejudice.[54] Professor Kretzmer, after examining the available historical and sociological data, concluded:

> Speech is the primary means by which human beings communicate ideas and beliefs . . . . It is evident, therefore, that speech may influence ideas, beliefs and attitudes. This truism is an essential ingredient of free speech theory, which regards speech as a means of influencing others. From [this general proposition] it follows that racist speech may induce nonracists to adopt racist beliefs . . . and may reinforce such beliefs and attitudes or ideas among nonracists. This means that racist speech may increase the incidence of racial prejudice and discrimination in society.[55]

By analogy, sexist speech reflects and reinforces a belief that women are sex objects, rather than productive and equal co-workers. Thus, prohibiting sexist speech from the workplace may help eradicate sexism in society and reduce discriminatory behavior in the employment setting.

Additionally, the state might regulate sexist speech not because of the ideology it espouses, but because it in fact discriminates; speech that causes inequality, rather than speech about inequality, would be silenced. Professor MacKinnon first proposed the censorship of speech during the recent attempts to ban pornography in order to eliminate discrimination.[56] An Indianapolis ordinance, for example, which allowed women to enjoin the production, sale, distribution or exhibition of pornography, was justified by the theory that pornography is a discriminatory practice based on sex which denies women equal opportunities in society.[57]

Similarly, under Title VII, sexual harassment is prohibited because such behavior subjects women to terms and conditions

---

[54] Kretzmer, *supra* note 15, at 462–63.

[55] *Id.* at 462.

[56] *See* MacKinnon, *supra* note 39, at 146–63.

[57] *See American Booksellers*, 771 F.2d 323 (7th Cir. 1985), *aff'd*, 475 U.S. 1001 (1986).

of employment which men need not endure.[58] By creating a hostile environment for women workers, sexist speech excludes women from full participation in the workforce. The determination of the extent to which the state may regulate speech that advocates discrimination and speech that in fact discriminates, however, must await the first amendment analysis later in this Article.

4. Ensuring an Efficient Workplace

All evidence indicates that sexist speech diminishes effective workplace performance. A study conducted by the United States Merit System Board conservatively estimated that, between May 1985 and May 1987, sexual harassment cost the federal government $267 million.[59] This cost reflected the expense involved in replacing employees who left jobs because of harassment, sick leave awarded for missed work, and money lost from decreased productivity.[60]

In a series of cases the Supreme Court recognized a state interest in ensuring the efficient performance of a public workplace, which, under certain circumstances, justifies the suppression of public employees' free speech rights.[61] Most recently, in *Rankin v. McPherson*,[62] the Court recognized "the interest of the state, as an employer, in promoting the efficiency of the public services it performs through its employees."[63] In such cases, the Court has considered whether the statement impairs discipline by superiors or harmony among coworkers, detrimentally affects working relationships when loyalty and confidence are necessary, hampers the performance of the speaker's duties, or interferes with the operation of the office.[64] When determining the constitutionality of regulating sexist speech in the workplace the courts must, therefore, weigh these considerations against the first amendment values of the employee's speech.

---

[58] Meritor Sav. Bank v. Vinson, 477 U.S. 57 (1986).

[59] Merit Systems Study Update, *supra* note 1 at 39.

[60] *Id.*

[61] *See* Rankin v. McPherson, 483 U.S. 378 (1987); Connick v. Myers, 461 U.S. 138 (1983); Pickering v. Bd. of Educ., 391 U.S. 563 (1968).

[62] 483 U.S. 378.

[63] *Id.* at 388 (quoting *Pickering*, 391 U.S. at 568).

[64] 483 U.S. at 388.

II. A First Amendment Analysis

One solution to the harms of sexist speech is to ban such speech from the workplace. Legislators in some cities have already proposed ordinances restricting sexist speech and others are beginning to consider such laws.[65] Sexist speech can also be regulated by imposing civil liability on those who use sexist speech or on employers when such speech occurs on their premises. Censoring speech in either fashion raises concern about the right to free expression.

In response, courts could conclude that the first amendment does not apply to sexist speech in the workplace. Although the first amendment appears to be written in absolute terms—commanding that no law shall abridge freedom of speech—it has often been interpreted to the contrary.[66] Narrow categories of speech have been found to lie outside of the first amendment's protective reach. If sexist speech were to fit within one of the existing exceptions, its regulation would pose no constitutional problems.

A. Existing Categories of Unprotected Speech

Certain categories of speech, such as fighting words, obscenity and perhaps group libel have been declared outside the purview of the first amendment.[67]

The fighting words doctrine was first enunciated by the Supreme Court in 1942. In *Chaplinsky v. New Hampshire*, the Court held that fighting words—words "which by their very utterance inflict injury or tend to incite an immediate breach of the peace"—are not protected by the first amendment.[68] The state did not need to demonstrate imminent violence.[69] Instead, the Court accepted the legislative assumption that there is a

---

[65] *See supra* note 10 and accompanying text.

[66] *See infra* note 67 and accompanying text.

[67] *See* Bose Corp. v. Consumers Union, 466 U.S. 485, 504 & n.22 (1984). Other unprotected categories include child pornography, New York v. Ferber, 458 U.S. 747 (1982); incitement of imminent lawlessness, Brandenburg v. Ohio, 395 U.S. 444 (1969) (per curiam); and defamation, New York Times v. Sullivan, 376 U.S. 254 (1964).

[68] 315 U.S. 568, 572 (1942) (footnote omitted).

[69] *Id.* at 574.

connection between abusive language and the outbreak of violence.

Since *Chaplinsky*, the Court has consistently construed the fighting words doctrine narrowly.[70] It has emphasized that fighting words may be punished only when they have a direct tendency to cause acts of violence by the person to whom, individually, the remark is addressed.[71] Thus, under current Supreme Court interpretations, any regulation of speech on the basis of the fighting words doctrine requires that: (1) the insulting and abusive words are hurled directly at another in a one-on-one confrontation; and (2) the words are likely to provoke violence by the person addressed.[72] It is assumed that words directed at an audience will not provoke violence, and it must be established that offensive words directed at an individual are likely to incite a breach of peace in the particular circumstances.[73]

Given these requirements, the state would have difficulty justifying its regulation of sexist speech in the workplace under the fighting words doctrine. Not all sexist speech is directed at an individual,[74] and none of the existing or proposed regulations are limited to situations in which such speech is likely to provoke acts of violence. Title VII of the Civil Rights Act, for example, prohibits speech which creates an offensive, hostile or abusive working environment.[75] It does not require that such speech be directed at an individual,[76] nor does it require an imminent breach of peace.[77]

---

[70] *See, e.g.*, Lasson, *supra* note 15, at 92.

[71] Cohen v. California, 403 U.S. 15, 20 (1971).

[72] *Id.*

[73] The Supreme Court has not upheld a conviction under the fighting words doctrine in over 25 years. *See* Gard, *Fighting Words as Free Speech*, 58 Wash. U.L.Q. 531, 536 (1980) (post-*Chaplinsky* Supreme Court decisions have rendered the doctrine "nothing more than a quaint remnant of an earlier morality that has no place in a democratic society dedicated to the principle of free expression").

[74] *See supra* note 35 and accompanying text.

[75] Title VII, 42 U.S.C. § 2000 (1981).

[76] Both directed and nondirected speech, however, must be sufficiently pervasive in the workplace to establish a cause of action. *See* Ross v. Double Diamond Inc., 672 F. Supp. 261, 269 (N.D. Tex. 1987) (Title VII is not an impenetrable shield protecting employees from mere utterances of sexual, ethnic or racial slurs which engender offensive feelings in the employee.); *cf.* Eaton v. City of Tulsa, 415 U.S. 697, 698 (1974) (per curiam) (single use in court of phrase "chicken shit," at least when not directed at the judge, was not punishable as contempt without a further showing that use of the expletive constituted an imminent threat to the administration of justice).

[77] *See* Meritor Sav. Bank v. Vinson, 477 U.S. 57, 68 (1986). *See also* legal definitions of sexual harassment described *supra* note 20.

More significantly, sexist speech is not likely to provoke violence. Women generally do not physically assault men, whether because of differences in size and strength or because of cultural norms.[78] The demoralizing effect of the speech itself, which reinforces the role of women as subservient and inconsequential, makes it even less likely that such speech would incite a breach of peace. Women historically have not reacted to sexist speech by physically fighting back.[79] It is only recently that woman have begun to "fight" back at all, and then only verbally, by complaining to management or by filing lawsuits.[80]

In addition to fighting words, the Supreme Court has also held that obscenity is not protected speech under the first amendment.[81] Although the test for obscenity has varied over time, the current formulation is a three-part test developed in *Miller v. California*.[82] Something is obscene under *Miller* if: (1) the average person, applying contemporary community standards would find that it, taken as a whole, appeals to the prurient interest; (2) it depicts or describes, in a patently offensive way, sexual conduct specifically defined by the applicable state law; and (3) taken as a whole, it lacks serious literary, artistic, political or scientific value.[83]

Some sexist speech bears no resemblance to obscenity as defined by these three requirements. Speech that is not sexually explicit—asking a woman in "polite terms" to have sexual re-

---

[78] *See* A. Montague, The Anatomy of Swearing (1967) (words which would provoke violence in men will cause emotional upset in women).

[79] The irony is that offensive language directed towards men may constitute fighting words if men are more likely to react aggressively. *Cf. Sexual Abuse: When Men are Victims*, L.A. Times, Jan. 10, 1989, § 5, at 1 (statement of Daniel Sonkin) ("[M]en who are sexually abused tend to act out their problems, while women internalize . . . women are more likely to have depression, anxiety and phobias; men are likely to be aggressive."). Thus, calling a man a "prick" may be unprotected fighting words if he is likely to respond violently, yet calling a woman a "cunt" might not. This result may provide support for those theorists who argue that the first amendment is not appropriate for analyzing the situation of women, that the first amendment was written by men for a patriarchal society. *See* C. MacKinnon, *Not a Moral Issue, supra* note 14, at 336.

The Supreme Court has made clear that the particular recipient of speech should be considered in judging the likelihood of violence. *See* Houston v. Hill, 482 U.S. 451, 462 (1987) (fighting words exception might require narrower application in cases involving police, who, properly trained, are less likely to respond belligerently to abusive language) (citation omitted).

[80] *See supra* note 4 and accompanying text.

[81] Roth v. United States, 354 U.S. 476 (1957).

[82] 413 U.S. 15 (1973). *See also* Pope v. Illinois, 481 U.S. 497 (1987).

[83] *Miller*, 413 U.S. at 24.

lations, calling her "honey," or ridiculing her for participating in the workforce—is not obscene under the *Miller* test. Even sexually explicit speech is likely not to appeal to the prurient interest. As noted above, most sexist speech, even sexually explicit language, is not about sex or arousing sexual desire. It is about developing and maintaining a power relationship.[84] Thus, regulation of sexist speech cannot be justified on the grounds that it is obscene.

Finally, regulation of sexist speech may be justified under the concept of group libel. This doctrine has its roots in a 1952 Supreme Court decision, *Beauharnais v. Illinois.*[85] The Court, in a 5-4 decision, held that the state, consistent with the first amendment, could ban speech which libeled or defamed a racial or religious group.[86] In so doing, the Court relied on then prevailing doctrine, that speech which libeled or defamed individuals was excluded from first amendment protection.[87] It also relied upon the holding in *Chaplinsky* that speech aired to a group of people, like that directed at an individual, could constitute a breach of peace.[88]

Reliance on a group libel approach to justify regulation of sexist speech, however, is unwise. First, *Beauharnais* likely is no longer good law. Both premises of the decision—that libel laws are not covered by the first amendment and that words aimed at groups could constitute breaches of peace—have since been rejected by the Court. The former premise was disavowed in *New York Times Co. v. Sullivan,*[89] where the Court held that defamation may be protected speech in certain circumstances.[90] The latter premise was limited by the Court's narrowing of the fighting words doctrine in *Cohen v. California.*[91] There the Court held that words must be directed at an individual and not simply at a group of people to constitute a breach of peace.[92] Virtually

---

[84] *See supra* note 51 and accompanying text.

[85] 343 U.S. 250 (1952).

[86] *Id.* at 263–64.

[87] *See* Note, *A Communitarian Defense of Group Libel Laws,* 101 Harv. L. Rev 682 (1988).

[88] *Id. See supra* notes 68–69 and accompanying text.

[89] 376 U.S. 254 (1964). *See also* Philadelphia Newspapers, Inc. v. Hepps, 475 U.S. 767 (1986).

[90] 376 U.S. at 279–83.

[91] 403 U.S. 15 (1971).

[92] *See supra* notes 71–73 and accompanying text.

all judicial consideration of *Beauharnais* conclude that the case, although never explicitly overturned,[93] is not reconcilable with contemporary first amendment theories.[94]

Moreover, even if *Beauharnais* were good law the group libel doctrine might not extend to sexist speech. Laws prohibiting group libel traditionally applied only to speech defaming racial or religious groups. Although there are commonalities between religious, racial and sexual defamation, the Illinois Supreme Court in *Beauharnais* upheld the state statute only insofar as it prohibited those utterances which had a strong tendency to cause violence. As shown earlier, sexist speech is not likely to induce breaches of peace.[95] Thus, the group libel doctrine, even if still valid, is likely inapplicable.

B. Creating a New Category: The Values of Free Speech

Sexist speech, therefore, does not fit within any of the existing categories of expression excluded from first amendment protection. Perhaps, however, a new categorical exception for sexist speech should be created. Justification for such a categorical exclusion would require that sexist speech not implicate the values underlying freedom of expression. On the other hand, if sexist speech should foster any of these values, regulating or punishing such expression requires a careful balancing of those values against the government's interests in regulation. Either way, consideration of the values underlying the first amendment is necessary.

---

[93] *See* Smith v. Collin, 439 U.S. 916, 919 (1978) (Blackmun, J., dissenting from denial of certiorari) (*Beauharnais* "has not been overruled or formally limited").

[94] *See* Collin v. Smith, 578 F.2d 1197, 1204 (7th Cir.), *cert. denied,* 439 U.S. 916 (1978) ("It may be questioned . . . whether the *tendency to induce violence* approach sanctioned implicitly in *Beauharnais* would pass constitutional muster today.") (emphasis in original); Tollett v. U.S., 485 F.2d 1087, 1094 n.14 (8th Cir. 1973); American Booksellers Ass'n v. Hudnut, 771 F.2d 323, 331 n.3 (7th Cir. 1985), *aff'd,* 475 U.S. 1001 (1986) (subsequent cases "had so washed away the foundations of *Beauharnais* that it could not be considered authoritative"); *see also* Post, *Cultural Heterogeneity and Law: Pornography, Blasphemy and the First Amendment,* 76 Calif. L. Rev. 297, 330 (1988) ("*Beauharnais* is . . . damaged goods.").

[95] *See supra* notes 78–80 and accompanying text.

There is no consensus about the purpose or meaning of the first amendment.[96] Numerous books and articles have suggested various reasons for valuing freedom of speech. The following justifications are most frequently offered: (1) speech enables citizens to make decisions required for self-governance; (2) speech advances the search for truth; and (3) speech enhances self-realization and the individual's potential for growth and advancement.[97]

1. Self-Government and Political Speech

The self-governance theory suggests that a predominant value of free speech is to facilitate democracy.[98] Because the people are sovereign, they need access to relevant information in order to participate intelligently in the electoral process, both in making decisions themselves and in communicating their wishes to elected officials. "Thus, the principle of the freedom of speech springs from the necessities of the program of self-

---

[96] See Shiffrin, *The First Amendment and Economic Regulation: Away from a General Theory of the First Amendment*, 78 Nw. U.L. Rev. 1212, 1252 (1983):

> [T]he Court has been unwilling to confine the first amendment to a single value or even to a few values. In recent years, the first amendment literature has exploded with commentary finding first amendment values involving liberty, self-realization, the marketplace of ideas, equality, self-government and more . . . . [T]he Court has been generous about the range of values relevant in first amendment theory, and unreceptive to those who ask it to confine first amendment values to a particular favorite.

See also BeVier, *The First Amendment and Political Speech: An Inquiry into the Substance and Limits of Principle*, 30 Stan. L. Rev. 299 (1978).

[97] See Cass, *The Perils of Positive Thinking: Constitutional Interpretation and Negative First Amendment Theory*, 34 UCLA L. Rev. 1405, 1411 (1987); Greenawalt, *Free Speech Justifications*, 89 Colum. L. Rev. 119 (1989). Constitutional scholars debate whether these values exist in a hierarchy, whether only one value is important, whether certain values subsume others, and how these values are even defined. See, e.g., Redish, *The Value of Free Speech*, 130 U. Pa. L. Rev. 591, 592 (1982); Baker, *Realizing Self-Realization: Corporate Political Expenditures and Redish's The Value of Free Speech*, 130 U. Pa. L. Rev. 646 (1982).

[98] See Mills v. Alabama, 384 U.S. 214, 218–19 (1966) ("[W]hatever differences may exist about interpretation of the First Amendment, there is practically universal agreement that a major purpose of that Amendment was to protect the free discussion of governmental affairs . . . includ[ing] . . . matters relating to political processes."). See also Karst, *Equality as a Central Principle in the First Amendment*, 43 U. Chi. L. Rev. 20, 24–25 (1975) (conception of self-government based on social contract theory among political equals); Schlag, *An Attack on Categorical Approaches to Freedom of Speech*, 30 UCLA L. Rev. 671 (1983).

government . . . . It is a deduction from the basic American agreement that public issues shall be decided by universal suffrage."[99]

Although the first amendment undeniably is concerned with speech that promotes self-governance, the question is what type of speech this includes. Some, most notably Judge Bork, argue that only "political speech," narrowly defined as criticism of public officials and policies, and speech addressed to the conduct of any government unit, is entitled to first amendment protection. As Judge Bork writes, "[c]onstitutional protection shall be accorded only to speech that is explicitly political. There is no basis for judicial intervention to protect other forms of expression, be they scientific, literary or that variety of expression we call obscene or pornographic."[100]

This, however, is a minority position. Even Alexander Meiklejohn, the "parent" of the self-governance theory, ultimately concluded that political speech includes expression about philosophical, social, artistic, economic, literary and ethical matters.[101] This expanded view of political speech recognizes that the ability to intelligently govern requires information from all spheres of life.

One could easily describe at least some sexist expression as political within the expanded definition of political speech. Certainly statements about a woman's role and responsibility in society, even when expressed in intemperate words, are expressions of political and social concern.[102]

The Supreme Court, however, increasingly has drawn a distinction between political speech and sexually explicit

---

[99] A. Meiklejohn, Free Speech and Its Relation to Self Government 39 (1948).

[100] Bork, *Neutral Principles and Some First Amendment Problems*, 47 Ind. L.J. 1, 20 (1971).

[101] Meiklejohn, *The First Amendment is an Absolute*, 1961 Sup. Ct. Rev. 245. The Supreme Court has noted that its cases "have never suggested that expression about philosophical, social, artistic, economic, literary or ethical matters . . . is not entitled to full First Amendment protection." Abood v. Detroit Bd. of Educ., 431 U.S. 209, 231 (1977). Certainly there is nothing in the language of the amendment that limits coverage to a narrow definition of political speech.

[102] F. Haiman, Speech and Law in a Free Society 96 (1981) (defamatory comments about groups of people are necessarily expression of political views: "If a speaker says that 'women's place is in the home,' he is, at one and the same time, defaming 51% of our population and expressing a fundamental political position on a major question of public policy.").

speech. The Court has recognized greater state authority to regulate sexually explicit expression than other types of speech, such as speech about self-government, which goes more to the "core" of the first amendment.[103]

Many scholars, most notably Professor Tribe, have argued that this hierarchical ranking of speech is unsound, and poses risks to freedom of expression:

> Once an expressive act is determined to be within the coverage of the first amendment, its entitlement to protection must not vary with the viewpoint expressed, and all attempts to create content-based subcategories entail at least some risk that government will in fact be discriminating against disfavored points of view.[104]

Others assert that if society is willing to march our children off to war to protect free choices in the political arena, it should be equally willing to send them off to protest against the state's power to determine what messages are worthless.[105]

---

[103] See NAACP v. Claiborne Hardware Co., 458 U.S. 886, 913 (1982) ("This Court has recognized that expression on public issues 'has always rested on the highest rung of the hierarchy of First Amendment values.'") (quoting Carey v. Brown, 447 U.S. 455, 467 (1980)); First Nat'l Bank of Boston v. Bellotti, 435 U.S. 765, 776 (1978) (speech on matters of public concern lie at the "heart of the first amendment's protection"); Buckley v. Valeo, 424 U.S. 1, 14 (1976) ("The First Amendment affords the broadest protection to . . . political expression in order to 'assure [the] unfettered interchange of ideas for the bringing about of the political and social changes desired by the people.'") (quoting Roth v. United States, 354 U.S. 476, 484 (1957)).

This hierarchical approach has often led to greater regulation of speech which the Court finds not to be at the core of the first amendment. Traditionally, the Court, when using a balancing test to determine the appropriate application of the first amendment, places a "thumb" on the side of the scale measuring the speech interest. That is, when the interest in free speech and the state's interest in censorship are of equal weight, the speech interest prevails. A compelling state interest, therefore, is necessary to overcome the presumption against infringing free speech rights. For speech at the outskirts of the first amendment, however, the Court has sanctioned regulation or curtailment of speech without reference to a compelling state interest. See Goldman, A Doctrine of Worthier Speech: Young v. American Mini Theatres, 21 St. Louis U.L.J. 281, 286 (1977).

[104] L. Tribe, American Constitutional Law 940 (2d ed. 1988). Other scholarly critics include: T. Emerson, The System of Freedom of Expression 326 (1979); Farber, Content Regulation and the First Amendment: A Revisionist View, 68 Geo. L.J. 727 (1980); Scanlon, Freedom of Expression and Categories of Expression, 40 U. Pitt. L. Rev. 519 (1979).

[105] Redish, supra note 97. Professor Redish makes this comment in response to Justice Stevens' remarks in Young v. American Mini Theatres, 427 U.S. 50, 70 (1976) ("few of us would march our sons and daughters off to war to preserve the citizen's right to see 'Specified Sexual Activities' in the theaters of our choice").

Feminists should find this hierarchical approach particularly troubling. Laws prohibiting sexually explicit language usually proceeded from antiquated notions of sexual propriety; the objective was not to promote sexual equality but to foster puritanical ideas.[106] Historically, legislators have used the state's censorship power to thwart objectives of the feminist agenda. For example, obscenity laws have often been used to ban materials that feminists would endorse, such as birth control information.[107] Censorship of sexually explicit language has not been motivated by a desire to promote sexual equality, but as a way to protect the "weaker sex" from exposure to sexual ideas and vulgarity. For example, the ordinance in *Cohen v. California*[108] prohibited individuals from using any vulgar, profane or indecent language within the presence of women or children. These laws and practices reflect the paternalistic assumption that women, like children, need protection from male speech that offends puritanical mores.

Ultimately, sexually explicit speech cannot simply be dismissed as non-political. Sexist speech—be it about sex, sexual relationships or a woman's body—may be deemed political under the feminists' own slogan that the personal is political.[109] The dynamics of interpersonal relationships and sexual conduct directly bear on the structure of social and political life. Telling a woman that she is a cunt may, in certain circumstances, convey a message about her social stature and political power— or powerlessness.

Finding that some sexist speech has political content suggests that categorical exclusion cannot be justified on the ground

---

[106] *See infra* note 107.

[107] Hoffman, *Feminism, Pornography and Law*, 133 U. Pa. L. Rev. 497, 522 (1985); Comment, *Anti-Pornography Laws and First Amendment Values*, 98 Harv. L. Rev. 460, 467 (1984) (feminists realize that laws appearing to proceed from attitudes about sexual propriety rather than equality can be turned against women).

[108] 403 U.S. 15 (1971).

[109] Amicus brief of Nan Hunter and Sylvia Law, submitted in *American Booksellers*, 771 F.2d 323 (7th Cir. 1985), *aff'd*, 475 U.S. 1001 (1986). *See also* Post, *supra* note 94, at 328 ("it is hard to understand how pornography can communicate attitudes of disrespect toward women if it is entirely devoid of propositional, emotive and artistic content"); Perry, *Freedom of Expression: An Essay on Theory and Doctrine*, 78 Nw. U. L. Rev. 1137, 1182 (1984) ("there is no denying that obscene pornography constitutes a political and moral vision"). *But see* Sunstein, *Pornography and the First Amendment*, 1986 Duke L.J. 589, 607 (fact that pornography conveys an ideology does not make it political speech).

that such speech lacks any social value. It does not mean such speech cannot be regulated; false speech about a public official, said with actual malice, is unprotected, even though it is about self-government.[110] Because sexist speech fosters first amendment values, the state's ability to prohibit or govern such speech must turn on a balancing of the state interests with the first amendment rights of the speaker. That balancing is accomplished in Section III of this Article.

2. Marketplace of Ideas

Political theorists argue for freedom of speech based upon the "marketplace of ideas" metaphor.[111] According to this theory, the "ultimate good desired is better reached by free trade in ideas—the best test of truth is the power of the thought to get itself accepted in the competition of the market. . . ."[112]

Free expression, according to this rationale, allows truth to prevail in several ways. If the opinion expressed is true, it may convince others who subscribe to a different opinion of the error of their position. Even if the opinion expressed is false, it compels proponents of the opposing position to muster arguments against it. This strengthens the true position, and bolsters the commitment of the people. If the opinion contains both true and false elements, "sifting the false from the true is best carried out by allowing opinions to clash."[113]

There are several weaknesses in the marketplace of ideas metaphor, especially when applied to the concept of sexist speech. The theory assumes that a recognizable and acceptable truth will usually prevail. Challenging this assumption, Professor Solum identifies two possible understandings of truth for purposes of evaluating the theory: truth as correspondence and truth as consensus.[114]

---

[110] New York Times v. Sullivan, 376 U.S. 254 (1964).

[111] J.S. Mill, On Liberty (1859).

[112] Abrams v. United States, 250 U.S. 616, 630 (1919) (Holmes, J., dissenting). *See also* Dennis v. United States, 341 U.S. 494, 546–53 (1951) (Frankfurter, J., concurring); Whitney v. California, 274 U.S. 357, 375–78 (1927) (Brandeis, J., concurring).

[113] Kretzmer, *supra* note 15, at 468.

[114] L. Solum, *Freedom of Communicative Action: A Theory of the First Amendment Freedom of Speech*, 83 Nw. U.L. Rev. 54 (1989).

The truth as correspondence idea provides that "a proposition is true if and only if the content of the proposition corresponds to an existing state of affairs."[115] People must act rationally if the marketplace is to produce truth as correspondence. They must reach conclusions based on the merits of the arguments. While this may occur in certain limited contexts, such as scientific inquiry,[116] there is no evidence that people generally reach decisions this way. A rational process is particularly unlikely when the topic of discussion is one fraught with ingrained and reinforced stereotypes such as sexist speech.[117] As Professor Kretzmer points out in relation to the analagous area of racist belief, "[l]iterature on racism reveals that a variety of psychological and sociological factors accounts for racist attitudes and beliefs. The notion that these beliefs and attitudes are acquired by a rational decision based on weighing conflicting arguments is no less than naive."[118]

Truth as consensus is based in the idea that the opinion which achieves consensus after open discussion is deemed the truth, while the view rejected becomes falsehood.[119] The theory is indifferent to the ultimate message adopted.[120] It permits the advocacy of any idea, creating the possibility that the idea will be accepted as truth.

Certain ideas, however, may be so unacceptable to a democratic society that even a consensus of opinion cannot validate them. Moreover, one must accept the underlying process or "marketplace" to support the truth as consensus theory. Society may be prepared to freely accept ideas that garner consensus in a "perfect" market—where arguments are presented fairly and

---

[115] *Id.* at 69. *See generally* Ingber, *The Marketplace of Ideas: A Legitimizing Myth*, 1984 Duke L.J. 1, 25.

[116] Even this claim may be suspect. *See* T. Kuhn, The Structure of Scientific Revolutions (2d ed. 1970).

[117] *See, e.g.,* Note, *Group Vilification Reconsidered*, 89 Yale L.J. 308, 312–13 (1979); Kretzmer, *supra* note 15, at 469–70.

[118] Kretzmer, *supra* note 15, at 470.

[119] It appears that Justice Oliver Wendall Holmes also viewed truth as consensus to be the basis of the marketplace of ideas theory. *See* M. Lerner, The Mind and Faith of Justice Holmes 290 (1954).

[120] *See* A. Bickel, *supra* note 41; Arkes, *Civility and the Restriction of Speech: Rediscovering the Defamation of Groups*, 1974 Sup. Ct. Rev. 281; Schauer, *Speech and "Speech"—Obscenity and "Obscenity": An Exercise in the Interpretation of Constitutional Language*, 67 Geo. L.J. 899, 915–16 (1979).

where rational discussion prevails—but society may not accept as truth those ideas that gain adherence through the use of force or misinformation.

This perfect marketplace, if it exists at all, does not exist with respect to sexist speech. In such a market, a false or undesirable message will be countered by a contrary message. Women, however, rarely respond when a male employer, supervisor or coworker directs an offensive comment to them.[121] In many cases, no reply is desired by the speaker, as he seeks only to shock and hurt. In other words, when women are called "bitches" or "whores" there is no marketplace of ideas at work because no discussion is invited or permitted. Even if a woman does respond to the sexist message, the destructive effects of the initial comment remain. In such circumstances, the process cannot be trusted to generate an acceptable "truth."[122]

Despite these significant weaknesses in the marketplace of ideas metaphor, experience still suggests that "the prospects for advancement of understanding are more promising in open climates than in closed ones."[123] Whatever flaws exist in the marketplace, it would be worse for courts to allow the state to decide which ideas will flourish and which will be denied discussion. Truth is more likely to prevail even in an imperfect market than under a system of government censorship.

Moreover, sexist speech conveys a message that would be lost if the speech were cleansed of its ugliness. It reminds society of the deplorable nature of such thoughts and ideas. The notion that the speech's very offensiveness may convey an important message has received support from the Supreme Court. For example, the plurality in *FCC v. Pacifica Foundation*[124] noted that the "fact that society may find speech offensive is not a sufficient reason for suppressing it. Indeed, if it is the speaker's opinion that gives offense, that consequence is a reason for according it constitutional protection."[125]

---

[121] *See generally* MacKinnon, *Not A Moral Issue, supra* note 14, at 337 (free speech rights of men silence free speech rights of women). *See also* Hoffman, *supra* note 107, at 522 (discussing same theory).

[122] *But see* Gertz v. Robert Welch, Inc., 418 U.S. 323, 339 (1974) ("Under the first amendment, there is no such thing as a false idea.").

[123] Greenawalt, *Speech and Crime*, 1980 Am. Bar. Found. Res. J. 647, 672.

[124] 438 U.S. 726 (1978).

[125] *Id.* at 745. *See also* Street v. New York, 394 U.S. 576, 592 (1969) (Harlan, J.,

Professor Farber expressed similar concerns when he discussed the dangers of limiting racist rhetoric like Nazi invective:

> [O]ffensiveness is often an important part of the speaker's message: use of offensive language reveals the existence of something offensive and ugly, whether in the situation described by the speaker or in the speaker's mind itself. In either event, the language reveals an important though unpleasant truth about the world. Suppressing this language violates a cardinal principle of free society, that truths are better confronted than repressed.[126]

At least in theory, then, sexist speech contributes to a marketplace of ideas. This does not mean, however, that sexist speech can never be regulated—"[e]ven protected speech is not equally permissible in all places and at all times"[127]—but determination of what constitutes permissible regulation must await consideration in Section III of the state's interest balanced against free speech concerns.

3. Self-Realization

The self-realization theory maintains that speech is essential to the development of the speaker's potential for "personal growth and self-fulfillment."[128] As the Supreme Court recognized, "[t]he First Amendment presupposes that the freedom to speak one's mind is . . . an aspect of individual liberty . . . and

---

concurring) ("It is firmly settled that under our Constitution the public expression of ideas may not be prohibited merely because the ideas are themselves offensive to some of their hearers.").

[126] D. Farber, *Civilizing Public Discourse: An Essay on Professor Bickel, Justice Harlan, and the Enduring Significance of Cohen v. California*, 1980 Duke L.J. 283, 302. *See also* F. Haiman, *supra* note 102, at 133 (epithets sometimes are a useful commodity in the marketplace of ideas).

[127] Cornelius v. NAACP Legal Defense & Educ. Fund, Inc., 473 U.S. 788, 799 (1985).

[128] F. Schauer, Free Speech: A Philosophical Enquiry 49 (1982). For a discussion of the self-realization theory, see M. Redish, Freedom of Expression: A Critical Analysis 15–40 (1984); Baker, *Scope of the First Amendment Freedom of Speech*, 25 UCLA L. Rev. 964, 990–1009 (1978); T. Emerson, The System of Freedom of Expression 6 (1971).

thus a good unto itself."[129] Freedom of expression aids the listener's human development by promoting independent judgment and autonomous decisionmaking.[130] Therefore, it could be argued that sexist speech promotes the speaker's self-realization by serving as a catharsis or as a way of venting frustration at the system.

A serious difficulty with the self-realization justification for freedom of speech is that almost any speech furthers an individual's development in some way. Since the theory does not permit normative judgment about the kind of development being fostered,[131] it would be virtually impossible for the state to regulate any speech.

Furthermore, the theory offers a particularly weak argument for protecting sexist speech since sexist speech harms the self-realization of the listener.[132] To the extent that sexist speech denies women their sense of self, their right to individual dignity and self-fulfillment, this justification for first amendment protection loses much of its force. The speaker's progress toward self-realization may also be hindered more than it is helped by sexist expression. The bigotry which is fostered by such speech may impede the speaker's social growth just as much as it impedes the listener's growth.[133]

4. Pragmatic Arguments Against a Categorical Approach

Even if sexist speech is not worthy of first amendment protection for its own sake, protection might be necessary to

---

[129] Bose Corp. v. Consumers Union, 466 U.S. at 503; *see also* Herbert v. Lando, 441 U.S. 153, 183 n.1 (1979) (Brennan, J., dissenting in part) ("Freedom of speech is itself an end . . . intrinsic to individual dignity. This is particularly so in a democracy like our own, in which the autonomy of each individual is accorded equal and incommensurate respect."); Procunier v. Martinez, 416 U.S. 396, 427 (1974) (Marshall, J., concurring) ("The First Amendment serves not only the needs of the polity but also those of the human spirit—a spirit that demands self expression."); Police Dep't of Chicago v. Mosley, 408 U.S. 92, 95–96 (1972) ("To permit the continued building of our politics and culture, and to assure self-fulfillment for each individual, our people are guaranteed the right to express any thought, free from government censorship.").

[130] Greenawalt, *supra* note 123, at 673.

[131] *See* Schauer, *Codifying the First Amendment*: New York v. Ferber, 1982 Sup. Ct. Rev. 285, 312.

[132] Note, *Anti-Pornography Laws and First Amendment Values*, 98 Harv. L. Rev. 460, 475 (1984).

[133] *Cf.* Delgado, *supra* note 15, at 175–76 (racial insults hurt self-realization of speaker because bigotry stifles moral and social growth of those who harbor it).

avoid incidentally censoring other speech that is valued. The determination of what is sexist speech is difficult. Is the presence of sexually explicit material in the workplace sexist speech? Is asking a woman for a date sexist speech? Not everyone agrees on which speech is degrading to women. For example, an employer's suggestion that I should be home with my two sons instead of working outside of the home would be degrading and destructive to my feelings as a professional worker. To others, the statement reflects sage advice.

There are significant gray areas involved in determining what words are offensive. State regulations may chill valued speech if speakers are unable to predict which speech will be considered offensive. Individuals, concerned that their speech will be punished, may temper their message or abstain from speech altogether.[134] In the first cases involving sexual harassment to reach the courts, many judges rejected the cause of action because of the fear of chilling speech. For example, one judge noted that if the claim of sexual harassment were to succeed, there "would be a potential federal lawsuit every time any employee made amorous or sexually oriented advances toward another. The only sure way an employer could avoid such charges would be to have employees who were asexual."[135] It seems unfair to punish individuals for using offensive speech when there is no clear understanding of what speech is prohibited.[136]

---

[134] For a general discussion of the chilling effect argument and first amendment jurisprudence, see Schauer, *Fear, Risk and the First Amendment: Unraveling the "Chilling Effect"*, 58 B.U.L. Rev. 685 (1978).

[135] Corne v. Bausch & Lomb, Inc., 390 F. Supp. 161, 163–64 (D. Ariz. 1975) (employers lamented that the rules against sexual harassment would force them to prohibit employees of the opposite sex from speaking to one another). *See* Significant Development, *New EEOC Guidelines on Discrimination Because of Sex: Employer Liability for Sexual Harassment under Title VII*, 61 B.U.L. Rev. 535, 537 n.14 (1981). *See also* Greene, *A Pattern of Fornication*, Forbes, June 16, 1986, at 66 (if sexual harassment laws upheld, "companies would face a ridiculous choice: either forbid fraternization between employees and supervisors, or monitor all relationships between employees"); Bennett-Alexander, *The Supreme Court Finally Speaks on the Issue of Sexual Harassment—What Did It Say?*, 10 Women's Rts. L. Rep. 65, 78 (workplace conversations about personal topics, especially between coworkers who are not personal friends, may be misunderstood, and therefore should be guarded against); *Hearings on Sex Discrimination in the Workplace*, 97th Cong., 1st Sess. 333, 464 (1981).

[136] This concern may be minimized by the fact that there are no criminal repercussions for using sexist speech. Only civil penalties are imposed. Under Title VII, for example, the employer may be liable for creating or permitting an offensive workplace

This difficulty in setting precise limits to sexist speech should not prohibit its regulation. Unless sexist speech is never punished, courts will still have to determine, case by case, if the speech is sufficiently offensive to regulate. Regardless of whether a court bases its judgment on the standard of a reasonable man or a reasonable woman in the situation, the court will have to utilize some objective measure to assess the speech.[137] Such line-drawing is not alien to the judicial system. In assessing obscenity, for example, a court must consider "contemporary community standards."[138] Moreover, in tort law, the reasonable person test is commonly utilized.[139] The point, then, is that the difficulty in defining punishable speech does not justify abandoning the task altogether. Rather, courts should determine liability in the context of a particular case, where the precise language and circumstances can be considered.

A somewhat different argument against categorical exclusion of sexist speech is based on the idea that control of sexist speech is content-based censorship: once society embarks on such governmental suppression, it has started down the slippery slope[140] towards greater acceptance of content regulation in other areas. Such a path is fraught with danger since content neutrality is a cardinal tenet of the first amendment.

Content-based distinctions are antithetical to freedom of speech. The Supreme Court, in an oft-repeated passage, noted that "[a]bove all else, the first amendment means that govern-

---

to persist, but the typical remedy is enjoining the offensive practice. Back pay and reinstatement are also available if the worker has left the job. The harassing coworker is not liable at all under Title VII.

The fact that no criminal consequences attach has been a factor considered by the Court in assessing the constitutionality of restraining speech. For example, in FCC v. Pacifica Found., 438 U.S. 726 (1978), the Court upheld the Commission's regulation of "indecent" language and distinguished Cohen v. California, 403 U.S. 15 (1971), in part by contrasting the different penalties in each case. "[T]he Commission imposed a far more moderate penalty on Pacifica than the state court imposed on Cohen. Even the strongest civil penalty at the Commission's command does not include criminal prosecution." Pacifica, 438 U.S. at 747 n.25 (citation omitted). Cf. L. Tribe, supra note 103, § 12-8, at 838 n.17 (drawing a distinction between state tort remedies for racial slurs which have been upheld as constitutional and criminal penalties which probably would violate the first amendment).

[137] See supra notes 31–34 and accompanying text.
[138] Miller v. California, 413 U.S. 15, 30–34 (1973).
[139] See, e.g., Prosser & Keeton on the Law of Torts § 32, at 173–93 (5th ed. 1984).
[140] See generally Schauer, Slippery Slopes, 99 Harv. L. Rev. 361 (1985).

ment has no power to restrict expression because of its message, its ideas, its subject matter or its content."[141] For better or worse, however, society has already taken that first step onto the slope of content-based discrimination. Content-based regulations such as obscenity laws have been upheld against constitutional challenge in the past.[142] In spite of these steps, the Court has generally not become more willing to allow the state to censor speech based on its content, nor is there any evidence for suspecting that regulating sexist speech would be the tipping point.

The slippery slope argument, however, does have some validity. It is an argument which is always present when one is advocating change. Given the risks inherent in pursuing new paths, the slippery slope argument is simply a "plea for caution in the face of an uncertain future."[143] That plea is heeded in the final section of this Article.

III. How Should Sexist Speech Be Regulated: The Balancing of Interests

A. The Balance

Previous sections of this Article set forth both the state's interests in curtailing sexist speech and the first amendment interests in free expression. This section balances the state interests against the values of free speech to determine whether sexist speech can be regulated in a manner consistent with the first amendment.

1. The Interest in Preventing Offense

The state's interest in preventing women from suffering psychological harm and taking offense from speech cannot outweigh the right of freedom of expression. The Supreme Court

---

[141] Police Dep't of Chicago v. Mosley, 408 U.S. at 95. *See also* Collin v. Smith, 578 F.2d 1197 (7th Cir.) (regulating the content of first amendment activities launches government on a slippery and precarious path), *cert. denied*, 439 U.S. 916 (1978).

[142] Roth v. United States, 354 U.S. 476 (1957).

[143] Schauer, *supra* note 140, at 376.

has consistently held that regulation of speech in order to protect against offense violates the first amendment.[144] As the Court most recently noted: "If there is a bedrock principle underlying the first amendment, it is that the Government may not prohibit the expression of an idea simply because society finds the idea itself offensive or disagreeable."[145] After all, speech is often supposed to offend, to arouse feeling and emotion. As Justice Harlan noted in *Cohen v. California*:

> To many, the immediate consequence of this freedom [of speech] may often appear to be only verbal tumult, discord and even offensive utterance. These are, however, within established limits, in truth necessary side effects of the broader values which the process of open debate permits us to achieve. That the air may at times seem filled with verbal cacaphony is, in this sense, not a sign of weakness but of strength.[146]

There may, however, be a difference between speech that simply offends and sexist speech in a workplace setting which has the potential to cause psychological and physical dysfunction. The Supreme Court decisions which address the problem of offensive speech involve only allegations of "offense." None of the cases involve individuals suffering from emotional distress as a result of hearing the offensive ideas.[147] Theoretically, the state's interest in the latter situation could be sufficient to override first amendment concerns.

Distinguishing between different gradations of offense for purposes of regulating speech, however, is unwise. Except in

---

[144] *See* Boos v. Barry, 485 U.S. 312 (1988); Cohen v. California, 403 U.S. 15 (1971); Street v. New York, 394 U.S. 576 (1969).

[145] Texas v. Johnson, 109 S. Ct. 2533, 2544 (1989).

[146] Cohen v. California, 403 U.S. at 24–25. *See* Schauer, *Response: Pornography and the First Amendment*, 40 U. Pitt. L. Rev. 605, 614–15 (1979) ("exclusion of the offensive . . . would limit commentary to polite commentary . . . and would exclude from public consideration many of the ideas of critics who often make the most signficant contributions to public debate").

[147] Note, *First Amendment Limits on Tort Liability for Words Intended to Inflict Severe Emotional Distress*, 85 Col. L. Rev. 1749 (1989). Even after acknowledging that a march by Nazis would seriously disturb some Skokie residents, the Seventh Circuit refused to draw a distinction for first amendment purposes between different levels of offense. Collin v. Smith, 578 F.2d 1197, 1200, 1206 (7th Cir.), *cert. denied*, 439 U.S. 916 (1978).

very limited circumstances, audiences should not be able to silence the advocacy of ideas, regardless of the level of offense engendered. The first amendment would be eviscerated if the recipient of the offensive speech were given such power. Even political speech, the most cherished form of expression, would be at risk. Though some southerners may have been deeply offended by civil rights demonstrations, and many anti-abortionists may be severely upset when confronted with pro-choice messages, such responses cannot justify censoring these forms of political speech.

2. The Interest in Protecting a Captive Audience

While the state interest in protecting the sensibilities of its citizens may not be compelling, the Supreme Court has struck a different balance when the offended parties are captive to the message. In *Frisby v. Schultz*[148] the Court recently concluded that the "First Amendment permits the government to prohibit offensive speech as intrusive when the 'captive' audience cannot avoid the objectionable speech."[149] Even political speech cannot be forced on an unwilling listener when the listener is captive.

Not surprisingly, the greatest concern for the captive audience arises when individuals are forced to receive unwanted communication in their homes, where privacy interests have always been considered most deserving of protection.[150] The Court has provided less protection to people outside of their homes because they are inevitably and inescapably captive to all kinds of objectionable speech.[151] In balancing the right to

---

[148] 108 S. Ct. 2495 (1988).

[149] *Id.* at 2503.

[150] *See* Rowan v. United States Post Office, 397 U.S. 728, 736–37 (1970). The decision in *Rowan* has been criticized because of the ease with which individuals can avoid exposure to offensive mailings. Unlike captive audience situations elsewhere, "it appears that any contact with objectionable material, no matter how fleeting, will constitute the recipient in the home a member of a captive audience . . . ." Nimmer, On Freedom of Speech 1–24 n.58 (1984). *See also* Kovacs v. Cooper, 336 U.S. 77, 86–87 (1949). The irony is that the protection of free expression is strongest in the home, yet at the same time protected expression can be restricted at home because of the fear of a captive audience. Meyerson, *The Right to Speak, the Right to Hear, and the Right Not to Hear: The Technological Resolution to the Cable/Pornography Debate*, 21 U. Mich. J. L. Reform 137, 240 (1988).

[151] *See* Frisby v. Schultz, 108 S. Ct. at 2502.

speak against the right to hear, therefore, courts have refused to view individuals as captive outside the home as long as they can walk or look away after initial exposure to the message. In *Erznoznick v. Jacksonville*,[152] for example, the Supreme Court held that an ordinance banning the exhibition of nudity from drive-in movie screens could not be upheld to protect the sensibilities of involuntary passers-by because they could simply avert their eyes after an initial viewing. The Court concluded:

> The Constitution does not permit government to decide which types of otherwise protected speech are sufficiently offensive to require protection for the unwilling listener or viewer. Rather . . . the burden normally falls upon the viewer to avoid further bombardment of his sensibilities simply by averting his eyes.[153]

The caveat that an audience is not captive if it has the ability to avoid the speech is important. Without it, the audience is granted too much power to censor speech with which it disagrees: "To regard such involuntary but merely momentary contact with the speech of others as enough to invoke a captive audience basis for suppressing the unwelcome speech would largely undermine the entire freedom of speech fabric."[154]

Employees at work, like residents in their homes, may qualify for captive audience status. Forced exposure to sexually explicit material, explicit sexual references, or sexual advances implicates significant privacy concerns, even outside the home. The balance of interests, however, requires that the worker bear some responsibility for avoiding the sexist speech. If a woman can simply avert her eyes to avoid a sexually explicit picture placed in a coworker's locker, then the employee should not be

---

[152] 422 U.S. 205 (1975).

[153] *Id.* at 210–11 (quoting Cohen v. California, 403 U.S. at 21). *But see infra* notes 186–188 and accompanying text.

[154] Nimmer, *supra* note 150, at 1–33. Similarly, the Seventh Circuit affirmed the rights of Nazis to march at the city hall in Skokie, Illinois, a town with a substantial Jewish population. The court emphasized the ability of the audience to avoid the speech: "There is room under the first amendment for the government to protect targeted listeners from offensive speech, but only when the speaker intrudes on the privacy of the home, or a *captive audience cannot practically avoid exposure*." Collin v. Smith, 578 F.2d at 1206 (7th Cir.), *cert. denied*, 439 U.S. 916 (1978) (emphasis added).

viewed as captive. Similarly, if a worker overhears an off-color joke and she can readily move out of hearing range, the burden of avoiding such speech should rest with her. On the other hand, when a coworker or supervisor *directs* the speech at the female worker, her ability to avoid such speech is severely limited, and a finding of captivity is reasonable.[155] In such circumstances, restrictions on sexist speech do not violate the first amendment.

3. The State Interest in Equality

a. Speech that Advocates Inequality

The desire to promote the ideology of sexual equality and to eliminate sexual stereotypes cannot outweigh the first amendment interest. Despite the attractiveness of the goal, suppressing speech to further equality in the workplace is still censoring speech based on its content. The state cannot censor speech in our society in order to promote a certain ideology or viewpoint, no matter how laudable.[156] When speech is censored in order to reach a desired state objective, there is no feasible stopping point.

For instance, the state cannot prohibit an individual speaking at an anti-ERA rally from advocating that women with young children stay at home to raise their families. Such a view, however, may serve to perpetuate inequality. How, then, can the government permit sexist speech generally, yet prohibit sexist speech on the job? When considering only the speech, and not the place or audience, no distinction can be drawn between public speech that advocates a particular social policy and sexist speech in the workplace.

It is tempting to say that equality is an ideal that society should be prepared to endorse, even if it means censoring speech. Others have analogously argued that advocacy of genocide should not be permitted because society has nothing to

---

[155] *See infra* notes 184–189.

[156] *See* American Booksellers Ass'n v. Hudnut, 771 F.2d 323 (7th Cir. 1985), *aff'd*, 475 U.S. 1001 (1986).

gain by promoting free speech on that topic.[157] While the first amendment generally precludes banning speech to promote a prevailing ideology, certain limited exceptions could be made for ideas that are universally accepted.

This suggestion, however, illustrates the evil of the state censoring speech to promote a certain end. If, for example, the Supreme Court overturns *Roe v. Wade*,[158] and a state government prohibits abortion, advocacy of the pro-choice position could be banned as advocating genocide. Even more problematic would be a ban on speech advocating inequality. Speech for and against affirmative action could conceivably be prohibited. The interest in achieving equality cannot support censoring speech that advocates, explicitly or implicitly, the subordination of women.

Feminists should be particularly loath to allow the state to determine which ideas should be adhered to, and which speech silenced to promote those ideas. Government censorship of speech does not usually further the feminist agenda. The abortion example demonstrates the danger in allowing the government to define which ideas may be expressed. This danger is one that the Supreme Court has recognized by consistently refusing to allow the regulation of speech in order to promote an idea.[159]

b. Speech that Discriminates

Although the state cannot constitutionally ban speech because it advocates discrimination, it may be able to regulate speech because the speech itself discriminates. That is, speech cannot be silenced simply because its message urges or pro-

---

[157] *See generally* Bollinger, *The Skokie Legacy: Reflections on an "Easy" Case and Free Speech Theory*, 80 Mich. L. Rev. 617, 624 (1982) (the Court could draw a narrow line, like prohibiting advocacy of genocide, that is not more difficult to define than current prohibitions on obscenity and libel); Delgado, *supra* note 15 (advocating a tort action for racist speech); Kretzmer, *supra* note 15 (advocating the curtailment of racist speech); Note, *A Communitarian Defense of Group Libel Laws*, 101 Harv. L. Rev. 682 (1988) (arguing that communitarianism provides a strong justification for group libel laws).

[158] 410 U.S. 113 (1973).

[159] *See* West Virginia State Bd. of Educ. v. Barnette, 319 U.S. 624 (1943); *American Booksellers*, 771 F.2d 323 (7th Cir. 1985), *aff'd*, 475 U.S. 1001 (1986).

motes abhorrent ideas. On the other hand, when that message causes women to leave their jobs, or to suffer impediments at work that men need not endure, that speech can be prohibited.

It has been argued that the first amendment permits no distinction between speech that discriminates and speech advocating discrimination.[160] Speech is powerful because it influences behavior and ideas: a message urging discrimination may cause, even if indirectly, discriminatory conduct. Therefore, both speech that discriminates and speech that advocates discrimination may ultimately result in the same harm.

There are, however, significant distinctions between speech that discriminates by its very utterance and speech that encourages discrimination by its message. Traditionally, the Supreme Court has placed great emphasis on the ability of countervailing speech to remedy harms caused by the advocacy of ideas.[161] At the heart of the marketplace of ideas theory is a presumption that more speech answers the evils in objectionable speech. The answer to speech that promotes sexual inequality is speech in favor of sexual equality. The "more speech" remedy, however, is no solution when speech itself is discriminatory. Whatever ability countervailing speech may have to minimize the spread of undesirable ideas, the harms of such speech are not erased by a response when the speech adversely affects women's job opportunities.

Moreover, regulation of speech that discriminates, unlike censorship of speech that advocates discrimination, is viewpoint-neutral. It does not matter whether the speaker tells the woman that she belongs in the bedroom or in the boardroom; a judgment need not be made about which statement, if either, subordinates or degrades women.[162] While the meaning of the words must be considered when determining whether there was discriminatory effect or intent, the particular point of view of

---

[160] Emerson, *Pornography and the First Amendment: A Reply to Professor MacKinnon*, 3 Yale L. & Pol'y Rev. 130, 131 (1984).

[161] *See, e.g.*, Whitney v. California, 274 U.S. 357, 377 (1927) (Brandeis, J., concurring). *See generally* L. Tribe, *supra* note 104, at 834.

[162] This fact would distinguish such a regulation from the pornography ordinance struck down in *American Booksellers*, 771 F.2d 323 (7th Cir. 1985), *aff'd*, 475 U.S. 1001 (1986). The primary reason given by the Seventh Circuit for invalidating the law was that its definition of pornography as sexually explicit materials portraying women as subordinate was viewpoint-based. 771 F.2d at 331–32.

the speaker is not important. Under Title VII, for example, the expression is prohibited if it creates an abusive and hostile work environment, regardless of the ideology of the speaker.[163]

On the other hand, a regulation prohibiting speech that promotes discrimination is not viewpoint-neutral; it is precisely because such speech expresses a view that denigrates women that it is suppressed. Significantly, the Court has consistently been more willing to regulate speech when the ideological message is not the basis for censorship.[164]

Finally, the two theories are distinguishable because the harm caused by speech that discriminates is direct and immediate, unlike the harm resulting from speech which advocates discrimination. Speech prohibited as discriminatory under Title VII, for example, is speech that in itself prevents the woman from participating fully in the workforce. Banning speech because it may influence someone's thinking, and cause that person in some undefined future circumstance to discriminate against women, regulates a more attenuated causal relationship. While the state may regulate speech that poses a "clear and present danger,"[165] it may not censor speech because of some possible future effect.[166]

For these reasons, the state has a recognizable interest in preventing speech that discriminates, which it does not have in regulating speech that merely advocates discrimination. Moreover, that interest is compelling and may outweigh the value of allowing discriminatory sexist speech. In other contexts, courts have found the goal of eliminating discrimination in the workplace to override other rights embodied in the first amendment, such as the right of freedom of association and the free exercise of religion.[167] As the Ninth Circuit explained in allowing the state to impose liability on a religious publishing house which retaliated against a female employee for filing a charge of discrimination:

---

[163] Title VII, 42 U.S.C. § 2000 (1981).
[164] *See* Sunstein, *supra* note 109, at 610; Stone, *Anti-Pornography Legislation as Viewpoint Discrimination*, 9 Harv. J.L. & Pub. Pol'y 461, 471 (1986).
[165] Schenck v. United States, 249 U.S. 47 (1919).
[166] *Id.*
[167] EEOC v. Pacific Press Publishing Ass'n, 676 F.2d 1272 (9th Cir. 1982).

[T]he retaliatory action taken against [the employee] will impose liability on [Pacific] Press for disciplinary actions based on religious doctrine. We find, however, that the government's compelling interest in assuring equal employment opportunities justifies the burden. *By enacting Title VII Congress clearly targeted the elimination of all forms of discrimination as a "highest priority." Congress' purpose to end discrimination is equally if not more compelling than other interests that have been held to justify legislation that burdened the exercise of religious convictions.*[168]

A statute like Title VII, which infringes speech interests only when a discriminatory intent or effect is discovered, may be justifed by the state's compelling interest in eliminating discrimination.

4. Efficiency in the Workplace

In certain limited circumstances, the efficient functioning of a public workplace may outweigh the free speech concerns. When balancing the state's interest in an efficient workplace against the values of free speech, the Supreme Court has distinguished purely private speech from speech on matters of public concern.[169] If the employee is dismissed for private speech, the employer's right to fire that employee is absolute. No balancing of interests occurs.[170] If a public employer fires an employee for speech on matters of public concern, however, the court must balance the right to speak against the degree of workplace impairment in each case.[171] Under this theory, in the public sector, much sexist speech could be suppressed without consideration of the actual harm suffered by the state. The Court has narrowly

---

[168] *Id.* at 1280 (citation omitted) (emphasis added).

[169] The first time the Court drew this distinction was in Connick v. Myers, 461 U.S. 138, 147 (1983). *See also* Rankin v. McPherson, 483 U.S. 378 (1986).

[170] *Connick*, at 147. *See, e.g.*, Mahaffey v. Kansas Bd. of Regents, 562 F. Supp. 887, 890 (D. Kan. 1983) (private speech regarding employee's salary, prerequisites, and position in college need not be reviewed by a federal court).

[171] *See Connick*, 461 U.S. 138, and *Rankin*, 483 U.S. 378.

drawn the category of speech on matters of public concern;[172] most sexist speech would qualify as private speech.

This approach to regulation, however, is problematic. The line between public and private speech drawn in *Connick v. Myers* and *Rankin v. McPherson* is amorphous, and has been justly criticized.[173] Even if this problem is set aside, and sexist speech is viewed as public, the balancing of interests is still troubling. Efficiency is a vague concept, and the Court has expressed fear that "public employers [would] use their authority over employees to silence discourse, not because it hampers public functions, but simply because superiors disagree with the content of employees' speech."[174] Perhaps for this reason, the courts seem to require more than just a dollar loss to the government. Rather, the speech must impair the efficient functioning of the overall workplace in order to outweigh the right to speak on matters of public concern.

It is conceivable, though not inevitable, that sexist speech would create such a result. A predominantly male workplace is unlikely to experience a cessation of functions if a few women employees are harassed. A different result may follow if women in a predominantly female workplace are harassed or if the women harassed occupy positions of importance.

In the final analysis, it seems dangerous to consider the state interest in efficiency, as developed in cases like *Connick* and *Rankin*, when justifying the regulation of sexist speech. Content-based distinctions, like that between public and private speech, traditionally have been antithetical to the first amendment. Moreover, as discussed earlier, calling sexist speech private or non-political, thereby permitting it less first amendment protection, is unwise.[175]

---

[172] *See Connick*, at 163 (Brennan, J., dissenting).

[173] *See* Note, *Developments in the Law: Public Employment*, 97 Harv. L. Rev. 1611, 1767–70 (1983); *The Supreme Court, 1982 Term*, 97 Harv. L. Rev. 70, 167 (1983). For example, in *Connick*, the views of staff members on office transfer policy and work conditions in the District Attorney's office were private but employees' views about being pressured to work on political campaigns were a matter of public concern. 461 U.S. at 148–49.

[174] *Rankin*, 483 U.S. at 390–91.

[175] If the principles of *Connick* are applied, it requires a case-by-case determination of the type of speech (public versus private) and the efficiency interests involved. It does not justify categorically excluding sexist speech from first amendment protection. Any regulation, moreover, must be carefully drafted to ensure censoring speech only if it causes the requisite level of harm.

In addition to creating practical difficulties, such an approach may not be necessary. If speech significantly impairs a workplace, it may very well cause employment discrimination and/or be directed at a captive audience. Accordingly, considerations of efficiency do not advance the first amendment analysis.[176]

B. Some Examples of the Balancing Approach

This section applies the balancing tests to the types of sexist speech set forth in Section I: (1) sexual demands or requests; (2) sexually explicit speech directed at the woman employee; (3) degrading speech directed at the employee; and (4) sexually explicit or degrading speech or expression that is not directed at the woman, but which she overhears or sees.

I conclude that in the first three categories, the state's interest in prohibiting such speech outweighs any possible first amendment arguments. Once the plaintiff alleges a cause of action under Title VII, and demonstrates a discriminatory intent or effect, the employer cannot successfully defend on first amendment grounds.[177] In a tort action, if a woman shows that the offensive speech was directed at her, and that she was captive to its message, the defendant cannot raise a first amendment defense.

The last category of speech requires a court to balance the specific interests in the particular circumstances. Courts must weigh the specific harms alleged from nondirected speech against the free speech interests asserted under the particular facts. Any statutory solution to sexist speech must reflect the distinction between directed and nondirected speech and must be narrowly drawn to reflect the legitimate state interests of preventing employment discrimination and protecting a captive audience from offensive speech.

---

[176] Moreover, in many of these cases, a supervisor can be fired not for his speech but for a lack of managerial responsiblity. Cf. Pickering v. Bd. of Educ., 391 U.S. 563, 573 n.5 (1968).

[177] Most Title VII lawsuits involve an assertion of directed speech, as defined in this Article. Moreover, it is unlikely that a claim of nondirected speech would succeed given the statute's requirement that the speech affect the terms and conditions of employment.

1. Sexual Demands or Requests

The state interest in preventing employers from coercing employees into sexual relationships, or from retaliating against employees based on a refusal to accede to sexual demands, outweighs any first amendment speech interest. In balancing the competing interests, the state's interest in preventing workplace blackmail is overwhelming. By compelling women employees to submit to a condition of employment that male workers need not endure, this speech necessarily discriminates against women. In addition, because sexual demands are directed at an individual employee and are spoken by someone with authority, the employee is a captive recipient of the message—she cannot escape the message or messenger. Accordingly, the state's compelling interest in protecting women from being forced to choose between acceding to sexual demands or enduring discriminating terms of employment justifies any infringement on freedom of speech.

Speech that truly does not constitute a sexual demand, but rather is a request for a personal relationship, sexual or otherwise, poses different concerns.[178] Such a request, if it is regulable at all, must constitute either sexually explicit or degrading speech directed at an individual. This type of speech is considered in the next two sections.

2. Sexually Explicit Speech Directed at an Employee

When an employer, supervisor or coworker tells a woman she is a "cunt," or makes suggestive remarks about her sex life, the state's interest in preventing such speech should outweigh any first amendment interests. If a hierarchical approach is accepted,[179] the state's interest would likely outweigh the minimal first amendment value accorded sexually explicit speech.

Even if courts reject such an approach (as I previously argued that they should), the state interests are compelling. If

---

[178] As indicated earlier, *see supra* note 21 and accompanying text, a "request" for a personal relationship made by a person of a position in power over the listener constitutes a demand because of the implicit threat of employment repercussions.

[179] *See supra* notes 103–105 and accompanying text.

sexually explicit speech affects the terms and conditions of the woman's employment, the state's interest in equality outweighs the value of such speech. Determining whether the speech affects work conditions in this way requires the court to inquire into the particular language used, and, more importantly, the pervasiveness of the taunts. Thus, although a single slur is unlikely to establish discrimination, persistent use of a sexually explicit message may be sufficient. The more "offensive" the slur, the less pervasive it need be before the plaintiff is able to demonstrate discrimination in the workplace.

Additionally, the state's interest in protecting a captive audience is implicated here. When the coworker or supervisor targets the women as the recipient of the speech, her ability to escape is limited, and she should be viewed as an unwilling captive to the speech.

3. Directed Speech that Is Degrading

What about directed speech that is not sexually explicit, but is degrading and destructive of a woman's feelings as a professional worker? Consider, for example, the scenario of a woman who works for the American Cyanamid Company in the pigments department. In that department, women are exposed to lead, a substance which could potentially lead to birth defects in fetuses.[180] A coworker constantly taunts a pregnant worker, calling her a "baby killer" because she refuses to leave work or transfer to a lower paying job in a different department. The male worker's expression of outrage at the woman's behavior certainly conveys a social and political message. While this is an extreme example, it is common for women to complain that

---

[180] This example is adapted from a real situation. In January 1978, American Cyanamid Company announced that all fertile women would be removed from exposure to toxic substances, including lead, at its Willow Island, West Virginia plant. Five women, faced with the "choice" between their jobs and their fertility chose to be sterilized. In 1980, a class action was filed against the company, alleging that the policy of excluding fertile women constituted sex discrimination in violation of Title VII. *See* Williams, *Firing the Woman to Protect the Fetus: The Reconciliation of Fetal Protection with Employment Opportunity Goals under Title VII,* 69 Geo. L.J. 641 (1981). Recently, the Seventh Circuit upheld a fetal protection policy against a Title VII challenge. UAW v. Johnson Controls, Inc., No. 88-1308 (7th Cir. Sep. 26, 1989).

they have been sexually harassed by male coworkers' comments that they do not belong in the workplace.[181]

Balancing the competing interests appears more difficult here. The speech, although offensive, is not sexually explicit. The speech clearly has a political message. Nevertheless, the woman should be able to successfully challenge the speech if she can prove that it was discriminatory. An employee told once that she should be at home would probably not suffice to establish discrimination under Title VII. Persistent and pervasive taunts, however, to the same effect may be illegal. Moreover, the woman could successfully challenge such speech if she were a captive audience and the speech were viewed as sufficiently offensive under the substantive tort requirements.

Concern about censoring political or social speech is minimized by the fact that banning sexist speech in the workplace does not censor such speech everywhere and for all time. The fact that individuals are presumably free to espouse sexist speech outside the workplace may weaken the free speech interest. Concededly, the Court has often declared that speech cannot be silenced on the ground that the message can be delivered elsewhere.[182] In a number of cases, however, the Court has been influenced by the fact that the challenged regulation did not greatly restrict overall access to lawful speech.[183] While sexist speech delivered elsewhere has its own set of harms, the injuries unique to the workplace will not be suffered. Without condemning sexist speech in all places, the Court need only determine that such speech does not belong in an employment context.

4. Degrading or Sexually Explicit Speech Not Directed at the Employee But Overheard or Seen by Her

Women persistently complain about sexist speech that exists as part of the workplace environment, but is not directed at

---

[181] See supra note 26 and accompanying text.

[182] See Southeastern Promotions Ltd. v. Conrad, 420 U.S. 546, 556 (1975) ("[O]ne is not to have exercise of his liberty of expression in appropriate places abridged on the plea that it may be exercised in some other place.").

[183] See Frisby v. Schultz, 108 S. Ct. 2495 (1988) (finding significant, among other factors, that ban on residential picketing left open ample alternative channels of communication); Young v. American Mini Theatres, 427 U.S. 50, 71–72 (1976).

an unwilling recipient. For example, an employee may keep obscene or pornographic material on his desk or in his locker, or male coworkers may exchange off-color jokes that are overheard inadvertently by a woman worker.

Balancing interests in the case of indirect speech differs from doing so in the foregoing categories, primarily because a court may not find discriminatory intent or effect. Title VII requires that speech be sufficiently pervasive to affect the terms and conditions of employment, and nondirected speech does not typically satisfy this requirement.[184]

Thus, the first amendment requires that courts consider the state's interest in protecting captive audiences from offensive speech. Finding a captive audience when speech is nondirected, however, is problematic. Although initial exposure to the offending message may occur, the woman, at least theoretically, maintains the ability to walk away and avoid further contact with the message. For example, if a woman inadvertantly notices a *Playboy* centerfold on a coworker's locker door, she can probably avoid exposure the next time she walks by.

On the other hand, it can be persuasively argued that a woman employee who knows that her supervisor keeps a poster of a naked woman in his office is in some sense captive to the message, even if she can avoid looking at it, indeed, even if she never saw it. She must daily work with the knowledge that such a degrading message persists in her workplace.

Yet for a court to view the woman as a captive recipient to the speech stretches the concept of captivity. At some point, the burden of rejecting speech must be placed on the potential listener. Otherwise, the Jews in Skokie could silence the speech of Nazis, not just from the streets of their suburb, but from a willing audience.[185] The free speech rights of individuals, which include the right to express themselves in sexually explicit terms and about sexual matters, presumptively should outweigh the

---

[184] Overheard speech may cause less harm than does directed speech. At least it cannot be presumed that nondirected messages restrict women's job opportunities or offend in the same manner as do directed messages. While one may find it offensive that a coworker enjoys looking at pictures of naked women on his desk, or that he enjoys talking about his sexual exploits to willing listeners, such events by themselves may not operate to significantly interfere with a woman's work performance.

[185] Collin v. Smith, 578 F.2d 1197 (7th Cir.), *cert. denied*, 436 U.S. 953 (1978).

state's interest in censoring nondirected speech. In other words, a male employee should have as much right to place a picture of a *Playboy* playmate in his office as he would have to place a "Bush/Quayle for President" poster there. The fact that both may upset other workers who know of their existence is not sufficient justification to prohibit them.

At some point, moreover, the desire to protect women from all sexually explicit or degrading speech in the workplace becomes paternalistic. Women do not need protection from every exposure to sexually explicit words or pictures. Some women may want to hear, and even to use, sexually explicit language. Some women are even offended when men avoid using "swear words," or telling "dirty" jokes in their presence.

Thus, unlike the previous categories of speech, courts cannot categorically exclude sexually explicit or degrading speech not directed at an individual from first amendment protection. The balancing of the first amendment interests against the harms of the speech must occur on a case-by-case basis.

Drawing the line between directed and overheard speech, however, is admittedly difficult. The courts should give the complaining party the opportunity to demonstrate that, in fact, she was unable to escape exposure to the speech. Once such a showing is made, the speech should be considered directed, causing her to be captive to the message. The Supreme Court has recognized such a common sense approach to the question of captivity. In *FCC v. Pacifica Foundation*,[186] the Court seemed to retreat somewhat from its position in *Erznoznick*[187] when it rejected the argument that the viewer could avoid further offense by turning off the radio or switching stations after the initial exposure. Such a solution, according to the Court, "is like saying that the remedy for an assault is to run away after the first blow."[188]

For example, if a "joke" requires that a woman listen in order to achieve its intended punchline, and if her escape is made difficult by the escalation of volume or the movement of the "jokesters" towards her, the speech should be considered

---

[186] 438 U.S. 726 (1978).
[187] 422 U.S. 205 (1975).
[188] *Id.* at 748–49.

directed rather than overheard. In such a circumstance, the speaker meant for the woman to hear the speech, and perhaps even to be offended. If the intent of the speaker is to speak to and/or offend the woman employee, then she should be considered captive. Although intent is not a necessary condition of finding directed speech, it should be a sufficient one.

In addition, pornographic pictures posted in conspicuous places, so that turning away is not feasible or would place too great a burden on the woman employee,[189] should be viewed as directed speech. The woman employee might demonstrate that the workplace was so permeated with pictures of naked women that avoiding exposure to the pictures was infeasible. In all these circumstances, the speech would fall within the category of directed speech, where the state's interest outweighs the right to free expression.

In practice, then, the area of nondirected speech is limited. It includes only a narrow range of behavior, like coworkers keeping pornographic pictures in their desks or in inconspicuous places, or coworkers discussing among themselves a sexually explicit joke which can be readily avoided by the worker who prefers not to hear it.

Conclusion

Sexist speech can be regulated in a manner consistent with the first amendment so long as the speech is made with discriminatory intent or causes a direct discriminatory effect, or if the offended listener constitutes a captive audience. A ban on nondirected speech which holds no one captive and which does not discriminate would on the other hand violate the constitution. The fact that government regulation of sexist speech usually does not pose a first amendment problem, however, does not mean that courts may dispense with a first amendment analysis. The inattention currently paid to potential constitutional limits on regulating sexist speech is a risky practice.

---

[189] A woman should not be forced to forego the free use of the office space in order to avoid offensive messages. For example, the inability to use a common area or having to take a circuitous route from her desk to the restroom to avoid a picture would be too significant a burden on the woman employee.

I must admit that when I first began to think about the problem of sexist speech and the first amendment ramifications, my initial reaction was fear: to recognize free speech interests would make it harder on women in the workplace, who already face immeasurable difficulties daily. As a teacher of a course in employment discrimination, and as a feminist, deeply concerned about the substantial inequality that still persists in the workplace, I was extremely troubled by the prospect of increasing barriers to women's effective participation in the workplace. Upon further reflection, however, I came to realize that ignoring first amendment issues posed even greater dangers.

First and most importantly, I concluded that ignoring free speech concerns risks infringing upon critical first amendment values. These values, while important to all in society, have particular relevance to women attempting to achieve equality. Many feminists recognized during the debate over the regulation of pornography that a broad reading of the right to free expression is critical to the overall feminist agenda.

Second, an analysis of the first amendment issues, where examination of the state's interests would receive careful, appropriate attention, minimizes the risk that too much weight will be placed on first amendment concerns. To ignore the analysis creates the possibility that judges or legislators, when first considering the issue, will find that the free speech interests are paramount, and therefore invalidate all state attempts to regulate sexist speech. Hopefully, this Article will help judges and legislators formulate an appropriate balance.

Finally, a responsible first amendment analysis serves as an indispensable reminder of the real evil of sexist speech. This is so because such an analysis requires a careful delineation of the conflicting interests, including the state's interest in banning sexist speech. It should not be forgotten that in the recent past, and perhaps subconsciously today, regulation of some forms of sexist speech was justified on paternalistic grounds. This country has historically sanctioned laws against offensive speech as a means of protecting women's sensibilities from crude language, not to promote sexual equality.[190]

---

[190] *See supra* note 108 and accompanying text.

Even today, some judges reveal a disturbing throwback to such paternalistic attitudes. Sexual harassment claims are often rejected when there is evidence that the woman also engaged in "lewd" language in the workplace.[191] The brevity of judicial analysis in these cases compels at least the suspicion that the claims were rejected because the woman, by joining in the behavior, no longer acted like a "lady." The judges, therefore, concluded that she was not deserving of their solicitude.

This Article reaffirms both a commitment to preserving the values of freedom of expression and the imperative of eliminating sexual inequality in the workplace. A victory over sexist speech in the workplace that perpetuates sexist stereotypes and trammels first amendment rights is a hollow one. Feminists would have won the battle, but lost the war. Only by careful analysis of the competing interests can the civil liberties of all and the civil rights of women be truly preserved.

---

[191] *See, e.g.,* Jordan v. Clark, 88 Daily Journal D.A.R. 6539, *aff'd*, 847 F.2d 1368 (7th Cir. 1988), *cert. denied*, 109 S. Ct. 786 (1989) (because both plaintiff and defendant engaged in flirtatious conversation, there was no abusive environment); Swentek v. USAir, 830 F.2d 552, 557 (4th Cir. 1987) (plaintiff's own foul-mouthed language, and activities such as placing a dildo in her supervisor's mailbox and grabbing the genitals of a male co-worker did not indicate that the complained-of behavior was unwelcome). *Cf.* Marmo, Arbitrating Sex Harassment Cases, 35 Arb. J., Mar. 1980, at 35, 37 (sometimes arbitrators, harboring protectionist sentiments, have established new and more stringent standards of behavior because women are present).

Women in the Workplace
and Sex Discrimination Law:
A Feminist Analysis
of Federal Jurisprudence

Francis Carleton

ABSTRACT. This article entails a critical analysis of federal sex discrimination law. A feminist perspective is employed to interpret the legal policies enacted by two federal courts (the U.S. Supreme Court and the District of Columbia's Court of Appeals) in the 1980s in regard to the workplace issues of sexual harassment and sex discrimination in promotion decisions. Specifically, the evaluative criteria of an ethic of care and victim empathy is used to gauge the value of federal sex discrimination jurisdiction for advancing the interests of women in the workplace. It is found that the federal courts currently expose legal policy that has contradictory and complex implications for women who participate in the American workforce. Analysis also reveals the value of legal briefs for those who wish to engage in a reconstructive jurisprudence of sex discrimination that is more responsive to the needs of women on the job.

Francis Carleton is affiliated with the University of Wisconsin at Green Bay.

Women & Politics, Vol. 13(2) 1993

INTRODUCTION

This article analyzes United States federal court cases dealing with sexual harassment and sex discrimination in promotion decisions. The aim is to arrive at significant insights into the usefulness of sex discrimination law for women in the workplace. Hence, it tries to understand and criticize the law from a (subjectively and broadly defined) feminist perspective. It argues that Alison Jaggar's contention that "women in our society constitute an oppressed group and . . . this oppression ought to be ended" is fundamentally correct, and that focusing on enhancing the participation of women in the workplace through legal means is one way to go about mitigating gender inequality in the United States. As Janet Rifkin argues, "patriarchy as a form of power and social order will not be eliminated unless the male power paradigm of law is challenged and transformed" (1980, 87).

The focus is on an explication and critique of current federal sex discrimination jurisprudence. This critique emphasizes the concept of law as ideology. Understanding the law's importance thus includes not only the concrete impact of particular judicial policies, but also the broader notion of law as expressive of a particular understanding of social reality. As Carol Smart has argued, "If we accept that law, like science, makes a claim to truth and that this is indivisible from power, we can see that law exercises power not simply in its material effects (judgements) but also in its ability to disqualify other knowledges and experiences" (1989, 11). This article, therefore, will include not only a careful analysis of particular federal court policies towards sex discrimination in the workplace, but also a critical review of each policy's underlying rationale. Finally, it endeavors to set forth a "reconstructive juris- prudence" that offers alternative legal policies which promise to mitigate the subordination of women in the workplace (West, 1991, 231). In this way a genuine and fruitful connection between theory and practice can be established.

The data base consists of cases decided by the Supreme Court of the United States and the District of Columbia Court of Appeals in the areas of sexual harassment and sex discrimination in promotion. This particular study encompasses several cases handed down between 1980 and 1989. It analyzes the majority opinion in each case and any legal briefs filed by interested parties (including defendants, plaintiffs, and amicus curiae). The jurisprudence analyzed below is based on the federal judiciary's interpretation of Title VII of the Civil Rights Act of 1964, which forbids, among other things, the practice of sex discrimination in the workplace.

It is argued that sexual harassment and gender discrimination in promotion decisions constitute two critical barriers to the participation of women in the workplace and therefore are deserving of attention. The federal courts first recognized sexual harassment in the workplace as sex discrimination in 1976. They did not deal with sex discrimination in promotion decisions until 1971, and only accorded regular legal recognition to this serious workplace harm after 1974. Women in the workplace have reaped very real and substantial benefits from legal decisions in these two critical areas of sex discrimination jurisprudence. However, the "revolution in the law" (Hoff-Wilson 1987) which began in the 1970s is incomplete at best, and is currently in danger of being halted or reversed by the increasingly conservative executive and judicial branches of the United States government. Catherine MacKinnon captures the essence of this dilemma when she argues that women must be concerned that "the law of sexual harassment will be taken away from us or turn into nothing or turn ugly in our hands" (1987, 105).

Sexual harassment is a primary manifestation and vehicle of the subordination of women in the workplace. It is an act that is overwhelmingly directed at women by men. The practice of sexual harassment discriminates systematically against women as a group and serves to keep them in an inferior position in the workplace. Men are frequently in a position of greater power than women and are able to threaten female employees with, for example, a loss of employment or an intolerably hostile work environment. Sexual harassment is remarkably widespread and ubiquitous, and has many adverse consequences for its victims. It is emotionally degrading and often results in physical symptoms that impede the performance of women in the workplace.

Harassment sometimes results in the resignation of female employees who feel they have no other viable options. Frustrated male overseers sometimes dismiss female subordinates who fail to respond to their unwanted advances, or they impede the victim's ability to perform effectively in the workplace. Women who file a complaint of sexual harassment often suffer retaliation as a result of their attempt to deal with a harmful situation (Farley 1978, MacKinnon, 1979). Eliminating or mitigating sexual harassment in the workplace, then, is critical to the success of women.

Sex discrimination in promotion decisions is also of great relevance to the success of women. Quite simply, if employers are permitted to discriminate against women by denying them upward mobility within the employment environment, women face an uphill battle indeed in their quest for equality. Some commentators have referred to this problem as the glass ceiling dilemma. That is, while women are currently entering the workplace in unprecedented numbers, they are being denied prestigious upper-management positions due, at least in part, to the problem of sex discrimination in promotion decisions.

Debra Blum points out in a recent article in the *Chronicle of Higher Education* that women in academe are still victimized by the problems of "gender discrimination and sexual harassment," and as a result are "paid less than men who hold jobs of equivalent rank, are more likely to hold lower-level positions, and receive fewer job promotions" (1991). A study just released by the Labor Department found that of 1,315 board members at America's 100 largest companies, only 7.5% were women (Shalal-Esa 1992). Another study of women in the American workplace established that "of 60 corporate appointments announced for January [1992] in the *Wall Street Journal* . . . only six went to women" (Kleiman 1992). It is apparent, then, that although women in the workplace have made great strides forward since the second wave of feminism was initiated in the 1960s, they have a long way yet to go.

AN EVALUATIVE MODEL

This paper will focus on two dimensions of a feminist jurisprudence that have been advanced by various feminist legal theorists. It argues that the concepts of empathy and an ethic of care promise to provide valuable insight into the relationship between women in the workplace and federal sex discrimination law. It discusses each of these concepts and their relationship to a feminist understanding of the law.

A feminist conception of an ethic of care, which has its origins in the work of Nancy Chodorow (1978) and Carol Gilligan (1982), entails a jurisprudence that recognizes the importance of taking responsibility for the well-being of vulnerable employees in the workplace. Advocates of a legal ethic of care desire a jurisprudence of sex discrimination that expresses a commitment to creating a more caring and humane workplace environment. Robin West (1991) argues that the law tends to find masculine expression because it embraces what she calls the 'separation thesis,' whereby people are conceived of in atomistic and individualistic terms. I contend that this masculine approach results in a focus on rights–on the right of people or institutions to relatively unrestricted autonomy within their own spheres of action. Cultural feminism, on the other hand, endorses the 'connection thesis,' which emerges from the insight that "Women are actually or potentially materially connected to other human life" through such experiences as menstruation, child bearing, and the nursing of newborn infants (West 1991). This material connection to others encourages a distinctive feminine voice of "responsibility, duty, and care for others" (211). I should note, however, that while there is a biological basis for a feminine "voice," biology does not *determine* this perspective. Robin West points out, for example, that "men can nurture life. Men can mother. Obviously, men can care, and love, and support, and affirm life" (1991, 232). And theorists such as Nancy Chodorow (1978) emphasize the social construction of women's commitment to an ethic of care. One's voice, then, is composed of both biological and learned (or socially constructed) behavior and is susceptible to change. This insight, presumably, would apply also to the malleable nature of the law's 'voice'; therefore, feminists can pursue with some hope a strategy of progressive legal change.

A traditionally masculine jurisprudence emphasizes a conflictual use of rights rhetoric. The drawback to de-emphasizing an ethic of care while advocating instead an adversarial notion of rights is the brute fact that rights rhetoric has often resulted in the triumph of politically powerful groups rather than vulnerable classes. Mortin Horwitz (1988) notes that the property rights of business have often trumped the rights of relatively powerless workers in the past and laments that the current Supreme Court is employing similar rights rhetoric to strike down government regulation of private enterprise. A feminist jurisprudence would de-emphasize a rights-centered approach to the law and promote instead a focus on an ethic of care and responsibility. It is primarily through the creation of such a jurisprudence that the participation of women in the workplace can be enhanced.

A feminist interpretation of legal empathy requires giving the victims of sex discrimination a stronger presence in the courtroom. Carol Smart (1989) believes this is the most valuable *potential* function of the law: to give women a significant voice within what has heretofore been a largely male institution. Empathy thus requires that the courts accord weight and legitimacy to the victim's experience of sex discrimination in the workplace. I argue that unless the law demonstrates a willingness to validate the victim's point of view, the very real harm of gender bias will pass by unnoticed. Siding instead with the perpetrator's perspective would render legal strategies of progressive change limited indeed.

Catherine MacKinnon argues that the law needs to incorporate and take seriously "[w]omen's lived-through experience, in as whole and truthful a fashion as can be" so that the harm of sex discrimination can be identified and mitigated (Pollack 1990, 42). A specific manifestation of what I am trying to express here can be found in Eleanor Bratton's argument that "men's views as to what constitutes sexual harassment differs from women's views and limits their acceptance of what is [and] how much of it there is" (1987, 99). As such, feminists must push for "a jurisprudential model which accurately and completely accounts for the experience of women" (100).

An important part of an empathic jurisprudence, of course, rests on the assumption that "(most) women and (most) men will sympathetically resist pain suffered by others, when that pain is meaningfully communicated" (West, 1987, 144). Although such an assumption may very well be problematic, it is also the case that "*without* a clear articulation of the content and meaning of our [women's] pain, it will not be sympathetically resisted by men who do not share it" (144). This insight makes it apparent that the concepts of empathy and an ethic of care cannot be considered in splendid isolation from one another, but rather should be understood as complementary criteria. And just as a victim-empathic jurisprudence will tend to promote an ethic of care, so will identification with the perpetrator push the law towards an ethic of rights. Empathizing with employers who have been shown to have used sexually discriminatory criteria in their promotion decisions, for example, will tend to produce an emphasis on preserving the right of employers to make personnel decisions as they see fit.

There is one final cautionary note before proceeding with the analysis. It is important to note that the analytical categories described above need not be construed as dichotomous in terms of feminist/antifeminist thinking. Rather, such conceptual categories as empathy and an ethic of care are used to *read* the complex content of legal rhetoric. That is, insight into the feminist nature of federal sex discrimination law may be gained by interpreting the language of the courts and other legal actors (as represented in legal briefs) through a lens constructed of the legal ideological concepts of empathy and an ethic of care. Thus, it is expected that the federal courts fall somewhere along a feminist/antifeminist continuum when measured by the evaluative criteria described above.

AN ANALYSIS OF FEDERAL JURISPRUDENCE

First, the concept of empathy as it applies to legal doctrine dealing with sexual harassment in the workplace is considered. Again, a feminist conception of the law emphasizes the necessity of giving predominantly female victims of sex discrimination in the workplace a strong presence in the courtroom. Determining the extent to which the law demonstrates a willingness to give the plaintiffs in Title VII sex discrimination suits a powerful voice constitutes a key test of the law as a force for progressive change.

Two federal court cases in the area of sexual harassment that speak to the concept of empathy are *Bundy v. Jackson* (1981) and *Meritor v. Vinson* (1986). The latter case was handed down by the Supreme Court, while the former case emanated from the District of Columbia's Court of Appeals.

The case of *Meritor v. Vinson*, which is the only case dealing with sexual harassment to reach the Supreme Court, deals with a female employee's claim that "she had been required to perform sexual favors for her supervisor . . . in order to maintain her employment" at what was to become Meritor Savings Bank (Robertson et al. 1987, 180). The employee, Mechelle Vinson, felt that denying the advances of her male supervisor would have led to her dismissal. Ms. Vinson eventually rose to the position of assistant branch manager. She stated, however, that "she was not required or asked to give sexual favors as a condition for promotion" (181). After about two years of coping with such workplace conditions, Ms. Vinson "left her job, taking indefinite sick leave, and was discharged two months later for excessive use of leave" (181).

Meritor, viewed through the interpretative lens of empathy, reveals a terribly ambiguous and contradictory jurisprudence of sex discrimination. One of the key holdings of Meritor is that sexual harassment, even absent tangible economic impact, is an actionable Title VII claim. Justice William Rehnquist, author of the Supreme Court's majority opinion, argues that sexual harassment, if it is sufficiently severe or pervasive to create a hostile or abusive work environment for the victim, is illegal even if it does not involve direct economic injury (the paradigmatic example of this latter harm, commonly referred to as quid pro quo harassment, would be a male supervisor who demands sexual favors from a female subordinate in return for job security or advancement). The Court validates the seriousness of Ms. Vinson's powerful experience of non-quid pro quo sexual harassment in the workplace, even absent tangible and direct economic harm. This holding lends at least some support to a feminist conception of an empathic jurisprudence. Meritor endorses the victim's point of view by creating legal redress for the victims of a hostile work environment.

Several significant limitations to the empathic nature of the above holding, however, cast great doubt over the feminist bent of the Supreme Court's sexual harassment jurisprudence. Justice Rehnquist, for example, argues that harassment in the workplace must exceed a certain (subjective) level of severity or pervasiveness before becoming actionable under Title VII. And the very severe manifestation of sexual harassment presented by the plaintiff in *Meritor* tells us little about how future courts will define the flexible standards enunciated in the instant case. The brief on behalf of Mechelle Vinson, for example, points out that she had been subjected to "40 or 50 episodes of undesired and traumatic sexual intercourse over a 20 month period. . . . Her physical and emotional suffering was testified to include bleeding and infections, inability to eat or sleep normally, loss of hair, . . . with one attack so violent that she bled from the vagina for weeks." Feminists must be concerned that an increasingly conservative federal judiciary will now have ready access to a legal loophole through which they may smuggle their hostility towards, or lack of understanding of, sexual harassment in the workplace. They may be reluctant indeed to find a sufficiently severe or pervasive presence of sexual harassment to justify legal intervention on behalf of the victims of such behavior.

A further limitation to the Court's empathy for the victim in *Meritor* can be found in their failure to award back pay or promotion to Ms. Vinson in the instant case. This is so because Rehnquist's finding of *environmental* harassment rather than quid pro quo harassment limits applicable remedies: "Those prevailing on hostile environment claims must settle for injunctive relief or reinstatement" (Vinciguerra 1989, 1733). Environmental harassment, however, often results in the constructive discharge of the victimized employee (a situation in which a harassed individual quits his/her job in the face of intolerable workplace conditions). Had the Court endorsed instead the presence of quid pro quo harassment, Ms. Vinson would have been eligible for an award of backpay and promotion. It may very well be time to erase the somewhat artificial distinction between environmental and quid pro quo sexual harassment and reconstruct a definition that encompasses more fully the victim's experience of this serious workplace harm. This would entail a definition that recognizes the serious impact that environmental harassment often has on its victims. Such a definition would need to include the fact that "a large number of working women respond to sexual harassment by quitting," even absent an explicit quid pro quo situation (Farley 1978). The Supreme Court thus fails to appreciate fully the serious impact of a hostile work environment on the victims of sexual harassment by failing to provide for a viable remedy in cases defined as hostile work environment rather than quid pro quo. To this extent, *Meritor* expresses a nonempathic understanding of sexual harassment.

The case of *Meritor v. Vinson* spawns a nonempathic legal brief by the Equal Employment Opportunity Commission (EEOC) which argues that the defendant's assertion of innocence in response to a charge of sexual harassment essentially negates the plaintiff's grim and detailed narrative of prolonged and severe sexual coercion. The EEOC claims that sexual advances and innuendo are ambiguous and, from the "viewpoint of the reasonable victim," no sexual harassment took place in the instant case. The EEOC thus advances a "reasonable victim" standard that is decidedly insensitive to Ms. Vinson's experience of sexual coercion in the workplace, thereby violating willfully a feminist understanding of empathy.

Another of the Supreme Court's holdings in *Meritor* permits the presentation of evidence about an alleged victim's manner of speech and dress. This decision is premised on the idea that such evidence is pertinent to the issue of sexual harassment. This argument contradicts the victim's point of view, which maintains that individuals should have the freedom to speak and dress how they wish without being blamed for subsequent harassment that is directed at them by others. Catherine MacKinnon argues that "men [who sexually harass women] wish to believe that women desire to be sexually attacked and to that end construct virtually any situation as an invitation" (1979, 50). *Meritor* thus affirms the perpetrator's viewpoint, which asserts the existence of a strong connection between how a woman dresses and speaks and subsequent sexual harassment.

A victim-empathic alternative to the above holding can be found in a brief for plaintiff Vinson, which argues that evidence about a victim's style of dress and verbal expression is simply not pertinent to the issue of sexual harassment. From the female victim's perspective, her manner of dress and speech patterns are an expression of personality and are not designed to be an open invitation to sexual harassment. The Women's Legal Defense Fund (WLDF) files an amicus curiae brief that makes a similar point, asserting that those who believe such evidence is germane to the issue of sexual harassment partake of the "discredited myth that only women who ask for trouble get it." The WLDF also argues that evidence concerning the victim's style of dress and manner of speech will evoke hopelessly stereotyped prejudices in the courtroom, and so should be excluded as irrelevant and prejudicial. From the woman's point of view, then, it is clear that the evidence considered in *Meritor* had no place in a case about sexual harassment.

Justice Rehnquist also finds in *Meritor* that Vinson's voluntary participation in sexual relations with her male supervisor is not the question that is relevant to her claim of sexual harassment. Rather, the crucial consideration is whether Ms. Vinson *welcomed* the sexual advances of her superior. The Supreme Court thus overturns a lower federal court which had argued that no sexual harassment was present since the alleged victim was not physically forced to have sex with her supervisor.

The Supreme Court's holding on the issue of welcomeness is empathic relative to the victim's coercive experience of workplace sexual harassment by a male superior, but only to a rather limited extent. Certainly Rehnquist chooses the proper standard to use in determining the presence of sexual harassment. The principle of welcomeness better captures a female employee's experience of sexual harassment from a male higher-up. A standard of voluntariness, conversely, willfully disregards the possibility that a female worker may, on the surface and in a very narrow sense, 'voluntarily' participate in a sexual relationship with a male manager and yet abhor and be negatively affected by this experience. The Court rightly rejects a standard of physical voluntariness that is clearly insensitive to the female victim's experience of workplace power dynamics. A partial failure of empathy on the part of the Supreme Court, however, is evidenced by Justice Rehnquist's implicit characterization of Ms. Vinson's conduct in her own oppression as voluntary. He seems to agree with the lower court's assessment of Ms. Vinson's voluntary participation in sexual relations with her supervisor, but rejects using such a standard to determine the presence of sexual harassment. A more feminist line of argument would include a strong rejection of the idea that Ms. Vinson's conduct was voluntary in any meaningful sense.

The brief for plaintiff Vinson, for example, notes that the sexual favors demanded by her male supervisor were "exacted by his intimidation and threats of reprisal." This supervisor, Mr. Taylor, "tampered with her personnel records, lodged false complaints about her with management, denigrated and abused her in front of other workers, entrapped her into work errors, escalated his campaign of fault-finding against her job performance, and threatened her life when she threatened to report him." Vinson's brief thus argues that she submitted "voluntarily" because she lacked the necessary workplace power to make her felt needs effective, she lacked viable economic alternatives had she left the employ of the bank (Ms. Vinson was a single black mother), and she feared the threatened consequences of reporting her supervisor's harassment. An understanding of the victim's point of view, therefore, reveals that Taylor's attacks on Vinson were not only unwelcomed by her, but also were not voluntary in any signficant way.

A seminal case involving sexual harassment in the workplace is that of *Bundy v. Jackson* (1981). In this case a female employee of the District of Columbia's Department of Corrections, Sarah Bundy, was repeatedly propositioned for sexual favors by her male supervisors. She was also sexually harassed by a male co-worker, Delbert Jackson, at this time. After Ms. Bundy filed a complaint about this sexual harassment, her supervisors began to complain about her work (no such criticism had been forthcoming prior to Bundy's formal complaint). After becoming eligible for promotion, Bundy was told that "because a freeze had been placed on promotions she could not be recommended for promotion. During this time, however, other employees of the Department were recommended for promotions and some were promoted" (Maxwell, 1981, 414). Ms. Bundy eventually filed a formal complaint with the Department. The director at this time, Delbert Jackson, found Bundy's charges to be groundless. She then "filed a complaint in the United States District Court for the District of Columbia, requesting declaratory relief for sexual harassment, and an immediate promotion and back pay for delay in promotion" (415). The District Court ruled that sexual harassment absent tangible economic harm did not constitute a violation of Title VII. This same court also held that Bundy had been denied promotion for legitimate, nondiscriminatory reasons. Bundy's claim for injunctive relief and immediate promotion and back pay were thus denied by the D.C. District Court. Ms. Bundy then appealed to the District of Columbia Court of Appeals.

The D.C. Court of Appeals reversed the lower court's holding in *Bundy v. Jackson*. J. Skelly Wright, Circuit Judge, held that sexual harassment that affects the psychological and emotional work environment, even absent any relation to tangible job benefits, constituted sex discrimination under Title VII of the Civil Rights Act of 1964. Wright argued that sexual harassment, "which injects the most demeaning sexual stereotypes into the general work environment and which always represents an intentional assault on an individual's innermost privacy," must not be considered outside the pale of Title VII's anti-discrimination provisions. This harassment, which the court calls environmental sexual harassment, is thus condemned by the D.C. Court of Appeals as illegal. This holding reveals the ability of the law to adopt an empathic understanding of the harm of sexual harassment in the workplace that may not involve an explicit bargain of sex for a job. The brief for Bundy makes clear the serious nature of such conduct: ". . . for Mrs. Bundy, the humiliation, degradation and discomfort caused by her employer's sexual advances was . . . severe. . . . An atmosphere in which unwelcome sexual advances are a normal condition of work destroys equality of opportunity for women. Such advances are emotionally and physically debilitating." The Court's holding in *Bundy* thus affirms the victim's experience of great harm in the workplace despite the lack of so-called tangible damage.

The D.C. Court of Appeals also decides that Bundy's strong showing of environmental sexual harassment should ease her burden of proof in seeking to obtain back pay and promotion. Judge Wright argues that since Bundy "has already proved that she is a victim of illegal discrimination as a matter wholly independent of her claim for back pay and promotion," subsequent efforts on her part to obtain a retroactive promotion and lost back pay should be facilitated. The Court of Appeals thus holds that Bundy's employer must refute her initial case for back pay and promotion with clear and convincing evidence rather than merely a preponderance of evidence.

An expression of empathy can be detected in Judge Wright's decision to facilitate the plaintiff's attempts to obtain back pay and promotion by establishing a heightened burden of proof for employers. The D.C. Court of Appeals thus questions vigorously the employer's perspective on workplace events and so expresses an empathic approach to the key issue of burden of proof standards. That is, the employer's perception of sexual harassment is not given a privileged place in the courtroom, but rather is subjected to a high level of scrutiny by Judge Wright. Indirectly, then, the victim's narrative is given greater legitimacy by this burden of proof ruling.

Supreme Court doctrine in the area of gender bias in promotion decisions also offers up a contradictory jurisprudence when measured by the feminist legal principle of empathy, although certainly it is the case that this area of the law is significantly less empathic than the sexual harassment jurisprudence reviewed above.

A pertinent case is *Price Waterhouse v. Hopkins* (1989). Ms. Hopkins, a senior manager and an officer in the accounting firm of Price Waterhouse, charged that she was rejected for partnership within the firm because of what several male partners considered to be unfeminine behavior. A male partner who was sympathetic to Ms. Hopkins, for example, advised her to "walk more femininely, talk more femininely, dress more femininely, wear make-up, have her hair styled, and wear jewelry" if she hoped to make partner. A less sympathetic senior member of Price Waterhouse advised her to take a course in charm school. Justice Brennan, writing for the majority, held that an employer may avoid liability in such cases by marshalling a preponderance of evidence in support of the contention that a legitimate reason would have resulted in the same personnel decision that the plaintiff, via a prima facie case, had already shown to be tainted with an illegal consideration of sexual stereotypes.

This holding is empathic to the extent that it involves shifting at least some of the burden of proof onto the defendant after the plaintiff has made out a prima facie (initial and reasonably persuasive) case of sex discrimination: "If an employer allows gender to affect its decision-making process, then it must carry the burden of justifying its ultimate decision." The Court also declines to allow the employer to present hypothetical motives that *could* have driven its behavior: "An employer may not . . . prevail in a mixed-motives case by offering a legitimate and sufficient reason for its decision if that reason did not motivate it at the time of the decision." These holdings question the employer's perspective to at least some extent, and do not place the entire burden of proof on the victimized employee.

Simultaneously, however, the Supreme Court draws back rather substantially from a full-bodied empathic understanding of sex discrimination in the workplace when it rejects a lower court holding that saddled employers with the more stringent burden of proof standard of clear and convincing evidence. The District Court for the District of Columbia, presided over by Judge Gerhard Gesell, had ruled that the employer must surmount just such an evidentiary barrier, and failed to do so in the instant case (a summary of Gesell's opinion can be found in *Hopkins v. Price Waterhouse*, 1987). The District Court's aggressive questioning of the employer's point of view, however, is reversed by the Supreme Court. Justice Brennan also enunciates the Supreme Court's commitment to holding employers liable for providing an affirmative remedy to employees only when personnel decisions *hinge* on an illegal consideration of gender. Brennan argues that one of Title VII's primary aims is the "preservation of an employer's . . . freedom of choice" (1786). A focus on actively remedying only sex discrimination that results in tangible and direct harm to the victim, however, denigrates the plaintiff's experience of sexual discrimination in the workplace and so violates an empathic understanding of such conduct. From the victim's perspective, *all* manifestations of sex discrimination result in very real harm, and so should be interpreted to render employers liable for such behavior.

The brief for respondent Hopkins, for example, argues that "Hopkins suffered not because of discrimination in the air but rather because of discrimination brought to the ground and visited upon her." This same brief also finds it particularly troubling that "Price Waterhouse knew what was happening and did nothing about it." Despite these victim-empathic arguments, however, the brief for Hopkins does *not* argue in favor of absolute liability in so-called mixed-motive cases (situations in which gender is only one among many considerations used to arrive at a personnel decision). Rather, Hopkins suggests that the moderate burden of proof assigned to defendants by a majority of the Justices (that of a preponderance of evidence) is too lenient and should be replaced by the more stringent standard of clear and convincing evidence. Hopkins also advocates an empathic alternative to the Court's ruling that sexual stereotyping must play a decisive role in an employment decision before an employer can be held liable for sex discrimination. Hopkins argues that liability should be fixed once the plaintiff can show that "one of the motives was unlawful." Hopkins thus indicates a sensitivity to the victim's experience of sex discrimination in the workplace that may not result directly in economic injury, but is very harmful nonetheless.

The Civil Rights Act of 1991 purports to reverse the holding of the Supreme Court in *Price Waterhouse*, but such a claim is doubtful. According to an analysis in a recent *Congressional Quarterly Weekly Report*, the 1991 legislation makes illegal any personnel decision in which "sex . . . was a motivating factor, . . . even when other factors also motivated the practice" (1991, 3621). The 1991 bill also specifies, however, that injunctive relief (a court order that an employer cease and desist from the practice of sex discrimination) may only be awarded if employees can prove that "they were denied a position *because of* an impermissible motive" (emphasis added). This section on legal relief implies strongly that sexually discriminatory motives must be shown to drive an adverse personnel decision. The Supreme Court gave just such an interpretation to the language "because of" in *Price Waterhouse*. As such, it appears that the Civil Rights Act of 1991 goes no further than the current legal status quo. A close reading of *Price Waterhouse* (1989) demonstrates that the Supreme Court spoke primarily to the question of liability: "We hold that when a plaintiff in a Title VII case proves that her gender played a motivating part in an employment decision, the defendant may avoid a finding of liability only by proving . . . that it would have made the same decision even if it had not taken the plaintiff's gender into account." The reading of *Price Waterhouse* is that the Court *does* find the presence of sexually discriminatory motives in a personnel decision to be a violation of Title VII, but hesitates to impose any liability on employers unless the above criteria are satisfied. Finally, it should be noted that the Civil Rights Act of 1991 permits only the award of injunctive relief, attorneys' fees, and court costs. "No compensatory or punitive damages would be permitted" (1991, 3621). This denial of such damages devalues the victimized employee's experience of sexual discrimination in the workplace, and so violates a feminist understanding of empathy.

The District of Columbia Court of Appeals manifests a nonempathic legal ideology in the case of *Clark v. Marsh* (1981). Judge Tamm, the presiding judge, firmly rejects the concept of punitive damages in a case where an employer was found guilty of consistently denying promotions to a female employee based on an illegal consideration of sex. Judge Tamm appeals to Title VII's explicit emphasis on make-whole relief and concomitant rejection of punitive damages. I argue that Judge Tamm fails to understand from the victim's perspective the serious harm of sex discrimination in the workplace, and so gives an improperly narrow meaning to make-whole relief. Had the D.C. Court of Appeals embraced a more victim-empathic understanding of the serious impact of any sex discrimination in the workplace, punitive damages could very well have been awarded as part of Title VII's commitment to make-whole relief. That is, an award of such damages would have indicated the court's ability to understand adequately the victim's experience of gender bias in the workplace setting.

A partial remedy to the above decision can be found in the Civil Rights Act of 1991 which allows for the award of punitive damages against employers found guilty of intentional gender discrimination. Congress, with the reluctant support of President Bush, has taken action that promises, at least in the abstract, to deliver a more empathic jurisprudence of sex discrimination. The Act's current provisions call for a $50,000 cap on damage awards involving small businesses, while the maximum liability of large companies has been set at $300,000. These caps, which do not apply to cases involving intentional racial or religious discrimination (racial minorities can obtain unlimited damages under Section 1981 of Title 42 of the U.S. Code, a Reconstruction-era federal law), signal a limit to Congress' sensitivity to the victim's experience of sex discrimination in the workplace (CQ Weekly Report 1991, 3620). Race discrimination, apparently, is to be taken more seriously than sex discrimination. It also remains to be seen just how willing the federal courts will be to permit such judgments against employers in cases involving gender bias in the workplace.

These various manifestations of a nonempathic legal ideology of sex discrimination jurisprudence emphasize the very real limitations of the law's usefulness as an emancipatory tool for women in the workplace. Most important, perhaps, is the fact that the legal ideology expressed in court cases dealing with sexual harassment is significantly more empathic than the ideology found in cases dealing with sex discrimination in workplace promotion practices. The reasons for this difference are crucial for an understanding of what role the law can play for women in the workplace.

Perhaps the presence of sexual harassment in the workplace is so obvious that the victims of such behavior have little difficultly in enlisting the empathy, and perhaps sympathy, of judges and justices. Also, it is apparent that those sexual harassment cases brought before the courts are likely to display clear-cut instances of wrong-doing by the perpetrator, and are not likely representative of the universe of sexual harassment that takes place in the American workplace. Sex discrimination in promotion, conversely, tends to consist of very subtle workplace dynamics and often involves decision-making processes that employers conduct largely in secret. It may also be that the elimination of sexual harassment may not threaten the status quo in the workplace as forcefully as the elimination of sex discrimination in promotion practices. Mitigating sexual harassment is aimed at giving women a chance to remain in the workplace and work in a humane environment, while remedying claims of sex discrimination in promotion entails allowing women greater upward mobility within the workplace. A more feminist jurisprudence of sex discrimination in promotion, therefore, may come at a greater cost to the status quo in the American workplace than a feminist jurisprudence of sexual harassment, and so encounter greater resistance in the judicial system. For these reasons, speculative though they may be, one can surmise that there exist significant limits to the law's willingness to invoke empathy for the victims of sex discrimination in the workplace.

A further function of this study's focus on two different areas of sex discrimination law is its potential to produce a cross-fertilization of ideas that can benefit the feminist goal of extending and deepening the participation of women in the workplace. For example, *Bundy v. Jackson*'s affirmation of the illegality of sex discrimination that does not entail tangible economic harm for the recipient (environmental sexual harassment) provides a valuable ideological alternative to the antifeminist legal doctrine espoused in *Price Waterhouse*. *Bundy*'s validation of using a finding of environmental sex discrimination to heighten the employer's burden of proof in refuting a victimized employee's prima facie case for an award of back pay and promotion (that of clear and convincing evidence, rather than merely a preponderance) could be used to inform *Price Waterhouse*'s decision to permit employers to fulfill only a minimal burden of proof when refuting a plaintiff's efforts to show that sex discrimination played a *decisive* role in a *particular* employment decision. *Bundy*, in other words, tells us that *Price Waterhouse* could demand that employers demonstrate with clear and convincing evidence that they would have made the same employment decision even absent the presence of sexually discriminatory behavior in the promotion process.

The second element of a feminist jurisprudence of sex discrimination law to be considered in this article involves the tension between an ethic of care and a hierarchical and competitive conception of rights. Legal rhetoric centered on rights tends to work against powerless groups and often justifies the triumph of the politically and economically powerful. Conversely, a legal focus on an ethic of care is rooted in a feminist dedication to preserving the well-being of vulnerable groups and individuals.

The case of *Meritor v. Vinson* (1986) offers valuable insight into the ability and willingness of the federal courts to embrace an ethic of care as it applies to vulnerable employees. Justice Rehnquist, writing for the Supreme Court, holds that employers are not automatically liable for compensating the victims of sexual harassment committed by management personnel. Rehnquist argues that Title VII "evinces an intent to place some limits on the acts of employees for which employers . . . are to be held responsible." The Supreme Court decides that absent a finding of quid pro quo sexual harassment, employers should only be held liable if they have actual knowledge of the behavior in question, or if the victim had no reasonable avenue of complaint. The Court's standard of conditional liability reveals a hesitancy to protect as fully as possible the victims of sexual harassment in the workplace. In all fairness to the Supreme Court, however, it does hold in the instant case that Meritor's "general non-discrimination policy did not address sexual harassment in particular, and thus did not alert employees to their employer's interest in correcting that form of discrimination." Furthermore, Rehnquist notes that Meritor's policy against discrimination required Ms. Vinson, the victim, to file a complaint with Mr. Taylor, her harasser. The Court thus holds Meritor liable for Mr. Taylor's sexual harassment. Nevertheless, I wish to argue that the Court's policy of conditional liability represents a moderate rather than aggressive commitment to an ethic of care in the workplace.

A more feminist alternative to the Supreme Court's holding in *Meritor* can be found in the brief for Ms. Vinson. This brief argues that it is the employer who is in the best position to provide "make-whole" equitable relief in cases involving sexual harassment, be it quid pro quo or environmental. Merely holding supervisory personnel liable for their actions fails to fulfill the intent of Title VII to remedy the harm of sex discrimination in the workplace. Several members of Congress sponsor a brief which asserts that only the employer can provide injunctive and monetary relief for victimized employees. Vinson's brief also notes that "most women, once forced to have sex, are too humiliated and intimidated to complain." Even the existence of "adequate" mechanisms for reporting sexual harassment, therefore, may very well fail to remedy the problem at hand. Congress's brief thus advocates a policy of strict liability, whereby employers would be held liable for the discriminatory acts of its management personnel, regardless of circumstances. Such a policy, argues Congress, would encourage employers to take an active and aggressive stance against sexual harassment in the workplace, and would most effectively serve the needs of victimized employees.

The Supreme Court adopts a similarly contradictory stance on the issue of responsibility in the workplace in cases dealing with sex discrimination in promotion practices. The case of *Hishon v. King and Spaulding* (1984), which deals with a female employee's claim that her employer (a large law firm) denied her promotion from associate to partner based on an illegal consideration of sex, endorses an ethic of care. The Supreme Court holds that partnership consideration at a law firm, while not a *right* of employment, is nevertheless covered by Title VII's prohibition of sex discrimination in the workplace, given the centrality of partnership consideration to such a job. This decision on the part of the Court, which gives women in the legal profession protection from sex discrimination in promotion decisions, reveals a willingness to restrict somewhat management's right to make personnel decisions without a healthy concern for the well-being of vulnerable employees.

The Supreme Court affirms an ethic of care in *Johnson v. Transportation Agency* (1987), which involves a claim of reverse discrimination by a male employee denied promotion in an occupation dominated by men (the repair and maintenance of roads), by emphasizing that employers need not prove a history of gender discrimination on their own part before implementing an affirmative action plan based in part on gender. The import of this holding is that discrimination flows, at least in part, from societal sources rather than just factors within the control of the employer. Requiring employers to demonstrate their own culpability for a workforce containing a disproportionately large number of males would fail to take into adequate account the fact that "women and men are subjected to different expectations and experiences, and that, as a result, they tend to express preferences for different types of work early in their lives" (Schultz 1991, 134). Permitting employers to implement affirmative action programs based in part on social forces also recognizes that "women's work preferences . . . [can be] . . . recreated in response to changing work conditions" (134). The Court thus demonstrates a full-bodied concern for the welfare of employees victimized by the practice of sex discrimination in both society and the workplace. The Supreme Court also recognizes the fact that few employers indeed would implement affirmative action plans if doing so required disclosing the prior practice of employment discrimination.

As in sexual harassment doctrine, however, there exists also a darker side to the law's treatment of responsibility in the workplace. In *Milton v. Weinberger* (1982), for example, the D.C. Court of Appeals argues that they are very hesitant to "second-guess an employer's personnel decision, absent demonstrably discriminatory motive," and so impose only a minimal burden of proof on employers who have been accused of sex discrimination. Judge Edwards thus displays a great deal of concern for maintaining a wide prerogative for employers while concomitantly evincing little concern for the fate of employees who claim sex discrimination, thereby denying minority groups access to the benefits of affirmative action.

The Supreme Court's decision in *Texas v. Burdine* (1981), a case dealing with the legality of a company's affirmative action program, also belittles an ethic of care as it applies to vulnerable groups in the American workplace. Justice Powell, writing for the majority, argues that employers cannot be made to "maximize" the number of minority and female employees hired or promoted, but rather should be given wide latitude to make personnel decisions without the threat of judicial intervention. Again, the Supreme Court affirms a stance against an ethic of responsibility towards vulnerable groups and focuses instead on an aggressive defense of employer rights in regard to personnel decisions.

A harsh approach to an ethic of care is demonstrated in a brief for King and Spaulding in *Hishon v. King and Spaulding* (1984). King and Spaulding argue that a law firm's right to freedom of association overrides the government's interest in prohibiting sex discrimination in the workplace. Partnership consideration, therefore, should not be governed by Title VII's prohibition of sex discrimination in the workplace. They emphasize the broad discretion that employers require when making personnel decisions. Such an argument demonstrates little concern is shown for the welfare of vulnerable employees who might be subject to workplace discrimination. King and Spaulding instead evince a great deal of concern with maximizing the employer's right to make personnel decisions with as little outside interference as possible.

CONCLUSION

Just what role do the legal ideology and judicial policies of the federal courts examined in this study play for women in the workplace? The findings seem to comport with the conclusion of E.P. Thompson in *Whigs and Hunters*: While the law frequently serves the needs of an unjust status quo, and so can inhibit the advent of progressive social change, it also can "afford some protection to the powerless" (1975, 266). This contradictory and complex nature of legal ideology thus acts as both a beacon of hope and a siren of despair for women in the workplace.

Ironically, the multifaceted and often contradictory composition of the legal ideology contained in sex discrimination jurisprudence is often manifested within the published opinions of the courts themselves. In *Meritor v. Vinson* (1986), for example, one can find both feminist and antifeminist elements of sex discrimination doctrine. It is also crucial to note that the legal policies pursued in one area of sex discrimination doctrine can sometimes be applied to others, thereby enhancing the feminist nature of federal law. *Bundy v. Jackson*'s (1981) validation of environmental sex discrimination, for example, could be used to inform the Supreme Court's understanding of sexual stereotyping in *Texas v. Burdine* (1981).

It is of great importance to emphasize the positive contributions that legal briefs can make to a more feminist jurisprudence of sex discrimination. They can highlight progressive directions which the courts might be persuaded to pursue in the future, or they can demonstrate the sort of legal argumentation that feminists must be prepared to counter as the federal judiciary shifts to the right. Just a few examples include the WLDF's brief in *Meritor* arguing that the dress of sexual harassment's victims is irrelevant to such behavior, and Ms. Vinson's brief in the same case arguing in favor of strict liability for employers in cases involving sexual harassment. Mari Matsuda has argued that legal briefs can be used to promote "innovations in legal concepts and changes in the law" (1988, 6). At the same time, of course, one can also find legal briefs that propose decidedly antifeminist legal innovations. Consider, for example, the brief for King and Spaulding in *Hishon* that argues against extending Title VII's protective umbrella to cover the female employees of law firms. These briefs can be used by feminists, perhaps, to prepare and sharpen legal rebuttals that could serve in the future to minimize the ground that will most certainly be lost to an increasingly conservative federal judiciary.

This last point probably deserves some attention, since there is no question that the ideological makeup of the courts that shape the doctrine of sex discrimination greatly affects how women should use legal avenues of social change. As Carol Smart contends, "[t]he case of access to legal abortions in the USA . . . and the constant threat to the notion that women should decide their own reproductive careers, reveals how vulnerable changes based on law reform can be" (1989, 81). This cautionary note emphasizes the danger of placing too much emphasis on a court-centered strategy of change.

Women should use a legal strategy of change in the workplace with a great deal of care. They must recognize the ultimately ambivalent position of the law with regard to a feminist ideology, and they need to acknowledge the precarious nature of legal progress. As such, women in the workplace should avoid placing all of their eggs in one basket, and should continue to pursue a multi-pronged attack on gender inequality. They might, for example, focus some of their efforts on lobbying Congress to overturn antifeminist court rulings. The Civil Rights Act of 1991, for example, with the support of both Congress and the President, seems to move the courts toward a more feminist law of sex discrimination, although the analysis of this legislation here reveals the limits to such an understanding. At the very least, however, this statute emphasizes the contribution that the legislative and executive branches can make to a feminist jurisprudence of sex discrimination. As such, it is critical to emphasize that advocates of a workplace more accepting of women must pursue a complex strategy of progressive change. Feminists must also lobby state legislatures for greater protection from such gender-linked harms as sexual harassment and sex discrimination in promotion practices, since state and local institutions tend to have a more direct impact on the lived experiences of citizens. Finally, and perhaps most crucially, it is incumbent on feminists to pursue a grass-roots strategy of educating people about the practice and harm of sex discrimination, since a broad-based strategy is most likely to result in lasting and significant change in society.

However, the law still constitutes a valuable vehicle for progressive social change for women in the workplace. Rejected here is Carol Smart's despair over the law ("law is so deaf to the core concerns of feminism that feminists should be extremely cautious of how and whether they resort to the law") (1989, 2) and embraced instead is E.P. Thompson's belief that "We ought to expose the shams and inequities which may be concealed beneath [the] law" (1975, 266) so that the more positive aspects of the law may be rescued in the pursuit of a more egalitarian society.

BIBLIOGRAPHY

Blum, Debra E. 1991. "Environment Still Hostile to Women in Academe, New Evidence Indicates." The Chronicle of Higher Education, 9 October.

Bratton, Eleanor K. 1987. "The Eye of the Beholder" An Interdisciplinary Examination of Law and Social Research on Sexual Harassment." New Mexico Law Review, v. 17, pp. 91-114.

Chodorow, Nancy. 1978. *The Reproduction of Mothering.* University of California Press.

Congressional Quarterly Weekly Report. 1991. "Civil Rights Act of 1991." 7 December, v. 49, pp. 3620-3622.

Farley, Lin. 1978. *Sexual Shakedown: The Sexual Harassment of Women on the Job.* McGraw-Hill Book Company.

Gilligan, Carol. 1982. *In A Different Voice.* Harvard University Press.

Hoff-Wilson, Joan. 1987. "The Unfinished Revolution: Changing Legal Status of U.S. Women." Signs: Journal of Women in Culture and Society, v. 13, pp. 7-36.

Horwitz, Morton. 1988. "Rights." Harvard Civil Rights-Civil Liberties Law Review, v. 23, pp. 393-406.

Jaggar, Alison. 1983. "Human Biology in Feminist Theory." In Carol Gould, editor, *Beyond Domination: New Perspectives on Women and Philosophy.* Rowman and Allanheld.

Kleiman, Carol. 1992. "By all accounts, Abacus partners are dancing on the glass ceiling." Chicago Tribune, 12 February.

MacKinnon, Catherine. 1979. *Sexual Harassment of Working Women.* Yale University Press.

MacKinnon, Catherine. 1987. *Feminism Unmodified: Discourses on Life and Law.* Harvard University Press.

Matsuda, Mari. 1988. "Affirmative Action and Legal Knowledge: Planting Seeds in Plowed-Up Ground." Harvard Women's Law Journal, v. 11, pp. 1-17.

Maxwell, Mary Joseph. 1981. "Case Note on Sex Discrimination Law." University of Cincinnati Law Review, v. 50, pp. 414-422.

Pollack, Wendy. 1990. "Sexual Harassment: Women's Experience vs. Legal Definitions." Harvard Women's Law Journal, v. 13, pp. 35-85.

Rifkin, Janet. 1980. "Toward a Theory of Law and Patriarchy." Harvard Women's Law Journal, v. 3, pp. 83-95.

Robertson, Robert K., Delaney J. Kirk, and Elvis C. Stephens. 1987. "Hostile Environment: A Review of the Implications of *Meritor Savings Bank v. Vinson.*" Labor Law Journal, March 1987, pp. 179-183.

Schultz, Vicki. 1991. "Telling Stories About Women and Work." In Katherine T. Bartlett and Rosanne Kennedy, editors, *Feminist Legal Theory.* Westview Press.

Shalal-Esa, Andrea. 1992. " 'Glass ceiling' remains hard to break, study says." Chicago Tribune, 12 August.

Smart, Carol. 1989. *Feminism and the Power of Law.* Routledge.

Thompson, E. P. 1975. *Whigs and Hunters.* Pantheon Books.

Vinciguerra, Marlissa. 1989. "The Aftermath of *Meritor*: A Search for Standards in the Law of Sexual Harassment." Yale Law Journal, v. 98, pp. 1717-1738.
West, Robin. 1987. "The Difference in Women's Hedonic Lives." Wisconsin Women's Law Journal, v. 3, pp. 81-143.
West, Robin. 1991. "Jurisprudence and Gender." In Katherine T. Bartlett and Rosanne Kennedy, editors, *Feminist Legal Theory*. Westview Press.

LEGAL DOCUMENTS

Bundy v. Jackson 641 F.2d. 934 (1981)
    Brief for Plaintiff Bundy.
    Clark v. Marsh 665 F.2d. 1168 (1981)
    Hishon v. King and Spaulding 104 S.Ct. 2229 (1984)
    Brief for Defendant King and Spaulding.
    Hopkins v. Price Waterhouse 825 F.2d. 458 (1987)
    Johnson v. Transportation Agency 107 S.Ct. 1442 (1987)
    Meritor v. Vinson 106 S.Ct. 2399 (1986)
    Brief for Plaintiff Vinson.
Brief for the United States and the Equal Employment Opportunity Commission as amicus curiae.
Brief amicus curiae of the Women's Legal Defense Fund, et al.
    Brief of amici curiae members of Congress.
    Milton v. Weinberger 696 F.2d. 94 (1982)
    Brief for Plaintiff Milton.
    Price Waterhouse v. Hopkins 109 S.Ct. 1775 (1989)
    Brief for Defendant Hopkins.
    Texas v. Burdine 101 S.Ct. 1089 (1981)
    Brief for Defendant Burdine.

SEXUAL HARASSMENT IN THE MILITARY

YXTA MAYA MURRAY*

I. INTRODUCTION

Women in the armed forces are often hampered by pervasive sexual harassment that threatens their careers as well as their physical and emotional well-being. Despite the various military regulations designed to prevent such harassment, the military has not addressed this problem adequately. Furthermore, the three branches of government have also failed to effectively counter sexual harassment in the armed forces. Congress, the executive branch, and the courts allow the military almost sole jurisdiction over sexual harassment claims even though the armed forces are characterized by a specious sexual culture and a tradition of sexually discriminating against women.

The government's inability to manage the topic stems from the uncomfortable relationship that exists between women and the military. The American military began to integrate uneasily in the early 1970s, and women now compose approximately eleven percent of all American armed forces.[1] Yet while the civilian world has slowly begun to take notice of sexual harassment, the military remains locked into archaic notions of gender inequality that preclude women's opportunities to safely and comfortably succeed there.

The executive branch has done little to combat this harassment, except to make a few inadequate investigations and express its disapproval of this increasingly evident problem.[2] Although the courts and Congress have addressed sexual harassment in the civilian workplace,

---

* Clerk for the 9th Circuit, 1994-95; J.D., Stanford University, 1993; B.A., University of California, Los Angeles; love and thanks to my husband, Andrew Brown; thank you also to David Sanford.

1. Eric Schmitt, *The Military Has A Lot to Learn About Women*, N.Y. TIMES, Aug. 2, 1992, at E3.

2. *See infra* part III.A.

251

their forays into the military workplace have been sporadic and inef-
fectual.[3] Judicial doctrines such as the "separate community" theory
and a general notion that the military's war missions require extreme
deference preclude much significant examination or regulation by any
governmental branch. These theories have helped create a severe crisis for women in the armed forces that has only recently come to
national attention.

Sexual harassment need not, however, become a permanent
aspect of military life. For example, extension of Title VII[4] to the uniformed military sphere would arm claimants with the investigative and
enforcement procedures that have worked in the civilian world. Until
the government is willing to intervene into the military's separate
sphere, the growing number of female military personnel will continue
to be deprived of the safe and supportive environment that their male
colleagues enjoy.

II.   SEXUAL HARASSMENT IN THE MILITARY

Formal studies and anecdotal evidence indicate that women in
the military face a shocking level of sexual harassment on the job.
One 1990 Pentagon study found that "more than a third of [women in
the military] experienced some form of harassment, including touching, pressure for sexual favors, and rape."[5] A Senate study in 1988
reported that "five percent of the women surveyed reported actual or
attempted rape . . . in the previous twelve months."[6] Other investigations and reports reveal an unsafe environment where sexual harassment is deliberately used to demean the professional status of military
women. Specific incidents include a Lieutenant Commander who was
made "the brunt of smutty skits" and was "forcibly removed from an
office by a man who did not want to take instructions from a woman,
then told that if she pressed charges she would be removed as a
department head."[7] Eighty percent of the female cadets at the Air
Force Academy say they hear sexist or demeaning remarks about

---

3.   *See infra* parts III.B-C.

4.   42 U.S.C. § 2000e *et seq.* (1991).

5.   *The MacNeil/Lehrer News Hour* (PBS Television Broadcast, July 1, 1992) (statement of
Washington correspondent Judy Woodruff).

6.   *Id.*

7.   Jane Gross, *Servicewomen's Families Speak Out on Abuse*, N.Y. TIMES, July 26, 1992, at
A16.

women *every day*.[8] Academics who study the problem link it to a pervasive ethos of sexism which exists and is tolerated in the military.[9] Moreover, straight women are not the only individuals who face sexual harassment. As the issue of gays and lesbians in the military becomes increasingly visible, so does the problem of their harassment.[10]

Yet despite the data, the mainstream public largely ignored the harassment until recently. In 1989, Annapolis female midshipman Gwen Dreyer was abducted by a group of male classmates, handcuffed to a urinal in a men's bathroom, and taunted as other male classmates photographed her.[11] Her attackers were given only demerits and reprimands.[12] Two years later, the 1991 "Tailhook scandal" erupted at a convention of the naval aviators' association, Tailhook. At the convention, which included "strippers and scantily clad bartenders,"[13] junior Navy officers participating in the revelries assaulted approximately eighty-three women.[14] In 1993, the *New York Times* reported that:

> The assaults varied from victims being grabbed on the buttocks to victims being groped, pinched and fondled on their breasts, buttocks and genitals .... Some victims were bitten by their assailants, others were knocked to the ground and some had their clothing

---

8. *Female Cadets Tell Air Force: Sexism is a Daily Routine*, ATLANTA J. AND CONST., Oct. 20, 1992, at A6.

9. *See, e.g.*, CHRISTINE L. WILLIAMS, GENDER DIFFERENCES AT WORK: WOMEN AND MEN IN NONTRADITIONAL OCCUPATIONS 69 (1989); Mary E. Becker, *Interdisciplinary Approach: The Politics of Women's Wrongs and the Bill of "Rights": A Bicentennial Perspective*, 59 U. CHI. L. REV. 453, 496 (1992).

10. *See* Carol Ness, *Gay Professionals More Open But Still Fearful*, S.F. EXAMINER, Oct. 10, 1993, at A1 (discussing harassment of openly gay and lesbian professionals and noting that "the debate on gays in the military (the nation's largest employer) has reinforced the need for caution"); Robert Reinhold, *Pentagon Shelves "Don't Ask" Policy*, HOUS. CHRON., Oct. 9, 1993, at A2 (quoting Michelle Benecke, co-director of the Service-Members Legal Defense Network as saying "gay service-members are likely to continue to face tenacious harassment and discrimination"); Eric Schmitt, *Anti-Gay Motive Questioned in Beating Death of a Sailor*, N.Y. TIMES, Feb. 27, 1993, at A9 (investigating allegations that sailor was murdered because of his sexual orientation).

11. *American Notes: Naval Academy: A Probe that Snowballed*, TIME, June 11, 1990, at 27; Molly Moore, *Navy Seeks to Improve Lot of Women: Secretary's Frank Memo Follows Report of Sexual Harassment, Rapes*, WASH. POST, Oct. 25, 1990, at A4.

12. Todd Spangler, *Defining Integrity, Honor of 'Mids': Academy Cheating Scandal Probed*, WASH. TIMES, Sept. 14, 1993, at C4.

13. *Admiral Testifies in Tailhook Case*, N.Y. TIMES, Nov. 30, 1993, at A22; Eric Schmitt, *Wall of Silence Impedes Inquiry into a Rowdy Navy Convention*, N.Y. TIMES, June 14, 1992, at A1, A34.

14. Schmitt, *supra* note 13, at A34.

ripped or removed . . . . Included in [a Pentagon] report is a photograph of a nude stripper straddling a clothed serviceman who is lying on the floor in a crowded room. Another photo shows aviators wearing T-shirts that declare, 'Women are Property.'[15]

Other events also highlight the problem, such as the 1993 suicide of an army private whose family says she shot and killed herself after being sexually harassed by two sergeants,[16] and the story of the Navy reservist who was forced to spend a three-day weekend in a locked psychiatric unit after she accused her boss of demanding sex in exchange for professional advancement opportunities.[17]

These incidents have created a brief but unrelenting spotlight on how the armed forces have dealt unsuccessfully with the relatively new arrival of women officers. After allegations surfaced of junior Naval officers' assaults on women at the Tailhook convention, the Navy's attempts to police itself revealed a disturbing pattern of outright sexism and corruption. The executive branch during the Bush Administration was also angered by the Inspector General's inability to investigate the allegations successfully.[18] The Inspector General and the Naval Investigative Service Command began preliminary investigations more than a month after the incident and concluded them only seven months later.[19] After more than 1500 interviews with officers and civilians who had been present at the convention, "investigators were able to identify only two suspects because of officers' refusals to talk about the incidents."[20] The Inspector General's report also revealed that certain commanding officers refused to order their subordinates to be photographed so that victims would not be able to identify their assailants.[21] One senior Marine Corps officer even intentionally misled investigators about whether a former aide had

---

15. Michael R. Gordon, *Pentagon Report Tells of Aviators' 'Debauchery,'* N.Y. TIMES, Apr. 24, 1993, at A1, A9. *See also* Eric Schmitt, *Navy Says Dozens of Women Were Harassed at Pilots Convention,* N.Y. TIMES, May, 1, 1992, at A14 (detailing the events at the convention and the subsequent "stone-walled" investigation).

16. Jim Doyle, *Suit in Death of Army Private,* S.F. CHRON., Sept. 16, 1993, at A9.

17. Eric Schmitt, *Harassed, Female and Navy: Lawyer Receives a Belated Apology,* N.Y. TIMES, June 5, 1994, at D2. The reservist, who had been scheduled for discharge, stated later, "[m]y record's been cleared, but there's no mechanism to rebuild it. That time has been lost, and I'm no longer competing for promotion with my year group." Eric Schmitt, *Navy Trying to Make Amends to Woman in Sex Harassment Case,* HOUS. CHRON., June 1, 1994, at A6.

18. *See* Eric Schmitt, *Navy Chief Quits Amid Questions Over Role in Sex-Assault Inquiry,* N.Y. TIMES, June 27, 1992, at A1.

19. Schmitt, *supra* note 13, at A34.

20. *Id.*

21. Schmitt, *supra* note 15, at A15.

attended the convention.[22] Moreover, the report revealed that many assaulted female officers were unwilling to report their complaints because they feared the publicity would jeopardize their careers.[23]

As the investigation progressed, scandal heaped upon scandal. H. Lawrence Garrett III, the Secretary of the Navy and the head of the Tailhook investigation, asked the Pentagon to take over the investigation when reports surfaced that he was present at the festivities and that fifty-five pages of documents that revealed his presence were deleted from the original reports.[24] He later resigned from the Navy.[25] In April of 1993, the Inspector General's inquiries into the Tailhook matter were more successful. Using lie detectors, undercover agents, and detailed computer analyses to dismantle the "wall of silence" that hampered earlier investigations, the Inspector General found that even more women than suspected had been assaulted and identified 175 naval officers for possible disciplinary action.[26] There were no reports that the Naval Investigative Services Command aided in this later, more fruitful, search.

However, despite the more intense investigations, very little punitive or remedial activity has been accomplished. Although 140 men were actually implicated in the Tailhook scandal, legal actions against seventy of them were dropped for insufficient evidence, while fifty others were merely fined or otherwise disciplined.[27] In the end, only

---

22. *Id.*

23. *See id.*

Navy Secretary John H. Dalton said today that it made his "blood boil" to hear testimony that sexual harassment goes unpunished in the military and that the Pentagon makes shoddy responses to women's complaints. Mr. Dalton's comments before the Senate Appropriations Defense Subcommittee came a day after four women, representing each of the military services, told lawmakers that they had been sexually harassed and then punished for reporting the offenses.

Eric Schmitt, *Women's Accounts Dismay Navy Chief*, N.Y. TIMES, Mar. 11, 1994, at A20.

24. Eric Schmitt, *Pentagon Takes Over Inquiry on Pilots*, N.Y. TIMES, June 19, 1992, at A20; Eric Schmitt, *Senior Navy Officers Suppressed Sex Investigation, Pentagon Says: Scathing Report Cites Hostility Toward Women*, N.Y. TIMES, Sept. 25, 1992, at A1, A20 [hereinafter Schmitt, *Senior Navy Officers*].

25. Schmitt, *Senior Navy Officers*, supra note 24, at A20. *See also* Eric Schmitt, *Officials say Navy Tried to Soften Report*, N.Y. TIMES, July 8, 1992, at A11 (discussing efforts by Navy officials to alter language in a report on the Tailhook convention to "make the incidents seem less offensive"); Eric Schmitt, *Pentagon Accuses Admirals of Sabotaging Investigation*, N.Y. TIMES, Sept. 27, 1992, at D2 [hereinafter Schmitt, *Pentagon Accuses Admirals*] (describing Pentagon report accusing senior Navy admirals of "deliberately sabotag[ing] their own investigation to protect fellow admirals").

26. Eric Schmitt, *Investigation of Sex Assaults by Pilots Had to Beat Wall of Silence in Navy*, N.Y. TIMES, May 2, 1993, at A24.

27. Eric Schmitt, *Judge Dismisses Tailhook Cases, Saying Admiral Tainted Inquiry*, N.Y. TIMES, Feb. 9, 1994, at A1, B7.

four cases reached trial, and three of those actions were later dismissed by a Navy judge who noted that Navy Admiral Frank B. Kelso II had been instrumental in manipulating and obfuscating the Tailhook investigation.[28] By the spring of 1994, Kelso retired with a four-star ranking, despite vigorous protests from all seven women in the Senate.[29] By early summer of that year, the Tailhook file was closed, and none of the 140 Navy and Marine Corps officers who were initially cited by Pentagon investigators ever went to trial.[30]

Neither the Navy nor the other segments of the armed forces has demonstrated that it can address sexual harassment in a neutral and effective manner. Instead, service-members who are sexually harassed in the Navy, if not all of the armed forces, have little hope of seeing a response to their complaints. The aftermath of Tailhook was a debacle complete with cover-ups,[31] colorful screaming matches,[32] congressional suspensions of thousands of Navy promotions, retirements, changes of command,[33] and promises of redress.[34] These events highlighted the executive branch's failure to combat harassment, Congress' ineffective muscle flexings, and the federal courts' inability or refusal to extend needed protection to these victims.

III.   THE THREE BRANCHES' APPROACHES TO SEXUAL HARASSMENT IN THE MILITARY

Congress, the executive branch, and the courts have paid only minimal effective attention to the sexual harassment that exists in the armed forces. A deeper analysis of each branch's response to sexual

---

28. *Id.*

29. Maureen Dowd, *Senate Approves a 4-Star Rank for Admiral in Tailhook Affair*, N.Y. TIMES, Apr. 20, 1994, at A1.

30. *Tailhook File Is Shut, No Cases Being Tried*, N.Y. TIMES, June 8, 1994, at A21 ("The Marine Corps has dismissed its last pending case stemming from the Tailhook scandal of sexual misconduct at a naval aviators' convention. The dismissal means that none of the 140 Navy and Marine Corps officers referred by Pentagon investigators for potential discipline in the scandal ever went to trial.").

31. *See* Schmitt, *Pentagon Accuses Admirals, supra* note 25, at D2.

32. *See* Schmitt, *Senior Navy Officers, supra* note 24, at A1 (describing a "screaming 'match'" in a Pentagon corridor about female aviators, in which the commander of the Naval Investigative Service compared female Navy pilots to "go-go dancers, topless dancers or hookers").

33. Eric Schmitt, *Navy Chief Quits in Assault Scandal Amid Questions Over Role in Sex-Inquiry*, CHI. TRIB., June 27, 1992, at C1.

34. *See* Eric Schmitt, *Navy Plans Training to Fight Sexual Harassment*, N.Y. TIMES, June 6, 1992, at 7.

harassment in the military reveals that all three have failed to develop an adequate solution.

A. THE EXECUTIVE BRANCH

Both the executive branch as a whole and its military arm have done very little to remedy sexual harassment. Regulations developed by the Department of Defense and within the armed forces are too vague to be helpful, do not give officials the power to take effective action, require victims to go through the chain of command, and suffer from a lack of proper enforcement.[35] Although the executive branch has some jurisdiction over sexual harassment issues, regulations generally give the military most power over these claims. The military has created a few mechanisms to handle personnel problems.[36] Some consist of avenues through which personnel may have their complaints heard and perhaps remedied.[37] Others are regulations which prohibit certain conduct.[38] While most of these regulations are quite general, at least one was designed to forbid sexual harassment.[39]

1. *Department of Defense Military Equal Opportunity Program*[40]

This program purports to regulate sexual harassment, but actually does nothing more than define both it and the program's policy to "[p]rovide for an environment that is free from sexual harassment by eliminating this form of discrimination in the Department of Defense."[41] The program's definition of sexual harassment does have the benefit of considering both *quid pro quo* and hostile environment harassment.[42] Nevertheless, the provision appears to be of little practical use. Although the Department of Defense ("DoD") denounces sexual harassment, it explicitly favors enforcement of its policy

---

35. *See, e.g., infra* notes 40-47 and accompanying text.
36. *See, e.g., infra* note 52-65 and accompanying text.
37. *See, e.g.,* 10 U.S.C. § 1552(a) (1988).
38. *See, e.g.,* Kevin W. Carter, *Fraternization,* 31 MIL. L. REV. 61, 101 (1986) (quoting Dep't of Army, Reg. No. 600-21, Personnel-General, Equal Opportunity Program in the Army, para. 2-2 (30 Apr. 1985)).
39. *Id.*
40. 32 C.F.R. § 51 (1989).
41. *Id.* § 51.4(e).
42. *Id.* § 51.3. This section defines sexual harassment as "[a] form of sex discrimination that involves unwelcomed sexual advances, requests for sexual favors, and other verbal or physical conduct of a sexual nature when" the harassment is a "term or condition" of a job, or factored into career and employment decisions. *Id.* In addition, sexual harassment is defined as conduct which interferes with "an individual's performance or creates an intimidating, hostile, or offensive environment." *Id.*

through the chain of command: "The chain of command is the primary and preferred channel for correcting discriminatory practices and for ensuring that human relations and EO matters are enacted."[43] Reliance on a chain of command has its dangers, since it "may discourage many women from bringing discrimination claims . . . . Many service-members apparently believe that such claims of discrimination processed under these circumstances will go unheeded or provoke retaliatory action."[44] Moreover, no specific guidelines explain the proper procedure for a complaint, nor are there any procedures to ensure proper investigation or resolution of complaints.[45] Finally, claims brought under the program are outside the jurisdiction of the Equal Employment Opportunity Commission.[46]

2. The Board for Correction of Military Records ("BCMR")[47]

Unlike the DoD's Military Equal Opportunity Program,[48] the BCMR avenue does not require a service-member to go through the chain of command.[49] The BCMR, composed of Defense Department civilian executives, is authorized to "correct an error or remove an injustice" in an individual's military records.[50] Yet this body is an inadequate means to redress sexual harassment complaints because it offers no aid unless a victim has a negative comment on her record as a function of, or in retaliation for, complaining about sexual harassment. Sexual harassment is rarely manifested by recorded admonishments. Moreover, "injustice" is not defined, service-members have no right to a hearing, and complainants rarely know when they have exhausted intramilitary remedies and earned the right to appeal to a

---

43. *Id.* § 51.4(b).

44. Robin Rogers, *A Proposal for Combating Sexual Discrimination in the Military: Amendment of Title VII*, 78 CAL. L. REV. 165, 184 (1990).

45. *See* C.F.R. § 51.4(b) (advocating use of chain of command); *id.* § 51.4(c) (asserting that "[d]iscrimination . . . shall not be tolerated"); *id.* § 51.4(e) (advocating a sexual harassment-free environment and the "elimination" of sexual harassment).

46. Gonzalez v. Dep't of Army, 718 F.2d 926, 927-28 (9th Cir. 1983). The Equal Employment Opportunity Commission ("EEOC") was established under Title VII to investigate and remedy alleged violations and to enforce the provisions of the Civil Rights Act of 1964. *See* 42 U.S.C. § 2000e-5 (1991).

47. 10 U.S.C. § 1552(a) (1988). A BCMR exists for each service. *See* 32 C.F.R. § 581.3 (1988) (Army); 32 C.F.R. § 723.1 *et seq.* (1988) (Navy and Marines); 32 C.F.R. § 865.1 *et seq.* (1985) (Air Force); 49 C.F.R. § 1.57 (1993) and 33 C.F.R. § 52.35-15 (Coast Guard).

48. 32 C.F.R. § 51 (1989).

49. *See, e.g.*, 32 C.F.R. § 581.3(c) (1988).

50. 10 U.S.C. § 1552(a) (1988).

civilian court.[51] Furthermore, civilian courts usually defer to the BCMR's decisions.

3. *Army Regulations*

Army regulations regarding sexual harassment range from the general to the specific. The sexual harassment policy of the Army, Army Regulation 600-21, explicitly defines and prohibits sexual harassment.[52] Generally, the policy prohibits abusive sexual contact, the repeated or deliberate making of sexually offensive comments or gestures, and the attempt to affect the career, pay, or job of a military member through sexual behavior.[53] Under this regulation, subordinates can be reprimanded for sexually harassing superiors.[54]

More generally, sexual harassment of a subordinate may also violate the Army's prohibition of fraternization.[55] This regulation recognizes that "[r]elationships between service-members of different rank which involve (or give appearance of) partiality, preferential treatment, or the improper use of rank or position for personal gain, are prejudicial to good order, discipline, and high unit morale."[56] Furthermore, the regulation requires commanders and supervisors to counsel or take other action against those involved in such relationships.[57] Although this regulation appears to cover only partiality, sexual harassment is within its scope since the senior member can use "rank or position for improper purposes such as . . . coercing sexual favors."[58] Sexual harassment can also "[c]ause an actual or clearly predictable adverse impact upon discipline, authority, or morale."[59]

Violations of either regulation generally call for "adverse administrative action."[60] Superiors can order that military personnel receive

---

51. *See* Hill v. Berkman, 635 F. Supp. 1228 (E.D.N.Y. 1986) (Article 138 appeal). *See also* Beller v. Middendorf, 632 F.2d 788 (9th Cir. 1980); Glines v. Wade, 586 F.2d 675, 678 (9th Cir. 1978), *rev'd*, 444 U.S. 348 (1980); Champagne v. Schlesinger, 506 F.2d 979 (7th Cir. 1974); Saal v. Middendorf, 427 F. Supp. 192, 197 (N.D. Cal. 1977), *rev'd*, 632 F.2d 788 (9th Cir. 1980).

52. *See* Carter, *supra* note 38, at 101 (quoting Dep't of Army, Reg. No. 600-21, Personnel-General, Equal Opportunity Program in the Army, para. 2-2 (30 Apr. 1985)).

53. *Id.* at 101-102.

54. *Id.* at 102.

55. *See id.* at 90-107.

56. *See id.* at 92 n.195 (quoting Dep't of Army, Reg. No. 600-20, Personnel-General, Army Command Policies and Procedures, para. 5-7*f* (15 Oct. 1980)).

57. *See id.* at 107-119.

58. *Id.* at 97.

59. *Id.* at 96 (quoting Headquarters, Dep't of Army Letter 600-84.2 (23 Nov. 1984)). *See also id.* at 90-94 (discussing the historical development of the Army's policies on fraternization).

60. *Id.* at 107.

counseling, reassignment, extra training or instruction, an administrative letter of reprimand, suspension of favorable personnel actions, or adverse evaluation reports.[61] Personnel may also face an administrative reduction in grade, a bar from re-enlistment, relief for cause, or administrative separation.[62] Superiors can also be criminally prosecuted for sexual harassment under the Army's criminal prohibition against fraternization.[63]

Although the Army's regulations seem to hold promise for combating sexual harassment in the military, service-members must still bring complaints of violations either through the chain of command or to the Board for Correction of Military Records, which has very little power to take affirmative action.[64] Moreover, superiors who are called on to discipline service-members for violations are instructed to use "the least severe option, or combination of options, necessary to correct the situation."[65] Thus, these regulations also fail to adequately address sexual harassment in the military.

B. Congress

> So when Xerxes heard of it, he was full of wrath, and straightaway gave orders that the Hellespont should receive 300 lashes, and that a pair of fetters should be case into it. Nay, I have even heard it said, that he bade the branders take their irons and therewith brand the Hellespont. . . . While the sea was thus punished by his orders, he likewise commanded that the overseers of the work should lose their heads.[66]

Congress produced some dramatic gestures in response to the Tailhook incident by manipulating the advice and consent powers; however, the action did little more than cost a few jobs and provide fodder for the media. Congress also remains inactive in the face of judicial decisions which refuse to extend Title VII protections to the uniformed military,[67] even though little suggests that lawmakers initially intended to exempt the military. The Uniform Code of Military Justice does give a general form of redress for all service-members,

---

61. *See id.* at 107-112.
62. *See id.* at 112-115.
63. *Id.* at 116-119.
64. *See supra* notes 48-51 and accompanying text.
65. Carter *supra* note 38, at 107.
66. HERODOTUS, THE PERSIAN WARS 511-12 (George Rawlinson, trans., The Modern Library 1942).
67. *See infra* part III.C.

but this provision is inadequate for sexual harassment purposes because it requires a victim to go through the intimidating chain of command.[68]

1. *Congress' Use of the Advice and Consent Power and Investigative Powers*

Congress takes only the most limited stance against sexual harassment, tolerating the harassment unless it is on a grand scale. After the Tailhook scandal erupted, the Senate Armed Services Committee announced that it would not allow Navy and Marine Corps promotions to go forward until junior officers were cleared of any involvement in the incident.[69] Congress suspended more than 4,500 promotions, retirements and changes of command until it received assurances from the Pentagon that the officers were not under scrutiny in the affair.[70] Although some jobs were lost and promotions were denied,[71] including in positions held by top brass,[72] Congress' actions against even such grand-scale harassment proved to be more symbolic than catalytic. Little has been done to accomplish systematic changes in the sexual politics of the military. Moreover, Congress, despite its gestures, has not created significant statutory protections against this sort of harassment.

2. *Title VII*[73]

In 1986, the Supreme Court held that under Title VII of the 1964 Civil Rights Act,[74] sexual harassment at the workplace constitutes actionable sex discrimination.[75] Since then, Title VII has been the primary vehicle for challenging sexual harassment in the civilian world. Section 717(a) of Title VII extends its protection against employment

---

68. *See infra* notes 80-87 and accompanying text.

69. Eric Schmitt, *Harassment Questions Kill 2 Admirals' Promotions*, N.Y. TIMES, July 18, 1992, at A1.

70. Eric Schmitt, *Navy Chief Quits Amid Questions Over Role in Sex-Assault Inquiry*, N.Y. TIMES, June 27, 1992, at C1, C7.

71. Schmitt, *supra* note 69, at A7; *Supporters Question Firing of Admiral*, L.A. TIMES, Aug. 10, 1992, at A21.

72. *See* Neil A. Lewis, *Tailhook Affair Brings Censure of 3 Admirals*, N.Y. TIMES, Oct. 16, 1993, at A1 (describing the censures given to admirals which "effectively [ended] their careers").

73. 42 U.S.C. § 2000e *et seq.* (1991).

74. *Id.*

75. Meritor Sav. Bank v. Vinson, 477 U.S. 57 (1986).

discrimination to "all personnel actions affecting employees or applicants for employment . . . in military departments as defined in section 102 of Title 5."[76] Nevertheless, several circuits have held that
"the term 'military departments' . . . can fairly be understood to
include only civilian employees of the Army, Navy and Air Force and
not both civilian employees and enlisted personnel."[77] These courts
base this military exception on legislative history which did not explicitly expand the Equal Employment Opportunity Commission's jurisdiction to include the armed forces.[78] Congress has remained silent
on the issue since it was first raised by the courts in 1978.[79] Whether
or not lawmakers initially intended to extend Title VII protections to
the uniformed military, Congress' silence on this issue over the years
has permitted the courts' own codification of this exception.

3. Article 138 of the Uniform Code of Military Justice[80]

The Uniform Code of Military Justice subjects all members of the
Armed forces to one set of disciplinary laws.[81] Article 138 provides
that any service-member "who believes himself wronged by his commanding officer" and is refused redress by that officer may complain
to any superior commissioned officer.[82] The Article further requires
the superior officer to forward the complaint to the officer exercising
general court martial jurisdiction over the officer against whom the
complaint is made, who shall examine the complaint "and take proper
measures for redressing the wrong complained of."[83]

Although Article 138 does give service people an avenue for
redress, it is not adequate for sexual harassment purposes because it
suffers the same flaw as the DoD's Equal Opportunity Program: it
requires the service-member to go through the chain of command for

---

76. 42 U.S.C. § 2000e-16(a)(1988).

77. Gonzalez v. Dep't of the Army, 718 F.2d 926, 928 (9th Cir. 1983). *See also* Doe v.
Garrett, 903 F.2d 1455, 1458 (11th Cir. 1990); Kawitt v. U.S., 842 F.2d 951, 953 (7th Cir. 1988);
Roper v. Dep't of Army, 832 F.2d 247 (2d Cir. 1987); Johnson v. Alexander, 572 F.2d 1219, 1222
(8th Cir. 1978), *cert. denied*, 439 U.S. 986 (1978). *Cf.* Hill v. Berkman, 635 F. Supp. 1228
(E.D.N.Y. 1986).

78. *Gonzalez*, 718 F.2d at 928.

79. *Johnson* was the first case to hold that Title VII did not apply to the uniformed military.
572 F.2d at 1224.

80. 10 U.S.C. § 938 (1956).

81. *Id.*; *see also* ROBERT S. RIVKIN & BARTON F. STICHMAN, THE RIGHTS OF MILITARY
PERSONNEL 124 (1977).

82. 10 U.S.C. § 938 (1956).

83. *Id.*

relief.[84] Recent events surrounding the Tailhook scandal and the responses of both the female service-members who were assaulted and their superiors display this weakness in the Article. When a Navy Lieutenant helicopter pilot filed a complaint with her boss, he replied, "That's what you get for going to a hotel party with a bunch of drunk aviators."[85] Another problem with Article 138 is that it applies only to wrongs committed by a commanding officer upon a subordinate.[86] The provision will not extend to sexual harassment between fellow enlisted personnel or to harassment which is visited upon a commander by a subordinate. Furthermore, depending on which service the victim is in, she may not even have the right to a military attorney.[87]

Thus, Congress' legislation does not adequately address sexual harassment in the military. This branch's failure to explicitly extend the Civil Rights Act to uniformed personnel, along with Article 138's requirement that complainants report through an intimidating chain of command, denies service-members a workable option for combating harassment.

C. THE COURTS

The courts' treatment of service-members' complaints of discrimination limits the latter's ability to seek redress under the Civil Rights Act of 1964.[88] The Civil Rights Act enables civilians to challenge sexual harassment on the job as illegal sexual discrimination under *Meritor Savings Bank v. Vinson*.[89] Many circuits, however, hold that Title VII's prohibition on gender or racial discrimination does not extend to the uniformed military.[90] Since the courts largely have held that Title VII does not prohibit sexual *discrimination* in the military, there are no federal civil cases involving Title VII, sexual harassment, and the military. We can only cite to federal cases which address the courts' approaches to general sexual discrimination in the armed forces.

---

84. *Id.*
85. Schmitt, *supra* note 13, at A34 (quoting a remark made by Rear Adm. John W. Snyder, Jr.).
86. 10 U.S.C. § 938 (1956).
87. *See* RIVKIN & STICHMAN, *supra* note 81, at 124-26.
88. 42 U.S.C. § 2000a *et seq.* (1992).
89. 477 U.S. 57 (1986).
90. *See supra* note 77 and accompanying text.

In *Brown v. General Services Administration*,[91] the Supreme Court ruled that Title VII "provides the exclusive judicial remedy for claims of discrimination in federal employment."[92] Civilian courts, however, have done little to provide military personnel with remedies for Title VII civil rights violations. In 1978, the Eighth Circuit held in *Johnson v. Alexander*[93] that Title VII did not extend to the uniformed military, reasoning that if "Congress had intended for the statute to apply to the uniformed personnel . . . it would have said so in unmistakable terms."[94] In the 1983 decision *Gonzalez v. Department of Army*,[95] the Ninth Circuit arrived at the same holding based on different grounds.[96] As of this date, there has only been one federal case holding that sexual discrimination in the military is actionable under Title VII. In *Hill v. Berkman*,[97] a federal court addressed facially discriminatory policies and found that Title VII could apply in a limited way to prohibit them. *Berkman*, however, is not strong precedent for cases involving sexual harassment. First, the *Berkman* court held that outrageous incidents of discrimination were actionable, but relatively small incidents could not be, since investigations into "day to day" military decisionmaking would be dangerously intrusive.[98] Second, the *Berkman* court did not tackle the issue of sexual harassment.[99] Although sexual harassment is an aspect of sexual discrimination,

---

91. 425 U.S. 820 (1976).

92. *Id.* at 835.

93. 572 F.2d 1219 (8th Cir. 1978).

94. *Id.* at 1224. The military exclusion articulated by the Eighth and Ninth Circuits has been followed by other courts as well. *See* Doe v. Garrett, 903 F.2d 1455, 1460 (11th Cir. 1990) ("[T]his Court has adopted [the *Gonzalez*] exception."); Kawitt v. U.S., 842 F.2d 951, 953 (7th Cir. 1988) (finding that the exception makes "compellingly good sense"); Roper v. Dep't of the Army, 832 F.2d 247, 248 (2d Cir. 1987) ("[W]e cannot agree to the extension of Title VII to uniformed members of the armed forces."); Salazar v. Heckler, 787 F.2d 527, 529 (10th Cir. 1986) (recognizing the *Gonzalez* and *Johnson* decisions). *But see* Ayala v. U.S., Assistant Secretary of the Navy, No. 86 Civ. 4963 (S.D.N.Y. May 15, 1987) ("[W]hether Ayala has a cause of action . . . under Title VII . . . remain[s] [an] open questio[n].").

95. 718 F.2d 926 (9th Cir. 1983).

96. That court held that when section 717(a) of Title VII extended the Civil Rights Act of 1964 to the "military departments" and transferred the Civil Service Commission's enforcement function to the EEOC, it was not meant to extend that authority to uniformed personnel. The court in *Gonzalez* stated that:

> there is no indication in the legislative history that the former jurisdiction of the Civil Service Commission was to be expanded upon the transfer of functions to the EEOC. Moreover, it is abundantly clear that the Civil Service Commission was never authorized to review or police discrimination within the armed forces.

Id. at 928.

97. 635 F. Supp. 1228 (E.D.N.Y. 1986).

98. *Id.* at 1241.

99. *Id.* at 1228.

Berkman remains a remarkably weak precedent for extending *Meritor's* prohibition on sexual harassment to the military.

1. *Deference In Perspective*

The judicial branch, then, has mostly abdicated review of sex discrimination claims based on sexual harassment in the military. On the rare occasion when a court hears the victim's case on the merits and believes that she is entitled to Title VII protection, she is still likely to lose her case because of judicial deference to military matters. More commonly, courts refuse even to hear these cases or extend relief to victims of discrimination in the military based on a version of "the separate community doctrine," a rationale for deference that was first articulated by the Supreme Court in 1953:

> [J]udges are not given the task of running the Army . . . . The military constitutes a specialized community governed by a separate discipline from that of the civilian. Orderly government requires that the judiciary be as scrupulous not to interfere with legitimate Army matters as the Army must be scrupulous not to intervene in judicial matters.[100]

Strains of this philosophy have been used to justify many instances of discrimination in the military. For example, in the 1983 decision *Chappell v. Wallace*,[101] the Supreme Court refused to allow victims of discrimination to sue military officers for discrimination or to successfully challenge discriminatory military policies under the equal protection clause of the Fifth Amendment. The Court based its holding on what it considered to be the "unique disciplinary structure of the Military Establishment"[102] as well as "Congress' activity in the field [that both] constitute 'special factors' which dictate that it would be inappropriate to provide enlisted military personnel a *Bivens*-type remedy against their superior officers."[103] In *Bivens v. Six Unknown Named Agents of Federal Bureau of Narcotics*,[104] the Court had established that the victim of a constitutional violation by a federal official has the right to recover damages against that official in federal court despite the absence of any statute conferring such a right.[105] Yet the

---

100. Orloff v. Willoughby, 345 U.S. 83, 93-94 (1953).
101. 462 U.S. 296 (1983).
102. *Id.* at 304.
103. *Id.* (citing Bivens v. Six Unknown Named Agents of Federal Bureau of Narcotics, 403 U.S. 388 (1971)).
104. 403 U.S. 388 (1971).
105. *Id.*

Chappell Court held that a *Bivens* remedy was inapplicable to the military because of "the need for unhesitating and decisive action by military officers and equally disciplined responses by enlisted personnel [that] would be undermined by a judicially created remedy exposing officers to personal liability at the hands of those they are charged to command."[106] Because of the Court's perceived need to avoid "the disruption of [the] peculiar and special relationship of the soldier to his superiors,"[107] service-members cannot bring a constitutional claim against a superior whose harassment violates their equal protection rights.[108]

Refusal to redress sex discrimination has also been justified by the more general premise of judicial deference to military matters set forth by the Supreme Court in the 1981 decision *Rostker v. Goldberg*.[109] In that case, the Court found the male-only draft registration constitutional on the basis that "[n]o one could deny that . . . the Government's interest in raising and supporting armies is an 'important governmental interest'."[110] Justice Rehnquist, in his majority opinion, took care to emphasize the proper degree of deference that military judgments deserved from the judiciary: "The case arises in the context of Congress' authority over national defense and military affairs, and perhaps in no other area has the Court accorded Congress greater deference."[111]

The Supreme Court's measure of appropriate deference under *Rostker* has been used to deny claimants redress for their claims of sex discrimination. In *Mack v. Rumsfeld*,[112] a case involving a regulation that prohibited the enlistment of single parents, a district court upheld the policy,[113] although it acknowledged the policy's disparate impact on women.[114] The court here based its holding on the Second Circuit's interpretation of *Rostker*, which mandated that "matter[s] provided for by Congress in the exercise of its war power and implemented by the Army [which] appea[r] reasonably relevant and

---

106. 462 U.S. at 303.
107. *Id.*
108. In *Chappell*, the plaintiff's claim was one of racial discrimination. *Id.* at 296.
109. 453 U.S. 57 (1981).
110. *Id.* at 69-72 (citing Craig v. Boren, 429 U.S. 190 (1976)).
111. *Id.* at 64-65.
112. 609 F. Supp. 1561 (W.D.N.Y. 1985), *aff'd*, 782 F.2d 356 (2d Cir.), *amended*, 784 F.2d 438 (2d Cir.), *cert. denied*, 479 U.S. 815 (1986).
113. 609 F. Supp. at 1569.
114. *Id.* at 1566-67.

necessary . . . should be treated as presumptively valid."[115] The court went on to find that the plaintiffs could not succeed "[e]ven if [they] could make a showing of discriminatory purpose."[116]

Similarly, in *Cobb v. U.S. Merchant Marine Academy*,[117] a district court held that a servicewoman had not stated a cause of action when she claimed that the Naval Reserve's refusal to commission her because of her pregnancy was illegal sex discrimination. The court, citing *Rostker* for support, found that "the Naval Reserve policy of not commissioning pregnant persons is not only rational, but is rational to such a degree as to make it unequivocally clear that the policy is not violative of the Fifth Amendment Due Process Clause."[118] Furthermore, one district court has unequivocally found that the "intermediate scrutiny" standard given to sex discrimination claims does not apply to the military. In *Lewis v. U.S. Army*,[119] a district judge asserted: "Based on my reading of *Rostker* . . . , I conclude that the standard outlined in *Craig* is not applicable to gender-based equal protection claims raised in the context of military affairs . . . ."[120]

Because of the pronounced deference with which courts treat military decisionmaking, service-members will not be able to successfully challenge their superiors' sexual harassment or the ineffectiveness or even nonexistence of policies which forbid and punish sexual harassment as a violation of their equal protection rights. They will also find it exceedingly difficult to challenge any other forms of sex discrimination as a violation of equal protection. And, as stated, service-members are also unlikely to obtain redress for sexual harassment under the Civil Rights Act of 1964.

IV. THE PROBLEM OF CULTURE, IGNORANCE, AND TRADITION THAT DIES HARD: WHY THE THREE BRANCHES FAIL

What remains is the failure of the legislative, the executive and the judicial branches to address the needs of women in the military. This abdication may be caused in part by the separate community doctrine outlined in *Orloff*.[121] The *Orloff* dictum gave courts and perhaps

---

115. *Id.* at 1564 (citing Katcoff v. Marsh, 755 F.2d 233 (2d Cir. 1985)).
116. *Id.* at 1567.
117. 592 F. Supp. 640 (E.D.N.Y. 1984).
118. *Id.* at 644.
119. 697 F. Supp. 1385 (E.D. Pa. 1988).
120. *Id.* at 1390 n.5 (citing Craig v. Boren, 429 U.S. 190 (1976)).
121. 345 U.S. 83, 93 (1953).

even Congress and the executive branch an excuse to eliminate their responsibility to check an abuse of military power.[122] The separate community doctrine also reinforces the cultural problems that exist in a military that considers itself apart from the norms of civilian life. One product of the doctrine is pervasive gender discrimination that would not be tolerated in civilian society.

An example of such discrimination was the military's former policy of barring women from all combat positions. Though upheld by a deferential Supreme Court,[123] this policy has been cited as one of the reasons women are treated so poorly in the military. The argument against women in combat has been stated quite baldly: "Women don't belong in combat. Women don't belong in the close confines of military lifestyle. The military is not the great social experiment of the '90s."[124] Retired Army Brigadier General Pat Foote, however, argues that this attitude exacerbates difficult sexual politics between male and female personnel: "[W]henever a person is denied the opportunity to prove that they [sic] have the skills . . . then that person will . . . be devalued. And behavior towards that individual frequently will be less than civil."[125] Commander Rosemary Mariner, the Navy's first female squadron commander, puts it more bluntly: "Until you remove all the combat restrictions on women, you're going to continue to have this problem . . . . If the institution says you're not good enough to fight or doesn't want you to, it's natural for people to think you're inferior."[126]

Although the Pentagon is making revolutionary changes by slowly including women in the military combat role,[127] the residue of the separate community philosophy will not abate readily and may continue to hamper women's equality in the military. As a separate community, the military subscribes to its own rules about gender. By relegating women to an unequal status, these rules, although some are now being dismantled, leave a precedent that fosters hostility toward women. Furthermore, the military's long history of removal from certain civilian norms results in an environment where that hostility is

---

122. *Id.*

123. Rostker v. Goldberg, 453 U.S. 57 (1981).

124. Rowan Scarborough, *PC Rankles in Military Ranks*, WASH. TIMES, Nov. 16, 1992, at A1.

125. *The MacNeil/Lehrer News Hour* (PBS Television Broadcast, July 1, 1992).

126. Schmitt, *supra* note 13, at A34.

127. *See Navy's New Chief Plans Push to Assign Women to All Ships, Subs*, HOUS. CHRON., May 4, 1994, at A18; Eric Schmitt, *Pentagon Plans to Allow Combat Flights by Women; Seeks to Drop Warship Ban*, N.Y. TIMES, Apr. 28, 1993, at A1.

expressed in highly exaggerated and dangerous ways. The Tailhook debacle, for example, illustrated the Navy's warped sexual culture. To reward officers for a successful venture in the Persian Gulf, the Navy rewarded them with alcohol, strippers and pornography. Its response to the scandal was itself replete with sexual stereotyping, continued harassment, and corruption. The military's demonstrated hostility to its gay and lesbian officers also reveals its guarded culture's rigid conception of sexuality, which, if offended, can give rise to a dangerous backlash.[128]

The rationale for the separate community doctrine is, as the Supreme Court in *Chappell* asserted, the "special nature of military life—the need for unhesitating and decisive action by military officers and equally disciplined responses by enlisted personnel . . . ."[129] A strain of this theory was also articulated by senior Navy officers who, when asked to contemplate the effects of Tailhook on their charges, "expressed concern that the lowered morale could lead to sloppy flying or even accidents."[130] These statements reveal the perception among the courts and within the military that the special nature of the armed forces mandates that there be no intrusions into military affairs. To intrude would risk disrupting the atmosphere of fraternity and community that is needed to maintain the rigid sense of loyalty and hierarchy. Yet the assumptions that the military can police itself and is justified in its discriminatory policies have been exposed as largely false since the Naval Investigative Service botched its 1991 Tailhook inquiries and women served so effectively in the Gulf War.[131]

The argument that the military must be left alone to operate well neglects the psychological and physical hazards that its atmosphere visits upon certain service-members. War exigencies do not require the current hands-off approach to sexual harassment and indeed, the failure to subject the military to some of the same social and legal

---

128. It must be noted that the Navy is attempting to alter its cultural landscape by writing a new sexual harassment handbook, but one wonders about its possible efficacy. *See* Eric Schmitt, *Word for Word*, N.Y. TIMES, Apr. 17, 1994, at E7 (discussing the handbook's use of "traffic-light colors to group acceptable and unacceptable forms of behavior," and its colorful instructive hypothetical questions, such as the one that asks the service-member whether it would be appropriate for officers to simulate sex acts with anatomically correct blow-up dolls at co-ed military parties).

129. 462 U.S. at 304 (1983).

130. John Lancaster, *Navy Pilots Say a Cloud is Hanging Over Them; Tailhook Sex-Abuse Scandal and News Media Seen as Unfairly Casting Shadow on All Aviators*, N.Y. TIMES, July 19, 1992, at A3.

131. *See* Schmitt, *supra* note 127, at A14.

prohibitions as the civilian world worsens the problems of women and homosexuals in the military. Intervention into military affairs is needed to remedy existing conditions.

1. Applying Title VII to the Military

The decision to remedy sexual harassment in the military must involve an examination of which body is best suited to change the current state of affairs. The courts will not make a good choice because they are too deferential in military matters. Although the courts could break with stare decisis and apply Title VII to the uniformed military as the *Berkman* court did,[132] if they continue to operate under the separate community theory, they may not act with needed aggression. Courts also are unlikely to act at all. They may continue to consider Congress' silence on the issue a manifestation of its intent not to extend Title VII protection to the military.

The executive branch is an obvious candidate to take action because of its close connection to the armed forces and the new Administration's apparent commitment to changing the military status quo. President Clinton may be amenable to the idea of promulgating an Executive Order that prohibits sexual harassment in the military. Indeed, the Clinton Administration has demonstrated a commitment to easing the way of straight women as well as gays and lesbians into the armed forces by eradicating most of the restrictions on women in aerial and naval combat,[133] and taking steps to limit sexual orientation discrimination in the military.[134] An Executive Order could use administrative law judges or Inspectors General to adjudicate and investigate claims. There are weaknesses, however, with this approach. For one, Executive Orders may be made by one President and invalidated by the next.[135] Furthermore, the Inspector General has already demonstrated its inability to address sexual harassment claims effectively.

---

132. *See supra* notes 97-99 and accompanying text.

133. *See* Eric Schmitt, *Navy Women Bringing New Era on Carriers*, N.Y. TIMES, Feb. 21, 1994, at A1.

134. *See Clinton Signs $261 Billion Defense Bill*, COURIER-JOURNAL, Nov. 20, 1993, at 6A (discussing the inclusion of a version of the "don't ask, don't tell" policy on gays and lesbians); Reinhold, *supra* note 10, at A2.

135. In 1990, for example, President Bush considered undercutting Executive Order 11246, which addresses affirmative action in federal hiring and federal promotion. *See Significant Differences Remain Between Vetoed Civil Rights Bill and White House Proposal*, DAILY LAB. REP., Nov. 5, 1990; Chris Black, *Buchanan Says He Would Abolish Quotas in Federal Employment*, BOSTON GLOBE, Mar. 3, 1992, at Nat./For. 8.

Congress, however, has a demonstrated capacity for building a system to effectively combat sexual harassment, which makes it the most attractive candidate. By including uniformed personnel in Title VII, claimants would have access to the battery of Title VII investigative and enforcement procedures that have worked so effectively in the civilian world. Although passing this amendment would be the subject of considerable Congressional debate and would be a lengthier process than an Executive Order, once passed there would be little danger of its revocation. Because of the damaging political implications, Congress rarely, if ever, decreases the potency of its civil rights laws.[136] Congress' tendency, in fact, is to bolster these laws once their cores have been established.

Extending Title VII to the military inclusion will require a careful balance between the armed force's perceived need for sole jurisdiction over its internal affairs and the problems with the current intramilitary chain of command procedure. Therefore, the extension of Title VII protection should retain some of the existing grievance procedures while also guaranteeing the service-member an impartial review of her complaint and the right to appeal military decisions to a federal civilian court.

First, a service-member would be required to bring an informal complaint simultaneously to her commanding officer as well as to an Equal Employment Opportunity counselor, who would review the problem with the service-member and attempt to resolve the conflict informally. The service-member would then have the right to file a formal complaint with the EEO officer, who would investigate the matter. Should the harassment complaint be verified, the commanding officer and the EEO counselor would work together to address the problem through the military disciplinary measures that already exist. The service-member would be able to have an EEOC hearing and, finally, bring a civil action.[137]

---

136. Consider, for example, the 1991 Civil Rights Act, which protected citizens' civil rights more than the courts had. *See generally* John P. Furfaro & Maury B. Josephson, *The Civil Rights Act of 1991*, 207 N.Y. L.J. 64 (1992) (concluding that the 1991 Act was meant to modify decisions by the Supreme Court that were widely perceived as regressive).

137. See 32 C.F.R. § 588.1 *et seq.* (1986) for federal regulations regarding the EEOC claims procedure. *See also* Rogers, *supra* note 44, at 184. Robin Rogers' note on sexual harassment in the military was one of the first articles to investigate the weaknesses in the military's current capacity to police sexual harassment. Her article was also one of the first to posit this sort of amendment structure.

In the civil suit, the service-member would have to prove that she was subjected to illegal sexual harassment. Service-members may also have an action for retaliatory discharge.[138] The armed forces, constituting an "employer," could be found liable for reinstatement, back pay, or any other equitable relief the court deems appropriate.[139] Scrutiny under Title VII should apply even to a single, egregious incident of sexual harassment; such a policy would give relief to victims like Gwen Dreyer and the women at the Tailhook convention.[140]

Extension of Title VII protections to the uniformed military would also place the remaining combat exclusions into question,[141] as well as other military policies which discriminate against women.[142] Although the combat exclusion and other facially discriminatory policies may pass muster as Bona Fide Occupational Qualifications, ("BFOQs")[143] the military would have to justify them. Mere stereotyped characterizations of the sexes would not be sufficient, since stereotypes are not a valid application of the BFOQ exception.[144] Although traditional judicial deference to military matters virtually ensures that any articulated justification for discriminatory policies will satisfy a BFOQ analysis, the extension of Title VII protections to the uniformed military would force the military to at least articulate its justifications and perhaps help begin to dismantle the biases that contribute to sexual harassment in the first place.[145]

Finally, applying Title VII may have another prodigious and unexpected result. As discussed above, the issue of gays and lesbians in the military looms larger as all three branches have taken steps to

---

138. *See, e.g.*, Tunis v. Corning Glass Works, 747 F. Supp. 951 (S.D.N.Y. 1990), *aff'd*, 930 F.2d 910 (2d. Cir. 1991).

139. 42 U.S.C. § 2000e-5 (1991).

140. For examples of courts finding that one incident of sexual harassment was actionable, *see, e.g.* Barret v. Omaha Nat'l Bank, 726 F.2d 424 (9th Cir. 1984); Gilardi v. Schroeder, 672 F. Supp. 1043 (N.D. Ill. 1986), *aff'd*, 833 F.2d 1226 (7th Cir. 1987). *See also* Harris v. Forklift Systems, Inc., 114 S.Ct. 367 (1993) (holding that verbal abuse is actionable even if it does not hurt the victim's job performance or mental health).

141. Although the Pentagon has lifted the ban on women flying in combat, women are still barred from combat cockpits and other combat positions. *See* Schmitt, *supra* note 127, at A1.

142. *See supra* notes 110-21 and accompanying text.

143. The BFOQ defense allows an employer to defend otherwise discriminatory employment practices in those instances where sex is a " 'BFOQ reasonably necessary to the normal operation of [the] particular business'." UAW v. Johnson Controls, 499 U.S. 187, 188 (1991) (quoting 42 U.S.C. § 703(e)(1) (1991)).

144. *See, e.g.*, Wilson v. Southwest Airlines, 517 F. Supp. 292 (1981).

145. Robin Rogers argues: "If the combat exclusion and any other gender-based restrictions were constrained to fit within legally supportable justifications, distinctions between men and women in the military would become less pervasive." *See* Rogers, *supra* note 44, at 189.

curb the military's historic ban on homosexuals.[146] Although Title VII itself does not include "sexual orientation" as a protected class, it is becoming increasingly clear that gays and lesbians face a considerable amount of harassment in the military. If the extension of Title VII to the military is viewed in concert with the new "don't ask, don't tell, don't pursue" policy, which has been approved by the executive and legislative branches, and which may even be expanded by the judicial branch, it seems reasonable and fair to conclude that gays and lesbians in the military who are harassed on the basis of their sexual orientation should have an actionable complaint. Although harassment of homosexuals may not be "sex discrimination" per se since either homosexual men or women can be harassed regardless of their sexual orientation, perhaps the harassment's connection with gender and the new policy against all-out discrimination against gays could be construed together as giving gays and lesbians a cause of action under the Civil Rights Act.

This discussion, of course, ignores the practical problems of implementing the extension of Title VII to the uniformed military. Any policy maker who attempted to do so would face a great deal of opposition from a military that is devoted to maintaining its inclusivity and dealing with its problems in private. Nevertheless, the United States armed forces are experiencing a great deal of immediate social and political scrutiny on practices that they have never before had to defend. Moreover, the recent media focus on more egregious events has made citizens intensely aware of military cultural matters. Although a move toward extending Title VII to the military would seem unprecedented and even, to some, catastrophic, we are witnessing a national reanalysis of how the military treats its service-members. Imposing Title VII's prohibitions appears to be a logical move where there is social discomfort with the armed force's insulated, precarious cultural norms and where those norms preclude effective remedial action.

---

146. President Clinton recently signed his "don't ask, don't tell" policy into law. *See Clinton Signs $261 Billion Defense Bill*, Courier-J., Nov. 20, 1993, at A6. The legality of the policy, and other policies which discriminate against homosexuals, however, is being questioned by the courts. *See Excluding Homosexuals From Military Denies Equal Protection CA DC Holds*, U.S.L.W., Nov. 23, 1993 (citing Steffan v. Aspin, D.C. Cir. No. 91-5409, Nov. 16, 1993 (holding that the pre-Clinton military exclusion of homosexuals failed equal protection tests because it had no rational basis)).

V. CONCLUSION

Combating sexual harassment in the military will prove to be a challenging task. Servicemen in the armed forces, who seem to equate their military duties with the privileges of operating within a different social framework, appear loathe to allow intervention into their separate sphere. Yet, even the military must face modern realities. Straight women, as well as gays and lesbians, make up a significant number of military personnel who excel in the armed forces[147] and have served this country well in its last two wars.[148] They are as entitled to work in a safe and supportive environment as are their straight male colleagues. Congressional intervention is required to ensure this equality.

---

147. *See, e.g.*, Jill Smolowe, *Conduct Unbecoming?*, TIME, Nov. 29, 1993, at 67 (discussing the impressive record of Joseph Steffan, a beleaguered gay student at the U.S. Naval Academy).

148. *See, e.g.*, *Sonya Live: Women, War & Equality* (CNN television broadcast, Nov. 11, 1992) (detailing the contributions made by women in the Vietnam and Persian Gulf Wars).

Gender Bias in the Legal Profession:
Women "See" It, Men Don't

Phyllis D. Coontz

ABSTRACT. Although the number of women in the legal profession has increased dramatically over the last 20 years, evidence shows that women continue to lag well behind men on every indicator of success. While the differences in the careers of women and men lawyers have been explained in terms of either structural organizational constraints or tokenism, neither adequately addresses the persistence of the gender-based pecking order in law. It is argued here that part of the reason why this two-tiered pecking order persists is related to the meanings attached to gender itself. No one has examined the social construction of gender in the legal profession. Thus, the analyses reported here add a new dimension to the research on the legal profession.

This paper focuses on the content of gender interpretations and the professional contexts in which these interpretations are found. I examine these by analyzing the attitudes of women and men lawyers and their observations of gender bias in professional situations. I predict that men lawyers will hold more traditional attitudes about gender roles than women lawyers and that women lawyers will observe more gender bias than men lawyers. Using data from a large

Phyllis D. Coontz is affiliated with the Graduate School of Public and International Affairs at the University of Pittsburgh, Pittsburgh, PA 15260.

Women & Politics, Vol. 15(2) 1995

survey of lawyers (N = 1,863) in the Pittsburgh Metropolitan area, I
compare (1) the gender role attitudes of women and men lawyers;
(2) the observations of gender bias in the professional interactions of
women and men lawyers; and (3) I analyze women lawyers'
accounts of their personal experiences with gender bias. The results
support the predictions, and these findings are augmented by analysis of in-depth accounts of actual experiences of gender bias by
women lawyers in the course of doing legal work.

INTRODUCTION

According to a recent article in *The Wall Street Journal*, gender bias[1] is
a problem throughout the legal profession (August 22, 1992). Although
women comprised 21% of all lawyers in 1992–moving them beyond
"token"[2] involvement–the empirical evidence shows that women continue to lag well behind men on every indicator of success (Chambers
1989; Coontz 1991; Curran 1986; Hagan 1990; Liefland 1986; Winter
1982). Women lawyers earn less than men, are not promoted, do not get
desirable assignments, are not given the same opportunities for litigation
experience, and are not even provided the same office amenities (Coontz
1991; Couric 1989; Vogt 1987; White 1967; Winter 1983). Women are
overrepresented in low prestige practice areas such as government, teaching, legal aid, and public defender work, and underrepresented in private
practice, the higher echelons of large law firms, and the judiciary (Abel
and Lewis 1989; Curran 1986; Hagan 1990). When women go into private
practice, they are more likely to practice solo or as associates in large firms
(Abel and Lewis 1989; Couric 1989; Simon and Garden 1981).

Women make up almost half of the students in law school today, come
from the same social backgrounds, go to the same law schools, earn the
same grades, and serve on the same law reviews as men. But once they
graduate, the similarities between women and men lawyers end. Women
are clustered in the lower prestige ranks while men are clustered in the
higher prestige ranks of the profession. A recent study examining the
structural transformation of the legal profession found that as more
women enter the profession, the career gap between women and men
lawyers widens (Hagan 1990, 840). In fact, the gap is greater between
women and men lawyers than it is between women and men in the general
labor force.[3] This, Hagan suggests, is because the legal profession remains
highly stratified by sex (1990, 848). Against the backdrop of 30 years of
feminism, the Equal Pay Act of 1963, the passage of Title VII, and the
influx of women into the profession, why is gender bias so persistent?

BACKGROUND

The workplace has always been segregated by sex; women have either worked in female dominated occupations or they have been restricted to the lower ranks of male dominated occupations. The elite professions have been especially inhospitable to women, but the legal profession is unique in that it has taken its own subject matter to restrict women's access (Kanter 1978; Morello 1986; Rhode 1988). Until the passage of Title VII, the percentage of women in law never exceeded 3% (Morello 1986). The number of women entering the profession since then has been nothing short of "revolutionary" (Abel 1989). In fact, 77% of all women currently practicing law entered the profession after 1970 (Rosenberg et al. 1990).

While the law can require that employers comply with Title VII provisions, such provisions do not guarantee an end to discrimination. Why? Because the values out of which discrimination arises are embedded in cultural beliefs, and it is these beliefs that get reflected in day-to-day informal workplace practices. When the goals of formal policy are incongruent with cultural beliefs, then discrimination can still occur. The persistence of gender bias in the workplace despite legal and formal policy prescriptives is in part related to wider cultural beliefs about gender roles and expectations for appropriate behavior. Women who enter the workplace are judged according to beliefs pertaining to their primary roles as wife and mother, female/male relationships, and differences (whether perceived or real) between women and men being innate (Reskin and Hartmann 1986).

Although there are few jobs in which sex is a bona fide occupational qualification (BFOQ), the workplace is stratified by sex, strongly suggesting that people, in fact, associate certain jobs with females and other jobs with males. Over half of all women who are now employed work in jobs that are at least 80% female. The majority of jobs that women hold are those that mirror traditional beliefs about women's roles, e.g., nursing, teaching, counseling. Women are characterized, albeit stereotypically, as more passive, dependent, and nurturing, and the sorts of jobs women hold reflect such views. The jobs that women are most likely to hold are also those that are unskilled, carry little or no responsibility, and are poorly paid. Jobs that men hold, on the other hand, are those that are skilled, carry a lot of responsibility, and are well-paid (Acker 1989; Cockburn 1986). A comparison of the earnings of women with those of men shows that, despite the Equal Pay Act of 1963 prohibiting the discrimination against women in wages, in 1990 women who were employed full-time year-round made just 70% of what men earned. In fact, the more female-dominated the occupation, the lower their relative earnings. In the legal profession the income disparity is even greater. Hagan found a consistent $40,000 income gap between women and men lawyers even when women had achieved comparable power and prestige within the profession (1990).

In an analysis of how women lawyers fare in the legal profession, Rhode (1988, 1188) argues that male dominance operates against women on three important levels: (1) through prototypes of lawyers; (2) schema which explain success and failure in the profession; and (3) scripts which set forth appropriate professional conduct. Prototypes of lawyers are cast typically in terms of male traits. In some practice areas, for example litigation, the prototype actually personifies male roles. A litigator has a penchant for conflict and is relentless, clever and, of course, aggressive. The dilemma for women operating in a male dominated environment is that every career decision involves actually two decisions: a substantive one and one involving whether and to what extent they are willing to conform to prototypical expectations. The risk of not modeling one's behavior after the prototype is to lose credibility and acceptance by one's colleagues.

The norms for success are prescribed through schema which also emphasize male traits. Thus, the traits more stereotypically associated with male roles, e.g., analytical ability, skill, finesse, strength, are the same traits assumed requisite for success in law. Men's success is interpreted in terms of ability and skill while failure is interpreted as being bad luck. Women's success, however, is interpreted in terms of luck, chance, or preferential treatment due to their sex while failure is due to a lack of ability and fortitude.

Scripts of the profession set forth interactional norms based on status–who can do what, to whom, and under what circumstances. Professional interaction provides a good example of how scripts work. Since men occupy positions of power and authority within the profession, they also control the structure and content of professional conversation. Thus, men can interrupt women, change topics at will, decide what is relevant to discuss, and terminate discussion without a reason (Rhode 1988, 1189). In a broader social context, men tend to control conversation (Lakoff 1975, Zimmerman & West 1975, 117) and this pattern is simply extended to the workplace. The message conveyed by scripts is about who has power and authority.

Overall, our understandings of gender roles shape our relationships and interactions with others. Thus, the concept of gender involves much more than simply classifying females and males into two distinct groups; it is a social category that we use to interpret, organize, and make sense of individual, social, and cultural phenomena (Stacy and Thorne 1985, 307). In short, gender conveys what it means to be female and male. In a workplace that is stratified and segregated by sex, the meaning conveyed is that women are not as valuable as men. The value of an employee is determined by the rank of the position held and the compensation for the position. Thus, higher ranking and paying jobs are associated with males while lower ranking and paying jobs are associated with women (Acker 1989, 221). In other words, worth on the labor market is determined by gender. Although there are no organic grounds for associating a given trait or characteristic (except for primary sex characteristics) exclusively with one sex or the other, people behave as though there were. Consequently, the assumptions we make about appropriate gender role behavior are carried into the workplace and form the basis for interpreting work roles and entitlement to work roles. For example, the provider role is still perceived primarily as men's responsibility; therefore it is automatically assumed that men belong in the workplace; whereas, for women work is secondary to their primary roles as wife and mother (Bielby & Bielby 1992).

Despite the central role gender plays in the social organization of the workplace, none of the research that has been done on gender and the legal profession has examined how gender affects professional relationships and interactions. Instead, research has focused on the impact of gender on the structural transformation of the profession (Abel 1986; Erlanger 1980; Hagan et al. 1988, 1990); the organizational constraints to women's upward mobility (Fuchs-Epstein 1990, 1981; Liefland 1986); and the impact of "tokenism" on women's legal careers (Kanter 1977). While these studies document gender differences in the profession, they tell us very little about the processes by which gender distinctions are actually made; that is, what the distinctions consist of and the contexts in which they occur. This study is a first step toward this goal and thus contributes to our understanding of the effect gender has on the professional lives of women and men lawyers by providing an empirical basis for analyzing how gender is made meaningful in professional interactions.

Since informal barriers to women's career parity reflect broader cultural beliefs about gender roles (Reskin and Hartmann 1986) and attitudes shape social relationships, women and men lawyers' attitudes about gender roles are examined. It is predicted that men's attitudes will be more stereotypical than women's. Similarly, since discrimination in the workplace is overwhelmingly directed against women (there is no comparable legislation to Title VII for men because men do not need it), it is assumed that women will be more attuned than men to discriminatory practices. There is growing evidence that women and men differ in perceptions of sexual harassment (Adams et al. 1983; Collins & Blodgett 1981; Kenig & Ryan 1986). Thus, women and men lawyers' observations of gender bias are examined and it is predicted that women lawyers will report more observations than men regardless of role, e.g., lawyer, judge, court employee, in the profession and that the form of observed bias will range in severity from comments about personal appearance to direct advances for sexual favors. Finally, actual experiences of bias are analyzed. Using the same logic in the predictions about differences in observations of bias, I also predict that women will report more actual experiences of bias than men. For this study I compare: (1) women and men lawyers' attitudes about gender roles; (2) women and men lawyers' observations of bias in their interactions with other legal professionals; and (3) women and men lawyers' experiences of gender bias.

METHODOLOGY

The data used in this analysis are from a large survey[4] of the Allegheny County Bar Association which is located in Western Pennsylvania. Allegheny County, in which the city of Pittsburgh is located, is a large metropolitan area ranked 19th in size of population according to the 1990 Census. A total of 6,501 surveys were mailed to the entire bar membership, and of these 1,870 were returned. Out of this number, 1,863 were usable and represent a 29% response rate.[5]

Measurement of Gender Role Attitudes

Gender role attitudes were measured using a 6-item scale asking respondents to indicate the degree to which they agreed with gender role statements on a 4-point scale of strongly agree, agree, disagree, and strongly disagree (higher scores reflect more progressive attitudes while lower scores reflect more stereotypical attitudes). The following items were included in this measure: "Too much attention is given to the gender wage gap"; "Mothers of pre-school age children should stay at home to care for them"; "It is more important for a wife to help with her husband's career than to have a career of her own"; "Decisions affecting the future of the family should be made by the husband"; and "A woman who works full time can establish just as warm and secure a relationship with her children as a mother who does not work." In coding the first and last statements, responses were reversed in order to produce an overall consistent score in one direction. Higher scores reflect more "progressive" attitudes while lower scores more stereotypical attitudes. The coefficient alpha for this measure is .74.

Measurement of Observed Bias

Observations of gender bias were measured by adapting questions used by Task Forces studying gender bias in the profession across the country. Seven different situations of gender bias were used, and respondents were asked to indicate on a 4-point scale the frequency with which these were observed with which professional groups, i.e., lawyers, judges, court employees, and coworkers. Specifically the types of bias presented included: "Remarks or comments about personal appearance of women when similar comments are not made about men"; "Women are interrupted or cut off while speaking when men are not"; "Women are addressed by first names or terms of endearment (e.g., honey or sweetie) when men are addressed by surnames or titles"; "Women are asked if they are attorneys whereas men are not"; "Women are characterized or referred to in a suggestive or sexual manner"; "Jokes or degrading comments are made about women"; and "Female attorneys are subjected to verbal or physical sexual advances." Responses were summarized for each group (lawyers' coefficient alpha = .90; judges' coefficient alpha = .91; court employees' coefficient alpha = .91; and co-workers' coefficient alpha = .88). High scores reflect frequent observations while low scores reflect no or few observations. In addition, respondents were asked whether they believed the outcome of the case was affected by the observed biased behavior. The responses to this question provide a picture, albeit limited, of the perceived impact of bias beyond the target.

Measurement of Experiences

Respondents were asked to share personal experiences of bias at the end of the survey. These responses were open ended and are used to examine the content and context of bias experiences.

FINDINGS

Women returned 29% of the surveys and men returned 71%. The sample was not a random sample and the findings should not be interpreted as representative. However, 29% of the bar membership is female (nationally, women comprise 21% of practicing attorneys) indicating that these findings reflect proportionately the female bar membership. Demographic information about survey respondents is presented in Table 1.

More men lawyers are employed full time than women lawyers; both typically practice in law firms; there is on average a seven-year age differ-

TABLE 1. Demographic Profile of Women and Men Lawyers

	Women	Men
Current Employment Status	80% full time	90% full time
	11% part time	5% part time
Type of Practice	Law firm	Law firm
Age	36 years old	43 years old
Average Billable Hours	1,991 hours/yr.	1,884 hours/yr.
Average No. Years Practicing	7 years	16 years
Marital Status	63% married	83% married
Average No. Hours Worked	47 hours/wk.	49 hours/wk.
Average Annual Salary Range	$35,000 -	$60,000 -
	$45,999	$79,999
Common Area of Practice	Family Law	Commerce

ence between women and men lawyers with women being younger (this is consistent with national demographics); women's average total billable hours worked translate into 13 more eight-hour work days a year than men's average; more men are married than women; women are more likely to specialize in family law while men specialize in commercial law (family law is a lower prestige practice area); and men's annual earnings are considerably higher than women's. These demographics roughly parallel national demographics.

The first question addressed is whether there are gender differences in attitudes toward gender roles. Gender role ideology is known to shape behavior in social groups (in and out of the workplace). Men have historically held more traditional views about gender roles than women (Bielby 1992). Thus, it was predicted that men lawyers would report more stereotypical attitudes than women lawyers and, as expected, they did. In fact, men lawyers are more stereotypical on every item of the attitude measure. Table 2 presents the mean scores for each item. Interestingly, the largest

TABLE 2. Women and Men Lawyers' Attitudes About Gender Bias

	Women			Men		
	Mean	SD	N	Mean	SD	N
Willing to Relocate	2.81	.71	512	2.53	.80	1207
Gender Wage Gap	3.30	.67	542	2.51	.76	1267
Mothers at Home	3.22	.71	530	2.58	.82	1242
Help Husband's Career	3.66	.54	543	3.14	.63	1256
Husband Makes Decision	3.80	.43	541	3.32	.61	1265
Combine Work & Motherhood	3.30	.78	537	2.60	.86	1253

(Higher scores more progressive, lower scores more traditional)

mean score difference between women and men was found on the gender wage gap item while the smallest mean score difference was found on the willingness to relocate item. These scores were collapsed into a summary score and further analysis using a t-test showed that attitude differences between women and men lawyers is significant (t-test = 25.47, df = 1822, $p < .000$).

The second question addressed here is whether there are gender differences in the observations of gender bias. It was predicted that since men occupy most of the positions of power, make the rules and set the standards for professional conduct, and reward or punish the degree of conformity to professional expectations within the legal profession, they would be less attuned to gender bias than women and thus report fewer observations. Observations of bias were examined by status groups, i.e., lawyers, judges, court employees, and co-workers. A summary score for all seven types of bias was calculated for each group (high scores reflect more numerous observations) and t-tests were performed to see whether differences between women and men lawyers' observations were significant. Mean scores, standard deviations, and t-test results are presented in Table 3 and these show that as predicted, women report observing bias more frequently than men and that the pattern holds true across all four status groups. The differences are significant at the $p < .000$ level.

When asked whether they believed any of the bias situations affected

TABLE 3. Mean Scores of Bias by Sex and Status Group

	Women			Men			
	Mean	SD	N	Mean	SD	N	t-test
Bias with Lawyers	1.77	.68	497	.88	.60	1113	26.39*
Bias with Judges	1.14	.69	380	.48	.52	895	18.82*
Bias with Ct. Employees	1.33	.71	362	.63	.59	843	17. 65*
Bias with Co-Workers	1.37	.74	485	.70	.57	1049	19.55*

*p = <.000
(0 = Never, 1 = Rarely, 2 = Sometimes, 3 = Often)

the outcome of the professional interaction, 26% (N = 101) of the women lawyers said yes while only 4% (N = 32) of the men believed outcome was affected. Unfortunately, this item was an overall assessment of impact since a separate item for each type of bias with each status group was not provided. Therefore, there is no way of knowing whether outcome was affected more with one professional group than another or whether there were perceived multiple or single effect(s) on outcome.

Although all respondents had an opportunity to share personal experiences at the end of the survey, 20% (N = 103) of the women lawyers, and only 5% (N = 65) of the men lawyers provided personal accounts. These accounts reflect individual interpretations of bias and reveal vividly those actions that were defined as bias, the content of bias, the contexts in which the bias occurred, and whether the bias resulted in negative reactions from other lawyers. The accounts that are presented here were not randomly selected, but were chosen because they "typify" the experiences that were shared. Rhode's (1988) conceptual framework of prototypes, schema, and scripts is used to organize and analyze these experiences. While ideally women's and men's experiences should be compared, this was not possible because too few male respondents (2% or one male out of 65) chose to recount a personal experience of bias. The overwhelming majority of the male respondents (N = 64) shared instead their personal views about the validity of gender bias. Consequently, the analysis that follows reflects women's experiences and men's viewpoints. The contrast in the nature of what was shared is not unimportant and represents another indicator of the degree to which gender bias is differentially recognized.

Prototypes

Prototypes serve as models against which to judge conformity to professional roles. Because the legal profession is dominated by men, the prevailing models of lawyers are male images. Evidence for this is found in the tendency to "qualify" professional status by prefacing status with sex when females are involved. An example of this practice is seen when a woman who is also a professional is described as a "woman-doctor," "woman-judge," or "woman-lawyer." This qualifier is not applied to men because it is taken for granted that professional status is appropriate for men. Schur (1985, 25) argues that while we criticize such designations, they are nevertheless ubiquitous throughout society. At a functional level, of course, prototypes preserve the professional status hierarchy. Underlying prototypes is the assumed incongruence between women's primary roles of wife and mother and secondary role of provider.

The following three examples show how the incongruence is operationalized in professional interactions. The first example is an account of interviewing for a position in Pittsburgh law firms. Despite this lawyer's background, prospective employers focused more on her gender than her qualifications. That questions about age, marital status, plans for pregnancy, and husband's occupation were asked, although it is illegal to do so, illustrates the powerful influence prototypes have in shaping professional behavior. Despite this woman's accomplishments, she was perceived first and foremost in terms of women's primary roles of wife and mother.

Case One

"Interviewing in Pittsburgh law firms is a bitch. I was eighth in my class in rank, had a prior career as a commercial banker lending to small and middle market sized companies, and what did I get asked by male lawyers: 'How old are you?' 'Married?' 'Any children?' 'Plan on having any?' 'What does your husband do?' When I told them he was also a lawyer, the reaction was: 'Why aren't you working for him?'"

The barriers created by prototypes are not limited to entry into the profession, but are also applied to women once practicing in the profession. The second case illustrates how the incongruence between the expectations of women and the prototype of a lawyer affected the assignment of professional responsibility.

Case Two

"With my first employer, a law firm representing unions, I was denied assignment to one of the unions that was represented because the union representative did not believe women should be attorneys. I learned this only after I asked why I was not being assigned to this union's cases. My male colleagues could not understand why I found this objectionable."

The third case provides yet another example of how the incongruence between women's primary role expectations and professional role expectations affects professional interaction. In this case not only didn't this lawyer fit the male prototype, but the judge involved determined that dealing with her was a waste of time for her male colleagues.

Case Three

"In Westmoreland County, two male attorneys and a judge made small talk about sports, then the judge turned to me and said, 'well young lady, you don't look like you've tried many cases. You'd better have some money ready for these gentlemen for wasting their time.'"

Whether one is applying for a job, being assigned responsibility within the profession, or interacting professionally, these three examples reinforce Rhode's (1988) assertion that prototypes in the profession are male, and also that incongruence with the dominant image affects getting a position, assignment of responsibility, and professional credibility. How discriminatory are prototypes? It is doubtful that had any of these situations been reversed and the lawyers involved male that they would have occurred at all.

Schema

Schema explain career milestones and rites of passage by reference to individual characteristics, the most notable of which is gender. Schema interpret success in the legal profession through lenses that associate success with traditional male attributes. The following three cases reveal just how important gender is to explanations of professional competence and accomplishment. In the first example, a 36-year-old attorney describes an experience in the courtroom in which her pregnancy was perceived not only by the opposing attorney, but also by the judge, as being incompatible with demands of being a lawyer.

Case Four

"I appeared at an argument in support of a motion when I was nine months pregnant. The attorney on the other side (male) made a big deal of being at a disadvantage arguing against a pregnant woman and said that my boss had deliberately sent me to the argument to exploit my condition. The judge concurred and nodded sympathetically. What did my pregnancy have to do with the argument? I was really annoyed that my pregnancy was mentioned."

Stereotypical depictions are demeaning and thus can affect perceptions of competence and credibility. In the next account, a 39-year-old attorney describes being admonished by a judge for speaking in a tone that is more stereotypically defined as female.

Case Five

"On one occasion, a judge admonished me for being 'shrill.' Several times with me, as well as other female attorneys, the judge appeared to have prejudged the case."

Objections are a standard device used to argue that an action is improper, unfair or illegal. As such, assessing the legitimacy of an objection should theoretically be based on merit and relevance. As the next case illustrates though, there appears to be a double standard for assessing objections when those raised by women are met with "outrage" and those raised by men ignored.

Case Six

"While I have not experienced sexual jokes or advances as a female attorney, I have noticed that men are more respectful of other men's objections or legal arguments than they are of women's. Often male attorneys are outraged at my objections, but they'll basically ignore objections made by other males. I've never had this experience with other female attorneys, and I've never seen female attorneys become outraged at other male attorneys' objections."

Schema justify the differential treatment of women lawyers by relying on stereotypical interpretations of individual characteristics. Thus, professional interactions are screened by gender. Gender works as a "master status"[6] (Becker 1963) so that the lawyer who happens to also be a woman is evaluated first and foremost as a woman. Other accomplishments or characteristics are secondary to being female. Thus, we see that female characteristics, i.e., pregnancy or a "shrill" voice, eclipse competence.

Scripts

Scripts set forth the norms of professional interaction. Like prototypes and schema, scripts reflect broader cultural beliefs about gender dominance, deference, and accommodation. Scripts indicate what is expected in the profession, and they reflect one's status. Scripts are most evident in the norms regulating verbal communication—when to speak, what is acceptable to talk about, when to change topics, and when to terminate talk. In the first two examples, women's physical appearance is an acceptable topic to discuss in professional contexts. In the first example, the object of the discussion, a 35-year-old attorney describes how her "looks" were discussed as though she were "invisible." Talking about others in their presence as though they were nonparticipants is what it means to objectify and devalue another.

Case Seven

"More than 50% of the time that I'm in a courtroom or judges' chambers, comments are made by the judge (if he's male which is usually the case) or by male attorneys about my good looks. I've been told, 'your collar is too high,' 'I wish I had legs like yours in my office,' 'your skirts are too long,' and 'I could watch you walk around here all day.' Often these comments are made as if I weren't present in the room. A few attorneys have said things to each other like, 'Hey Joe, she has a definite advantage over you with those looks,' or 'It's hard to concentrate with her around.' Even judges, some of whom I view as otherwise progressive and enlightened, have done this. I've never heard a woman comment about my or anybody else's looks."

In the next example, a 27-year-old attorney describes how her "good" looks were translated into a "distraction" by the opposing attorney. By allowing the opposing attorney to make this comment, the judge in effect has signaled to the approximately 45 other attorneys that it's acceptable to complain about the "looks" of opposing women attorneys.

Case Eight

"After I filled out my survey, but before depositing it in the mail, I had the following experience. I had to argue preliminary objections to a complaint to join additional defendants in front of Judge McCue. Counsel for the third party plaintiff was Arrow of Wing, Arrow & Pott. The complaint Mr. Arrow had filed on behalf of his client was dreadfully deficient, and as far as we could tell, utterly failed to state any cause of action against our client whatsoever. Shortly after I started my argument, Judge McCue asked me a question, and following my response, Mr. Arrow interjected that every time he is involved in a legal matter with my client, they send the 'best looking' woman attorney they can to give oral argument, and he doesn't stand a chance. Judge McCue merely chuckled rather than tell

Mr. Arrow that he was out of line. Further, there were approximately 45 other attorneys in the courtroom–only two of whom were women–and all of the men found this comment very amusing. I found this experience to be extremely humiliating, and it destroyed any credibility I could have had that morning. I was not given an opportunity to finish my argument. The outcome was that the opposing party was required to file a more specific complaint and our demurrer was denied."

The following two examples illustrate the impact that conversational styles have on conferring and reinforcing status differences between women and men. Both women attorneys in these examples describe being interrupted in the interaction with men lawyers.

Case Nine

"In motion court I found that it was characteristic for the judges (all of whom were male) to defer to the male attorney who characteristically was more aggressive and monopolized argument time as well as took more time to present argument. The male attorney usually started off the argument regardless of whether it was appropriate and it usually took a long time. Then, when female attorney's turn came up, the judge was either impatient, interrupted, looked bored, cut off argument, or argued for male attorney's point of view."

Case Ten

"Once Judge Reed did not allow me to speak throughout the entire hearing on a motion to suppress. Every time I attempted to present the government's arguments, he interrupted me. I believe the outcome of the hearing would have been different if he had allowed me to present the government's case. (In fact, he'd already ruled once in the government's favor.) In that case, opposing counsel was a male. The last time I appeared before Judge Reed, both attorneys were female. He treated my opponent with total disrespect–even accusing her of lying and presenting him with false documents. These accusations were wholly unfounded."

All of these personal experiences reveal just how deeply embedded gender is in day-to-day interactions of lawyers and show that gender bias arises in myriad contexts: questions about women's marital status; comments about women's looks; stereotypical characterizations of women's behavior; treating women as objects; and interrupting women's professional speech. Women attorneys are routinely reminded that in the eyes of their male colleagues being female overrides their professional ability, competencies, and accomplishments.

While gender bias could theoretically affect both women and men, these experiences indicate that women are far more likely to experience bias than men. This is consistent with other research showing that women are the targets of bias (particularly sexual harassment) in the overwhelming majority of cases (Gutek 1985). Because the survey was voluntary and only one male out of the total sample (N = 1,309) reported bias, it is reasonable to conclude that this single response reflects the reality of men's experiences of bias, i.e., it occurs much less frequently among men. This is not surprising or even unexpected in the legal profession since men occupy the higher positions of power and status. The lone respondent who did share his experience wrote:

> In two of my jobs, women have discriminated against me because of my sex. When asked by them to perform physical and menial labor I refused. Consequently they stopped sending me legal work. This is why I'm unemployed. Why don't we hear about this?

The remaining 98% who did respond shared views that either challenged or criticized the validity of gender bias. The following examples typify these responses.

A 37-year-old male respondent asserted the following:

> The problem with women is that they don't have a sense of humor and can't take a joke.

A 43-year-old male respondent wrote:

> In my opinion there is no satisfactory substitute for the mother remaining at home a majority of the time with children until age 5 regardless of career or economic ambitions. Mothers with working spouses who are unwilling to stay at home with their children should not have a child or should give up working.

Another 38-year-old male respondent wrote:

> In my opinion this so-called 'gender bias' is purely fiction–an invention brought about by a small faction of women lawyers who are emotionally and intellectually immature. Some women want equality, but don't want the burden of the negative effects of equality. Negative treatment at times is part and parcel of practicing law–it has absolutely nothing to do with this mythical 'gender bias' which to me simply does not exist.

Finally, a 30-year-old male exclaimed: "Hey girls, if you want to play with the big boys, you'd better grow up."

What conclusions can be drawn from these personal accounts? While we know that the profession is highly stratified by sex, the meaning attached to gender cannot be captured by examining the structure of the profession. Thus, these accounts reveal vividly what it means to be a woman in a male dominated profession. The accounts are not "war stories," but reflect the ordinary ways in which bias occurs. Not only do women's and men's professional experiences differ (women experience bias and men question its validity), but these accounts show that gender serves as a screen for participation in the profession. Although it is clear the gender bias is not uniformly experienced in every professional interaction, with every colleague, or in every context, it nevertheless occurs and with enough frequency that it cannot be considered an aberration. A fifth of the women who responded reported personal experiences of bias. And their experiences are disturbing on two counts. First, gender bias is a phenomenon that is not the sole domain of older men lawyers who have not been exposed to feminist ideology, but occurs at the hands of younger men who were exposed to the ideology of the women's movement, feminist theory, and shifts in women's behavior. Despite this exposure, the overwhelming majority of views shared by men respondents of all ages reflects the underlying prevalence of highly sexist attitudes. These accounts are also disturbing for what they reveal about the general acceptance of gender bias in the profession. Although gender bias occurs in a variety of forms, contexts, and with all other legal status groups, it does not result in negative sanctions–it does not even evoke a raised eyebrow. In none of the examples presented here (or in any of the other personal accounts not selected) was there any suggestion that the bias behavior was viewed as inappropriate except by those who experienced it.

DISCUSSION

The findings presented here go one step further than other research examining gender differences in the legal profession by showing concretely how gender enters into day-to-day professional interactions and the professional contexts in which gender is raised. While gender bias is ubiquitous, it is interpreted as a problem only by those against whom it is directed: women lawyers. Gender differences were found in attitudes toward gender roles, observations of gender bias, and personal experiences of bias. The two predicted patterns of gender differences were confirmed. Specifically, men lawyers are more stereotypical than women in their attitudes toward gender roles, and women lawyers observe bias more frequently than men. In addition to these two patterns, based on actual accounts of bias, this study found that bias affects women more than it does men. Despite the removal of formal barriers to the profession, these findings show that formidable obstacles still exist impeding women's full integration into the profession.

While certainly the sharp increases in the number of women entering the profession have been influenced by changes in women's roles in general, such changes do not tell the whole story. That is, the sharp jump in the number of women in the profession is probably less a function of a shift in gender role ideology than it is with structural changes in the profession itself. These findings present concrete evidence that while women are more progressive in gender ideology, men are still highly traditional. The dramatic growth in the number of women in the profession parallels sharp increases in the number of lawyers in general and suggests larger structural changes. That is, the ratio of lawyers to the general population, the size, type, and organization of law firms, and the regional distribution of the legal practice, have all changed dramatically over the last 50 years (Halliday 1986; Hagan 1990). There is little evidence that this transformation of the legal profession has had an effect on the gender gap since other research finds it continues to be quite large (Hagan 1990, 849). The importance of the results presented here is that they show the ways in which gender remains an issue.

An influx of women into the profession was expected to have significant effects on the way law is conceptualized, practiced, and interpreted. But as seen from the findings presented here, in the day-to-day activities of the profession, women have yet to be accepted as equal members to the profession. The contrast of women's status within the profession against a backdrop of the Equal Pay Act of 1963 and Title VII based employment policies, and 30 years of feminism, points to the real limitations inherent in relying solely on formal policy to change workplace practices. While there is no question that formal policies have been significant in advancing equality in the workplace, the findings presented here underscore the limitations inherent in formal policy for achieving equality. A review of Title VII litigation as well as Department of Labor statistics on wages indicate the range of discriminatory practices as well as the magnitude of pay inequity. Legal responses are inadequate by themselves because they are based on a theoretical tradition that focuses on individual choice rather than social forces. Individual choice is central to theories of occupational inequality, especially human capital theory, but as these findings reveal, individual choice has little to do the underlying beliefs upon which gender bias rests. Moreover, a growing body of empirical evidence shows that only half of current gender disparities can be accounted for by individual choice (Cockoran & Duncan 1979; Reskin & Hartmann 1984). Gender bias is a part of the professional culture that subscribes to a gender ideology that views women in highly traditional terms. Since more than two-thirds of the lawyers who responded to the survey are men, the findings show that the dominant view in the profession is that while women take on the role of lawyer, it is still perceived as secondary to their primary roles. A consequence of this perspective is the marginalization of women lawyers within the profession. Moreover, these traditional attitudes are reflected in the differences reported in both the observations and experiences of bias–women "see" and experience bias, but men don't. Formal policy can require employers to abide by Title VII provisions, but they by themselves are insufficient for ending occupational inequality. What is needed are strategies aimed at reconceptualizing gender and women's place in the workplace. Such strategies should target the sources of gender bias: socialization and educational practices that channel females and males into traditional gender roles; assumptions about family responsibilities that are gender-based; and cultural images that portray women and men in stereotypical ways.

NOTES

1. I use Reskin and Hartmann's (1984) definition of gender bias which is that gender bias refers to situations where, although irrelevant, gender is made to make a difference.

2. Kanter set the threshold for overcoming "tokenism" at 20% (1976, 10). According to Dept. of Labor statistics, by 1992 women comprised 21% of all lawyers practicing in the United States, thus moving them slightly beyond "token" involvement. In her analysis of "token" women, Kanter (1977) observed that they were found in "skewed" groups where one type of employee, e.g., men, dominated over types of employees, e.g., women. Further tokenism was distinguished from other conditions by: conspicuous visibility of minority group; minority group's differences are accentuated by their presence; and reference to their attributes as evidence for why token group is treated differently (1977, 206-42).

3. Although the gender gap is smaller in the general labor force than it is in the legal profession, the gap appears to be widening in occupational categories. Tienda et al. (1987, 206) argue there are two reasons for the growth of the gender gap: one relates to the extent to which a job category is segregated and the other to the proportion of women in the job category.

4. The catalyst for the survey was an incident involving a federal judge who ordered a female attorney presenting a case before him to use her married name (which she had never used before) or face a night in jail for contempt of court. She

refused to use her name, and although the lawyer did not end up in jail, the incident drew national attention for what it revealed about gender bias in the courts. Local attorneys used this incident to mobilize interest in the issue and formed an ad hoc task force made up mostly of female attorneys. This group was instrumental in the establishment of the Women in the Law Committee of the Allegheny County Bar Association which then was successful in convincing the Bar's Board of Governors to sponsor the survey. I was hired to develop the survey and analyze the results. The survey covered a wide range of issues related to the practice of law, i.e., legal background, demographic background, current working conditions, household responsibilities, weekly use of time, child care and family responsibilities, and family constraints were covered along with questions aimed directly at gender role attitudes, professional interactions, and personal experiences.

5. While a higher response rate is desirable, 29% is acceptable for statistical purposes. Possible reasons why the response rate was not higher could be: (1) it was a mail survey without followup efforts encouraging participation; (2) participation was not compensated and totally voluntary; (3) the survey was long (14 pgs.); (4) and a stamped return envelope was not provided to respondents.

6. Becker formulated this idea to apply to deviant behavior. It involves the imputation of an identity such that it overrides all other characteristics. Individuals are then responded to on the basis of their identity in the devalued group. As it applies to gender, being a "woman" serves as the master status through which all other characteristics and traits are filtered.

REFERENCES

Abel, R.L. (1986). "The Transformation of the American Legal Profession." *Law & Society Review,* 10:7-17.

Abel, R.L. (1988). "Lawyers in the Civil Law World" in R.L. Abel & PSC Lewis (eds) *Lawyers in Society, Vol. 2 The Civil Law World,* Berkeley, CA: Univ. of Calif. Press.

Acker, J. (1989). *Comparable Worth.*

Adams, J.W., Kottke, J.L., Padgitt, J.S. (1983). "Sexual Harassment of University Students." *Journal of College Student Personnel,* 24, 484-490.

Becker, H. (1963). *Outsiders.* New York: The Free Press.

Bielby W.T. and D.D. Bielby. (1992). "I Will Follow Him: Family Ties, Gender Role Beliefs, and Reluctance to Relocate for a Better Job." *American Journal of Sociology,* 5:12441-67.

Chambers, D. (1989). "Accommodation & Satisfaction: Women & Men Lawyers and the Balance of Work & Family." *Law & Social Inquiry.*

Cockoran, M. & G. Duncan (1979). "Work History, Labor Force Attachment, and Earnings Differences Between the Races and Sexes." *The Journal of Human Resources,* 15:3-20.

Collins, E.G.C. & Blodgett, T.B. (1981). "Sexual Harassment: Some See It, Some Won't." *Harvard Business Review,* March-April, 77-95.

Coontz, P. (1991). "ACBA Women in the Law Survey." *Pittsburgh Legal Journal,* 13:3-35.

Couric, E. (Dec. 11, 1989). "Women in the Large Firms: A High Price of Admission." *National Law Journal.*

Curran, B. (1986). "American Lawyers in the 1980's: A Profession in Transition." *Law and Society Review,* 20:19-52.

Erlanger, H. (1980). "The Allocation of Status Within Occupations: The Case of the Legal Profession." *Social Forces,* 58:882-903.

Fuchs-Epstein, C. (1981). *Women in Law.* New York: Basic Books.

Gutek, B. (1985). *Sex and the Workplace.* San Francisco: Jossey-Bass.

Hagan, J., M. Huxter, P. Parker. (1988). "Class Structure and Legal Practice: Inequality and Mobility Among Toronto Lawyers." *Law & Society Review,* 22:9-55.

Hagan, J. (1990). "The Gender Stratification of Income Inequality Among Lawyers." *Social Forces,* 68:836-855.

Halliday, Terence C. (1986). "Six Score Years and Ten: Demographic Transitions in the American Legal Profession." *Law and Society Review,* 20:53.

Holstein, J. (1987). "Producing Gender Effects on Involuntary Mental Hospitalization." *Social Problems,* 34:141-156.

Kanter, R. (1977). "Some Effects of Proportions on Group Life: Skewed Sex Ratios and Responses to Token Women." *American Journal of Sociology,* 82:965-975.

Kanter, R. (1978). "Reflections on Women and the Legal Profession: A Sociological Perspective." *Harvard Women's Law Journal,* 1.

Kenig, S. & Ryan, J. (1986). "Sex Differences in Levels of Tolerance and Attribution of Blame for Sexual Harassment on a University Campus." *Sex Roles,* 15, 535-549.

Lakoff, R. (1975). *Language and Woman's Place.* New York: Harper Colphon Books.

Liefland, L. (1986). "Career Patterns of Male & Female Lawyers." *Buffalo Law Review,* 36:601-631.

Morello, K. (1986), *The Invisible Bar: The Women Lawyers in America: 1638 to the Present.* Boston, MA: Beacon Press.

Reskin, B. & H. Hartmann. (1986). *Women's Work, Men's Work.* Washington, D.C.: National Academy Press.

Rhode, D. (1988). "Perspectives on Professional Women." *Stanford Law Review,* 40:1163-1207.

Rosenberg, J., H. Perlstadt, & W. Phillips. (1990). "Politics, Feminism and Women's Profession Orientation: A Case Study of Women Lawyers." *Women & Politics,* 10:19-48.

Schur, E. (1984). *Labeling Women Deviant.* New York: Random House.

Schutz A. (1970). *On Phenomenology and Social Relations.* Chicago: Univ. of Chicago Press.

Simon & Garden. (1981). "Still the Second Sex." *Student Law.*

Stacy, J.& B. Thorne. (1985). "The Missing Feminist Revolution in Sociology." *Social Problems,* 32:301-316.

Tienda, M., S. Smith, V. Oritz. (1987). "Industrial Restructuring, Gender Segregation and Sex Differences in Earning." *American Sociological Review,* 52:195-210.

Vogt, L. (1986). "From Law School to Career: Where Do Graduates Go and What Do They Do: A Career Paths Study of Seven Northeastern Area Law Schools." Cambridge, MA: Harvard Law School Program in the Legal Profession.

The Wall Street Journal. (August, 1992). "Gender Bias is Widespread in the Legal Profession."

White, J. (1967). "Women in the Law." *Michigan Law Review,* 65.

Winter, 1983. "Survey: Women Lawyers Work Harder, Are Paid Less, But They're Happy." *ABA Journal.*

Zimmerman, D. & C. West. (1975). "Sex Roles, Interruptions and Silences in Conversation," in *Language and Sex Difference and Dominance.* Rowely, MA: Newbury House.

The Combat Exclusion and the Role of Women in the Military

JUDITH WAGNER DECEW

I first discuss reasons for feminists to attend to the role of women in the military, despite past emphasis on antimilitarism. I then focus on the exclusion of women from combat duty, reviewing its sanction by the U.S. Supreme Court and the history of its adoption. I present arguments favoring the exclusion, defending strong replies to each, and demonstrate that reasoning from related cases and feminist analyses of equality explain why exclusion remains entrenched.

Many women and feminists have for years been identified with antiwar and antimilitarist efforts, and have been both initiators and staunch supporters of pacifist movements. However, as increasing numbers of women are serving in the military beyond traditional roles such as nursing, administration, and communications, and as the sexism, harassment, and inequity in the military is being more highly publicized, women scholars are beginning to address issues surrounding the role of women within the military.[1]

I begin by describing central themes in the feminist debate about military values and gender, urging that despite the feminist emphasis on antimilitarism and nonviolence, there are important reasons to attend to the desirability of struggling for women's equality in the military. I then turn to the exclusion of women from military combat duty, an exclusion given implicit legal sanction by the Supreme Court in 1981 in *Rostker v. Goldberg*,[2] a decision holding that there was no gender-based discrimination in requiring men but not women to register for the draft. I argue that Rehnquist's majority opinion in *Rostker* endorses, despite his disclaimers, unsubstantiated judgments about the "proper role" of women, relies on an overly narrow interpretation of Congress's stated purpose for draft registration, and accepts the combat exclusion based on a mistaken reading of the history of its adoption, thus undermining his arguments and perpetuating inequality for women in the military.

Hypatia vol. 10, no. 1 (Winter 1995) © by Judith Wagner DeCew

To make the last point I review and assess the history of the adoption of the combat exclusion, showing that the exclusion was never given adequate justification by Congress. Next I examine further arguments that have been given in favor of the combat exclusion, many of which were not reflected in the earlier debates. I argue that there are strong replies to each and that most are based on sociopolitical considerations rather than military need. I then present additional reasons for lifting the combat exclusion.

We might well wonder why, given the wealth of arguments against the exclusion, it continues to be hotly debated and strongly supported by many. I suggest that related case arguments as well as feminist analyses of equality help explain why so many continue to defend the exclusion despite weak justifications and strong counterarguments. In conclusion, I point out why lifting the combat ban to gain equal opportunity for women has implications for treatment of military women in the areas of sexual harassment and abuse.

THE FEMINIST DEBATE ON WOMEN AND THE MILITARY

It is important to note that there is no single feminist position on the exclusion of women from combat. For years feminists committed to equality have been divided over issues concerning the role of women in the military, and it would be a mistake not to recognize this diversity of views.[3] Nevertheless, there is a long tradition of antiwar and antimilitarist sentiment among many women and feminists, which has sometimes precluded discussion of the combat exclusion for women in the military.

Feminist scholars who have examined the relationship between gender, violence, and war have often associated violence with male sexuality and nonviolence with mothering and nurturing. Thus, for example, Catharine MacKinnon (1989) has repeatedly emphasized the relationship between male sexuality and force, particularly violence against women in the form of rape, battery, and sexual harassment, Nancy Hartsock (1989) has traced ways in which virility and violence are commonly linked, and Cynthia Enloe (1983, 13-14) has called attention to respects in which the notion of combat is fundamental to the concepts of manhood and male superiority. Virginia Held writes that Betty Reardon (1985) claims:

> that sexism and the war system arise from the same set of authoritarian constructs. A social order based on competition, authoritarianism, and unequally valued human beings, upheld by coercive force controlled by male elites, gives rise, on her view, to both sexism and the system of war. The profile of men who abuse women is similar to that of soldiers; some view the similarity as "deliberate and necessary." Military combat train-

ing uses women hating as part of its method of turning men into
soldiers. (Held 1993, 146)

Amy Swerdlow (1989), Judith Stiehm (1983), and Sara Ruddick (1980),
among others, have emphasized in addition the relationship between a commitment to nonviolence and the activities of caring for and raising children.
Ruddick notes the incompatibility between a mother's aim to preserve life and
military destruction, and she traces parallels between peacemaking by mothers
and nonviolence techniques advocated by Ghandi and Martin Luther King.

Given this context of feminist discussion and the widespread feminist
commitment to peace and pacifism, it may seem incompatible with feminist
ideals to be concerned with women's equality in the military and the exclusion
of women from combat duty. Indeed, Virginia Held has suggested that many
feminists find it bizarre or sick or at least misguided for women even to seek
an equal right to fight, to kill, or to participate in the institutions of the military
on a par with men. These feminists believe that women should strive for a
much more meaningful equality, one that would empower women to prevent
war, to make military combat obsolete, and to make military service unnecessary for anyone.[4] In this context it is not surprising that most recent feminist
writing on the subject has not even addressed the issue of an equal right for
women to participate in military combat.

Feminists may believe that a right to serve in combat in the military exists
but that it should take low priority for feminist thinkers, given the many rights
denied women around the world. Or, more strongly, they may reject any female
participation in U.S. interventionist and military endeavors, particularly
under male orders. They may believe an equal right to carry out U.S.
military orders, which they find both morally outrageous and internation-
ally illegal, is a right they would prefer not to have. By arguing against the
combat exclusion, however, I am not thereby endorsing current military
activities. I believe we can and must discuss the egalitarian concerns raised
by the exclusion independently of assessments of general military policies,
procedures, and objectives.

There are, furthermore, two considerations that make the inequality of the
combat exclusion relevant for a wide range of feminists. First, we can idealize
the military in such a way that we see it as the kind of institution that will be
needed even in a largely peaceful and demilitarized world, to deal with the
kinds of peacekeeping efforts that will continue to be necessary in a world
without the military institutions and activities with which we are currently
familiar. Second, we must realize how nonideal this world is and can be
expected to remain. It is arguable that military establishments and military
efforts are necessary and even justifiable, when, for example, they are used to
prevent atrocities and violations of human rights such as those we have seen
in such places as Bosnia and to provide aid in crises like that in Rwanda.[5] If

this is correct, there is good reason for feminists to be concerned about the combat exclusion, the importance of women gaining equal treatment in the military, and their ability to be promoted to positions where they can transform military practices. Although my argument provides just one liberal feminist approach, it is, I believe, a compelling one.

THE ROSTKER LEGACY

The Military Selective Service Act required registration of males but not females for possible military service. The purpose of such registration, as stipulated by Congress, was to facilitate conscription of military personnel. Rehnquist's majority opinion in Rostker sets forth a two-pronged argument justifying the registration of men but not women. Note that I am not arguing for the draft (indeed I have great misgivings about a draft for men and women), but I utilize the Rostker case because it has major implications for the combat exclusion.

The majority's primary argument relies on deference to the legislature. Rehnquist claimed that the scope of congressional power is especially broad in the military context. On his view, courts should not in general substitute their own judgments concerning which policies will be desirable, and this customary deference is enhanced in military affairs and national defense contexts where courts are far less competent than Congress to pass judgment. Emphasizing that "deference does not mean abdication" (70), Rehnquist argued that since Congress specifically considered the question of the registration of women for the draft and recommended against it, their decision was not an "accidental byproduct of a traditional way of thinking about females" (74) and hence it was inappropriate to overturn their legislative decision. He claimed, in fact, that the Constitution required this deference to the legislature. Rehnquist also explicitly chided the district court for exceeding its authority and ignoring Congress's conclusions that the need for women in noncombat roles could be met by volunteers and that staffing noncombat positions with women during a mobilization would be "positively detrimental" to the important goal of military flexibility.

Rehnquist's second argument addressed the equal protection issue more specifically. He agreed that Congress's determination that any future draft would be characterized by a need for combat troops was sufficiently justified by testimony at the hearings. Because women were excluded from combat by statute in the navy and air force, and by military policy in the army and marines, he concluded that "men and women are simply not similarly situated for purposes of a draft or registration for the draft" (78). Thus, he continued, excluding women from registration did not violate the due process clause of the Fifth Amendment.[6] Congress was entitled to base the decision on military need over equity.

301

Note that the district court had rejected the defendant's deference to Congress argument as well as the plaintiff's request that the constitutional standard used be "strict scrutiny" and had instead relied on the midlevel "heightened scrutiny" or "important government interest" test articulated in previous sex discrimination cases (see *Craig v. Boren*, 429 U.S. 190 [1976]). In contrast, Rehnquist distinguished such cases as *Reed v. Reed* (404 U.S. 71 [1971]) and *Frontiero v. Richardson* (411 U.S. 677 [1973]), which involved overbroad classifications, and cited other recent cases such as *Schlesinger v. Ballard* (419 U.S. 498 [1968]), as supportive of his view. *Schlesinger*, which had challenged the navy's policy of allowing females a longer period than males to attain promotions needed for continued service, was cited as a case where the "different treatment of men and women naval officers . . . reflects, not archaic and overbroad generalizations, but, instead, the demonstrable fact that male and female line officers in the Navy are not similarly situated with respect to opportunities for professional service" (66).

Combat restrictions formed the clear basis for Congress's decision to exempt women from the draft registration. Given that women had been excluded from combat through statute and policy, Congress concluded that they would not be needed in the event of a draft, and therefore decided not to register them. Thus, while we think of *Rostker* as the draft case, it is also crucially a combat exclusion case. According to Rehnquist, *Rostker*, like *Schlesinger*, relied appropriately on a Senate report that said in part, "In the Committee's view, the starting point for any discussion of the appropriateness of registering women for the draft is the question of the proper role of women in combat" (S. Rep. No. 96-826, cited by Rehnquist at 67). Rehnquist stressed in his own words that "Congress was fully aware not merely of the many facts and figures presented to it by witnesses who testified before its Committees, but of the current thinking as to the place of women in the Armed Services" (71). Clearly the idea was that women should be protected from combat situations. Furthermore, it is explicit in the opinion that the reason men and women were not "similarly situated" for a draft or registration for one was "because of the combat restrictions on women" (78). Rehnquist added gratuitously that women would not actually be excluded by the decision because they could always volunteer for military service.

It should be clear at this point that despite his disclaimers, Rehnquist repeatedly relied on and reasserted Congress's emphasis on the "proper role" of women in the military. This "proper role" was invoked as the justification for the combat exclusion, which in turn formed the basis for the exclusion of women for registration for the draft. In reply to the district court he also cited further problems associated with registering women which had been raised in hearings: that "training would be needlessly burdened by women recruits who could not be used in combat," and "other administrative problems such as housing and different treatment with regard to dependency, hardship and physical standards" (81). Rehnquist's claims to the contrary, these arguments raise questions of convenience, not military need.

Second, while the case does not judge the combat restriction per se, the exclusion is accepted uncritically by Rehnquist and then given as the basis for the conclusion that men and women are not similarly situated in this instance and thus, as unlike cases, may be treated differently with no equal protection violation. The exclusion thus plays a pivotal role in the argument. Yet we can now see that Rehnquist's interpretation of the stated purpose of the registration, to facilitate preparation for a draft of combat troops, justifies his conclusion only when read far more narrowly than is reasonable. That is, even if the combat exclusion is accepted, preparing for a draft of combat troops does *not* imply that only combat positions will need to be filled. Approximately one-third of the positions were acknowledged to be roles where women could serve effectively. Including women in a draft to gain their skills in communications, radar repair, navigation, jet engine mechanics, drafting, surveying, meteorology, transportation, administrative and medical specialties, and so on, could save the time needed to train men in those fields and could release men from noncombat jobs to move to combat positions, thus facilitating rather than hindering a mobilization.

Third, Rehnquist's primary argument, relying on deference to Congress, is of course a common one. But it leaves the combat exclusion itself unchallenged from a constitutional point of view. It is thus staggering to discover that the combat exclusion for women was, when first enacted, merely an addition not originally part of the bill and not ever adequately justified in congressional testimony (see Gordon and Ludvigson 1991).

HISTORY OF THE ADOPTION OF THE COMBAT EXCLUSION

The original Senate bills establishing a regular corps of women in each of the services were introduced in 1947 and did not contain any provisions that would have excluded women from combat roles. At the Senate Armed Services Committee hearings little attention was paid to the possibility of legislating a mandatory combat exclusion, although some discussion indicated the services' intentions not to use women in combat situations. General Eisenhower, for example, testified concerning the value of women in the military, but his compliments were laced with comments about the roles for which women were well suited (Gordon and Ludvigson 1991, 4). In the House of Representatives, during the air force portion of the hearings there was no discussion of adding a combat exclusion for women. It was only during navy testimony that Representative Vinson proposed a legislative exclusion:

> I propose an amendment, if somebody will draft it. I am just throwing it out for what it is worth. Those are my views. I think

it will strengthen the bill to have it positively understood by Congress that ships are not places to which these women are going to be detailed and nobody has authority to detail them to serve on ship.

Of course, they are not going to be detailed to serve on ships, but you cannot tell what happens, you know, because somebody might say they need a few of them up there to do communications or other kinds of work and I do not think a ship is the proper place for them to serve. Let them serve on shore in the Continental United States and outside of the United States, but keep them off the ships. Of course, they ought to be on hospital ships. (Quoted in Gordon and Ludvigson 1991, 8).

Despite testimony from Captain F. R. Stickney of Navy Personnel that "we do not feel, though, that it was [sic] necessary to write that into law, Mr. Vinson" (Gordon and Ludvigson 1991, 8), the proposed amendment appeared later in the hearing. There was further objection to the amendment, but the bill considered the following year included combat exclusions for the navy and the air force. During the House debate, Representative Short commented, "we have put in those safeguards which I think are wise. We do not want our women killed" (Gordon and Ludvigson 1991, 11). There was no other specific discussion on combat exclusions. There seemed merely to be a general understanding that women would fill noncombat roles. The bill passed the House with the exclusion amendment. When submitted to the Senate it was described as essentially the same bill that originally passed by the Senate, with no mention of the addition of the combat exclusion. Moreover, the conference report made no reference to the rationale behind the combat amendment.

Consider, however, related House testimony that displays an attitude toward women in the military that was probably typical of the time:

> All these positions that will be filled by women at the present time are of a so-called housekeeping nature such as your excellent secretaries in many of your offices . . . women that men would have to replace.

> For every job ashore filled by a Wave [sic] officer you deny a male officer, who, after several years at sea, [has] the right to come ashore and occupy such an assignment.

> Enlisted men objected to the idea of having to take orders from a WAVE officer. Put yourself in the position of an enlisted man and I am sure you will agree with them. (Quoted in Gordon and Ludvigson 1991, 12)[7]

Clearly there was a prevailing view that if women were to serve in the military at all, it would be to do "women's work," and this presumably influenced views on the combat exclusion. But in all the congressional discussions on the issue, no military purpose for the exclusion seems to have been articulated. It appears that the only reasons for the exclusion were paternalistic protectionism and stereotypical views about what work women were suited for.

We find corroboration for this conclusion in Judge John Sirica's 1978 opinion in *Owens v. Brown* (455 F. Supp. 291 [D.D.C. 1978]), which held that the absolute ban on assignment of female personnel to sea duty, except in certain ships, violated the equal protection guarantee of the Fifth Amendment:

> The part of Section 6015 being challenged . . . was added casually, over the military's objection and without significant deliberation. . . . The provision was not directed at enhancing military preparedness . . . (n)or was it inserted to take account of the practical considerations associated with integrated ship-bound personnel. . . . Instead, the sense of the discussion is that Section 6015's bar against assigning females to shipboard duty was premised on the notion that duty at sea is part of an essentially masculine tradition. ("The Combat Exclusion Laws" 1991, 4)

It is worth remembering that despite all its restrictions,[8] the 1948 act ultimately provided permanent status to women in all the armed forces (both regular and reserve) and so provided for a group of trained women who could be mobilized in an emergency. This was a first step toward moving women from their second-class status as citizens allowed only in auxiliaries.

ARGUMENTS FOR AND AGAINST THE COMBAT EXCLUSION

Subsequently, there has been considerably more discussion of arguments both in favor of and against the combat exclusion for women. We would do well to describe them in categories. One argument, exemplified in the quotation given above from Representative Short, mirrors the early paternalistic and protectionist justifications for the exclusion, namely that women should not be hurt or killed in combat. In General Westmoreland's words, "No man with gumption wants a woman to fight his Nation's battles. I do not believe the American public wants to see a woman . . . do a man's job and that is to fight."[9] The underlying premises are that only certain jobs are appropriate for women and that the public expects and demands that women will be kept out of harm's way so they do not become victims. One obvious reply is that women have often served at substantial risk of injury in noncombat and semicombat positions and have been POWs as well. They are surely exposed to combat when serving as nurses or administrative assistants at the front lines. These women are not out of harm's way and may be doubly vulnerable if they have received little training in self-protection.[10] Note, in addition, the ironic relation between service and risk for women:

> U.S. military history in fact demonstrates that when the nation's level of military activities is reduced, women are no longer needed in service and their military activity is commensurately reduced; however, when military emergencies arise a role for women in service is quickly rediscovered. This results in the irony that women have served in the military in greater numbers precisely when the risks were the greatest, but their military participation was less acceptable when the risks were lower.[11]

Furthermore, as the definition of "combat" changes over time or due to different guidelines in the four services, the protection afforded women by the combat exclusion is diminishing. Finally, battle versus homefront lines may be irretrievably blurred in nuclear warfare so that there is no choice about whether or not women "go to war." Some women receive training in nuclear/biological/chemical (NBC) defense; yet if women not "in combat" are subject to the threat of an NBC attack, the combat exclusions are obsolete to the extent they are based on the fear of risk to women.

A second common argument favoring the combat exclusion cites the physical disadvantages of women, such as strength, stamina, and muscle. This diminished physical ability of women is often cited as the reason women cannot meet the physical demands of ground combat, including tasks such as carrying and lifting. Therefore, the argument continues, their presence impairs military efficiency (Tuten 1982, 247). Of course men who lack upper body strength are not for that reason prohibited from combat duty. Moreover, the statutes exclude women from combat ships and aircraft, not land activities. In reply, others point out that physical strength is only one of many attributes necessary to perform successfully as sailors and aviators, and physical conditioning may compensate for much lack of strength for ground troops. In addition, many have emphasized that the small physical stature of the Viet Cong and North Vietnamese did not lead to military success for the American forces whose troops were usually of larger stature. The issue is not one of lowering standards for performance to allow women to participate. Rather, it seems that efficiency should dictate gender-neutral determinations of whether or not an individual (male or female) has the competence, skill, and strength to serve in any given position. Note also that with the growing complexity of modern weapons systems, technical ability and education are becoming far more important than physical strength in determining eligibility and qualifications for many military positions.

Another popular argument used to justify the exclusion of women stresses the purported psychological differences between men and women. It is often claimed that women are less able than men to withstand the stress of combat, that women are too emotional and volatile to perform under combat stress. There are two strong replies to this argument. First, critics note the overall performance record of women in World War II, Korea, Vietnam, and more recently in Panama, Operation Desert Storm, and elsewhere, not only as nurses on the front lines but also as military police, pilots, flight engineers, and so on. Second, they point to the record of women who serve as urban police and firefighters under analogous stress. There does not seem to be documented evidence to establish the claim that women will deal less well than men with combat pressure.

Fourth, pregnancy and child-rearing are cited as reasons women cannot serve effectively in combat. It is claimed that pregnancy hinders military readiness, the ability to deploy rapidly, and the length of women's service careers (see Mitchell 1989; Yarborough 1985, 31, cited in "Combat Exclusion Laws" 1991, 25). These concerns may stem from a social perception of the "proper role" of women. But whatever their origin, they do not seem to acknowledge that women are pregnant only a short part of their lives, that some women never become pregnant at all, and that readiness procedures and policies could well accommodate the 5-10 percent of military women who are pregnant at any given time. Men as well as women have child care responsibilities, and all military personnel are expected to take responsibility for dependent care arrangements in case of a mobilization.

A fifth reason cited for excluding women from combat is the fear that some women will fail to develop a "team spirit" or "bond" with men in combat (see D'Amico 1990, 7). The assumption underlying this argument is that males will bond with males, and females with females, but bonding will not occur across the sexes. This argument mirrors similar claims about group cohesion used against allowing blacks in the military, indicating that fear and prejudice are at least partially at its base. Respondents argue that bonding is important, especially in military emergencies, but that it is more dependent on leadership, trust, organization for a common goal, the pressure of imminent danger, and a willingness to sacrifice than on any considerations relevant to sex differences. Respondents suggest the problem is not that women will not be active participants on the "team," but men's attitudes: men will not accept women with a "team" spirit unless encouraged to do so.

A sixth reason cited against allowing women in combat is that the presence of women will lead to sexual relationships and disruption of discipline. But this argument relies on the dubious assumptions that existing rules against sexual "fraternization" will not be obeyed and that sexual relationships will be more of a threat in combat situations than elsewhere in the military.

Seventh, some have expressed worries that if women participate in combat, the image of the U.S. armed forces will suffer. The simple reply to this is that Canada and Great Britain have now made it a violation of law to bar women from combat or to place restrictions on their number, and Israel conscripts women into the military. These countries, and others that include women in the military, do not appear to have a tarnished image of military strength and preparedness. Preparations to commit women to combat might, in contrast, demonstrate especially strong resolve.

Finally, a somewhat darker and more malevolent interpretation of the combat exclusion is that it is an expression of the belief that women are inherently inferior and therefore should have subordinate status. The nineteenth-century *Dred Scott* case provides an interesting analogy. When Justice Taney sought to explain why the drafters of the Constitution could not have intended to include blacks within the term "citizens," he relied in large part on the long-standing exclusion of blacks from service in the military. Taney understood how law can be used to express and reinforce subordinate status. He also understood the fundamental nature of the activity of defending one's country as an indication of one's worthiness.[12]

It is clear from this summary of justifications and replies that most of the arguments against allowing women in combat are based on sociopolitical considerations, some quite dubious, rather than military need. Not only are there readily available replies to these arguments favoring the combat exclusion, but there are also a variety of additional justifications for abolishing the exclusion. The most often cited is the impact on individual women in the military who face fewer job opportunities and choices (and therefore less access to medical, educational, retirement, and veterans' benefits), less opportunity for promotion and career advancement, as well as less opportunity to gain the experience needed to gain promotion. Sheila Tobias has argued that women's exclusion from combat has been a barrier to their political success as well (Elshtain and Tobias 1990, 163-88). Advocates for the exclusion argue that opening career opportunities for women is not a function of the armed forces.[13] But for years career opportunity has been an argument used to promote the military services for men.

More difficult to document is the morale problem for women who are capable of doing a job but who are nevertheless excluded and who are thus not able to get recognition for the tasks they can perform or the risky service they endure. A flip side of the morale problem is the resentment felt by males who feel they must hold more than their share of some undesirable duties because women trained to do them are precluded from that service. Low morale surely can affect military capability and management. Excluding women from combat can also limit military flexibility. Shifting and disrupting a crew in wartime damages cohesiveness and military readiness, for example. And troop movement can be delayed while military officials try to determine whether or not female personnel can participate. As Senator William Proxmire commented in 1986,

> Barring women from combat has resulted in complex and arbitrary restrictions that limit our military. (Congressional Record, March 21, 1986: S3182-3183, cited in Gordon and Ludvigson 1991, 16)
>
> The first consideration in any issue of military personnel must always be national security, and, indeed, that is my primary concern. The combat exclusion policies deprive our forward battle areas of available personnel resources and limit our flexibility. . . .
>
> I am not saying that every position should be open to every soldier. Of course no soldier should be assigned to a position for which he or she is not qualified. . . . Gender-neutral physical requirements would address this concern without arbitrarily excluding qualified candidates. . . . We are wasting our personnel resources. . . .
>
> It is important that those women feel that they are a valued part of our armed services and that they be regarded with ample opportunities for advancement. We owe them that. The women in the military serve our country faithfully, and, despite the combat exclusion policy, many women risk their lives every day at dangerous posts like the Mx and Minuteman launch sites. They must not be treated like second-class soldiers. (Gordon and Ludvigson 1991, 16-17)

Finally, there is the serious problem of defining "combat duty." Military definitions differentiate combat missions, close combat, direct combat, combat support, and combat service support, to name a few. The definitions are not always consistent from one branch of the services to another, leading to confusion and inconsistency in determinations of which positions are or are not open to women ("Combat Exclusion Laws" 1991, 11-14). Redefinition of positions in which women can serve results in reassignment, retraining, and career uncertainty, which in turn can affect retention and morale.

EQUALITY AND FEMINIST ANALYSIS

Bernard Williams has said: "Equality is a popular but mysterious political ideal. People can become equal (or at least more equal) in one way with the consequence that they become unequal (or more unequal) in others. . . . It does not follow that equality is worthless as an ideal" (Williams 1981, 185). Differentiating types of equality does not lessen the importance of equality.

Equal opportunity and equal treatment are two of the most distinctive conceptions of equality, and both are at issue for women in the military. During the 1970s there were many gains in these areas, achieved through the federal courts. Women won the right to the same benefits for dependents as males, the right to remain in the military after bearing children, the right to attend military academies, and the right to a lengthier discharge time frame than men, given that women had fewer promotional opportunities. Despite these successes the combat exclusion has remained in effect, and despite the numerous arguments and replies defending elimination of the exclusion, it is still widely supported both within and outside the military. Why is this? Why has the combat exclusion remained so entrenched? Why does the legacy of *Rostker* remain, leading many to deny the equality issues at stake?

Let me suggest two reasons. First, equality for women in the military has been precluded by subtle arguments that reappear. In 1979 in *Personnel Administration v.Feeney* (442 U.S. 256 [1979]) the Supreme Court upheld Massachusetts's absolute hiring preference for veterans, notwithstanding its obvious negative impact on women. The Court concluded that the legislature had no intention of discriminating against women, only the intention of helping veterans who just happened to be overwhelmingly male. *Feeney* is particularly relevant in two ways. It illustrates the economic subordination that comes with the military's exclusion of women. In addition, the opinion uses a two-step reasoning process similar to the *Rostker* analysis. In *Feeney* the Court assumed the legality of the previous exclusion of women from the military and focused only on the hiring preference. As explained above, in *Rostker* the Court assumed the legality of the combat exclusion and focused only on the draft exclusion. This sort of sequential reasoning is useful for condoning inequality and subordination. The inequality can be made to disappear if one assumes away its antecedent.

Second, feminist analysis applied to equal protection of the law can help us understand why the combat exclusion persists, and that understanding can in turn help us determine strategies to gain further equality for women through its abolition. Martha Minow has recently discussed ways of applying feminist analysis to the legal doctrine of equal protection of the law. She calls attention in particular to three assumptions underlying that doctrine:

> Feminist theorists stress and challenge three assumptions that usually remain unstated in analyses of equality and discrimination. The first is that the perspective of the excluded or subjugated person or group is irrelevant or untrustworthy in evaluating claims of discrimination: the perspective presumed relevant is that of those with the power to structure social institutions and to rule on charges of discrimination. The second assumption is that the equality inquiry does and should

use as the norm for whether likes are treated alike those who have been privileged in the past: generally, white, male, Christian, English-speaking, able-bodied persons. The third assumption is that the status quo in social and economic institutions is sufficiently fair and uncoerced, and resists change.

In making these assumptions explicit, feminists suggest that the assumptions are themselves contestable and that alternative starting points should be used. (Minow 1991, 639)

Consider the first assumption that the only relevant perspective for evaluating equal opportunity claims is that of those in power, not the perspectives of the complainants. We see this clearly at play in *Rostker* as well as in later arguments. Rehnquist, for example, does not see *Rostker* as a legitimate equal protection case. But the history of the adoption of the combat exclusion shows that deference to the legislature is very suspect in that case. First, almost no women in the military were questioned during the original hearings on the 1948 bill and the exclusion amendment. One male representative suggested its addition, and it was tacked on in a haphazard manner. Second, even in 1981, deference to the legislature basically meant deferring to the white males in power. It allowed virtually no input from women in general or women in the military. Even if not explicit or intended, women were treated from the early hearings to the *Rostker* decision as if they had no valuable or relevant input on the question. This is emphasized throughout later hearings when most testimony is from men who repeatedly refer to "them" or "those women." Clearly the perspective advanced is not that of women in the military.

Consider next the second assumption cited by Minow concerning who makes the determination when cases are "alike" or "similar" enough to require equal treatment. There is continued focus, from *Rostker* on, on the "proper role" for women, the need to protect women from harm, on physical strength, psychological ability to handle stress, on male bonding, and problems of pregnancy. That these are used repeatedly to differentiate men and women gives strong indication that the determination is being made by individuals who are reinforcing stereotypical views about women as fragile, emotional, and weak, who should be home tending their children, and who are thus not similar enough to men to be treated like them. The tendency to disregard the many counterarguments and contrary evidence on women's interest in serving in the military even under severe risks, on their effectiveness in military and civilian positions under combat-like stress, on their physical conditioning in the military, and on their qualifications for positions relying on education more than physical strength, points out that the norm being applied is one of a physically strong and unemotional male needed for ground combat. Given the contrast between the norm used and the stereotype of women appealed to, it is hardly surprising that women are judged not to be similarly situated to men, and are thus automatically excluded.

The refusal of advocates of the combat exclusion to allow career advancement to be considered a relevant or important military goal for women, despite repeated emphasis on it as a legitimate goal for men in service, shows as well that the female perspective is being ignored and that the norm being used necessarily excludes women. But it also illustrates reliance on the third assumption, that the status quo in social and economic institutions is viewed as sufficiently fair by those making decisions about women's role in the military. According to those defending the exclusion, men need the jobs, and there is no need to provide for or guarantee positions or promotions for women. The military is doing just fine as it is.

In sum, the arguments favoring the combat exclusion repeatedly ignore the perspective of women, rely on stereotypical views of their needs and abilities, and assume there is no difficulty with the status quo of the military, thereby ensuring that women cannot and will not be deemed similar enough to men to be treated alike. Using Minow's analysis, therefore, we can see that the question of whether or not to allow women in combat generates a paradigm equal protection case.

If this is correct, then there may be hope for change as more women are able to speak up and be heard in positions of authority and power. Since Sheila Widnall has been appointed Secretary of the Air Force, we can expect to have more military women called into hearings to voice their views on the qualifications and need for women in the services. Similarly, more military men and congressional leaders are taking views like that of Senator Proxmire. For example, former President Bush's Navy Secretary, Sean O'Keefe, urged (before he left office) that the navy should permit women to fly combat aircraft and serve on all navy ships and amphibious vessels (*Boston Globe*, January 7, 1993). Although his comments are not binding, they do signal a new attitude. We can also look forward to more women joining Representative Pat Schroeder on the Senate Armed Forces Committee. And we now have the new voice of Ruth Bader Ginsberg on the Supreme Court as a justice who is already articulately defending the strengths and abilities of women. These show, I believe, that we can expect and should demand future testimony and arguments to expose and reject the common assumptions made in the past.

CONCLUSION

Military policy has changed to allow women to serve in more positions, though this has often had less to do with logic and argumentation than with powerful events such as the navy's Tailhook scandal. However, combat restrictions still remain. Maintaining the exclusion for special flight operations units and for ground troops, for example, continues to reinforce stereotypes and perpetuate inequality for women. A blanket ground combat exclusion is unacceptable. The relevant question must be who is qualified to do the job. What is required is full acknowledgment that the issue of women in the military *is* a question of equal opportunity and that assumptions and arguments supporting the exclusion from the past to the present are deeply flawed.

Over the last twenty years arguments against women's combat service have changed to de-emphasize claims about the instability of women, but concerns about unit cohesion are still featured, and considerations of strength keep reappearing, particularly for the army and the marines. Future discussion must focus instead on the relevant considerations, equity and military need, both of which provide strong justifications for abolishing the combat exclusion.

One final point. I have focused until now on the combat exclusion, merely alluding to the sexual abuse and harassment now well documented in the armed services. (Tailhook is only one case. There are also reports of rape and sexual assault in the Persian Gulf during Operation Desert Storm and reports of various levels of sexual harassment including demeaning sexual jokes and demands for sex.) But combat exclusion and sexual harassment are closely connected.

Harassment and abuse are made worse by the exclusion. Wherever women are barred, their absence leads to a culture that breeds sexism and domination. It is arguable that integrating woman and giving them equal opportunity can lead to gains in equal treatment and can decrease sexism more effectively than instruction for men about sexual harassment. While harassment may initially increase with more inclusion of women, over the long term it will ease. Consider, for example, the experience in the air force where 97 percent of the jobs are open to women as opposed to only 59 percent of the jobs in the navy. The women in the air force who understand the technology are rarely harassed (*Time*, July 13, 1992). Until women can compete based on the same standards as men, they are likely to remain vulnerable to harassment and mistreatment. If they are not allowed to use their full abilities, it will continue to be easy for them to be treated as if they do not have the skills and to be stereotyped as unable, unqualified, and unneeded, as "detriments" to military effectiveness rather than the assets they are. Thus, another major argument for the elimination of the combat exclusion is its effectiveness in minimizing sexual harassment and abuse in the military.

NOTES

An earlier version of this paper was presented at a conference on Feminist Ethics and Social Policy at the University of Pittsburgh Graduate School of Public and International Affairs, November 6, 1993. Portions of this paper are reprinted in Bushnell (1995). I am grateful to participants at the conference as well as to Cynthia Enloe, Virginia Held, Susan

Brison, James Sterba, and the referees from *Hypatia* for helpful material and comments, though they may not all agree with my conclusions.

1. Recent books addressing the role of women in the military include Muir (1993) and Stiehm (1989). See Katzenstein (1993) for a review of both books.

2. *Rostker, Director of Selective Service v. Goldberg et al.*, 453 U.S. 57 (1981). Quotations from this case are noted in the text by page numbers. Note that *Rostker* involved a male plaintiff and the executive branch at the time supported registering women for the draft, but Congress disagreed.

3. The National Organization for Women, for example, submitted an amicus brief in *Rostker* supporting the draft of women as well as men. Other feminist groups disagreed. Similarly, with respect to the combat exclusion, women both within and outside the military hold different views.

4. From comments presented at a conference on Feminist Ethics and Social Policy at the University of Pittsburgh Graduate School of Public and International Affairs, November 6, 1993.

5. I am indebted to Virginia Held for these points.

6. The guarantee of equal protection is found in two amendments to the U.S. Constitution. The Fourteenth Amendment applies to actions of state governments, whereas the prohibitions of the Fifth Amendment apply to actions of the federal government and so are at stake here. Although the text of the Fifth Amendment does not expressly guarantee equal protection of the law, the U.S. Supreme Court has held that this guarantee is included within the due process clause of the Fifth Amendment in *Bolling v. Sharpe*, 347 U.S. 497 (1954).

7. Comments from Representative Andrews followed by two comments from Representative van Zandt. Cong. Rec. 2 June 1948: 6969 and 6869-70. Beginning in 1943, women serving in the Naval Reserve had been known as Women Accepted for Voluntary Emergency Services (WAVES).

8. Other restrictions included a separate rank and promotion structure for women and men, different minimum age restrictions on enlistment for women and men, a limitation on total female enlisted strength of 2 percent of personnel on duty in each service, a 10 percent ceiling on female officers who could serve as permanent regular lieutenant colonels and navy commanders, and a 20 percent ceiling in the navy for the number of lieutenant commanders. Many of these restrictions on rank and percentage limits were reversed in 1967 ("Combat Exclusion Laws" 1991, 3-5).

9. Hearings on Women in the Military, 1979 at 75 ("Combat Exclusion Laws" 1991, 9).

10. Susan Brison has pointed out to me that combat training provides important self-defense skills useful in nonmilitary contexts, and is arguably of equal or even greater value for women than for men.

11. "Combat Exclusion Laws" (1991, 22). See also Enloe (1983) for a description of how the government campaigned hard during the war to recruit women for military service and factory jobs (to replace the men who went off to war), and then after the war engaged in a full scale propaganda blitz to send women back to their homes so men could have their civilian jobs back.

12. I am grateful to a referee from this journal for this point.

13. For example, see opposing statements by J. Philip Anderegg and Nicholas Kamillatos, in "Combat Exclusion Laws" (1991, 49, 51).

My thanks to the NEH for a fellowship supporting this research.

REFERENCES

Bushnell, Dana. 1995. *Nagging Questions*. Lanham, MD: Rowman & Littlefield Publ. Inc.

D'Amico, Francine. 1990. Women at arms: The combat controversy. *Minerva: Quarterly Report on Women and the Military* 8(2): 1-35.

Elshtain, Jean Bethke and Sheila Tobias. 1990. *Women, militarism, and war: Essays in history, politics, and social history*. Lanhan, MD: Rowman and Littlefield.

Enloe, Cynthia. 1983. *Does khaki become you? The militarization of women's lives*. Boston: South End Press.

Gordon, Marilyn A. and Mary Jo Ludvigson. 1991. A constitutional analysis of the combat exclusion for air force women. *Minerva: Quarterly Report on Women and the Military* 9(2): 1-34. First published in different form in *U.S. Air Force Journal of Legal Studies* 1(1990), and *The Naval Law Review* 1(1990).

Harris, Adrienne and Ynestra King, eds. 1989. *Rocking the ship of state*. Boulder, CO: Westview.

Hartsock, Nancy. 1989. Masculinity, heroism, and the making of war. In *Rocking the ship of state*. See Harris and King 1989.

Held, Virginia. 1993. *Feminist morality*. Chicago: University of Chicago Press.

Katzenstein, Mary Fainsod. 1993. The right to fight. *The Women's Review of Books* 11(2): 30-31.

MacKinnon, Catharine. 1989. *Toward a feminist theory of the state*. Cambridge: Harvard University Press.

Minnow, Martha. 1991. Equalities. *The Journal of Philosophy* 88(11): 635-644.

Mitchell, B. 1989. *Weak link: Feminization of the American military*. Washington, DC: Regnery Gateway.

Muir, Kate. 1993. *Arms and the woman*. London: Hodder and Stroughton.

Reardon, Betty. 1985. *Sexism and the war system*. New York: Teachers College Press.

Ruddick, Sara. 1980. Maternal thinking. *Feminist Studies* 6: 342-67.

Stiehm, Judith. 1983. The protected, the protector, the defender. In *Women's and men's wars*. New York: Pergamon Press.

Stiehm, Judith Hicks. 1989. *Arms and the enlisted woman*. Philadelphia: Temple University Press.

Swerdlow, Amy. 1989. Pure milk, not poison: Women strike for peace and the test ban treaty of 1963. In *Rocking the ship of state*. See Harris and King 1989.

The combat exclusion laws: An idea whose time has gone. 1991. The Association of the Bar of the City of New York Committee on Military Affairs and Justice. *Minerva: Quarterly Report on Women and the Military* 9(4): 1-55.

Tuten, Jeff M. 1982. The argument against female combatants. In *Female soldiers-combatants or noncombatants: Historical and contemporary perspectives*, ed. Nancy Loring Goldman. Westport, CT: Greenwood.

Williams, Bernard. 1981. What is equality? Pt. 1 of Equality of welfare. *Philosophy and Public Affairs* 10(3): 185-224.

Yarborough, J. 1985. Sex and the military: The feminist mistake. *Current*, 27-32.

LISE VOGEL

Considering Difference: The Case of the U.S. Family and Medical Leave Act of 1993

The 1993 Family and Medical Leave Act (FMLA) has been widely hailed as a significant step forward in U.S. social policy. For the first time, American women's need for maternity leave has been addressed by national legislation. The statute requires employers to provide time off to employees for a variety of reasons, including pregnancy, childbirth, and care of a newborn.[1] Leave is unpaid but jobs and benefits are protected. About 60 percent of the workforce is covered by the FMLA.

Meager though the FMLA's benefits actually are when measured by international standards (Smirnov 1979; Stoiber 1989), politicians and the media claim its passage constitutes a sea change. At last the notion that the state should help its citizens meld family and work responsibilities has been put on the U.S. policy agenda. In Vice President Albert Gore's words, "American families will no longer have to choose between their families and their jobs" (Clymer 1993).

U.S. feminists likewise welcome the new legislation but add words of caution. During the eight years it was under congressional consideration, the FMLA attracted substantial feminist criticism. Its benefits were dismissed as too limited to be useful to those most in need. Its gender-neutral legal form was viewed as problematic, given the particular needs of women and the structural realities of the U.S. workplace.

Social Politics   Spring 1995

Its ideological implications were characterized as assimilationist—constructing women as just like men in all relevant respects—and thereby insensitive to gender differences.

In this agenda I examine the feminist critique of the FMLA. In particular, I challenge the common assumption that the legislation's gender-neutral design necessarily entails an assimilationist vision. Far from assimilationist, the FMLA takes account of special needs. Despite its substantive limitations, the legislation represents, I argue, an important new direction in U.S. social policy.

The Critique

Two charges exemplify feminists' misgivings about the Family and Medical Leave Act. The first targets its supposed disregard of the gender specialness of pregnancy and motherhood. Critics note that pregnancy is a physiologically normal process. As the physician and feminist activist Wendy Chavkin puts it (1984, 202), pregnancy "is not an illness. Rather, it is a unique condition that may be accompanied by special needs and sometimes by illness." The FMLA's treatment of pregnancy as if it were a medical problem is thus, in the critics' view, inappropriate. The legislation also ignores, it is suggested, the unique social contribution of mothers, who are largely responsible for nurturing society's next generation. By taking pregnancy to be akin to a disability, the FMLA thus fails to consider women's special difference and mothers' special role.

The second charge focuses on social class. Along with conservatives who have tagged the FMLA a "yuppie bill" (e.g., Winston and Bane 1993, 239–46), feminist critics claim the legislation will mainly cover women with professional and other high-status careers. Working-class women—the vast majority of women workers—are less likely to have access to family and medical leave because they tend to work in smaller firms and to have more intermittent employment. Even when covered, the critics argue, working-class women can't afford to take unpaid leaves. Thus the historian Alice Kessler-Harris worries that the Family and Medical Leave Act would benefit those who least need it—"women and men who could in any event take the time off" (quoted in Bacchi 1990, 119). The legal scholar Martha Minow suggests more generally that the statute ignores not only social class but also a range of alternative family lifestyles: "problems of exclusion hobble the bill and expose it to charges of cultural, racial and class myopia" (1990, 155).

These two charges center on the extent to which the FMLA seems to require denial of the special physiological and social character of motherhood, on the one hand, and of class and other group differences, on the other.[2] The legislation is said to posit a single normative experience that is supposedly gender-neutral but is actually male. The failure of the FMLA derives, in other words, from its assimilationist assumption that women can and should behave just like men—indeed, just like white, upper-middle-class men.

Feminists who make these charges often identify with the more progressive sectors of the contemporary women's movement. Their qualms about gender neutrality and assimilationism reflect their commitment to addressing the needs of working-class women, poor women, and women of color. Looking longingly at European-style welfare programs, they belittle the ideological adequacy of the FMLA as much as they criticize its practical usefulness.

Equality, Gender Neutrality, and Assimilationism

Feminist questions about the Family and Medical Leave Act draw on more than a decade of critique of the concept of equality.[3] This literature argues that equality notions are embedded in Enlightenment constructions of citizens as identical abstract individuals. Yet the universal citizen turns out to be not only gendered as male but also disembodied, strangely unencumbered, and, perhaps, of a dominant class and race. State policies that appear to be neutral thus in fact presume citizens to have gender (and class and race) specificity. Armed with these insights, scholars have unmasked the gendered character and group-specific workings of the modern welfare state.

In these accounts, difference is central while equality and gender neutrality appear to be scams devised to benefit men. The issues came compellingly to the attention of the U.S. women's movement in the early 1980s, as litigation concerning maternity policy in the workplace moved through the courts (Kay 1985; Vogel 1990). Given the special demands of pregnancy and motherhood on women workers, feminists asked, can treating women equally be fair? What about the family obligations for which women have disproportionate responsibility? Don't gender-neutral policies deny the unique character of women? Feminist scholars and activists divided in acrimonious debate. Confronted with the apparently unbridgeable opposition between equality and difference, many rejected equality and the gender-neutral policy framework of liberal feminism. Female specificity now seemed the policy approach most likely to accommodate the needs of women.

According to the FMLA's critics, in short, gender-neutral policies wear a mantle of fairness but actually disadvantage women by insisting they renounce special needs. That is, gender neutrality in policy is assumed to be unavoidably coupled with a vision of the just society as assimilationist. Is this assumption warranted?

319

Assimilationism constructs women as fundamentally the same as men and supposes men to be the unencumbered abstract individuals of liberal theory. Targeting obstacles to women's full participation in society, assimilationism seeks policies that treat women and men in an identical manner. It therefore has difficulty incorporating the specificities associated with childbearing. Traditionally, assimilationists ignored them by focusing on the so-called public sphere. More recently, they have addressed physiological sex differences by making a close analogy or equation of female-specific traits to already recognized characteristics—converting pregnancy, for example, into a temporary disability.

Although assimilationism was implicit in the efforts of most U.S. feminist policy activists during the 1960s and 1970s, it is not the only possible position on the equality side of the equality-versus-difference dichotomy. A range of positions actually stretches across the distance between the dichotomy's poles, nearly all of which call for recognizing "difference" (i.e., specificity) alongside equality. In the mid-1970s, for example, androgyny, a new understanding of feminist objectives, became popular. Like assimilationism, androgyny uses analogy to deal with the stubborn specificity of sex-unique traits. But it shifts the object of the analogy from physiological characteristics to persons. That is, it invokes analogies not in order to convert sex-specific physical conditions to a supposedly universal basis, but to draw out the commonalities in the lives of differently-sexed persons.

Androgyny and assimilationism offer different analyses and have divergent practical implications. In the case of pregnancy, for example, the assimilationist likening of pregnancy to disability obliterates the embodied specificity of gender. By contrast, androgyny constructs pregnant women as different from their coworkers but with analogously special needs when temporarily unable to work. In this way androgyny can acknowledge the special character of pregnancy within a gender-neutral legal framework. The 1978 Pregnancy Discrimination Act, for example, is a gender-neutral measure that implies androgyny, not assimilationism (Vogel 1993). It does not define pregnancy as a temporary disability but instead requires employers to make analogies across the bodily diversity of their employees—temporarily disabled or able-bodied, women or men.

A third vision of the meaning of equality has recently been proposed by the political scientist Susan Moller Okin. In her view, which I call "genderlessness," gender would be eliminated in the ideal future. As in assimilationism, a person's sex would become as irrelevant as eye color in shaping his or her social experience. But Okin recognizes, as assimilationists do not, that removing obstacles is not enough. To achieve the gender-free society requires a massive restructuring of social institutions and Okin proposes an array of practical measures: parental leave, subsidized day care, flexible working hours, more equitable post-divorce parenting arrangements, and so on. In the long run, she argues, a genderless society will provide the best context for both the development of human capacities and the realization of social justice.

Still on the equality side of the debate, I have suggested (Vogel 1993) a fourth approach: differential consideration. If we take differential consideration as our perspective, we envision a society in which individuals are diverse, embodied, and at times burdened with special needs and responsibilities, yet also deserving of equal treatment.

Each of these equality positions—assimilationism, androgyny, genderlessness, and differential consideration—can be put into practice by means of gender-neutral measures. No necessary association links gender neutrality as a policy approach to assimilationism as a social vision. While some gender-neutral policies are indeed normatively male, others are gender-inclusive, even diversity-inclusive. That is, gender-neutral policies are not intrinsically unable to recognize human heterogeneity and connection. The trick, here, is in the specifics.

The Family and Medical Leave Act

The Family and Medical Leave Act of 1993 is a statute whose complex structure is not well understood. Feminist critics impugn its gender neutrality, but the media and popular opinion believe it to be a special-treatment policy to help working mothers care for their children. In reality, the FMLA is gender-neutral legislation that manages to address special needs. Because of widespread confusion about the statute, it is useful to review its provisions.

As its name suggests, the FMLA provides two distinct kinds of job- and benefit-protected leaves. Family leave has drawn the most attention, for it represents an innovation in U.S. employment policy. Family leave allows an employee time off to care for family members—a newborn, a newly adopted child, or a seriously ill child, spouse, or parent. Family leave will, of course, benefit women, who still bear primary responsibility for family caretaking. But family leave for men is not unimportant. Some will use it to care for a new baby or to accompany a sick child to the hospital. Others will take the leave to care for a mother with Alzheimer's or a father with a fractured hip.

Medical leave, the rarely mentioned other half of the FMLA, is not a new kind of benefit. Traditionally called disability leave, medical leave gives an employee time off to recover from her or his own temporarily disabling health condition. Many workers will find the FMLA's medical leave component at least as important to them as family leave. Only five U.S. states and Puerto Rico require employers to allow a temporarily disabled employee to take time off. Until the passage of the FMLA, the majority of American workers had no job-protected disability leave. For a worker felled by a medical emergency, job-guaranteed medical leave will be the FMLA's unexpected boon.

In sum, the FMLA provides benefits for a variety of off-the-job needs to women and men participating in a spectrum of household and family arrangements. Whether they need to care for others or for themselves, employees can take time off and then return to their jobs with seniority and health coverage intact. As for maternity leave, the legislation entitles a new mother to both medical leave (for difficulties of pregnancy and recovery from childbirth) and family leave (to care for the new baby). By dividing maternity leave in this way, public policy can now consider the special needs of working mothers without disregarding those of their coworkers.

In my interpretation, the Family and Medical Leave Act is an example of differential consideration. It does not provide preferential treatment for women as a special group, but neither are its benefits rigidly the same for all. Instead, it recognizes that workers all have personal needs and family responsibilities that their employers should acknowledge. By addressing a diversity of special needs within a formally gender-neutral framework, the legislation assumes employees to be heterogeneous, embodied, encumbered, sometimes specially needy, but also equally entitled. That is, it posits a new sort of normative worker. However restricted its coverage and benefits, the FMLA creatively rethinks an old dilemma and marks a new path for U.S. public policy in the 1990s.

The Critique Revisited

The media, the public, and many feminists do not appreciate the innovative design of the Family and Medical Leave Act. Relying on a set of familiar pairings, they interpret the statute in terms of dichotomies: equality/difference, same-treatment/special-treatment, gender-neutrality/female-specificity, and so forth. Thus they miss the way the FMLA resists such oppositions by constructing the normative worker in a new way. And they make the charges that the measure cannot encompass women's special difference and that it is a class-biased or "yuppie" bill.

Yet, as demonstrated in the previous section, the FMLA does not disregard the specialness of pregnancy and motherhood. The strength of differential consideration as a policy orientation is precisely its ability to affirm specificity without giving up universalism. Feminists designed the FMLA to address women's particular situation as mothers and simultaneously offer benefits on an equal basis to all. Launched to help women workers, the statute turns out to have a broader scope. Indeed, I suspect that the general lack of job-guaranteed temporary disability leave in the U.S. workplace will make medical leave for nonmaternity purposes the most frequently used benefit in the FMLA's package.

The critics' inability to see the FMLA as a differential consideration policy in part flows from an underestimation of the range of available policy options. Believing they must choose between equality in the form of parental leave and difference in the form of maternity leave, they opt for difference.[4] But parental leave is only one—and not the best— of several possible gender-neutral policies that can address the needs of working mothers.

The rejection of the FMLA as class-biased legislation is problematic on several counts. It is of course true that the 40 percent of the workforce not covered are those perhaps most in need of its benefits. But the statute's limited scope is a typical outcome of the difficult and conflict-ridden process of enacting reforms (Bunch 1987; Smart 1989; Eisenstein 1990). Feminist academics who wish to produce better policies for women too often assume it is possible to design legislation without considering context and history. Backing female-specific measures in emulation of European-style welfare provision, they overlook the peculiar trajectory of twentieth-century U.S. social policy. In particular, where European female-specific policies have always been embedded in comprehensive welfare programs, the most powerful legacy of U.S. female-specific legislation is discrimination. Recent reforms have eliminated the legal basis for most sex discrimination, but the tradition of paternalist yet discriminatory protection remains.

As history suggests, female-specific policies can all too easily be used to deny benefits to women. For example, the female-specific California statute (Kay 1985, 12n. 69) that triggered litigation and the 1980s' equality-versus-difference debates covered women in small firms with ambiguous consequences. Its requirement that employers provide pregnancy disability leave represented an important benefit. Yet the same legislation allowed firms to exclude pregnancy from their health plans. Working-class women have a pressing need for both kinds of benefits, but I doubt they would choose access to *unpaid* disability leave over coverage of the medical costs of pregnancy.

Feminist critics of the FMLA also misread the legislation's utility for those working-class women it covers. Here again, the baseline for comparison is not Europe but the United States. Faced with a family crisis, American workers have traditionally had no protection. Thus, the job- and benefit-guaranteed leave offered by the FMLA sets an important new labor standard. Painfully limited though the benefits are, they are significantly better than nothing. As Karen Nussbaum, then of the Service Employees International Union (SEIU) and now director of the Women's Bureau, said in testimony to Congress: "Though it is hard for a low-wage worker to take an unpaid leave, it is harder to lose your job entirely and start looking for a new one after the birth or illness of a child" (Senate 1987, 219).

Conclusion

Whether female-specific or gender-neutral, U.S. public policy is not likely soon to provide the benefits women workers need: income replacement while on leave, adequate health care, quality child care, better schools and housing, and so on. The American women's movement has been struggling for years simply to get a bit of unpaid leave. Employers continue to get away with not providing what little the law requires, particularly in small firms where working-class women often work. In the contemporary U.S. context—a stingy welfare state, a tradition of discriminatory protection, divide-and-conquer management, propensity to backlash, and persistent economic recession—female-specific measures remain risky.

With all its limitations, the Family and Medical Leave Act offers a significant new approach to social provision in the U.S. workplace. Employers must henceforth acknowledge the off-the-job needs of their workers. And they must do so in a way that respects their employees' diversity—in gender, parenthood, family status, household structure, stage in the life cycle, and so forth. The FMLA may also become the basis for an expansion of such specificity-affirming benefits. Even in the difficult economic climate of the late twentieth century, some state and local family and medical leave legislation already goes further—covering workers in smaller firms, providing longer leaves, and defining family membership and caretaking needs more broadly (Lenhoff and Becker 1989; Sementilli-Dann et al. 1991; WLDF 1992). Paid leave may also be entering the policy agenda. Feminist policy analysts point, for example, to the effectiveness of mandatory temporary disability insurance (TDI) programs (IWPR n.d. [1993]). Currently in force in only five states and Puerto Rico, TDI laws require even tiny firms to give time off with pay to temporarily disabled employees. Costs are spread widely by collecting small premiums from the state's many employers and/or employees. Why not use the same approach to fund paid family and medical leave for all workers?

The Family and Medical Leave Act shows that the alternative to female-specificity is not necessarily an uncaring yuppie-style assimilationism. Feminists can refuse to be pushed to one side of the supposed equality/difference dichotomy. And they can look more creatively for policies that embody the kind of radical approach to heterogeneity I am calling differential consideration.

NOTES

1. As detailed below, the FMLA actually offers leave to both male and female employees who need time to care for family members or to recover from their own serious health problem.

2. A third feminist charge against the FMLA suggests that it risks triggering discrimination by employers against women of childbearing age. Unlike the two critiques considered here, this charge originates in the mainstream feminist community, which is wary of any policy that can be perceived to single women out and treat them in a special manner.

3. For a sampling of this literature, see Phillips (1987), Meehan and Sevenhuijsen (1991), and Barrett and Phillips (1992).

4. Those who pose such choices do not always make clear what they mean by maternity leave (e.g., McDonald 1993). The term maternity leave traditionally refers to leave taken by biological mothers during pregnancy, for childbirth, and to care for infants and young children. In the late twentieth-century U.S. policy context, maternity leave has been differentiated into a combination of pregnancy disability leave and parental leave.

REFERENCES

Bacchi, Carol Lee. 1990. *Same Difference: Feminism and Sexual Difference.* Sydney, Australia: Allen and Unwin.

Barrett, Michele, and Anne Phillips. 1992. *Destabilizing Theory: Contemporary Feminist Debates.* Stanford, Calif.: Stanford University Press.

Bunch, Charlotte. 1987. *Passionate Politics: Feminist Theory in Action.* New York: St. Martin's Press.

Chavkin, Wendy. 1984. "Walking a Tightrope: Pregnancy, Parenting, and Work." Pp. 196–213 in *Double Exposure: Women's Health Hazards on the Job and at Home,* ed. Wendy Chavkin. New York: Monthly Review Press.

Clymer, Adam. 1993. "Congress Passes Measure Providing Emergency Leaves." *New York Times,* Feb. 5.

Eisenstein, Hester. 1991. *Gender Shock: Practicing Feminism on Two Continents.* Boston: Beacon Press.

Institute for Women's Policy Research (IWPR). n.d. [1993]. "Research-in-brief: What Is Temporary Disability Insurance?" Washington, D.C.: Institute for Women's Policy Research.

Kay, Herma Hill. 1985. "Equality and Difference: The Case of Pregnancy." *Berkeley Women's Law Journal* 1 (Fall): 1–38.

Lenhoff, Donna R., and Sylvia M. Becker. 1989. "Family and Medical Leave Legislation in the States: Toward a Comprehensive Approach." *Harvard Journal on Legislation* 26 (Summer): 403–63.

McDonald, Marian. 1993. Review of *For Whose Protection? Reproductive Hazards and Exclusionary Policies in the United States and Britain,* by Sally J. Kenney. In *Women's Review of Books* 10 (Sept.): 25–26.

Meehan, Elizabeth, and Selma Sevenhuijsen, eds. 1991. *Equality Politics and Gender.* London: Sage.

Minow, Martha. 1990. "Adjudicating Difference: Conflicts among Feminist

Lawyers." Pp. 149–63 in *Conflicts in Feminism*, ed. Marianne Hirsch and Evelyn Fox Keller. New York: Routledge.

Okin, Susan Moller. 1989. *Justice, Gender, and the Family*. New York: Basic Books.

Phillips, Anne, ed. *Feminism and Equality*. New York: New York University Press.

Sementilli-Dann, Lisa, with Eva Gasser-Sanz, Alison Lowen, Stephen T. Middlebrook, Glenn Northern, Janice Steinschneider, and Sharon Stoneback. 1991. *Family and Medical Leave: Strategies for Success*. Washington, D.C.: Center for Policy Alternatives.

Smart, Carol. 1989. *Feminism and the Power of Law*. London: Routledge.

Smirnov, S. A. 1979. "Maternity Protection: National Law and Practice in Selected European Countries." *International Social Security Review* 32:420–44.

Stoiber, Susanne A. 1989. *Parental Leave and "Woman's Place": The Implications and Impact of Three European Approaches to Family Leave Policy*. Washington, D.C.: Women's Research and Education Institute.

Vogel, Lise. 1990. "Debating Difference: Feminism, Pregnancy, and the Workplace." *Feminist Studies* 16 (Spring): 9–32.

———. 1993. *Mothers on the Job: Maternity Policy in the U.S. Workplace*. New Brunswick, N.J.: Rutgers University Press.

U.S. Senate. 1987. Subcommittee on Labor-Management Relations and Subcommittee on Labor Standards of the Committee on Education and Labor. *Family and Medical Leave Act of 1987* (FMLA). 100th Cong., 1st sess., Feb. 25 and Mar. 5. Karen Nussbaum's testimony.

Winston, Kenneth, and Mary Jo Bane, eds. 1993. *Gender and Public Policy: Cases and Comments*. Boulder, Colo.: Westview Press.

Women's Legal Defense Fund (WLDF). 1992. *State Laws and Regulations Guaranteeing Employees Their Jobs after Family and Medical Leaves*. Washington, D.C.: Women's Legal Defense Fund.

What's Sex Got To Do with It?

Miranda Oshige*

Plaintiffs in Title VII hostile work environment cases must prove that the sexually oriented misconduct they suffered was both pervasive and unwelcome. In this note, Miranda Oshige argues that these requirements conflict with the language and purpose of Title VII because they insulate from liability some discrimination against women in the workplace. Ms. Oshige proposes that the hostile work environment violation be conceived as simply a form of gender-based disparate treatment, rather than as "sexual" harassment. Accordingly, she argues, welcomeness should be reconfigured as an affirmative defense, and pervasiveness considered only when measuring damages, not as an element of the claim. Thus conceived, Ms. Oshige contends, hostile work environment doctrine would more faithfully reflect Congress' mandate to achieve equality in the workplace regardless of gender.

Charles Hardy treated Teresa Harris differently than the men who worked for him. He dropped things on the floor and asked her to pick them up.[1] He suggested she go with him to the local Holiday Inn to negotiate her raise.[2] He asked her to retrieve coins from the front pocket of his pants.[3] He called her a "dumb ass woman."[4] He told her in front of other workers that she must have promised a customer sex to get him to sign a deal with the company.[5] Harris sued him under Title VII, claiming that Hardy's actions discriminated against her by creating a hostile work environment.[6] Title VII of the Civil Rights Act of 1964 prohibits an employer from discriminating "against any individual with respect to . . . compensation, terms, conditions or, privileges of employment, because of such individual's . . . sex."[7] Although the language of Title VII plainly seems to condemn boorish behavior like Hardy's, Harris lost her case in both the district and circuit courts.[8] While the Supreme Court reversed the circuit court's decision, it did so on a narrow ground that fails to clarify the doctrinal confusion that caused Harris to lose her case in the lower courts.

Congress originally enacted Title VII of the Civil Rights Act of 1964 to prohibit discrimination in the workplace on the basis of race, color, religion, or

---

* Third-year student, Stanford Law School. This is for David, who makes everything possible.
1. Harris v. Forklift Sys., Inc., 114 S. Ct. 367, 369 (1993).
2. *Id.*
3. *Id.*
4. *Id.*
5. *Id.*
6. *Id.*
7. 42 U.S.C. § 2000e-2(a)(1) (1988).
8. *Harris*, 114 S. Ct. at 369-70.

national origin.[9] The prohibition against discrimination on the basis of sex was added to Title VII only as a last-minute amendment.[10] As a result, judges have little to guide them in the attempt to define the contours of sex discrimination in the workplace. At the very least, the language of the statute suggests that Title VII should guarantee women an equal working environment. That guarantee, however, has gone unfulfilled, particularly with respect to working women who are subjected to abusive conduct at their place of employment.

In this note I examine the inadequate judicial treatment of sex discrimination claims. In particular, I focus on the hostile work environment doctrine and analyze its application by the courts. Currently, in order to win a Title VII hostile work environment claim, an employee must prove that: (1) her employer subjected her to abusive conduct of a sexual nature, (2) she did not welcome it, (3) the conduct was both severe and pervasive enough that it unreasonably altered her working conditions, and (4) that it would have done so for a reasonable person in her situation.[11] Because the burden of establishing these facts rests with the plaintiff, women subject to discriminatory workplace conduct often find that they must endure degrading and humiliating inquiries about their sexual histories, as defendants attempt to cast them as unworthy of protection by Title VII. Under the perverse structure of current law, a female employee who brings criminal rape charges against her supervisor is protected from such inquiries in a criminal trial. But a woman who brings a civil suit for a hostile work environment against her supervisor based on the same conduct may expect every aspect of her life—from past boyfriends to her dress to her sense of humor—to be fair game for discovery and manipulation before a trier of fact.[12]

A close analysis of the hostile work environment doctrine and its development reveals a judicial assumption that society generally desires, and therefore that courts should tolerate, flirtation and other sexually based interactions, even in the workplace. Thus, courts have developed a standard for hostile work environment claims that require proof of "unwelcome" and severe or pervasive sexual harassment, presumably to protect "normal" and "desirable" sexual behavior at work. I argue that this fear of penalizing (and thus chilling) "normal" behavior in the workplace pollutes the hostile work environment doctrine and undermines the role of women in the workplace.

Framing the hostile work environment cause of action in terms of "sexual" harassment creates unnecessary hurdles for plaintiffs alleging discrimination. First, the current case law unnecessarily burdens plaintiffs by requiring them to prove that they did not welcome the discriminatory conduct. Moreover, under current doctrine, a woman can state a claim only if she has suffered outrageous conduct that courts deem beyond the boundaries of normal courting. Because courts require plaintiffs to establish the severity and pervasiveness of the objec-

---

9. H.R. Rep. No. 914, 88th Cong., 2d Sess. 2 (1964).
10. 110 Cong. Rec. 2577 (1964).
11. *Harris,* 114 S. Ct. at 370; Meritor Sav. Bank v. Vinson, 477 U.S. 57, 65-68 (1986).
12. *See* note 86 *infra;* text accompanying notes 86-88 *infra.*

tionable conduct, implicitly they condone a certain level of discriminatory conduct in the workplace.

To eliminate the substantial problems caused by these deficiencies, I propose that the hostile work environment cause of action be reconfigured simply as *gender-based disparate treatment*. Under such a configuration, Title VII liability would depend upon: (1) whether the employer subjected the plaintiff to disparate treatment; (2) whether the disparate treatment would not have occurred if the plaintiff had been a man—that is, because of the plaintiff's gender; and (3) whether the disparate treatment reflected invidious stereotypes about women.[13] In determining whether a plaintiff welcomed the conduct at issue, courts should strictly limit their inquiry to whether the plaintiff actually initiated the conduct. Welcomeness should also be reconfigured as an affirmative defense, and defendants should bear this burden. Further, stricter evidentiary rules should govern the admission of evidence as to whether the plaintiff welcomed the discriminatory behavior. Finally, the question of the pervasiveness of the hostile work environment should only arise in connection with damages, not in the liability phase of the trial.[14] As a result, an employer who argues that his discriminatory conduct was not severe enough to amount to "real" harassment will not escape liability for discrimination. On the other hand, employers will only be liable for the damages they cause: Employers causing little harm will pay little, but employers causing substantial harm will pay more substantial damages.

I. *HARRIS, MERITOR*, AND THE LIMITS OF THE HOSTILE WORK ENVIRONMENT CAUSE OF ACTION

During oral argument before the Supreme Court in *Harris*, some of the justices posed a fundamental question for Title VII sexual harassment claims: Why was there any real argument over what should have been an obvious violation of Title VII under a hostile work environment theory?[15] More specifically, as Justice Ginsburg inquired during oral argument and in her concurrence, why is it not enough for Title VII purposes that Hardy's misconduct forced Harris to endure different working conditions because she is a wo-

---

13. This formulation borrows from 14th Amendment gender equal protection jurisprudence, which in evaluating whether disparate treatment constitutes invidious discrimination looks to whether the discrimination reflects "archaic and stereotypic" generalizations about women. *See* Mississippi Univ. for Women v. Hogan, 458 U.S. 718, 725 (1982) (holding that a university's refusal to admit men into its nursing school violates the 14th Amendment because it perpetuates the stereotype that nursing is exclusively a woman's job).

14. Such an approach would parallel the mixed-motive cause of action. In a mixed-motive case, if a defendant employer considered race, gender, or other impermissible factors in its decision to hire, fire, or not promote an employee, it is liable under Title VII. Liability attaches even if the employer had independent, nondiscriminatory reasons for its decision. 42 U.S.C. § 2000e-2(m) (Supp. V 1993). That the employer would have made the same decision regardless of discriminatory motive only mitigates damages. *See id.* § 2000e-5(g)(2)(B) (stating that in such a case a court may grant attorneys' fees and costs or declaratory or injunctive relief). An employer in a hostile work environment case, reconfigured as I propose as a gender-based disparate treatment case, similarly would not be able to escape liability for its discrimination by arguing that the discrimination was minimal. The degree of discrimination, as in mixed-motive cases, would be relevant only to assess damages and not to determine liability.

15. Lyle Denniston, *Ginsburg: Not a Tentative Beginner*, AM. LAW., Dec. 1993, at 84, 84-85.

man?[16] Unfortunately, the *Harris* Court did not confront the challenge Justice Ginsburg's question posed. Instead, the Court analyzed Harris' case as a hostile work environment claim and held that Harris lost in the trial and appellate courts simply because the lower courts had simply misinterpreted the Supreme Court's landmark hostile work environment case, *Meritor Savings Bank v. Vinson*.[17] The Court's conclusion that the district and circuit courts had misinterpreted *Meritor* does not speak well for the clarity of the rule set forth in that case. More importantly, any legal standard that could lead the district and circuit courts to characterize *Harris* as a "close case"[18] cannot offer a plausible interpretation of Title VII.

According to the Court, the Sixth Circuit erred in requiring Harris to prove that the defendant's conduct had inflicted tangible psychological injury.[19] The Court overturned that requirement, holding that "[w]hen the workplace is permeated with 'discriminatory intimidation ridicule, and insult,' that is 'sufficiently severe or pervasive to alter the conditions of the victim's employment and create an abusive working environment,' Title VII is violated."[20] This standard, which incorporates the language of *Meritor* that led the Sixth Circuit to impose a "tangible psychological injury" test in the first place, seems unlikely to provide any real guidance to courts faced with hostile work environment claims.

Perhaps aware that such a vague standard would provide little guidance to lower courts, the Court discussed some factors to be considered in determining whether an employer's conduct had crossed the line from being merely offensive to creating a hostile or abusive work environment. Lower courts must examine "all the circumstances"[21] and evaluate the "frequency of the discriminatory conduct; its severity; whether it is physically threatening or humiliating, or a mere offensive utterance; and whether it unreasonably interferes with an employee's work performance."[22]

The Court's opinion implies two further holdings of paramount importance to Title VII hostile work environment claims. First, the Court reiterated *Meritor*'s conclusion that the " 'mere utterance of an . . . epithet [that] engenders offensive feelings in a[n] employee,' does not sufficiently affect the conditions of employment to implicate Title VII."[23] By minimizing such behavior, the

---

16. *Harris*, 114 S. Ct. at 372 (Ginsburg, J., concurring).
17. *Id.* at 371. Meritor Savings Bank v. Vinson, 477 U.S. 57 (1986), held that sex discrimination under Title VII is not limited to tangible economic injury and that employees are entitled to a work environment free of "discriminatory intimidation, ridicule, and insult." *Id.* at 65.
18. *Harris*, 114 S. Ct. at 369.
19. *Id.* at 370.
20. *Id.* (quoting *Meritor*, 477 U.S. at 65, 67) (footnotes omitted).
21. *Id.* at 371.
22. *Id.*.
23. *Id.* at 370 (quoting *Meritor*, 477 U.S. at 67) (footnote omitted). In *Meritor*, the Court noted in dicta for the first time that a single epithet could not alone violate Title VII. 477 U.S. at 67. *Meritor* relied on Rogers v. EEOC, 454 F.2d 234 (5th Cir. 1971), *cert. denied*, 406 U.S. 957 (1972). The 5th Circuit in *Rogers* was the first to recognize that race-based comments in the workplace could form the basis of a cause of action under Title VII if they created a working environment "so heavily polluted with discrimination as to destroy completely the emotional and psychological stability of minority group workers." 454 F.2d at 238. Interestingly, although *Meritor* and *Harris* quote *Rogers* with approval in

Court creates a safe harbor for discrimination: Calling a woman one offensive gender-based name does not amount to cognizable disparate treatment in the workplace. Second, and more generally, under *Harris* an employer does not violate Title VII even if the employer treats female employees differently than male employees. Some disparate treatment—that is, some discrimination—is permissible in the workplace so long as the employer's discriminatory conduct does not *unreasonably* interfere with the employee's ability to do her work. What the Court means by "unreasonably" is not entirely clear; one can only wonder what "reasonable" interference with a woman's work would look like.

Title VII's language certainly does not compel either of these requirements; to the contrary, a persuasive argument may be made that the requirements are fundamentally at odds with both Title VII's language and its purpose. Title VII sets a standard that would prohibit behavior far less egregious than what the courts presently require to establish a hostile work environment claim. In order to make the doctrine consistent with the statute, a plaintiff should only have to prove that the employer's conduct, in Justice Ginsburg's words, makes "it more difficult [for the plaintiff] to do the job."[24] In light of Title VII's plain language, the Court has an uphill battle in justifying why it would require plaintiffs to show pervasiveness and unreasonable interference with their ability to do work in order to state a hostile work environment claim. The Court did not offer any justification in either *Meritor* or *Harris*. These requirements appeared *ipse dixit*, with little discussion and nothing that approaches a persuasive justification.

Analytically, Justice Ginsburg's concurrence breaks further with the majority in *Harris* than her conciliatory language suggests. She does not just argue that a plaintiff should only have to show that her employer's conduct made it more difficult for her to do her job. Her concurrence reflects a more basic disagreement with the *Harris* majority's understanding of hostile work environment. As she put it, "The critical issue, Title VII's text indicates, is whether members of one sex are exposed to disadvantageous terms or conditions of employment to which members of the other sex are not exposed."[25]

---

dicta, *Harris*, 114 S. Ct. at 371, *Meritor*, 477 U.S. at 67, *Harris* struck down the 6th Circuit's application of a hostile work environment standard similar to the standard applied in *Rogers*. The Court rejected the standard set out in Rabidue v. Osceola Refining Co., 805 F.2d 611, 620 (6th Cir. 1986), *cert. denied*, 481 U.S. 1041 (1987), requiring that a plaintiff show that her employer's discriminatory behavior was so severe as to affect seriously her psychological well-being in favor of a standard that required a lesser showing of abusiveness. *Harris*, 114 S. Ct. at 370.

24. *Harris*, 114 S. Ct. at 372 (Ginsburg, J., concurring) (quoting Davis v. Monsanto Chem. Co., 858 F.2d 345, 349 (6th Cir. 1988)) (internal quotation marks omitted).

25. *Id.* Justice Ginsburg claimed to be in agreement with the majority's opinion and approach to hostile work environment claims. "The Court's opinion . . . seems to me in harmony with the view expressed in this concurring statement." *Id.* at 373. Yet it appears that Justice Ginsburg's formulation diverges from the majority opinion significantly. The majority requires a much higher showing of interference with the plaintiff's ability to work than Justice Ginsburg would. She agrees with the Court's standard of "unreasonable interference" but implicitly defines "unreasonable interference" as conditions that simply make it more difficult for the plaintiff to do her job than it is for men in the office. *Compare id.* at 370 (explaining the majority's standard) *with id.* at 372 (explaining Justice Ginsburg's proposed standard).

The standard I propose in this note tracks Justice Ginsburg's stance and suggests doctrinal reforms to implement it: If a supervisor treats his female subordinates differently than he treats his male subordinates because of their gender, and that disparate treatment reflects invidious stereotypes about women, then such disparate treatment *alone* should be enough to establish liability under Title VII. I draw a distinction here quite consciously between the treatment of female subordinates by their supervisors and the treatment of female workers by coworkers, and the standard I propose should only be read to apply to behavior in the former case. Because supervisors generally have the power to hire, fire, promote, or, at the very least, evaluate a subordinate's work so that others may make these decisions, supervisors have much more power over subordinates than coworkers have over one another. Thus, "[t]he position [of] power of the supervisor . . . may operate as an enabling force in sexual harassment."[26] Even if a supervisor does not intend to take advantage of his position of power over a subordinate, "the employee may perceive and respond to the authority inherent in the position."[27] In comparison to those of a coworker, a supervisor's actions toward subordinates will more likely affect the terms and conditions of a woman's employment.

As I elaborate further in Part II, in interpreting Title VII courts have tacitly assumed that flirtation and sex are natural behaviors worthy of protection in the workplace. This assumption lies at the root of judicial reluctance to find Title VII violations in nonpervasive instances of workplace harassment and is reflected in the courts' characterization of the hostile work environment as "*sexual* harassment" rather than "disparate treatment based on gender." Thus, courts have developed a standard that requires proof of severe or pervasive sexual behavior in the workplace to ensure that the law does not sanction "normal" and "desirable" sexual behavior. The courts' fear of penalizing or chilling "normal" behavior in the workplace distorts the entire hostile work environment doctrine, even though much of the disparate treatment in the workplace bears no resemblance to mutual flirting or consensual sexual behavior of any kind.

II.   The Problems with Treating Gender Harassment Claims As Something Different from Disparate Treatment

A.   Current Doctrine Unjustifiably Distinguishes Between Discrimination Based on Sexual Conduct and Discrimination Based on Nonsexual Conduct

In order to establish a successful Title VII hostile work environment claim based on gender, a plaintiff must meet a heavier burden than plaintiffs who allege other kinds of Title VII discrimination. A hostile work environment plaintiff must demonstrate that: (1) her employer subjected her to conduct of a sexual nature, (2) that she did not welcome this conduct, (3) that the conduct

---

26. Jeanette N. Cleveland & Melinda E. Kerst, *Sexual Harassment and Perceptions of Power: An Under-Articulated Relationship,* 42 J. Vocational Behav. 49, 54 (1993) (footnote omitted).
27. *Id.* at 55.

was severe or pervasive enough to create a work environment that was objectively hostile or abusive, and (4) that subjectively it did alter her work environment.[28] While the concept of a hostile work environment cause of action originated in racial discrimination cases,[29] in the gender discrimination context the hostile work environment cause of action evolved from the quid pro quo sexual harassment cause of action. That lineage is responsible for some confusion in the doctrine. In cases of quid pro quo harassment, an employer implicitly or explicitly demands sexual favors from an employee as a condition of her continued employment, her hiring, or her promotion.[30] In the late 1970s and early 1980s, many courts began to realize that quid pro quo harassment represented only one kind of discrimination women regularly endured in the workplace.

Much of the discriminatory treatment women suffer does not implicitly or explicitly extort sexual favors for continuing employment or advancement. Rather, much discriminatory treatment involves conduct that constitutes gender-based disparate treatment. An employer or supervisor might, for example, flirt with a woman, ask her out on dates, grope her, or call her gender-based names—a whole range of behavior that belittles, undermines, or objectifies a woman without formally putting her job on the line. This treatment creates employment conditions different from those a woman's male coworkers face.

The Equal Employment Opportunity Commission (EEOC) recognized this unequal state of affairs in the early 1980s and established guidelines defining hostile work environment sexual harassment as a form of sex discrimination prohibited under Title VII.[31] The EEOC guidelines define prohibited sexual

---

28. *See* Harris v. Forklift Sys., Inc., 114 S. Ct. 367, 370 (1993); Meritor Sav. Bank v. Vinson, 477 U.S. 57, 65-69 (1986); Henson v. City of Dundee, 682 F.2d 897, 903-04 (11th Cir. 1982); *cf.* Ellison v. Brady, 924 F.2d 872, 875-76 (9th Cir. 1991) (establishing a "reasonable victim" standard for determining whether the conduct at issue created an abusive environment). In contrast, a plaintiff alleging racial or gender discrimination in hiring or firing decisions initially faces a light prima facie burden of proof as established in McDonnell Douglas Corp. v. Green, 411 U.S. 792 (1973). In such a case a plaintiff need only prove that (1) she belongs to a protected class; (2) she applied for and was qualified for a job for which the employer was seeking applicants; (3) despite her qualifications she was rejected; and (4) that after her rejection the position remained open and the employer continued to seek applicants from persons with the plaintiff's qualifications. *Id.* at 802. Winning a case under *McDonnell Douglas* is admittedly more difficult than stating a prima facie case, however. If the defendant rebuts the plaintiff's prima facie case with evidence of reasons other than discrimination for the plaintiff's rejection, plaintiff must show that the legitimate nondiscriminatory reasons the employer offered to justify not hiring the plaintiff were mere pretexts for invidious discrimination. *Id.* at 804. Nevertheless, in a *McDonnell Douglas*-style case, the Court has clearly defined the prohibited conduct—discrimination. Unlike the law covering hostile work environment claims, *McDonnell Douglas* does not require proof of severity or pervasiveness of the discrimination. Thus, a court need not engage in an amorphous search for evidence of those "elements."

29. *See* Rogers v. EEOC, 454 F.2d 234, 238 (5th Cir. 1971), *cert. denied,* 406 U.S. 957 (1972) (reasoning that Congress' broad mandate to eliminate ethnic and racial discrimination encompasses protection against a discriminatory work environment).

30. *See Meritor,* 477 U.S. at 62 (noting that EEOC guidelines prohibit sexual harassment, including conduct that conditions employment benefits on sexual favors).

31. A cause of action for discrimination based on a hostile work environment has its roots in *Rogers.* In that case, a circuit court recognized for the first time that a workplace "heavily charged with ethnic or racial discrimination" could in and of itself violate Title VII by creating a hostile work environment. *Rogers,* 454 F.2d at 238. Yet the early EEOC guidelines for hostile work environment based on gender were much narrower than the cause of action established in *Rogers* for racial harassment

harassment as "[u]nwelcome *sexual* advances, requests for *sexual* favors, and other verbal or physical conduct of a *sexual* nature . . . [that] ha[ve] the purpose or effect of unreasonably interfering with an individual's work performance or creating an intimidating, hostile, or offensive working environment."[32] In many ways the EEOC guidelines expanded women's bases for claims of employment discrimination because they recognized that an employer does not have to threaten a woman's employment directly for her to have been discriminated against in the terms and conditions of her employment.

Why the EEOC guidelines emphasize the *sexual* nature of the conduct is not entirely clear. Perhaps the EEOC simply thought that in the gender discrimination context the hostile work environment claim was merely an extension of the quid pro quo cause of action rather than a distinct cause of action in its own right. That the EEOC addressed the elements of both the quid pro quo and the hostile work environment causes of actions in the same set of guidelines buttresses this interpretation.[33] Although the EEOC guidelines expand the relief available to women for disparate treatment on the job, they do not fully address the problem of gender-based disparate treatment in the workplace.

B. *Neither the Language of Title VII nor Empirical Research Supports a Distinction Between Sexual and Nonsexual Conduct*

By defining the hostile work environment cause of action in terms of sexual conduct rather than in terms of gender-based disparate treatment,[34] the courts and the EEOC have established an interpretation of Title VII at odds with its language. This interpretation holds that some amount of sexual conduct at work between supervisors and their employees is perfectly acceptable. Courts are reluctant to recognize a woman's claim of sexual harassment as discrimination unless the conduct is of the kind that would be inappropriate *outside* of the workplace. As Judge Posner puts it, the proper definition of sexual harassment "exclude[s] mere flirtations and solicitations."[35] Judge MacKinnon echoed this view: "Sexual advances [in the workplace] may not be intrinsically offensive .

---

because they emphasize the *sexual* nature of the conduct. In addition, the EEOC guidelines for gender-based discrimination are narrower in that they require a plaintiff to show that the conduct in question was unwelcome.

32. EEOC Guidelines on Discrimination Because of Sex, 29 C.F.R. § 1604.11(a) (1994) (emphasis added).

33. *See id.*

34. Indeed, the new proposed EEOC guidelines on nonsexual, gender-based harassment explicitly distinguish between nonsexual and sexual conduct. Only plaintiffs who allege a hostile work environment based on gender-based conduct of a sexual nature must prove that such discriminatory conduct was unwelcome. Unwelcomeness is presumed for nonsexual gender harassment. As the EEOC put it, "Sexual harassment continues to be addressed in separate guidelines because it raises issues about human interaction that are to some extent unique in comparison to other harassment . . . ." Guidelines on Harassment Based on Race, Color, Religion, Gender, National Origin, Age, or Disability, 58 Fed. Reg. 51,266, 51,267 (1993) (to be codified at 29 C.F.R. § 1609) (proposed Oct. 1, 1993) [hereinafter Guidelines on Harassment].

35. Richard A. Posner, *An Economic Analysis of Sex Discrimination Laws,* 56 U. Chi. L. Rev. 1311, 1331 (1989).

. . . [for they involve] social patterns that to some extent are normal and expectable."[36]

The assumption that some level of flirtation or dating behavior is acceptable or desirable at work seems to command broad support.[37] But the empirical research performed to date indicates that even "mere flirtations" can demean a woman and interfere with her ability to work. Flirtatious behavior and sexual "compliments" about a woman's appearance have been shown to cause "sex role spillover," a term used to describe the process by which attitudes and expectations regarding women's behavior outside the workplace are transferred into the workplace.[38] "Sex role spillover" means that women are defined by reference to their traditional, circumscribed roles as helpers or sex objects, rather than as original thinkers or serious professionals.[39] Defining women at work as "women" rather than as workers circumscribes expectations of the kind of work women can do and thus discriminatorily limits their work horizons. "Mere flirtation" is no small matter for women; such acts may hinder women's ability to succeed in the workplace by perpetuating "sex role spillover" and similar forms of adverse disparate treatment of women.[40] In other words, flirtations and flirtatious compliments cast women in dual roles: as workers and as sex objects, or worse, as sex objects conveniently located at work.[41] In the latter case, a woman can be transformed from an attorney or an accountant into

---

36. Barnes v. Castle, 561 F.2d 983, 1001 (D.C. Cir. 1977) (MacKinnon, J., concurring).

37. One commentator has asserted, "[A]ttitudes toward nonharassing sexual behavior are generally favorable and . . . such behavior is prevalent at work." Sharon A. Lobel, *Sexuality At Work: Where Do We Go from Here?*, 42 J. VOCATIONAL BEHAV. 136, 142 (1993).

38. BARBARA A. GUTEK, SEX AND THE WORKPLACE: THE IMPACT OF SEXUAL BEHAVIOR AND HARASSMENT ON WOMEN, MEN, AND ORGANIZATIONS 15-17 (1985). According to Gutek,

> *Sex role spillover* is a term used . . . to denote the carryover into the workplace of gender-based roles that are usually irrelevant or inappropriate to work. Sex role spillover occurs, for example . . . when women are expected to serve as helpers (as in laboratory helper), assistants (as in administrative assistant), or associates (as in research associate) without ever advancing to head of the laboratory, manager of the office, or principal member of the research staff.
>
> When men are expected to behave in a stereotypical manner—to automatically assume the leader's role in a mixed-sex group, pay for a business lunch with a female colleague . . . sex role spillover also occurs.
>
> . . .
>
> . . . If people at work behaved within the narrow confines of work roles, [instead of within the confines of sex roles,] then sexual jokes, flirtatious behavior, sexual overtures, and sexual coercion would not exist in most workplaces.

Id.

39. *Id.; see also id.* at 167 ("A woman cannot be an analytical, rational leader and a sex object at the same time. When she becomes a sex object, her status as a sex object overpowers other aspects of her sex role and completely overwhelms the work role she is trying to occupy."); *id.* at 67 (arguing that "men who make serious sexual overtures toward women tend to treat women as women" rather than as serious employees); *id.* at 165 ("[W]hen an employee is complimented for physical attractiveness . . . a subtle side effect may be to draw attention away from work accomplishments.").

40. *See* Barbara A. Gutek, *Understanding Sexual Harassment At Work*, 6 NOTRE DAME J.L. ETHICS & PUB. POL'Y 335, 350 (1992) (arguing that behavior not commonly considered sexual harassment, such as dating, quasi-sexual touching, and compliments about physical appearance, also have "negative work-related consequences for women workers, although even they are not always aware of them").

41. *Id.* at 354-55 (arguing that "women do not seem to be able to be sex objects and analytical, rational, competitive, and assertive at the same time . . . . [because the sexual aspects of the female role] swamp or overwhelm a view of women as capable, committed workers").

"smart, attractive SWF, 49."[42] The consequences of such a role are substantial. Who will promote a "SWF, 49," when they can promote a "real" attorney?

The empirical research to date supports this analysis, indicating that women dislike "mere" flirtations, sexual jokes, innuendos, and comments in the workplace, and that such conduct impedes women's ability to do their jobs.[43] Such conduct thus places women at a disadvantage relative to otherwise similarly situated men. In Barbara Gutek's survey of 1232 working adults in Los Angeles County, most respondents initially assumed that men and women felt flattered to receive sexual advances from someone at work, particularly from a propositioner. But in contrast, when asked how they themselves would feel if propositioned at work, only 17 percent of the women said they would feel flattered. Sixty-seven percent of the men, on the other hand, said they would be. Moreover, 63 percent of the women said if propositioned, they would feel insulted, while only 15 percent of the men said they would take offense.[44] The research also suggests that "mere" flirtations hinder women's ability to work effectively and consequently blocks their ability to advance in their careers.[45] Nearly 7 percent of women who responded to Gutek's survey, for example, reported losing a job at some point for refusing sexual advances, versus 2 percent of men. Women were also nine times more likely to quit a job or abandon efforts to get a job because of sexual harassment and twenty-five times more likely to seek a job transfer.[46] Women's reactions to sexual overtures, propositions, and compliments about their physical appearance at work bolster the contention that women rarely like such comments.[47]

Perhaps women "realize that being attractive to men is not their prime motive for working."[48] Indeed, women who experience this type of conduct, "including sexual comments meant to be complimentary, are less satisfied with their jobs than other women are."[49] Gutek also points out that "an emphasis on workers' gender in the workplace is generally not necessary for the effective

---

42. *See Personals,* N.Y. REV. BOOKS, Apr. 7, 1994, at 51.

43. Indeed, the most commonly reported sexually harassing behavior at work was of the kind not thought of as the "most serious," including requests for dates, unwanted physical contact, the use of offensive language, and sexual propositions that were not conditioned on future employment or success. *See* Paula M. Popovich, DeeAnn N. Gehlauf, Jeffrey A. Jolton, Jill M. Somers & Rhonda M. Godinho, *Perceptions of Sexual Harassment as a Function of Sex of Rater and Incident Form and Consequence,* 27 SEX ROLES 609, 611-12 (1992).

44. GUTEK, *supra* note 38, at 20, 96-97.

45. For example, a woman who has an affair at the office, especially with her supervisor, can seriously undermine her credibility and thus damage her career. *See* Gutek, *supra* note 40, at 350.

46. GUTEK, *supra* note 38, at 54. A recent University of Arizona study backs up Gutek's findings. This study found that fewer than 1% of women would be flattered if propositioned by a man at work, while 13% of men would. Furthermore, about half of the women said they would be insulted, while only 8% of men would. Asra Q. Nomani, *Work Week,* WALL ST. J., Jan. 3, 1995, at A1.

47. *Id.* at 161-62; *see also* Meg Bond, *Division 27 Sexual Harassment Survey: Definitions, Impact, and Environmental Context, in* MICHELE A. PALUDI & RICHARD B. BARICKMAN, ACADEMIC AND WORKPLACE SEXUAL HARASSMENT: A RESOURCE MANUAL 189, 191-93 (1991) (reporting that graduate students asserted that they found conduct by professors, including jokes with sexual themes, invitations for dates, sexually suggestive comments, suggestive eye contact, and hinting or joking pressure for sex, to be generally "unsupportive" of women).

48. GUTEK, *supra* note 38, at 162.

49. *Id.*

conduct of work . . . [and is in fact] probably detrimental to productivity."[50]   In contrast, because sexual harassment has caused many women to quit their jobs, request transfers or reassignment,[51] the "[p]rofessionalization and desexualization of work . . . are good for business, for effective work organizations."[52]

Women may be unable to view sexual conduct at work in the same way as men may[53] because they realize that at work they are "too readily seen as potential sexual partners . . . and *too reluctantly seen as serious employees. . . .* They may be understandably concerned that when their sexuality is noticed, their work is not. When men make sexual comments, they are interpreted as insults because they draw attention away from [women's] work" performance.[54]   When supervisors engage in this conduct, it can be even more damaging than that when coworkers do.[55]   Both overtly threatening and "innocuous" sexual conduct at work between supervisors and subordinates decreases women's productivity[56] and their job satisfaction and imposes barriers on their ability to excel as workers.[57]   If Title VII mandates, as its language states, that women are not to be subjected to adverse differential treatment at work because of their gender, it follows that sexual conduct at work, and the concomitant introduction of sex roles to the workplace, creates working conditions that discriminate against women in violation of Title VII.[58]

---

50. *Id.* at 121; *see* notes 45 *supra* & 56 *infra.*

51. According to a United States Merit Systems Protection Board report, "[d]uring a recent 2-year period, over 36,000[ ] federal employees quit their jobs, were transferred or reassigned, or were fired because of sexual harassment. [And] [a]mong 88 cases filed with the California Department of Fair Employment and Housing, almost half [of the women] had been fired and another quarter had quit out of fear or frustration." Barbara A. Gutek & Mary P. Koss, *Changed Women and Changed Organizations: Consequences of and Coping With Sexual Harassment,* 42 J. Vocational Behav. 28, 31 (1993) (citations omitted).

52. Gutek, *supra* note 38, at 128.

53. I say "may" here because although Gutek's study tends to show that men are less threatened by sexual comments at work than women are, she focuses mainly on women's reactions to sexual conduct at work. *Id.* at 96-97.

54. *Id.* at 100-01 (emphasis added).

55. Gutek, *supra* note 40, at 341 ("The relationship between the two people is also important. The situation is . . . more serious . . . when the initiator is a supervisor of the recipient rather than an equal or a subordinate . . . .").

56. While a woman may not become less diligent at her job because of harassment, her productivity may nonetheless suffer because "lack of access to information and support from others in the work environment may well have an indirect effect on her work performance." Gutek & Koss, *supra* note 51, at 32. The federal government has estimated that sexual harassment alone cost the federal government $267 million over a two-year period in lost productivity. This figure includes the cost of replacing employees who left their jobs, sick leave for missed work, and lower group and individual productivity. This figure excludes any personal costs to the victims. U.S. Merit System Protection Board, Sexual Harassment in the Federal Government: An Update 39 (1988) [hereinafter Sexual Harassment in the Federal Government].

57. Courts are not necessarily blind to this fact. The 4th Circuit noted relatively early in the development of sexual harassment doctrine that "[s]exual harassment erects barriers to participation in the work force of the sort Congress intended to sweep away by the enactment of Title VII." Katz v. Dole, 709 F.2d 251, 254 (4th Cir. 1983).

58. The problem with supervisors initiating dating relationships with their subordinates or making comments about a woman worker's physical appearance is that a woman who may not have chosen to introduce her sex role into the workplace may have it foisted upon her anyway:

> What is doubly troublesome about this inability to be sexual and a worker at the same time is that women are not the ones who usually choose between the two. . . . More often . . . [a]

Finally, courts' implicit assumption—which *Harris* did not dispute—that a certain amount of flirting and sexual attention at work is acceptable reflects the apparent acceptance of the view that women do not object to being cast as sex objects at work, and the concomitant view that being cast as a sex object does not materially alter a woman's work environment. According to this view, "[b]eing attractive to men is extremely important to women, and overtures and advances are an indication of that attractiveness."[59] Unfortunately, being recognized at work as sexually attractive is at best double-edged. Not only does it make most women feel uncomfortable, it also diverts attention away from a woman's ability to perform her job and thus reinforces and reflects the misconception that women are less competent workers.[60] Because women must prove serious sexual misconduct at work before they can state a cognizable claim under Title VII, they have little ability to control the introduction of harmful sexual stereotyping into their work environment. So long as women are forced to battle the imposition of traditional, subservient sex roles at work, women will continue to face discriminatory barriers at work in violation of any plausible interpretation of Title VII.[61] Until the courts recognize that sexual conduct at work is just a subset of disparate treatment, myths about the appropriateness of sexual conduct in the workplace will persist, and only plaintiffs who have endured truly disabling, as opposed to simply discriminatory, misconduct in the workplace will be able to seek redress for the discrimination they have endured.

III. Doctrinal Effects of Framing Gender-Based Disparate Treatment in the Workplace in Sexual Terms

As currently understood, the hostile work environment cause of action reflects society's misplaced tolerance for sexual conduct in the workplace, resulting in a doctrine that excuses a great deal of gender-based disparate treatment. The notion that some sexual conduct in the workplace between supervisors and their subordinates is acceptable affects the doctrine in two fundamental ways: First, courts require a plaintiff to prove that the conduct she experienced was "unwelcome," a requirement I argue is gratuitous in theory and vicious in practice. Second, courts require a plaintiff to demonstrate that the conduct to which she was subjected was pervasive or severe enough to create an *abusive* working environment. I argue that this requirement creates a perverse safety zone in which women may be subjected to gender-based discriminatory treatment for which Title VII offers no remedy.

---

working woman chooses not to be a sex object but [is] so defined by male colleagues or supervisors anyway, regardless of her own actions.
Gutek, *supra* note 40, at 355.

59. Gutek, *supra* note 38, at 97.

60. *See id.*

61. Because of women's tenuous position in the workforce, they often feel as though they have no choice but to go along with the sex role to maintain the worker role. " 'I'll never get a good recommendation from him . . . if I don't go along with him.' " Paludi & Barickman, *supra* note 47, at 30 (listing "common reactions to being sexually harassed" as reported by victims); *see also* Alba Conte, Sexual Harassment in the Workplace: Law and Practice 5 (1990) ("Sexual harassment degrades women by reinforcing their historically subservient role in the workplace.").

A.   *The Unwelcomeness Requirement: An Unjust Element of the Hostile
     Work Environment Cause of Action*

The Supreme Court has referred to "unwelcomeness" as the "gravamen of
any sexual harassment claim."[62] That characterization presents a serious problem. The unwelcomeness requirement is gratuitous, punitive, and reflects some
of society's most insidious and outdated stereotypes about women and sexual
behavior.[63] Not only is the unwelcomeness requirement theoretically irrelevant
to whether a woman is subject to a different work environment because of her
gender, in practice it also forces a woman to prove both that she "did not solicit
or incite" her supervisor's conduct, and that she "regarded the conduct as undesirable or offensive."[64] The kind of evidence the Court has held as admissible
to rebut the plaintiff's assertion of "unwelcomeness" is every feminist's
nightmare: The Court has concluded that evidence of the sexual provocative-
ness of a plaintiff's "speech or dress" is "obviously relevant" to the merits of a
plaintiff's claim of discrimination.[65]

In this Part I show that the unwelcomeness requirement imposes an unnecessary and unreasonable burden on women bringing Title VII claims. This burden is based on the nonsensical assumption that a woman might welcome any
conduct that would be offensive enough to interfere "unreasonably" with her
work. Despite the inherent flaw in such a contention, courts have adopted the
unwelcomeness requirement because they continue to assume that some sexual
conduct is desirable at work, and thus the doctrine must distinguish between
"proper" and "improper" sexual advances.[66] But Title VII is a civil rights statute designed to guarantee women's *equality*, not to guarantee that sexual advances will be made courteously. If we recognize and reconceptualize sexual
harassment as one form of disparate treatment of women, as I recommend, my
point becomes even clearer: No one "welcomes" discriminatory treatment.

1.   *The unwelcomeness requirement imposes an unreasonably harsh
     burden on plaintiffs.*

Meritor makes the unwelcomeness requirement the gravamen of any sexual
harassment hostile work environment claim, and in *Harris* the Court continued

---

62. Meritor Sav. Bank v. Vinson, 477 U.S. 57, 68 (1986).
63. *See, e.g.,* Susan Estrich, *Sex at Work,* 43 STAN. L. REV. 813, 826-34 (1991) (arguing that the
unwelcomeness inquiry is either gratuitous when the environment is not objectively hostile or punitive
when the environment is objectively hostile); B. Glenn George, *The Back Door: Legitimizing Sexual
Harassment Claims,* 73 B.U. L. REV. 1, 28-30 (1993) (analogizing the unwelcomeness requirement to
the "did she ask for it" inquiry in rape trials); Michael D. Vhay, Comment, *The Harms of Asking:
Towards a Comprehensive Treatment of Sexual Harassment,* 55 U. CHI. L. REV. 328, 344 (1988) (arguing that the "unwelcomeness test is at root the product of an outdated stereotype").
64. Henson v. City of Dundee, 682 F.2d 897, 903 (11th Cir. 1982).
65. *Meritor,* 477 U.S. at 69.
66. Indeed, the newly proposed EEOC guidelines on gender, national origin, and religious harassment cite the need to distinguish proper from improper sexual advances as the reason for treating hostile
work environments based on sexual conduct under a different standard. Guidelines on Harassment,
supra note 34, 58 Fed. Reg. 51,267 ("Sexual harassment continues to be addressed in separate guidelines because it raises issues about human interaction that are to some extent unique in comparison to
other harassment and, thus, may warrant separate emphasis.").

to apply that requirement. In some circuits, proving unwelcomeness imposes a difficult burden indeed. For example, the First Circuit effectively holds that a plaintiff cannot state a hostile work environment claim unless she has explicitly taken action against her supervisor to head off the disparate treatment. *Lipsett v. University of Puerto Rico*[67] starkly articulated the plaintiff's responsibility to communicate to her supervisor that she did not welcome his behavior:

> [A] determination of sexual harassment turns on whether it is found that the plaintiff misconstrued or overreacted to what the defendant claims were innocent or invited overtures. A male supervisor might believe, for example, that it is legitimate for him to tell a female subordinate that she has a "great figure" or "nice legs." The female subordinate, however, may find such comments offensive. . . . [T]he man may not realize that his comments are offensive, and the woman may be fearful of criticizing her supervisor. . . . The [supervisor] must be sensitive to signals from the woman that his comments are unwelcome, and the woman . . . *must take responsibility for making those signals clear.*[68]

Similarly, in *Dockter v. Rudolf Wolff Futures, Inc.*[69] the Seventh Circuit revealed its tolerance for employers who create a hostile work environment:

> For the first few weeks, [Plaintiff's boss], as he occasionally did with other female employees at the office, made sexual overtures to—in the vernacular of the modern generation, "came on to"—her. Although Plaintiff rejected these efforts, her initial rejections were neither unpleasant nor unambiguous, and gave [the boss] no reason to believe that his moves were unwelcome.[70]

Because the district and circuit courts in *Dockter* accepted the propriety of some sexual conduct between supervisors and their employees, the plaintiff could not simply point to her rejection of the advances to prove their unwelcomeness. The kind of response that would be sufficient to prove unwelcomeness remains unclear. If a woman's response is at all ambiguous, either because she is not firm enough in her rejection (perhaps because she fears losing her job if she offends her boss) or because she happens to dress attractively, she not may be entitled to relief, as the plaintiff in *Dockter* found.[71] The woman therefore faces the dilemma of rejecting her boss convincingly enough to satisfy the court's demands while taking care not to be so forceful as to risk retribution.

Moreover, placing the burden of explicit communication on the plaintiff imposes unrealistic demands. While most workers may fear that criticizing their supervisors puts their jobs at risk, the problem may be magnified for wo-

---

67. 864 F.2d 881 (1st Cir. 1988).

68. *Id.* at 898 (emphasis added). The court did note that a woman may be able to communicate her disapproval in some circumstances if she consistently failed to respond to the supervisor's suggestive comments. *Id.*

69. 913 F.2d 456 (7th Cir. 1990).

70. *Id.* at 459 (quoting Dockter v. Rudolf Wolff Futures, Inc., 684 F. Supp. 532, 533 (N.D. Ill. 1988)). In fairness, the 7th Circuit's approach may be evolving. *See* Carr v. Allison Gas Turbine Div., GMC, 32 F.3d 1007 (7th Cir. 1994) (reversing the trial court's dismissal of a hostile work environment claim involving harassment by coworkers).

71. *See* Estrich, *supra* note 63, at 829 (arguing that the outcome in *Dockter* means that "unwelcomeness may be judged not according to what the woman meant, but by the implication that the man felt entitled to draw. . . . [C]ourts, however, privilege *his* interpretation.").

men. Susan Estrich suggests that "less powerful, and economically dependent" women cannot be expected to express unwelcomeness.[72] Indeed, she questions whether there ever can be "such a thing as truly 'welcome' sex between a male boss and a female employee who needs a job."[73] Women who rely on their paychecks to support themselves and their families cannot go to great lengths to communicate the unwelcomeness of discriminatory behavior. Further, many women mistakenly think that an indirect approach to combat behavior they do not welcome is the most effective way to end it. For example, women may deflect offensive comments, make jokes back, or try to ignore the behavior.[74]

If we reconceptualize hostile work environment cases as gender-based disparate treatment rather than a form of *sexual* harassment, the absurdity of the unwelcomeness requirement comes into stark relief. Very little discriminatory behavior could ever be construed as "welcome." For example, few women welcome being the target of gender-based epithets or having their competence called into question because they are women. Similarly, most women *do not* welcome being "hit on" by their bosses at work,[75] much less having their bosses fondle them. The contrary assumption may stem from the misconception that hostile work environment claims are about sexual misconduct and not about discriminatory conduct.[76]

It is hardly surprising, therefore, that the "unwelcomeness" requirement has no analog in other types of discrimination law.[77] In the racial harassment context, courts *presume* that a plaintiff did not "welcome" being subjected to racial epithets.[78] Similarly, under the *McDonnell Douglas* disparate treatment framework, which governs both racial and gender discrimination cases, a plaintiff need not allege that she did not welcome being discriminated against in hiring or firing decisions.[79] We simply assume that plaintiffs do not welcome disparate treatment because of their race or sex—any suggestion to the contrary would strike us as bizarre indeed. If an employee is treated differently because of race or gender, that is enough. In this respect, hostile work environment claims should be treated no differently than other types of discrimination claims.

---

72. *Id.* at 828.

73. *Id.* at 831.

74. *See* Gutek & Koss, *supra* note 51, at 37-38, 39-40 (citing numerous studies showing that many women use indirect strategies to cope with sexual harassment, even though they are not particularly effective in stopping harassment).

75. *See* notes 43-47 *supra* and accompanying text.

76. *See* texts accompanying notes 32, 35-36 *supra*.

77. I am not the first to make this observation. *See* Vhay, *supra* note 63, at 344 (stating that victims of discriminatory conduct based on race, national origin, or religion need not prove the unwelcomeness of the conduct).

78. *See, e.g.,* Rogers v. EEOC, 454 F.2d 234, 238 (5th Cir. 1971) (stating that a work environment can be "so heavily polluted with discrimination as to destroy completely the emotional and psychological stability of minority group workers"), *cert. denied,* 406 U.S. 957 (1972).

79. *See* Texas Dep't of Community Affairs v. Burdine, 450 U.S. 248, 252-56 (1981) (applying the *McDonnell Douglas* burden-shifting framework to gender discrimination); McDonnell Douglas Corp. v. Green, 411 U.S. 792, 802 (1973) (setting out the elements of a prima facie case alleging racial or gender discrimination in hiring or firing decisions); note 28 *supra*.

Further, no other area of Title VII jurisprudence imposes on a plaintiff the burden of proving that he did nothing to encourage discrimination. Disparate treatment based on race or gender simply does not belong in the workplace. Yet, in the gender hostile work environment context, because the courts have presumed that a certain amount of sexual activity is desirable in the workplace,[80] a plaintiff must go to great lengths to establish that the conduct at issue in her particular case was beyond the pale. Since unwelcomeness is not at issue outside of the hostile work environment context in other gender-based disparate treatment cases, courts should accordingly assume that sexual behavior is presumptively offensive.

It is also perverse to rely on prevailing notions of what constitutes commonly acceptable behavior in the workplace in defining an objectionable workplace. As the Ninth Circuit observed in *Ellison v. Brady*,[81] doing so runs the risk of reinforcing prevailing discrimination: "Harassers could continue to harass merely because a particular discriminatory practice was common . . . ."[82] But Title VII was meant to change the workplace by replacing disparate treatment with equality, not to ensconce a discriminatory status quo. If, as the Supreme Court has stated, Title VII was "intended to strike at the entire spectrum of disparate treatment of men and women resulting from sex stereotypes,"[83] then the legal rules governing workplace behavior, including the elements of a claim for a violation of Title VII, must be tailored to enable women to have an equal position in the workplace. The standard for establishing liability in a Title VII hostile work environment claim should mirror this principle, because the whole point of the statute, and thus its enforcement, is to define what behavior is and is not acceptable in the workplace by reference to the principle of equality. Unacceptable behavior may cause only slight harm, but degree of harm is only an issue of damages. The failure to establish such a standard will necessarily produce slippage between the statutory guarantee of equality and the reality of the workplace; as a practical matter, supervisors may have little incentive to avoid conduct for which they will not be held liable.

There is a further problem with the unwelcomeness requirement. It shifts the inquiry from the discrimination itself to whether by her own conduct the plaintiff invited the discriminatory conduct.[84] By shifting the focus to the plaintiff's conduct and to her efforts to communicate her dislike of the defendant's behavior, the unwelcomeness requirement imposes an unfair burden on the plaintiff to protect herself from her supervisor's discriminatory conduct. Conversely, "no burden is placed on [the supervisor] to refrain from abusing his position of power"[85] by flirting with or propositioning his female subordinates.

---

80. *See* text accompanying notes 34-36 *supra*.

81. 924 F.2d 872 (9th Cir. 1991).

82. *Id.* at 878.

83. Price Waterhouse v. Hopkins, 490 U.S. 228, 251 (1989) (quoting Los Angeles Dept. of Water and Power v. Manhart, 435 U.S. 702, 707 n.13 (1978)) (internal quotation marks omitted).

84. Estrich, *supra* note 63, at 827.

85. *Id.* at 828.

2. *The unwelcomeness requirement unjustifiably deters plaintiffs from bringing suit.*

Besides placing an unreasonable burden on plaintiffs to prove that they did not welcome the discriminatory conduct, the unwelcomeness requirement also deters plaintiffs from bringing meritorious claims. As currently configured, the unwelcomeness requirement enables and encourages defense attorneys to engage in discovery tactics that deter both "imperfect" and "perfect" plaintiffs from filing suit. Even with "perfect" plaintiffs, the unwelcomeness requirement provides an opportunity for defense attorneys to seek discovery about all aspects of a woman's sexual life, and many take full advantage of that opportunity to discourage plaintiffs from pursuing their claims.[86] If evidence of plaintiff's speech, dress, and expressions of sexual fantasies at work are "obviously" relevant,[87] then evidence of any involvement with other men at work—or any men at all—would be relevant as well. The fear of having her personal life, with all of its imperfections,[88] exposed and paraded in court by adverse attorneys most likely overwhelms and discourages the average plaintiff and prevents her from bringing a legitimate claim.[89]

Additionally, the criminal law analog to sexual harassment—rape—excludes evidence of the victim's reputation or of prior sexual conduct with a person other than the defendant offered to prove consent.[90] Although courts do

---

86. Evidence about a woman's sexual history may be introduced to show that the woman welcomed the conduct, or under the pervasiveness requirement, to show that her reaction to the conduct at issue was not reasonable because her past sexual history has made her unreasonably sensitive. "[D]efense lawyers, contending they are only doing their duty to clients, are going straight into the bedroom. In sexual harassment cases, they are challenging the way women talk, dress and behave in an effort to prove that the plaintiff 'welcomed' a boss's behavior . . . ." Ellen E. Schultz & Junda Woo, *Plaintiff's Sex Lives Are Being Laid Bare In Harassment Cases*, WALL ST. J., Sept. 19, 1994, at A1. Using such evidence, and the discovery process to elicit it, to discredit a plaintiff or to discourage her from pursuing her claim is becoming more and more commonplace, ironically since the 1991 Civil Rights Act passed. The Act makes it easier for women to recover damages for sexual harassment by allowing them to recover for emotional distress and punitive damages. 42 U.S.C. § 1918a(a), b (Supp. V 1993). The Act "raised the stakes so sharply that defense lawyers are increasingly resorting to harsh tactics, asking about sex lives, childhood molestation, abortions and venereal disease." Schultz & Woo, *supra*, at A1. Since sexual harassment cases are now more expensive, they can no longer be settled by defendants; they must be won. *Id.* Margaret A. Harris, chair of the Sexual Harassment Committee for the National Employment Law Association, says that she regularly faces discovery battles with defense attorneys seeking to pry into the sexual history of her clients: "My day-to-day sexual harassment pretrial litigation involves defense attorneys trying to portray my clients as whores." Telephone Interview with Margaret A. Harris (Oct. 25, 1994).

87. *See* Meritor Sav. Bank v. Vinson, 477 U.S. 57, 69 (1986) (stating that evidence of the plaintiff's sexually provocative speech or dress and her sexual fantasies was "obviously relevant").

88. As Estrich points out, perfect hostile work environment plaintiffs are few and far between. *See* Estrich, *supra* note 63, at 830-31 (noting that the behavior of both "traditional" women who act femininely and "untraditional" or "unfeminine" women will be used against them under the unwelcomeness analysis).

89. As Estrich argues,

> Under the old rule in rape cases, a woman's sexual history might be relevant regardless of the circumstances of the assault. In most cases, the effect was not to improve the truth-seeking process of the courts, but to discourage women from filing complaints in the first instance. "Welcomeness"—defined in sexual harassment doctrine to include the woman's dress, language, habits, and even sex life—may play a similar role.

Id. at 833.

90. FED. R. EVID. 412.

permit prosecutors to present accounts of the victim's dress and demeanor at the time of the rape, evidence about the victim's general demeanor, method of dress, or prior sexual experiences is not allowed.[91] Rule 412 of the Federal Rules of Evidence at least calls into question whether the kind of evidence *Meritor* classifies as "obviously relevant" to whether a woman welcomed the harassing conduct[92] is indeed relevant. As with rape shield laws, courts should allow evidence of a plaintiff's consent to a particular act or previous consent only with respect to the same defendant. *Meritor's* endorsement of evidence that Rule 412 regards as inadmissible is unjustified and punitive,[93] especially since in a criminal rape trial a defendant has much more at stake in proving his innocence than does a civil defendant in a hostile work environment case. If the justice system is willing to exclude arguably legally relevant evidence to a criminal defendant's innocence in order to protect women victims from humiliating questioning, civil cases should strike a similar balance.

Although the unwelcomeness requirement is both unreasonable and unnecessary, the EEOC pushed for an "unwelcomeness" requirement in its brief to the Supreme Court in *Meritor*,[94] contending that consensual sex in the workplace should not form the basis of a Title VII action.[95] The implicit argument is that women who have engaged in consensual relationships at work that have failed will use Title VII as a retaliatory measure against their former lovers.[96] The threat of the scorned woman charging her supervisor with creating a hostile work environment without cause is, as in the rape context, completely overblown. The costs of filing a lawsuit, which include damaged relationships at work and severe loss of privacy, are prohibitive. As Estrich argues,

> Start with embarrassment, loss of privacy, and sometimes shame. . . . Empirical studies suggest that possibly actionable harassment is widespread, even endemic, but the number of lawsuits, not surprisingly, does not bear out this possibility. Anything [that] adds another disincentive [to bringing a lawsuit to vindicate one's rights under Title VII], as the . . . unwelcomeness requirement surely does, ought to be supported by a strong justification. . . . [T]he unwelcomeness inquiry certainly is not.[97]

---

91. *See, e.g.,* Wood v. Alaska, 957 F.2d 1544, 1550-54 (9th Cir. 1992) (excluding as irrelevant evidence that the rape victim posed nude for *Penthouse*, acted in pornographic movies, and excluding as prejudicial that the victim told defendant about her movies and showed defendant her *Penthouse* pictures); United States v. Saunders, 943 F.2d 388, 391-92 (4th Cir. 1991) (upholding the trial court's exclusion of evidence that a rape victim had sexual relations with defendant's friend and had a reputation for being a prostitute), *cert. denied,* 112 S. Ct. 1199 (1992); Doe v. United States, 666 F.2d 43, 47-48 (4th Cir. 1981) (ruling inadmissible evidence of a rape victim's general demeanor and reputation as sexually promiscuous).

92. *Meritor,* 477 U.S. at 69.

93. *See* Estrich, *supra* note 63, at 827, 833 (arguing that the evidentiary focus on the woman puts the victim on trial and may deter women from pursuing valid claims).

94. Brief for the United States and the Equal Employment Opportunity Commission as Amici Curiae at 13, Meritor Sav. Bank v. Vinson, 477 U.S. 57 (1986) (No. 84-1979).

95. *Id.*

96. *Id.* at 15 (arguing that courts must "ensure that sexual harassment charges do not become a tool by which one party to a consensual sexual relationship may penalize the other").

97. Estrich, *supra* note 63, at 833-34.

We should not expect that women would file more fallacious hostile work environment claims than plaintiffs in any other civil actions would. If anything, the costs involved likely cause women to sue less frequently than the law allows. In fact, a major federal study estimated that women report only 5 percent of harassing behaviors.[98] Given this backdrop of extreme underreporting, courts should not worry that a significant number of women will abuse the court system with fallacious hostile work environment claims.

B. *The Pervasiveness Requirement: An Unfairly High Hurdle*

Judicial tolerance for some level of sexual conduct in the workplace underlies the pervasiveness requirement, just as it does the unwelcomeness requirement. To state a successful hostile work environment cause of action, a plaintiff must show that the discriminatory conduct was "severe or pervasive enough to create an objectively hostile or abusive work environment."[99] As the Court first stated in *Meritor* and repeated approvingly in *Harris*, a "mere utterance of an . . . epithet [that] engenders offensive feelings in a[n] employee" is not sufficient to constitute actionable disparate treatment in the workplace.[100] Other courts have asserted this threshold even more strongly: "[C]asual or isolated manifestations of a discriminatory environment, such as a *few . . . slurs, may not raise* a cause of action."[101]

---

98. SEXUAL HARASSMENT IN THE FEDERAL GOVERNMENT, *supra* note 56, at 27, *cited in* Mary F. Radford, *By Invitation Only: The Proof of Welcomeness in Sexual Harassment Cases,* 72 N.C. L. REV. 499, 523 (1994).

99. Harris v. Forklift Sys., Inc., 114 S. Ct. 367, 370 (1993).

100. *Id.* (quoting *Meritor,* 477 U.S. at 67) (internal quotation marks omitted) (alteration in *Harris*). This analysis first appeared in Rogers v. EEOC, 454 F.2d 234, 238 (5th Cir. 1971), *cert. denied,* 406 U.S. 957 (1972), which involved racial harassment.

101. Downes v. FAA, 775 F.2d 288, 293 (Fed. Cir. 1985) (applying a rationale originally addressing ethnic and racial slurs to a gender hostile work environment case) (quoting Bundy v. Jackson, 641 F.2d 934, 943 n.9 (D.C. Cir. 1981)) (internal quotation marks omitted). Even the EEOC guidelines reflect this permissive attitude toward sexual conduct at work, suggesting that a single request for a date from a supervisor, absent coercive demand, is not actionable under Title VII because it does not alter the working conditions of the plaintiff. *See* Cobbins v. School Bd. of Lynchburg, No. 90-1754, 1991 U.S. App. LEXIS 526, at *7 (4th Cir. Jan. 14, 1991) (interpreting the EEOC guidelines to mean that "a single request, absent a coercive demand or ultimatum, most likely would not amount to the establishment of a hostile work environment") (unpublished case); *see also* Caihleen Marie Mogan, Note, *Current Hostile Environment Sexual Harassment Law: Time to Stop Defendants from Having Their Cake and Eating It Too,* 6 NOTRE DAME J.L. ETHICS & PUB. POL'Y 543, 559-60 (1992) (discussing *Cobbins*). *But see* King v. Hillen, 21 F.3d 1572, 1581 (Fed. Cir. 1994) (holding that the EEOC guidelines require a court to look at the totality of the circumstances, not at each isolated incident). Many courts reflect this attitude in their rejection of claims that represent disparate treatment based on the employee's gender. For instance, in *Downes* the court found that the plaintiff failed to demonstrate that the discriminatory conduct to which she was subjected was pervasive enough, even though her employer speculated in her presence about the frequency of her sexual relations after her divorce, called her the office "Dolly Parton," and touched her hair on two occasions. *Downes,* 775 F.2d at 293-94.

1. *The pervasiveness requirement allows instances of disparate treatment to go unpunished.*

The pervasiveness requirement sanctions a certain amount of gender-based disparate treatment in the workplace. *Jones v. Flagship International*,[102] for example, reflects this tolerance of some sexual conduct at work. In *Jones*, the plaintiff's supervisor propositioned her on three separate occasions, even after she had asked him to stop. On another occasion, he told her his wife did not know he was back in town and that the plaintiff "needed the 'comfort of a man.' "[103] And yet another time he informed her that she was "off the hook" because one of his friends was interested in her.[104] The court failed to find that Jones suffered any tangible job detriment and concluded that her supervisor's conduct was not severe enough to have created a hostile work environment in violation of Title VII.[105]

Furthermore, the courts' imposition of the pervasiveness requirement has prevented women from asserting valid claims of a hostile work environment. The Sixth, Seventh, Federal, and Eleventh Circuits, for example, applied a pervasiveness standard that required a plaintiff to demonstrate serious psychological harm,[106] until the Supreme Court struck that standard down in *Harris*.[107] That courts would apply such an onerous standard reflects a judicial belief that sex in the workplace is generally unobjectionable. According to these courts, conduct tolerated under Title VII could include referring to women as "cunts" and "fat ass" and referring to their "tits,"[108] prominently displaying photographs of nude or partially clad women,[109] asking a woman to negotiate her

---

102. 793 F.2d 714 (5th Cir. 1986), *cert. denied,* 479 U.S. 1065 (1987). Although this case predates *Meritor,* the 5th Circuit applied the same general analysis. *Compare Meritor,* 477 U.S. at 67 ("For sexual harassment to be actionable, it must be sufficiently severe or pervasive 'to alter the conditions of [the victim's] employment and create an abusive working environment.' ") (quoting Henson v. Dundee, 682 F.2d 897, 904 (11th Cir. 1982)) (alteration in *Meritor*) *with Jones,* 793 F.2d at 719-20 ("[T]he sexual harassment must be sufficiently pervasive so as to alter the conditions of employment and create an abusive working environment . . . .").

103. *Jones,* 793 F.2d at 716.

104. *Id.*

105. *Id.* at 720-21. Unfortunately, other courts have tolerated gender-based discriminatory treatment in the workplace. *See, e.g.,* Hicks v. Gates Rubber Co., 833 F.2d 1406, 1409-10, 1415 (10th Cir. 1987) (overturning the district court's conclusion that two supervisors' acts of grabbing plaintiff's breasts, touching her buttocks, and rubbing her thigh were merely isolated incidents and were not pervasive enough to create an abusive working environment); Christoforou v. Ryder Truck Rental, Inc., 668 F. Supp. 294, 298-300 (S.D.N.Y. 1987) (holding that a supervisor's conduct was not pervasive enough to create a hostile work environment even though he propositioned plaintiff, touched her thigh and hair, and told her to "be more modern in her attitudes" toward having affairs, because the conduct was nothing but a few "scattered incidents").

106. *See* Brooms v. Regal Tube Co., 881 F.2d 412, 418-20 (7th Cir. 1989); Vance v. Southern Bell Tel. & Tel. Co., 863 F.2d 1503, 1510 (11th Cir. 1989); Rabidue v. Osceola Refining Co., 805 F.2d 611, 620 (6th Cir. 1986), *cert. denied,* 481 U.S. 1041 (1987); Downes v. FAA, 775 F.2d 288, 292 (Fed. Cir. 1985).

107. *Harris,* 114 S. Ct. at 370-71.

108. Rabidue v. Osceola Refining Co., 584 F. Supp. 419, 423 (E.D. Mich. 1984), *aff'd,* 805 F.2d 611 (6th Cir. 1986), *cert. denied,* 481 U.S. 1041 (1987).

109. *Id.*

raise at the local motel,[110] telling her that her "ass was so big" that if she wore a bikini there would be an eclipse,[111] and querying whether the woman had to sleep with a client to get him to sign an important deal.[112] The courts did not find this conduct severe enough to affect seriously the plaintiffs' psychological well being. While the Supreme Court may have thought it remedied this problem in *Harris,* because that case relies on the *Meritor* standard, which gave rise to such cases in the first place, there may be little reason for such optimism.

While there is no compelling reason why a plaintiff should have to prove that the discriminatory behavior she endured was "pervasive," there are powerful reasons why a plaintiff should not have to. The type of incidents that some courts have dismissed as trivial affect women deeply.[113] Many may agree that a supervisor should never be allowed to call his subordinates gender-based epithets, and many may even agree that one such incident should be actionable. Yet the courts have never seriously entertained a "zero tolerance" stance toward supervisors' asking their subordinates out on dates. Even Gutek hesitates to condemn dating in the workplace altogether,[114] although her analysis on sex role spillover could be read to support such a stance.[115] We may hesitate to desexualize a workplace by forbidding relationships between supervisors and their subordinates and consider such a position extreme.[116] The costs and benefits involved in prohibiting a supervisor from asking his subordinate out on a date, flirting with her, or complimenting her on her new hairstyle, however, weigh in favor of prohibiting such conduct to the extent that it involves an unequal power arrangement. Because of the inherent power differential in relationships between supervisors and subordinates, being asked for a date may put a subordinate in a very uncomfortable situation, and being complimented on physical appearance may make a woman feel that her appearance garners more attention than her work. Moreover, since supervisors exercise control over a

---

110. *See* Brief for the United States and the Equal Employment Opportunity Commission as Amici Curiae at 3, Harris v. Forklift Sys., Inc., 114 S. Ct. 367 (1993) (No. 92-1168).

111. *Id.* at 3 n.3.

112. *Id.* at 4. The magistrate in *Harris* recognized that these comments were offensive but nonetheless concluded that Harris was not harmed severely enough psychologically to allege a Title VII violation. Harris v. Forklift Sys., Inc., 60 Empl. Prac. Dec. (CCH) ¶ 42,070, at 74,250 (M.D. Tenn. 1990), *aff'd,* 976 F.2d 733 (6th Cir. 1992), *rev'd,* 114 S. Ct. 367 (1993). The district court reached this conclusion even though Harris testified that she could not sleep, lost all desire to go to work, cried frequently, began drinking heavily, and that her personal relations suffered. *Id.* at 74,247.

113. *See* notes 40-57 *supra.*

114. *See* GUTEK, *supra* note 38, at 173 (rejecting a "return to 'outlawing' dating").

115. *See* notes 38-39 *supra* and accompanying text.

116. Barring supervisors from asking subordinates out on dates, complimenting them on their physical appearance, or touching them does not represent an extreme position and may be the only truly effective way to prevent harassment. Even *Parade,* a Sunday newspaper insert not generally known for its extreme left-wing, radical-feminist positions, recommends that males in the workplace err on the side of caution and refrain from what the courts would generally consider nonactionable behavior. *Parade*'s recommendations included, for example, relying on courtesy rather than contact (offer handshakes rather than hugs, and encouraging words, not pats on the back); using a same-sex standard (ask yourself whether you would tell a male colleague you liked the way he styled his hair); and complimenting female colleagues on the quality of their work rather than their appearance. Dianne Hales & Dr. Robert Hales, *Can Men and Women Work Together? Yes, If . . .,* PARADE MAG., Mar. 20, 1994, at 10, 11. The authors put it succinctly, "A kiss is still a kiss, a hug is still a hug, a joke is still a joke—except at work, where they could spell trouble." *Id.* at 10.

subordinate's career path, such requests or comments, even well-intentioned ones, may be inherently coercive. A subordinate may not feel as free to turn down her supervisor as she would someone outside of the workplace or even a coworker, nor may she feel as free to tell a supervisor that his compliments about her appearance make her feel uncomfortable. This means that women are being treated differently than men, and that is enough.

Recognizing the danger of the power imbalance in these situations, some universities have recognized the inherent potential for coerciveness in professor-student relationships and have banned even "mutual" relationships between professors and their students.[117] Professor-student relationships are somewhat different from supervisor-subordinate relationships—they are at once both more and less coercive. They are more coercive because professors are generally much older than students, which may make students more vulnerable. They also may be less coercive in the sense that a student may have less at stake. While a student may risk getting a bad grade from a professor, at least at the undergraduate level, she may be able to avoid him by taking classes with other professors in the future. Her ability to avoid both the objectionable behavior and its consequences may be greater than in the employment context. Most likely, the student's future career is not on the line. In contrast, if a subordinate turns down a supervisor for a date and angers him, her career and livelihood may be at stake. Transferring to another job may also be more difficult than dropping classes. None of this suggests that harassment of an undergraduate by a professor should be taken lightly or tolerated. I suggest only that school administrators have acknowledged the potential for coercion and have implemented bans on dating and the like in settings where less may be at stake than in the workplace.[118]

In the workplace context, at least one San Francisco law firm has recognized the coerciveness inherent in the differential power of supervisors and subordinates. This law firm requires that if two attorneys are dating, and one is in a supervisory relationship to the other, they cannot work on the same case,

---

117. Harvard University, for example, bans all professor-student dating because

[a]morous relationships that might be appropriate in other circumstances are always wrong when they occur between any teacher . . . and any student for whom he or she has a professional responsibility. . . . Implicit in the idea of professionalism is the recognition by those in positions of authority that in their relationships with students there is always an element of power . . . . with which they are entrusted . . . .

PALUDI & BARICKMAN, *supra* note 47, at 10 (quoting the Harvard University Policy on Sexual Harassment). The University of Iowa takes a similar stance:

A faculty member who fails to withdraw from participation in activities or decisions that may reward or penalize a student with whom the faculty member has or has had an amorous relationship will be deemed to have violated his or her ethical obligation to the student, to other students, to colleagues, and to the University.

Id. (quoting the University of Iowa Policy on Sexual Harassment).

118. The Harvard and University of Iowa bans on professor-student dating extend to relationships between graduate students and professors, *see* note 117 *supra,* which may be more closely analogous to workplace dating between supervisors and subordinates than undergraduate student-professor dating. Graduate students may work for professors on long term projects and rely heavily on the development of that relationship to further their careers. Graduate students may also work closely with only one professor because of specialization in study.

and one of them must be transferred to another work assignment.[119] Thus, some workplaces and universities have recognized that our general acceptance of workplace dating and flirtation may be more harmful than we tend to treat it, at least when it involves persons in positions of unequal power. Our gut reaction that a certain amount sexual conduct is desirable, or at least not harmful at work, needs rethinking.

2. *Title VII should not tolerate any instances of disparate treatment.*

Requiring that the disparate treatment of women be pervasive is at odds with Title VII's language. According to *Meritor*, Congress intended Title VII's requirement that an employer refrain from discriminating against an employee "with respect to his compensation, terms, conditions, or privileges of employment because of such individual's . . . sex"[120] to " 'strike at the *entire spectrum* of disparate treatment of men and women' in employment."[121] This language does not support a requirement that discrimination be pervasive before it can be actionable. Thus, in adopting the pervasiveness requirement, *Meritor* adopted a standard that squarely contradicts the purpose of Title VII as Congress envisioned it.

Despite its continued insistence that a plaintiff demonstrate that the discriminatory treatment she endured was pervasive, the Court has never offered a persuasive justification for this restriction in hostile work environment causes of action.[122] The Supreme Court and lower courts likely have feared creating a cause of action that enables plaintiffs literally to make a "federal case"[123] out of stray remarks in the workplace. In other words, judges may believe that recognizing claims based on gender discrimination will open the floodgates to "frivolous" lawsuits. Early cases that resisted recognizing gender-based hostile work environment claims stated this concern openly. One court feared that recognizing hostile work environment claims based on an employer's asking an employee out on a date would require "4,000 federal trial judges instead of

---

119. Law Firm Policy Regarding Employee Relationships (Aug. 16, 1994) (redacted copy on file with the *Stanford Law Review*) (firm name withheld by request).

120. 42 U.S.C. § 2000e-2(a)(1) (1988).

121. *Meritor*, 477 U.S. at 64 (quoting Los Angeles Dept. of Water and Power v. Manhart, 435 U.S. 702, 707 n.13 (1978)) (emphasis added).

122. Courts have repeatedly cited Rogers v. EEOC, 454 F.2d 234 (5th Cir. 1971), *cert. denied*, 406 U.S. 957 (1972), as support for the pervasiveness requirement. *Rogers* was the first case to recognize that harassment in the workplace (in *Rogers*, racial harassment) could in and of itself violate Title VII. *See id.* at 238 (asserting that Title VII should be interpreted broadly to proscribe conduct that creates "a working environment heavily charged with ethnic or racial discrimination"). Importantly, the language for which *Rogers* is repeatedly cited, "that an employer's mere utterance of an ethnic or racial epithet [that] engenders offensive feelings in an employee" does not violate Title VII, *id.*, is dicta. The 5th Circuit did not say that such conduct could not violate Title VII, just that the court was not willing to recognize such a low threshold at that time. If, as Justice Holmes said, "[i]t is revolting to have no better reason for a rule of law than that . . . it was laid down in the time of Henry IV," Oliver Wendell Holmes, The Path of the Law, Address at Boston University School of Law (Jan. 8, 1897), *in*, 10 HARV. L. REV. 457, 469 (1897), the pronouncement of the 5th Circuit in 1971 can hardly be the last word on the subject.

123. George, *supra* note 63, at 22.

some 400."[124] Another worried that recognizing hostile work environment claims would result in "a potential federal lawsuit every time any employee made amorous or sexually oriented advances toward another,"[125] while yet another predicted that "flirtations of the smallest order would give rise to liability."[126] It is also possible that this concern arises from the unrealistic fear of women bringing retaliatory suits against former lovers.[127]

Yet administrative concerns alone are an insufficient basis for denying women relief for the discrimination they suffer. Judicial fear of opening the floodgates simply cannot by itself provide an adequate response to the charge that disparate treatment in working conditions *is* disparate treatment, no matter how unpervasive it is.[128] First, given that women file very few hostile work environment claims, as a practical matter the fear of opening the floodgates is utterly overblown.[129] Second, given the costs associated with asserting hostile work environment claims, it is unlikely that women will abuse the cause of action to bring frivolous lawsuits.[130] And finally, if a doctrine that allows women to bring valid claims of gender-based disparate treatment creates a flood of claims, so be it. Ultimately, Title VII is a tool to vindicate a person's right to be free from discriminatory treatment. If there is so much discriminatory treatment against women that it creates a flood of claims, that should not stand in the way of a woman's vindication of her rights. If anything, the courts' refusal to deal with actual cases of disparate treatment will only encourage continued discrimination against women.

3. *The pervasiveness requirement confuses a question of damages with a question of liability.*

The courts' reliance on the pervasiveness of the harm confuses liability with damage. A requirement like pervasiveness is irrelevant to whether discrimination has actually occurred. Whether a supervisor or employer discriminated against an employee does not and logically cannot turn on the employee's reaction to the discrimination.[131] Similarly, the occurrence of disparate treat-

---

124. Tomkins v. Public Serv. Elec. & Gas Co., 422 F. Supp. 553, 557 (D.N.J. 1976), *rev'd,* 568 F.2d 1044 (3d Cir. 1977).

125. Corne v. Bausch & Lomb, Inc., 390 F. Supp. 161, 163 (D. Ariz. 1975), *vacated,* 562 F.2d 55 (9th Cir. 1977).

126. Miller v. Bank of Am., 418 F. Supp. 233, 236 (N.D. Cal. 1976), *rev'd on other grounds,* 600 F.2d 211 (9th Cir. 1979).

127. *See* text accompanying notes 94-98 *supra.*

128. Suppose an employer purposely paid an African-American employee $1 less on only one occasion. Certainly such an action would violate Title VII, although the plaintiff's damages might be limited to $1. I argue that the same standard should apply to gender-based disparate treatment when it concerns derogatory comments or sexual requests. *Cf.* George, *supra* note 63, at 21-22 (making a similar argument with respect to the triviality of gender-based harassment, but favoring a sliding scale standard for liability to vary with pervasiveness). Professor George argues that the more trivial the conduct, the more pervasive it ought to be before it counts as a Title VII violation. *Id.*

129. *See* text accompanying note 98 *supra.*

130. *See* texts accompanying notes 86-89 & 97 *supra.*

131. Notably, none of the other Title VII causes of action for discrimination require a plaintiff to prove that she suffered emotional harm to state a cause of action for discrimination. *See, e.g.,* Price Waterhouse v. Hopkins, 490 U.S. 228, 239-42 (1989) (stating the requirements for a mixed-motive

ment does not depend on whether an objectively reasonable person would be offended by the discrimination. Disparate treatment is an objectively verifiable event: At bottom, whether discrimination has occurred depends on whether an employer treats an employee differently from other employees because of her gender. Nothing more, nothing less.

In short, current doctrine has it backwards. Sexual conduct at work between supervisors and subordinates *is* disparate treatment and should therefore be presumed illegitimate.[132] We similarly should refuse to tolerate disparaging comments that target women based on their gender. As Professor George put it,

> The courts' underlying assumption in hostile environment cases remains unchallenged: [W]hen men and women work in the same environment, some "flirting" or other comparable behavior is inevitable and appropriate. Our assumption should be just the opposite: [S]exually oriented conduct or discussions in the workplace are generally demeaning to women and, therefore, improper.[133]

If we reverse our assumptions about the appropriateness of sexual conduct between supervisors and subordinates at work, we can no longer countenance supervisors asking their subordinates out on dates without the "employer . . . bear[ing] the risk that the supervisor's conduct [may disturb] the victim to the extent that she [would be] willing to pursue a claim."[134] If our goal truly is to achieve gender equality in the workplace and to fulfill Title VII's mandate to "strike at the entire spectrum" of disparate treatment in the workplace based on gender, this sacrifice does not seem too high a price to pay. In the end, after all, the workplace is for work.[135] And if certain behavior discriminates against

---

cause of action); McDonnell Douglas Corp. v. Green Corp., 411 U.S. 792, 802 (1973) (enumerating the prima facie requirements for a disparate treatment cause of action).

132. George, *supra* note 63, at 18 (arguing that if a supervisor fondles a subordinate or comments on her anatomy, the conduct is discriminatory).

133. *Id.* at 22-23.

134. *Id.* at 23.

135. Some may fear that a Title VII standard as stringent as the one I propose poses 1st Amendment problems. Although a 1st Amendment challenge to Title VII has never reached the Supreme Court, the Court's continued acceptance of Title VII restrictions on speech suggests that the Court recognizes that the workplace is different than a street corner or a public meeting place. Indeed, workplace restrictions on speech, including political speech, have been upheld by the Court when interference with the work environment has been shown. For example, in Cornelius v. NAACP Legal Defense & Educ. Fund, 473 U.S. 788 (1985), the Court upheld an executive order expressly excluding legal defense and political advocacy groups from the charities included in the Combined Federal Campaign—a fundraising drive conducted by federal employees during work hours. The Court upheld this restriction on political speech because "[t]he federal workplace, like any other place of employment, exists to accomplish the business of the employer. . . . [Thus], the Government has the right to exercise control over access to the federal workplace in order to avoid interruptions to the performance of the duties of its employees." *Id.* at 805-06 (footnotes omitted). In light of *Cornelius*, even stringent Title VII workplace restrictions on nonpolitical speech that are specifically aimed at enhancing workers' ability to do their jobs likely will not collide with the 1st Amendment. *See* Connick v. Myers, 461 U.S. 138, 154 (1983) (upholding the discharge of a government employee for circulating a questionnaire concerning internal office affairs because the "limited First Amendment interest involved here does not require that [an employer] tolerate action which he reasonably believe[s] would disrupt the office . . . and destroy close working relationships"); David F. McGowan & Ragesh K. Tangri, Comment, *A Libertarian Critique of University Restrictions of Offensive Speech*, 79 CAL. L. REV. 825, 902 n.377 (1991) ("Speech in the

women in the workplace and interferes with women's ability to be effective employees, we should be willing to curtail such behavior in favor of productivity. As my discussion above indicates, even one respectful request for a date from a supervisor can harm women in the workplace.[136] Because the request itself may be inherently coercive, it can undermine their position as workers, highlight their position as sex objects, and affect their work environment adversely.[137]

IV. REDESIGNING THE HOSTILE WORK ENVIRONMENT CAUSE OF ACTION: RECOGNIZING A CAUSE OF ACTION BASED ON "DISPARATE TREATMENT"

Courts should reconceptualize hostile work environment claims as gender-based treatment that affects the conditions of an employee because of her gender, rather than as a form of sexual harassment. Such a reconceptualization would establish that a hostile work environment action is simply a cause of action for disparate treatment and would dispel confusion over whether an instance of sexual conduct or a sexual comment are inappropriate in the workplace. Discrimination is always presumptively inappropriate in the workplace.

A. *Eliminating "Unwelcomeness" As a Requirement To Prove Liability*

Reframing sexual harassment as gender-based disparate treatment has ramifications for the unwelcomeness requirement as well. Currently, courts seem to characterize hostile work environment cases as involving essentially unobjectionable and harmless behavior taken too far. Because courts generally perceive less egregious forms of sexual conduct as harmless, a plaintiff must show that she actually did find the particular behavior unwelcome. In contrast, if we instead presume that sexual conduct or gender-based disparagement is unacceptable workplace conduct because it is inherently discriminatory, logic leads us to the conclusion that disparate treatment in gender hostile environment cases is, as in all other kinds of disparate treatment cases, presumptively unwelcome.

Plaintiffs should not bear the burden of proving that they found the disparate treatment unwelcome. As in other areas of Title VII jurisprudence, courts should presume such conduct is unwelcome. In order to protect defendants

---

workplace is controlled in part because work is compelled for the majority of people—workers are a true captive audience. If they leave their posts to avoid offensive speech, they will either literally be leaving their jobs or they will be fired.").

136. Admittedly, Gutek shies away from condemning dating in the workplace. GUTEK, *supra* note 38, at 173 ("I am not advocating a return to 'outlawing' dating . . . ."). If we take her analysis that the introduction of sex roles in the workplace undermines women's status to its logical conclusion, however, dating in the workplace does indeed undermine women's positions at work.

137. This hard-line stance obviously does not come without tradeoffs. "An uncompromising judicial stance on sexual harassment may effectively dissuade some men from all warm, personal interaction with female subordinates . . . for fear of being charged with sexual harassment." George, *supra* note 63, at 24. This would be a gross overreaction, though. "[M]en can support their female colleagues in a warm and personal manner without risking misinterpretation. . . . [Men can, for example,] support women employees through compliments about their work instead of their appearance." *Id.*

from retaliatory suits, a supervisor should be able to assert as an affirmative defense (and bear the burden of proof) that the plaintiff indeed welcomed the conduct.[138] To assert the affirmative defense, the defendant should be required to prove that the plaintiff initiated the particular conduct in question. In other words, if whether a plaintiff welcomed her supervisor telling her dirty jokes in the workplace is at issue, a defendant should have to prove that the plaintiff initiated the telling of dirty jokes. Evidence that plaintiff took part should not be sufficient to demonstrate welcomeness. A plaintiff may join in behavior that she finds distasteful and offensive simply because she does not want to "make waves" or she believes it will help her "fit in" or cope with an unpleasant situation.[139] Similarly, if a defendant asserts that a plaintiff actually welcomed him asking her out on dates or propositioning her, he should have to prove that she initiated such conduct.

Courts should also strictly limit the kind of evidence admissible to prove welcomeness; otherwise defendants could turn discovery into a fishing expedition to discourage a plaintiff from pursuing an otherwise meritorious lawsuit. *Meritor's* holding that evidence of a plaintiff's dress and personal fantasies are plainly admissible to prove welcomeness should be reversed, either by Congress or the Supreme Court at the earliest possible opportunity. Aside from being of questionable probative value in proving whether a plaintiff "welcomed" particular conduct from her supervisor, evidence of the plaintiff's clothing, comments about the people she dates, or her dating habits with men other than the defendant, should not be admissible to prove whether the plaintiff initiated the questioned conduct. Instead a defendant should have to show unequivocally that a plaintiff initiated the conduct to rebut the presumption of unwelcomeness.

Such a position is not as extreme as it may sound at first blush. Under this new approach, a supervisor who initiates sexual contact with a subordinate will be liable for any harm he causes, no matter how insignificant. What is wrong with that? The likely consequences would be to deter supervisors from initiating such contact unless they were quite certain that it would be welcomed and to encourage them to avoid intimidating conduct entirely. In spite of such results, people will still manage to find mates. But some might object further that a supervisor could still be liable even if he *was* reasonably sure that his advances would be welcome and even if he did avoid taking advantage of his

---

138. George also suggests transforming the unwelcomeness requirement into an affirmative defense. *Id.* at 19, 29. His definition of "welcomeness," however, gives employers more room to maneuver than does my argument that the plaintiff must actually have initiated the conduct in question to have welcomed it. He suggests that a defendant may prove welcomeness by "establishing that the plaintiff 'welcomed' the behavior through specific words or gestures to which the supervisor responded in kind." *Id.* at 19 (footnote omitted). The problem with a standard like George's is that it leaves the door open for courts to infer welcomeness from what the defendant may have interpreted as the plaintiff's "provocative" behavior. In other words, George's standard allows supervisors to initiate conduct and then to justify that conduct *post hoc* based on assertions that the plaintiff had actually welcomed it.

139. *See* Morris v. American Nat'l Can Corp., 730 F. Supp. 1489, 1495 (E.D. Mo. 1989) (holding that joining in profanity and nonsexual pranks could have been part of plaintiff's effort to fit in, and did not imply welcomeness of sexually explicit conduct and materials), *aff'd in part and rev'd in part,* 941 F.2d 710 (8th Cir. 1991).

superior position of power. This is so. In such an event, of course, the supervisor is unlikely to be liable for much, because he will have caused little or no harm. The fact of the matter is that the line of liability cannot be perfectly drawn. As it is now, women are subject to unwanted advances that, however polite, divert attention from their roles as workers, force upon them the role of sex objects, and impede their ability to do their work. This state of affairs must exist, the present doctrine says, because it is better than a state of affairs where men might be deterred from polite sexual advances and where women might bring "trivial" lawsuits. The latter concern forces women to suffer an actual harm to forestall a hypothetical and unlikely burden. The former concern is, under Title VII's mandate for equality, too insignificant to justify the present doctrine. Whatever harm might occur to polite suitors or subordinates too shy to initiate contact on their own is outweighed by the harm to *all* women in the status quo.

The current standard allows for confusion on both sides due to miscommunication and misinterpretation. A narrower, bright-line rule provides employers and employees with a clearer idea of when sexual conduct at work is welcome and appropriate and when it is not. If a defendant were required to prove that a plaintiff initiated the conduct in question, we would no longer have to worry that the plaintiff miscommunicated "welcomeness" by remaining silent about conduct she found objectionable because she feared negative consequences.[140] This bright-line rule would also ameliorate our concern about whether subordinates can ever truly consent to sexual advances from their supervisors because of the power differential inherent in the relationship. In other words, if a defendant could only successfully defend himself on welcomeness grounds by demonstrating that a plaintiff actually initiated the conduct, we would not have to worry that the plaintiff acquiesced to her boss's advances because she feared saying no.

B. *Pervasiveness: Merely a Question of Damages*

A plaintiff should not have to demonstrate that the conduct or comments she suffered were pervasive or severe enough to create an objectively or subjectively abusive working environment in order to state a claim under Title VII. She should need only to demonstrate that (1) because of her gender, (2) she was treated differently than men in the office, and (3) that this treatment reflected invidious stereotypes about women. In developing this prong of the test, hostile work environment jurisprudence should follow the general contours of Fourteenth Amendment sex discrimination jurisprudence. Under the Fourteenth Amendment, if women are treated differently than men and that treatment reflects invidious stereotypes about women, the discriminatory treatment

---

140. *See* text accompanying notes 72-74 *supra.* Women may also intentionally hide their feelings of unwelcomeness: "Perhaps she does not want to hurt the man or is afraid of negative repercussions if she were open about her feelings. This fear of repercussions is understandable since women are more likely than men to suffer adverse consequences of such encounters." GUTEK, *supra* note 38, at 58-59.

is actionable, unless a defendant provides a firm basis for the differential treatment.[141]

Conduct and comments that courts have previously considered trivial take on new significance when viewed in light of the stereotypes on which they are based. In *Downes v. FAA*, for example, a supervisor stroked the plaintiff's hair because he said he thought it was important to women to be complimented on physical appearance.[142] The court did not find such behavior actionable because the court did not find it sufficiently pervasive.[143] Under the standard I propose, such conduct would be actionable under Title VII. The supervisor's conduct toward his subordinate embodied a negative stereotype about the woman's desire to be treated as an attractive sex object at work. Similarly, comments that imply the negative stereotype that a woman's gender prevents her from doing her job effectively, like the kind of comments Teresa Harris suffered from her boss, would also be actionable.

Liability should attach even if the incident involved a single discriminatory comment or incident. Employers should not escape liability for gender discrimination simply because they do not engage in it often.[144] Under the *McDonnell Douglas* disparate treatment analysis, the law does not tolerate instances of de minimis discrimination.[145] Since the conduct that creates a hostile work environment essentially constitutes disparate treatment, we should not tolerate such discriminatory behavior simply because it does not rise to some standard of "pervasiveness."

Instead, the question of severity should be reserved, as it is in disparate treatment causes of action, to mitigate damages. In order to prevent the question of pervasiveness or severity from affecting determinations of liability, courts should bifurcate hostile work environment into separate liability and damages phases, as courts do in mixed-motive cases.[146]

V.   CONCLUSION

Title VII prohibits discrimination in the workplace based on gender. It does not create a code of conduct for courting at work. To the extent a woman's work environment invidiously takes note of her gender, she suffers discrimina-

---

141. Mississippi Univ. for Women v. Hogan, 458 U.S. 718, 724-26 (1982).

142. 775 F.2d 288, 294-95 (Fed. Cir. 1985). As the supervisor described the incident, he went "by her desk and [placed his] fingers on a couple of strands of [her] hair . . . and said, '. . . your hair looks great that way.'" *Id.* at 294. He explained, "It was a gesture of friendliness or whatever you want to call it, or understanding or appreciation of her hair. I might tell a man he had a nice necktie on that day. That's all it amounted to, as far as I was concerned." *Id.* at 295. One wonders, however, how a heterosexual man would react if his gay supervisor were to stroke his tie while telling him how nice he looked that day.

143. *Id.* at 293.

144. *See* George, *supra* note 63, at 21.

145. *See* note 128 *supra.*

146. The analogy to mixed-motive cases is strong. If a racial or sexual stereotype enters into a promotion or hiring decision, even if the defendant based its decision not to hire or promote the plaintiff on a nondiscriminatory reason, the defendant is still liable under Title VII. 42 U.S.C. § 2000e-2(m) (Supp. V 1993). The defendant can only introduce evidence that shows that it would have reached the same employment decision absent discrimination to mitigate its damages. *Id.* § 2000e-5(g)(2)(B).

tion of the type Title VII, properly interpreted, forbids. Such discrimination need not be sexual to be actionable. The current focus on sexuality rather than gender-based discrimination has created a doctrine that does not protect women's full range of rights in the workplace. The doctrine should be revised to prohibit invidious disparate treatment based on gender regardless of whether such treatment is "sexual."

Acknowledgments

Hill, Ann Corinne. "Protection of Women Workers and the Courts: A Legal Case History." *Feminist Studies* 5 (1979): 247–73. Reprinted with the permission of the publisher, FEMINIST STUDIES, Inc., c/o Women's Studies Program, University of Maryland, College Park, MD 20742.

Ellis, Judy Trent. "Sexual Harassment and Race: A Legal Analysis of Discrimination." *Journal of Legislation* 8 (1981): 30–45. Reprinted with the permission of the University of Notre Dame.

Scales-Trent, Judy. "Comparable Worth: Is This a Theory for Black Workers?" *Women's Rights Law Reporter* 8 (1984–85): 51–58. Reprinted with the permission of the *Women's Rights Law Reporter*.

MacKinnon, Catharine A. "Sexual Harassment: Its First Decade in Court." In *Feminism Unmodified: Discourses on Life and Law* (Cambridge: Harvard University Press, 1987): 103–16, 251–56. Reprinted by permission of the publisher. Copyright 1987 by the President and Fellows of Harvard College.

Evans, Sara M. and Barbara J. Nelson. "Comparable Worth: The Paradox of Technocratic Reform." *Feminist Studies* 15 (1989): 171–90. Reprinted with the permission of the publisher, FEMINIST STUDIES, Inc., c/o Women's Studies Program, University of Maryland, College Park, MD 20742.

Scarborough, Cathy. "Conceptualizing Black Women's Employment Experiences." *Yale Law Journal* 98 (1989): 1457–78. Reprinted by permission of The Yale Law Journal Company and Fred B. Rothman and Company.

Ehrenreich, Nancy S. "Pluralist Myths and Powerless Men: The Ideology of Reasonableness in Sexual Harassment Law," *Yale Law Journal* 99 (1990): 1177–1234. Reprinted by permission of The Yale Law Journal Company and Fred B. Rothman and Company.

Strauss, Marcy. "Sexist Speech in the Workplace." *Harvard Civil Rights-Civil Liberties Law Review* 25 (1990): 1–51. Permission granted. Copyright 1990 *Harvard Civil Rights-Civil Liberties Law Review*, and by the President and Fellows of Harvard College.

Carleton, Francis. "Women in the Workplace and Sex Discrimination Law: A Feminist Analysis of Federal Jurisprudence." *Women and Politics* 13 (1993): 1–26. Reprinted with the permission of Haworth Press, Inc. Copyright 1993.

Murray, Yxta Maya. "Sexual Harassment in the Military." *Southern California Review of Law and Women's Studies* 3 (1994): 279–302. Reprinted with the permission of the *Southern California Review of Law and Women's Studies*.

Coontz, Phyllis D. "Gender Bias in the Legal Profession: Women 'See' It, Men Don't." *Women and Politics* 15 (1995): 1–22. Reprinted with the permission of Haworth Press, Inc. Copyright 1995.

DeCew, Judith Wagner. "The Combat Exclusion and the Role of Women in the Military." *Hypatia: A Journal of Feminist Philosophy* 10 (1995): 56–73. Reprinted with the permission of Indiana University Press.

Vogel, Lise. "Considering Difference: The Case of the U.S. Family and Medical Leave Act of 1993." *Social Politics* 2 (1995): 111–20. Copyright (1995) by the Board of Trustees of the University of Illinois. Used with the permission of the author and the University of Illinois Press.

Oshige, Miranda. "What's Sex Got To Do With It?" *Stanford Law Review* 47 (1995): 565–94. Reprinted with the permission of the Board of Trustees of the Leland Stanford Junior University. Copyright (1995).